MEMOIRS

OF THE

Lower Ohio Valley

———

PERSONAL AND GENEALOGICAL

WITH PORTRAITS

———

VOLUME I

———

Book Publishers

Southern Historical Press, Inc.
Greenville, South Carolina

Originally Published 1905

SOUTHERN HISTORICAL PRESS, INC.
PO BOX 1267
Greenville, SC   29601

ISBN #978-1-63914-077-0

Printed in the United States of America

MEMOIRS

OF THE

LOWER OHIO VALLEY

PERSONAL AND GENEALOGICAL

WITH PORTRAITS

VOLUME I

HON. MELVILLE EZRA-INGALLS, president of the Cleveland, Cincinnati, Chicago & St. Louis railway, more popularly known as the "Big Four," was born at Harrison, Me., Sept. 6, 1842, his parents being Ezra T. and Louisa Ingalls, descendants of that old New England stock whose industry, patriotism and inherent love of honesty have been such potent factors in moulding the character of American institutions. His youth was passed on his father's farm, and in attendance upon the common schools during the winter months. At the age of sixteen he was granted a teacher's certificate and from that time until he reached his majority he was engaged in the onerous labor of the country schoolmaster or in attending higher institutions of learning. After graduating from Bridgeton academy he entered Bowdoin college in 1860, but his finances running low he did not finish the course. In 1862 he entered the Harvard law school, from which he graduated the following year, receiving one of the prizes for a legal essay. Shortly afterward he opened a law office at Gray, Me., but, the place be'ng small, he decided to remove to a larger center of population, and in 1865 he located in the city of Boston, where he was associated with Judge Charles Levi Woodbury. Mr. Ingalls soon won the attention of bench, bar and the public in his new home, and in 1867 he was elected to the State senate. At the close of his term he declined a re-election and turned all his attention to his profession. About this time his successful management of several corporation cases attracted wide attention, and when, in 1871, the old Indianapolis, Cincinnati & Lafayette railroad became seriously involved he was requested by the stockholders to assume the management of its financial affairs. Notwithstanding the magnitude of the undertaking, Mr. Ingalls accepted the receivership and in a short time restored order out of chaos. He was then elected president of the company in recognition of his executive ability, but in 1876 the company was again confronted with bankruptcy and he was again appointed receiver. Four years later the company was reorganized under the name of the Cincinnati, Indianapolis, St. Louis & Chicago railroad, Mr. Ingalls being elected to the presidency. Now began the real work of Mr. Ingalls' life—the building up of a great railroad system. In 1889 the interests of his company were consolidated with the Cleveland, Columbus, Cincinnati & Indianapolis railway (the old "Bee Line Route"), and the present name adopted. Mr. Ingalls was elected president of the new organization and has held the position ever since. The wonderful growth of the Big Four is due in a large degree to his executive ability and foresight. From about four hundred miles in 1889, the system at present comprises more than two thousand miles. Track, rolling-stock, roadbed and buildings have been improved, and few railway systems stand higher in the popular favor than the Big Four. Besides his interests in this company, Mr. Ingalls was president of the Kentucky Central from 1881 to 1883, and of the Chesapeake & Ohio from October, 1888, to January, 1900. In 1879 he was elected by the Cincinnati chamber of commerce one of the commissioners of the industrial expositions, and the following year was chosen president of the board. He was also instrumental in securing the fifty-three subscriptions, of one thousand dollars each, to build the art museum, and upon the death of the first president, Joseph Longworth, was chosen to succeed him. For some time he was president of the Cincinnati Commercial club, an organization limited to fifty of the city's leading business men, and having for its object the promotion of the commercial prosperity of the city. Mr. Ingalls is a member and president of the Unitarian church of Cincinnati, and as such is active in promoting all worthy movements tending to better the moral and spiritual condition of the masses. He is not narrow in his religious views, is liberal and charitable in the extreme, and is one of the most approachable men in the country. He is noted for his literary taste, and, although a busy man, he finds time to cultivate the acquaintance and association of scholars. On Jan. 19, 1867, Mr. Ingalls was united in marriage to Miss Abbie M. Stimson, of Gray, Me., and to this union have been born six children. The Ingalls home is the abode of happiness and social culture.

JULIUS FLEISCHMANN was born at Riverside, Cincinnati, on June 8, 1872. His father, Charles Fleischmann, the well-known banker and manufacturer of compressed yeast, which made the name internationally famous, was of Austrian ancestry. The family of his mother, who was a Miss Henriette Robertson, was of Scottish origin, settled in Germany. Mr. Fleischmann's early education was received in the public schools of Cincinnati, and the Franklin school, also of that city, from which he graduated. His first business experience was in the occupation of clerk in his father's house, which business was then as now conducted under the firm name of Fleischmann & Co. He familiarized himself with this vast business in such a thorough manner that in 1884 he became manager, which position he held up to the time of his father's death, in 1897, when, in conjunction with his brother, Max Fleischmann, he assumed control of all the various Fleischmann interests, among which may be enumerated the following, in the management of every one of which Mr. Fleischmann takes an active part, being president of the Union Grain and Hay Company, the Market National bank, the Security Savings bank and Safe Deposit Company, the Riverside Malting and Elevating Company, all of Cincinnati; Illinois Vinegar Manufacturing Company; the Fleischmann Manufacturing Company, of New York, and vice-president of the Cincinnati, Newport & Covington Street Railway Company. Aside from the numerous interests which engage his time, of which the foregoing are some of the most important, Mr. Fleischmann, withal, finds ample opportunity for social diversion and attention to public matters. In military affairs he has always taken the deepest interest, having served with distinction on the staff of William McKinley, when governor of Ohio. He also served in the same capacity under Governors

Bushnell and Nash. Politically, Mr. Fleischmann has affiliated with the Republican party since attaining his majority, but despite the consistency of his partisanship, a public-spirited recognition of his capacity for the high office to which he was elected on April 2, 1900, rallied to his support the conservative business element irrespective of political creeds. At the municipal election held in April, 1903, Mr. Fleischmann was re-elected mayor by the largest plurality ever given a candidate for that office. His administration during the four years of his incumbency in office has been such as to challenge universal admiration. His progressive ideas, his unquestioned executive ability, his breadth of mind and warmth of heart have earned for him popularity to a degree never before enjoyed by any mayor of Cincinnati. Mr. Fleischmann is a governor of the Queen City club, director of the Phoenix club, and member of the Commercial club, and the Riding club, of Cincinnati; the New York Yacht and the Atlantic Yacht clubs, of New York; a thirty-second degree Mason, an Elk, Cincinnati Lodge No. 5, and a Knight of Pythias. He has also been the recipient of many civic honors, a fact which is attributed to the ardent interest which he has taken in the city of Cincinnati and its progress. In yachting he takes a lively interest, as is witnessed by his ownership of the magnificent floating palace, "Hiawatha." Mr. Fleischmann was married on April 12, 1893, to Miss Lilly Ackerland, of Cincinnati, and three children have been born to them, Louise, Charles, and Julius Fleischmann, Jr.

HON. HARRY L. GORDON, a prominent attorney and vice-mayor of the city of Cincinnati, O., was born in the picturesque little village of Metamora, Franklin county, Ind., Aug. 27, 1860. He is a son of M. B. and Sophia (Tracy) Gordon, the father being one of the leading farmers of the Whitewater valley until his death, which occurred in 1892. Harry L. Gordon was reared on his father's farm, assisting in the cultivation of the crops during summer and attending the public schools in the winter, until he was eighteen years of age. He then left his country home to attend college. After a season in the Normal college of Ladoga, Ind., he entered DePauw university at Greencastle, from which institution he was graduated with honors in 1882, receiving the degree of Ph. B.

Three years later, after post-graduate work, he was honored with the degree of Master of Arts. He entered the law office of McDonald, Butler & Mason, one of the leading law firms of Indianapolis, Ind., in 1882, and remained in the office until 1887, being the chief clerk nearly all that time. In January, 1887, he went to Wichita, Kan., where he opened a law office and soon won a high standing at the bar. There he practiced successfully for ten years, and during that time filled several offices of trust and responsibility. For some time he was assistant prosecuting attorney of Sedgwick county, was then city attorney for Wichita, and in 1895 was elected a member of the Kansas state senate. In June, 1897, he removed to Cincinnati, where he became a member of the legal firm of Renner, Gordon & Renner and soon became well known in all the courts as one of the successful lawyers of the city. Subsequently he retired from this firm and established offices in the Union Trust Building, where he carries on a large and profitable law practice. Mr. Gordon is a Republican in his political affiliations and stands high in the councils of his party. In 1899 he was appointed to a place on the board of supervisors of Cincinnati, and the following year was made president of the board, a fitting recognition of the high order of his executive ability and his progressive ideas of municipal affairs. This position he continued to hold until April 1, 1903. On June 26, 1902, he was appointed by Gov. George K. Nash to fill the vacancy in the office of lieutenant-governor caused by the resignation of Hon. Carl L. Nippert, and served until the expiration of the term in 1904, discharging the duties of the position with credit to himself and to the entire satisfaction of the people of Ohio. In April, 1903, he was elected vice-mayor and president of the council of the city of Cincinnati, which position he now holds. In all the official positions occupied by Mr. Gordon he has received the unqualified support of the better class of people because of his championship of law and order, public morality, education, and all those things that go to mark a community progressive and refined. In social life Mr. Gordon is a well-known figure, being a Scottish Rite Mason, a Knight Templar, a Noble of the Mystic Shrine, a member of the Itan-Nic-Nic club, as well as several other leading clubs and business organizations of the city. Although an indefatigable worker in his profession and the duties of official position he finds time to attend his lodge and club meetings occasionally, where he is always welcomed because of his genial disposition and entertaining qualities. On April 20, 1892, Mr. Gordon led to the altar Miss Esther L. Langtree, of Aurora, Ind., and to this marriage there has been born one son, Harry L., Jr., now ten years of age.

WILLIAM HENRY ELDER, D.D., archbishop of Cincinnati, is a descendant of one of the oldest Catholic families in America. His great-grandfather, William Elder, came from England and was one of the early settlers of Maryland. In the early half of the eighteenth century, when the anti-Catholic sentiment procured the passage of the law prohibiting the celebration of the mass except in private homes, William Elder built a large log house about two miles south of Emmitsburg, in which was one room large enough to accommodate all the Catholics in the vicinity, and here the Holy Sacrifice of the mass might be attended by all who desired to do so. This building, which was made historic because of its associations, was occupied by some of his descendants until a few years ago, when it was torn down. Thomas Elder, the grandfather of the archbishop, was born in Maryland and lived there during the early years of his life, but later removed to Bardstown, Ky., where he died at a ripe old age. His son, Basil, married Elizabeth Miles Snowden, of Maryland, and they reared a family of ten children to maturity, the archbishop being the ninth. William H. Elder was born in the city of Baltimore, March 22, 1819, his father having taken up his residence in that city some seventeen years before, to engage in the grocery and commission business. In 1831 the archbishop entered Mt. St. Mary's college, Emmitsburg, Md., then under the charge of John B. Purcell, D. D., afterward the second bishop and first archbishop of Cincinnati. In 1837 he graduated, and in 1842 left for the Propaganda, Rome. He was ordained priest on Passion Sunday, 1846, returned to his native diocese, and was soon after appointed professor of dogmatic theology in his alma mater. In 1855 the death of Rt. Rev. J. O. Van De Velde left a vacancy in the See of Natchez, and the choice of his successor fell upon Dr. Elder. At that time the diocese included the whole State of Mississippi, with the people few in numbers, poor in purse, and badly scattered over the large area. Notwithstanding all this, the new bishop, after his consecration at Baltimore by Archbishop Kenrick, May 3, 1857, entered with commendable zeal upon the discharge of his duties and remained there until appointed coadjutor to Archbishop Purcell in 1880. During these years the great Civil war and the yellow fever scourge made his work far from pleasant, but in the most trying times he never left his post of duty. Always ready to assist and encourage the priests and nuns of his church, who were daily and hourly making sacrifices in behalf of suffering humanity, he endeared himself to all who came in contact with him, Catholics and Protestants alike. He fell a victim to the dread disease, and for a time his life was despaired of, but he recovered, greatly to the delight of his co-workers and followers. In 1879 he was offered the archbishopric of San Francisco, and while he did not directly refuse, he did ask to be permitted to remain with his diocese because of its deplorable condition. The Pope, pleased with this manifestation of self-sacrifice, refrained from ordering his acceptance and he remained at Natchez until late in the year 1879, when Archbishop Purcell, of Cincinnati, asked for a coadjutor owing to his declining years and the financial troubles of the archbishopric. On Jan. 30, 1880, Doctor Elder assumed the duties of coadjutor to Archbishop Purcell, who retired to St. Martin's convent, leaving all the administration of the affairs of the diocese to his assistant. The death of Archbishop Purcell occurred in 1883, and on December 13th of that year Dr. Elder became the archbishop. For nearly three score years Archbishop Elder has devoted his best energies to the cause of the Master, and to relieving the sufferings of his fellow-man. He has officiated at the altar, when two happy hearts have been made as one; he has christened the innocent, smiling infant, and in later years confirmed it into the church; he has crossed the hands of the dead upon the breast and pronounced the final benediction as the lifeless clay was lowered into its last resting place. Thus he has stood by the cradle, the altar and the tomb, speaking words of cheer or consolation, and now in his old age he peacefully awaits the command of his Master to "Come-up higher."

WILLIAM M'CALLISTER, comptroller-assessor of the city water works, of Cincinnati, O., was born in that city in 1844. He attended the city schools until his sixteenth year, and in 1860 entered the employ of the Little Miami railroad (now operated by the Pennsylvania company), and was for thirty-nine years with the Pennsylvania company, working his way up from messenger boy to the position of Cincinnati agent for the Union fast freight line. For five years, beginning in 1895, Mr. McCallister was a member of the city school board. He was president of the union board of high schools in 1897-98, and during the same period was also president of the Cincinnati chamber of commerce. In 1899 he was elected a member of the board of city affairs, and after serving one year was appointed to his present position. Since coming into this office he has increased the revenue of the department over $100,000, which speaks well of his executive ability, and tells better than words could possibly do the story of his unimpeachable integrity. Mr. McCallister is a Republican in politics, but believes in doing rather than talking. He is, therefore, not a noisy politician, but one who tries to carry out in practice the principles advocated by his party. He is an Odd Fellow, a Royal Arch Mason, and a Presbyterian, and in, church, lodge and the community he has a deservedly high standing.

CAPT. ELIAS RIGGS MONFORT, A.M., LL.D., postmaster at Cincinnati, O., was born at Greensburg, Ind., March 2, 1842. His father, J. G. Monfort, D.D., LL.D., was a descendant of the Huguenots, and his mother, whose maiden name was Hannah Riggs, was a daughter of Rev. Elias Riggs, one of the pioneer clergymen of New Jersey. Her brother, also named Elias, was for sixty years a missionary to Turkey, under the auspices of the American board of Christian missions. From ancestry composed of sturdy English, Irish, French, Dutch, Welsh and Scotch blood, Mr. Monfort inherited those vigorous traits of character that have contributed in a large degree to his successful career. In 1855 his parents removed to Cincinnati, and the following year his father became president of the Glendale female college, one of the leading educational institutions of Ohio. Elias received his early education in the schools of Cincinnati and Glendale, and in 1859 entered Hanover college as a sophomore. Before completing his course the Civil war broke upon the country, and he was one of the first to give up the peaceful life of the student to take up arms in defense of his country. On June 18, 1861, he enlisted as a private in Company A, Sixth Ohio volunteer infantry. On October 8th, of the same year, he was made a second lieutenant and transferred to the Seventy-fifth Ohio infantry. He was commissioned captain Jan. 12, 1863, and served in that capacity until discharged from the service in January, 1864. His regiment was in more than twenty severe engagements, among them being the second Bull Run, Laurel Hill, Carrick's Ford, Franklin, Va., Cross Keys, Fredericksburg, Chancellorsville, Chantilly, and Gettysburg. In all these engagements Captain Monfort was with his company and several times distinguished himself by his coolness and bravery. At Gettysburg, July 1, 1863, he was severely wounded in the hip, which at first was feared would prove fatal, but he recovered and was honorably discharged by a military board for total disability early in January, 1864. He was also wounded at the second Bull Run, but remained at his post of duty. Returning home, he re-entered Hanover college, completed the remaining two years of the course in one year, and graduated in 1865. He then entered the Cincinnati law school, graduated in 1867, and was admitted to practice in the Ohio courts the same year. He located in his native town of Greensburg, where he served as district attorney and prosecuting attorney for a number of years. In 1874, his old wound so impaired his health as to interfere with the practice of law and he came to Cincinnati, at the request of his father, to accept a position as associate editor of *The Herald and Presbyter,* a Presbyterian weekly. Later he became the business manager, remaining with the publication until 1896. During these years he helped to increase the influence of the paper by his strong editorials and by his business ability placed it upon a more secure footing. Captain Monfort has for many years been one of the active and influential elders in the church. In 1869 Hanover college conferred upon him the degree of A. M., and in 1885 he received from Highland university the degree of LL.D. For many years he was one of the trustees of Hanover college and also of Lane Theological seminary, of which he was treasurer for eight years. He has twice been a member of the General Assembly of the Presbyterian church, and in 1888 was appointed by that body as one of the representatives to the meeting of the alliance of reformed churches, held at London, England. In 1896 he was appointed to the office of county clerk of Hamilton county, by the board of county commissioners, and served until his successor was elected, Sept. 1, 1897. In 1899 he was appointed postmaster, and at the expiration of his term was reappointed by President Roosevelt. Although primarily engaged in church work, Captain Monfort has not lost his military spirit, and neither age nor his wound has dampened his patriotic ardor. He is a member of the Loyal Legion, and in 1900 was the department commander of the Grand Army of the Republic of Ohio. He is a member of F. C. Jones Post, No. 401, Grand Army of the Republic, and is prominent in Masonic circles, being a Knight Templar, a thirty-second degree member of the Scottish Rite, and a Noble of the Mystic Shrine. He has also taken a great interest in municipal affairs, and as a member of the Cincinnati board of education played an important part in securing the Walnut Hills high school, which has the finest and best equipped school building in Ohio.. Captain Monfort married Miss Emma Taylor, daughter of Eli Taylor, a prominent business man, and a sister of Capt. J. G. Taylor, who served on the staff of Gen. Gordon Granger during the war. They have three children: Joseph Taylor, Hannah Louise, and Margaret Morehead.

ORLANDO T. HOLLOWAY, superintendent of the fifth division railway mail service, composed of the States of Ohio, Indiana, Kentucky and Tennessee, with headquarters in Cincinnati, O., was born on a farm in Fairfield township, Columbiana county, O., Dec. 2, 1854. When he was about seven years old his father, Gen. E. S. Holloway, removed to the village of Columbiana, where he became owner and editor of the *Independent Register*, a weekly publication of general circulation. Orlando graduated from the Columbiana high school in 1871, and then attended and graduated from the Duff Commercial college at Pittsburg, after which he entered his father's office and learned the printer's trade, becoming in time part owner and foreman of the office. He continued in this occupation until 1881, when he entered the railway mail service as a postal clerk, being assigned to first duty on a line between Pittsburg, Pa., and Cincinnati, O., and later to the line between Pittsburg and Chicago. After working his way up through all the grades of the service, he was assigned as chief clerk in charge of a number of lines and located at Crestline, O., where he continued until again promoted in 1897 and assigned as superintendent of the division above noted, with headquarters at Cincinnati. Mr. Holloway is a member of Salem Commandery, No. 42, Knights Templars; a thirty-second degree member of the Ancient and Accepted Scottish Rite, Ohio Valley, Cincinnati; and of Syrian Temple, Nobles of the Mystic Shrine, also of Cincinnati, and affiliates with the Methodist Episcopal church. He was married in 1873 to Lomie S., daughter of Lafayette Stuckman, of Columbiana. They have no children living.

JOHN W. CARROLL, inspector of police, Cincinnati, Ohio, was born at Springfield, in the same state, Feb. 2, 1852. His father, Williard W. Carroll, was born in the North of Ireland in 1822, but came in his early manhood to America. For a number of years he was in the grocery business in Cincinnati, and died there in 1862. The family removed to Cincinnati when John W. was about seven years of age, and he received his education in the schools of that city. At the age of seventeen he learned the plumbing trade and worked at it for about fifteen years. About the time he began learning his trade he became a member of the First regiment, Ohio National Guard, and remained in the service for seventeen years, rising from private to the rank of major. While captain of Company C, March 17, 1887, he was appointed drill master of the Cincinnati police force, with the rank of sergeant. Three years later he was made lieutenant, and on June 4, 1903, he was made inspector, with the title of major. Mr. Carroll is a Republican in his political affiliations and takes a deep interest in political contests. He is a thirty-second degree Mason, a Knight Templar, and a Noble of the Mystic Shrine. He is a past chancellor of his lodge in the Knights of Pythias, has taken the Grand Lodge degrees, and belongs to the Uniform Rank. He was married March 17, 1890, to Miss Ida Foster, of Cincinnati, and they have two children, Williard W. and Avis C.

BENJAMIN RUSH COWEN, of Cincinnati, was born in Moorefield, Harrison county, O., Aug. 15, 1831, his parents being Benjamin Sprague and Anne Wood Cowen. For many years his father was presiding judge of the court of common pleas. Until he was twenty-six years of age Benjamin R. Cowen lived at St. Clairsville, O., obtaining his education in the classical institute of that village. He then learned the printers' trade, working at it for several years and studying medicine in the meantime. For nine years he was editor and proprietor of the *Belmont Chronicle* at St. Clairsville, afterward engaging in the mercantile and real estate business at Bellaire. In 1860 he was elected chief clerk of the lower branch of the Ohio legislature, and since that time he has been a prominent figure in state and national affairs. In April, 1861, he enlisted as a private in the Fifteenth Ohio volunteer infantry, and was soon after appointed first lieutenant and assistant commissary of subsistence, serving three months. In June following he was appointed additional pay-master by President Lincoln, and served with the army of the Potomac and in West Virginia until January, 1864. In October, 1861, he was elected secretary of state, of Ohio, on the ticket with Governor Tod, but resigned the succeeding May and returned to the field. In 1864 he was appointed adjutant-general of Ohio by Governor Brough, on a leave of absence without pay from the army, holding the office through the administrations of Governors Anderson and Cox. For organizing and sending out the "hundred days' men" in 1865 he was brevetted brigadier-general by President Johnson. Prior to 1856 he was a Whig, but in that year he voted for John C. Fremont, and since that time has affiliated with the Republican party. He was a delegate to the Republican national conventions of 1856 and 1868, being secretary of the latter. From 1865 to 1867 he was chairman of the state Republican committee. He was a candidate for the nomination for governor in 1867 and was defeated by General Hayes by ten votes. Declining the nomination of lieutenant-governor the same year he was appointed supervisor of internal revenue in 1869 for the states of California, Nevada, Arizona, and Utah, but a year later was transferred to the southern district of Ohio. From 1871 to 1877 he was assistant secretary of the interior department under President Grant; commissioner to appraise lands in the Indian Territory, in 1871; commissioner to visit Sitting Bull's tribe in Montana, in 1872; commissioner to survey and appraise certain Indian lands in California, in 1873; commissioner, with Admiral Rodgers, to investigate the race troubles in New Orleans, in 1874, and wrote the report of the commission; commissioner in the spring of 1875 to investigate the Mormon troubles in Utah. In 1880 he returned to the field of journalism as editor of the *Ohio State Journal,* at Columbus, and continued in that capacity until November, 1884, when he was appointed clerk of the Federal district and circuit courts for the southern district of Ohio. General Cowen is a Scottish Rite Mason; a member and past commander of the Loyal Legion; Fred Jones Post, Grand Army of the Republic; ex-president Sons of the Revolution; member of the Society of the Colonial Wars and the War of 1812; ex-president of the Cincinnati Literary club; ex-president of the New England society; a member of the Methodist Episcopal church, and was for ten years secretary of the Elizabeth Gamble Deaconess Home association and Christ's hospital. On Sept. 19, 1854, he was married to Miss Ellen Thoburn, of Belmont county, O., daughter of Matthew and Jane Lyle Thoburn, natives of County Antrim, Ireland. She is a sister of Bishop J. M. Thoburn, of India and Malaysia, and of Col. Joseph Thoburn, who was killed at the battle of Cedar Creek while in command of a division of the Union army. Of the eight children born to General and Mrs. Cowen, only three survive. They are James Lyle, of Tokio, Japan; Benjamin Sprague, manager of the Associated Press at Cincinnati, and Sidney Joseph, also of that city.

CHARLES A. BOSWORTH, assistant treasurer of the United States, in charge of the sub-treasury at Cincinnati, O., was born at Wilmington, Clinton county, O., in the year 1853. After a primary training in the schools of his native city he entered the University of Michigan, at Ann Arbor, and graduated in 1877 with the degree of Bachelor of Arts. He then became the vice-president of the First National bank of Wilmington, of which his father was the president, and in 1888 succeeded to the presidency. He continued to hold the position at the head of the bank's affairs until 1895, although he came to Cincinnati in 1890, entered into partnership with United States Senator J. B. Foraker, having studied law with Mr. Foraker from 1878 to 1880, and was admitted to the bar in 1880. This partnership lasted until 1893, and the law firm of Black & Bosworth still continues to exist. Mr. Bosworth was appointed to his present position as assistant treasurer in 1898. He is a member of the Methodist Episcopal church. In Masonic circles he is a prominent figure, being a thirty-second degree member of the Scottish Rite, a Knight Templar, and a Noble of the Mystic Shrine.

HORACE JOHNSON STANLEY, deceased, late chief engineer of the city of Cincinnati, O., was born at Mayfield, Fulton county, N. Y., Aug. 12, 1846. His father, Thomas Samuel Stanley, was born at Hartford, Conn., in the year 1817. He was a farmer and lumberman by occupation. He married Abigail Burr, a daughter of Nathan Burr, of Kingsboro, N. Y., and they had the following children: Adeline Burr, wife of Joseph Birch, of Amsterdam, N. Y.; Roxana Leonard, wife of Jeremiah Watson, of Staunton, Mass.; Eugenia Mills, who married Charles Deal, of Amsterdam, N. Y., and Horace Johnson, the subject of this sketch. Horace J. Stanley received his elementary education in the public schools of his native town and Kingsboro, and in 1869 went to Cincinnati, where he entered the office of R. C. Phillips, starting in to learn the profession of civil engineer. On the first day of May, 1870, he entered the office of the city engineer of Cincinnati as a draughtsman and from that time until his death he was connected with the office, to which he devoted the greater portion of his active business life and energies. From draughtsman he was promoted to the position of assistant city engineer, and in March, 1880, was made chief engineer by the board of public works, which position he held until his death, on Feb. 9, 1905. Had he lived about a month longer he would have been chief engineer a quarter of a century. During the time he filled the office he discharged his duties with signal ability and fidelity, as may be witnessed by the long time he held the position. Mr. Stanley was a Republican, firm in convictions, yet he had a host of Democratic friends who respected him for his many sterling qualities aside from his difference of political views from their own. He was married on Jan. 16, 1873, to Miss Mary J., daughter of Michael Tempest, and this union was blessed with the following children: Clarence, Lincoln, Susie Burr, Horace Tempest and Helen Abigail. Mr. Stanley was Presbyterian in his religious views, and was a consistent practitioner of the tenets of his faith in his daily conduct with his fellow-men.

J. A. ARCHIBALD, chief of the Cincinnati fire department, was born in that city Jan. 21, 1859. He attended the city schools until he was seventeen years of age, when he went into an architectural iron works, where he learned the trade of finisher. In January, 1882, he was appointed to the position of pipeman in the fire department. His promotions in the department were rapid and well deserved: lieutenant in 1884; captain in May, 1887; and chief, March 1, 1893. This record of advancement is due to his temperate habits, his robust physique, his clear mentality, and his even disposition. As an executive officer he has few equals and no superiors. His coolness and courage in trying moments during great fires have excited the admiration of the populace, while his justice and impartiality have won the confidence and respect of the men under his control. Called to the position of chief when thirty-four years of age, he has, by his quick intellect and indefatigable energy, during the eleven years of his administration, placed the department upon a high plane and made it the peer of any in the country. Having r.sen from the ranks, he knows the duties and trials of the humblest fireman, commends each one for the faithful performance of duty, and sympathizes with those who fail because of unforeseen contingencies. His orders are promptly executed, because the men know that they are based on a thorough knowledge of the demands of the department, and the result is that perfect discipline and good fellowship prevail. Mr. Archibald does not drive men into perilous situations. His position is that of a leader, and he is generally in the forefront, his cry of "Come on" inspiring others to follow his example. Politically Mr. Archibald is a Republican, but he never takes an active part in campaigns. His business is to protect property. He is a thirty-second degree Mason, a Noble of the Mystic Shrine, a Knight of Pythias, and a member of the Fraternal Order of Eagles. In all these societies "Jack," as he is familiarly called, is a popular fellow, to whom the "glad hand" is always extended when his duties will permit his attendance at the lodge meetings. He is also a member of the Presbyterian church.

F. D. COMSTOCK, local treasurer of the Big Four Railroad Company, at Cincinnati, O., is a native of the Badger State, having been born at Fox Lake, Wis., June 23, 1856. When he was about four years of age his parents, both of whom were natives of Ohio, removed to Cleveland. There the subject of this sketch was educated in the public schools, and when about seventeen or eighteen years old he began his business career as agent for an oil company. He continued in this line of employment until 1881, when he entered the service of the Cleveland, Columbus, Cincinnati & Indianapolis railroad, usually referred to as the "Bee Line." In 1889 this company was merged into the Big Four, Mr. Comstock going with the new organization. Since then he has continued in the employ of the company, filling various positions of trust and responsibility, until 1892, when he was appointed to his present position. Mr. Comstock is well known to railroad men all over the country as a careful and efficient official. During the twelve years that he has been local treasurer, thousands of dollars have passed through his office, but his affairs are always in such a shape that an examination of his books at any time would only add to his already well established reputation. Mr. Comstock is a member of the Presbyterian church.

CLARK W. DAVIS, M.D., health officer, Cincinnati, O., was born in that city, Dec. 14, 1863. He received his general education in the city schools, read medicine with his father, William B. Davis, who was one of the well-known physicians of the city, and in 1886 was graduated from the medical department of McMicken university, now the Miami Medical college. Upon leaving college he became associated with his father in practice and continued with him until his death in 1893. Since the death of his father, Dr. Davis has practiced alone. He is a member of the American Medical association and the Cincinnati Academy of Medicine. He was a member of the staff of Christ's hospital from the founding of the institution until 1900, and since 1893 has been medical director of the Union Central Life Insurance Company, of Cincinnati. In 1900 he was appointed to his present position as health officer, and since then has given a great deal of attention to the promotion and preservation of the public health. Dr. Davis is a member of Lafayette Lodge, Free and Accepted Masons; is a Knight Templar, a life member of Cincinnati Lodge, No. 5, Benevolent and Protective Order of Elks, and belongs to the Clifton Methodist Episcopal church.

WILLIAM THOMAS PERKINS was born in Xenia, Greene county, O., Dec. 8, 1834, his parents being John S. and Elizabeth C. Perkins. He obtained his education at the Xenia academy and in the public and high schools of Cincinnati, to which city his parents removed when he was but a little boy. His business life began as an errand boy in a dry goods store on West Sixth street for $1.00 per week. This was in 1845 and 1846. Next he became a clerk in the old Eagle white lead factory of this city, then a clerk in the banking house of Groesbeck & Co. In 1862 he began the banking business for himself on Third street. Two years later he went to Knoxville, Tenn., and started the First National bank of that city. Subsequently he returned to Cincinnati and became the cashier of the Central National bank. Closing out his banking interests he went South, and became a cotton planter. His next business venture was as a Cincinnati newspaper man, connecting himself with the old *Cincinnati Chronicle*—afterward the *Times-Chronicle.* On Jan. 1, 1891, he became a member of the firm of John J. Perkins & Co., with which he was associated for a number of years. He was an enthusiastic Republican as long ago as in 1856, when, during the Fremont campaign, he was made secretary of the first young men's Republican club of Cincinnati. Mr. Perkins was appointed fire trustee by Mayor Mosby on May 4, 1893, and served for over eight years in that capacity. He has been for years a director and treasurer of the Young Men's Mutual Life association of Cincinnati; was president of the Merchants and Manufacturers' association of Cincinnati and Hamilton county, and is president and treasurer of the American District Telegraph Company. In 1903 he was elected city auditor of Cincinnati for a term of three years. He is an active member of the Young Men's Blaine club of Cincinnati and also a member of Cincinnati Lodge No. 5, Benevolent and Protective Order of Elks. Mr. Perkins was married to Miss Sallie E. DeCamp, daughter of Hiram and Elizabeth DeCamp, May 3, 1859. Four children have been born to them, only one of whom survives, George B. Perkins. Their home is on East Walnut Hills.

JAMES H. WHITNEY, examiner of weights and measures, Cincinnati, O., was born at Corry, Pa., Oct. 11, 1861. In the public schools of his native town he acquired a good practical education, after which he went to work in a grocery store. Four years later he started a retail fruit and confectionery store. Later he went into the fruit business in a wholesale way in Corry, remaining in that line until 1896, when he came to Cincinnati and entered the employment of a wholesale fruit house there. In 1897 he started in the wholesale fruit business for himself and carried it on until 1900, when he was appointed to his present position by Mayor Fleischman. His long experience in handling groceries and fruits has made him thoroughly acquainted with weights and measures and given him the very best qualifications for the successful discharge of his duties. His four years of service have demonstrated the wisdom of the mayor in selecting him for the position. Mr. Whitney belongs to no secret order nor church organization. He is an enthusiastic Republican and a member of both the Blaine and North Side Republican clubs.

FRANK A. TUCKER, superintendent of the city infirmary, Cincinnati, O., is a native of that city, having been born there in 1848. After attending the public schools he graduated from Bartlett's business college at the age of nineteen, after which he became associated with his father, George W. Tucker, in the manufacture of trunks, continuing in that line of business for about seven years. He was then engaged in the manufacture of rugs and mats for several years. In 1875 he was elected to the city board of education; re-elected two years later; elected alderman at large in 1878 in a district overwhelmingly Democratic, and the same year chosen as a member of the union board of high schools, holding all three positions at once. In 1880 he was re-elected alderman for four years but resigned in 1881 to become a member of the board of public works. In 1886 he was re-elected to the board of public works for another five-year term, but before the expiration of that time the office was abolished by the legislature. In May, 1888, he was appointed chief deputy and private secretary to George B. Cox, inspector of oils for Ohio, and served in this capacity for two years. He was a delegate to the Republican national convention of 1888, and two years later successfully managed the campaign of Hon. Bellamy Storer, candidate for Congress in the first district. Shortly after the election in November, 1890, Mr. Tucker was appointed superintendent of the street cleaning department and remained at the head of the department for three years, when he resigned to accept the position of manager of the Sanitary Extracting Company, which had the contract for disposing of the city's garbage. Here he remained until 1902, when he came into his present position. Mr. Tucker is one of the leading Republicans of the city and as a worker has few equals. For about eight years he was a director of the Blaine club, of which he is a member. He is a Mason and a member of the Lincoln Park Baptist church. He was married in 1899 to Miss Anna B. Hudson, of Cincinnati.

GEORGE H. KOLKER, appraiser of merchandise in the United States custom house, Cincinnati, O., was born in that city, Jan. 27, 1853. In 1872 he graduated from the Woodward high school and began life as a bookkeeper. After a year in this occupation he started in to learn the trade of stair builder, but two years later he changed his mind and began the study of law. In 1878 he graduated from the Cincinnati law school and practiced for several years. In 1882 he was elected journal clerk in the Ohio legislature and served in that capacity at every session of the general assembly for twelve years. In 1893 he was appointed deputy clerk of the Ohio supreme court, serving in that position until October, 1896, when he went into the Hamilton county auditor's office as chief deputy. In June, 1898, he was appointed to his present position by the late President McKinley. In all the positions he has occupied Mr. Kolker has been distinguished for his thorough and methodical way of doing business, and for his courteous treatment of all who happened to have dealings with him.

ELMER E. GALBREATH, national bank examiner, Cincinnati, O., was born at Georgetown, Brown county, O., Feb. 1, 1864. His education was obtained at the public schools of Ripley, O., prior to the time he was eighteen years of age. At that time he went into the Ripley National bank as assistant cashier, his father being the cashier. Upon the death of his father in 1899 he succeeded to the position of cashier and held it until February, 1902, when he was appointed to his present place. Mr. Galbreath's long experience in the banking business gives him a peculiar fitness for the position of examiner, to which his sterling integrity adds strength and confidence. Those who know him best speak of him in high terms as being "the right man for the place." Mr. Galbreath is prominent in fraternal society circles, being a Royal Arch Mason and Knight of

Pythias. He is also a member of the Presbyterian church. As a Republican he has always taken an active part in political work and has frequently been called on to serve as delegate to state and local conventions. He acted as chairman of the committee on credentials at the convention of the National League of Republican clubs at Omaha, Neb. In 1889 he was married to Miss Bessie I. Torrence, daughter of Rev. J. W. Torrence, of Ripley, O., and they have five children—four boys and one girl.

JOHN A. PENTLAND, wharfmaster, Cincinnati, O., is a descendant of an old Scottish family that later settled in Ireland, in the childhood of his grandfather, who was the youngest of four brothers. Among the highly respected descendants of this great-uncle were Dr. Pentland, of Black Hall, in the neighborhood of Drogheda, Ireland; his son married a Miss Barrington, daughter of Sir I. Barrington; Dr. Pentland, of Kells; Dr. Shekleton, father of the Royal Advisers and S. V. P. of the Free and Accepted Masons of Ireland. R. Shekleton, Sir Hugh Childers, Canon Brady, Maria Henn and Mrs. Thirsby are collectively cousins of the subject of this sketch. The paternal grandfather of John A. Pentland was a respected and wealthy merchant and ship owner, who lived in Roseville, near Dublin, Ireland. He married a Miss Murray and they had two daughters and four sons: Harriet, Louisa, Charles, Henry, William and Thomas, the last named being the father of the subject of this sketch. Harriet was joined in wedlock to Sir Connory, the eminent chancellor; Louisa remained single; Charles wandered to Rio de Janeiro and died single; Henry married a Miss Manley, and his granddaughter was married not long ago to Rev. Frederick Bevan of Australia; William likewise crossed the ocean and settled in Canada. One of his sons, Samuel Pentland, was at one time the owner of the Neil House at Columbus, O., and another son, Charles, married a young lady of a distinguished French family. Of the family of Grandmother Pentland but little is known. Thomas Pentland, the father of John A., was for many years the rector of the parish of Drumreilly, in the diocese of Killmore, County Leitrim, Ireland, and died there in 1877, at the age of seventy-seven years. He married Miss Florence Sadlier and of the eleven children born to them six are still living, viz.: Mrs. F. Gumley, Mrs. Louisa H. Alexander, Mary, Henry, William F. and John A. Pentland. Mrs. Gumley is the widow of the late R. Gumley, who was rector of a church in Killedeas, Ireland; Louisa is the wife of Rev. Hugh Alexander of Black Lion, near Enniskillen, Ireland; Henry is a physician living in Black Rock Castle, Mohill, Ireland; William is a practicing physician in London, England, and John A. is the subject of this sketch. The relatives of Mr. Pentland on the maternal side embrace several distinguished families, among whom may be named the "Sadliers," the "Yelletts," the "Atkinsons," the "Digbys," the "L'Estranges," etc. John A. Pentland was born at Aughovilla, County Leitrim, Ireland, in April, 1851, and received his education in the Raneleagh school at Athlone, on the banks of the river Shannon. On Sept. 22, 1870, he sailed from Liverpool for America, and upon reaching this country made his way directly to Cincinnati. He went to work for the firm of Proctor & Gamble, the great soap manufacturers, and remained with them for seventeen years. In the year 1888 he went to Knoxville, Tenn., as a stockholder and superintendent of the Unaker Soap Works. But the venture was not a profitable one, and after about fifteen months he returned to Cincinnati. Mr. Pentland had married in Cincinnati a cousin of Benjamin Harrison, ex-president of the United States. When he returned to Cincinnati he received, through a letter his wife wrote to President Harrison, a position in the United States revenue service, under the collector of the district, Col. D. W. McClung, and held that position until President Cleveland came into office in 1893. Mr. Pentland then became notice clerk in the city engineer's office for six or eight months, when he went into the county auditor's office under Eugene Lewis and remained there for four years. He next occupied the position of paymaster of the water works, and on Aug. 29, 1900, was appointed to his present position. Mr. Pentland takes great interest in social and political affairs. He is an honorable member of Vattier Lodge, Free and Accepted Masons; member of the Young Men's Blaine club and the Republican club of the fourteenth ward, and is a member of the Episcopal church. In 1874 he was married to Miss Carrie M. Smith, of Cincinnati, and they have two children living: Florence May, wife of William F. Belmer, of H. Belmer & Co., and Bessie L., at home. The maiden name of Mrs. J. A. Pentland's mother was Elizabeth Irwin. She was the eldest sister of the late John and William P. Irwin, of Clarksburg, W. Va., merchants and capitalists of that city. Her relatives embrace several of the most distinguished families of Cincinnati, past and present, among whom may be named the Irwins, General Findlay, the Harrisons, Torrances, etc. Mr. Pentland lives with his family at No. 845 Poplar street, and has his office at No. 7 Main street.

WILLIAM RUEHRWEIN, superintendent of the city workhouse, Cincinnati, O., was born in Westphalia, Prussia, Feb. 21, 1840. While he was still in his infancy his parents came to America, settled in Cincinnati, and there the father, whose name was also William, worked at his trade of tailor until his death in 1893, in the eighty-third year of his age. Until he was about twelve years old the son attended the city schools. For the next two years he worked at odd jobs and when he was fourteen he went into the machine shop of Antone Mueller to learn the trade of machinist. He remained with Mr. Mueller until 1860, when he entered the employment of Fay & Co. (now the Fay & Eagan Company), and was associated with this company until 1894, being superintendent of the tool department for twenty-seven years. For a number of years Mr. Ruehrwein was a member of the city board of education and of the union board of high schools. In 1893 he was elected on the Republican ticket to the state legislature and was re-elected in 1895. Before the expiration of his second term he resigned to accept the appointment of state labor commissioner, tendered him by Gov. Asa Bushnell. He served two years as commissioner and in May, 1898, was appointed to his present position. Mr. Ruehrwein was married in 1861 to Miss Sarah, daughter of Henry Stegner, of Cincinnati, and they have one son, Samuel, and seven daughters. Mr. Ruehrwein is a thirty-second degree Mason, a Knight Templar and a Noble of the Mystic Shrine, an Odd Fellow, a Knight of Honor and a member of the First German Reformed church, in which he has served as deacon and elder. He is an active Republican, frequently going as a delegate to state and district conventions.

PETER W. DURR, superintendent of the county infirmary of Hamilton county, Ohio, was born in the city of Cincinnati, Dec. 15, 1861. His education was obtained in the public schools and at the age of sixteen years he went to work in the malleable iron works of

James L. Haven & Co. After about five years with this firm he went into the employ of Proctor & Gamble, the great soap manufacturers, and remained with them for eleven years, working his way up to superintendent of the stamping and packing department. While with this company he was elected trustee of Mill Creek township, being elected the first time in 1886 and re-elected for six successive terms. During this time he also served three terms as mayor of Elmwood Place. In 1893 he received an appointment as United States gauger and served until the end of President Harrison's administration. He was then made deputy sheriff of Hamilton county, under Robert Archibald, to fill a vacancy, and held the place until the end of the term. He then went into the county auditor's office as chief deputy and remained there until April, 1903, when he was made superintendent of the county infirmary. Mr. Durr has been a member of the Republican state central committee since 1894, was chairman of the committee from 1900 to 1902, and before that had served two years as secretary. He was an alternate delegate to the national convention of 1904, and has frequently been a delegate to state and congressional conventions. He is a director of the First National bank of Elmwood Place, and a member of numerous societies.

HARRY C. CRAGG, M.D., of Cincinnati, O., is a native of the Buckeye State, having been born at Groesbeck, Hamilton county, July 23, 1869. His parents, Richard H. and Julia A. (Ponder) Cragg, were of English descent, though the father was a native of Cincinnati. During the Civil war he served as a member of Company A, One Hundred and Thirty-seventh Ohio volunteer infantry, participating in all the battles and skirmishes in which his regiment was engaged. After the war he returned to Cincinnati, where he continued to reside until his death, which occurred Aug. 31, 1898, in his fifty-eighth year. Doctor Cragg received his general education in the common and high schools of his native county and in 1901 was graduated from the Miami Medical college of Cincinnati, standing high in his class. Through the dean of the faculty he was offered the position of interne in the United States marine hospital, but he declined, preferring to build up a practice for himself.

This showed him to be a young man of strong determination and self-reliance, and subsequent events have sustained his decision at that time. Locating in Cincinnati soon after leaving college he has devoted his energies to his practice and he occupies a high place in the profession. He is a member of the American Medical association and of the Cincinnati Academy of Medicine. Doctor Cragg is a member and past chancellor of Crescent Lodge No. 42, Knights of Pythias, and of some of the leading Republican clubs of the city, being somewhat active in furthering the interests of that party in political contests. On July 11, 1900, he was married to Miss Florence Ware, daughter of Charles H. Ware, an old resident and one of the early dentists of Cincinnati, amassing a comfortable fortune by the practice of his profession. Doctor Cragg and his wife attend the Episcopal church of which he is a member.

FRED MAAG, superintendent of the street cleaning department, Cincinnati, O., has been a resident of that city all his life. He was born July 20, 1854, educated in the public schools until he was about ten years of age, when circumstances compelled him to quit school and begin the battle of life for himself. Later he learned the trade of silversmith and worked at it until 1875, when he began working in the street cleaning department as hostler. He has been in the department ever since, except the years 1884-85, when he was connected with the street railway service, and again in 1890-91, when he was in the same line of employment. From 1891 to 1898 he was a clerk in the department and since 1900 has occupied the position of superintendent. Mr. Maag has worked his way up from the bottom and knows the work of street cleaning in all its details. His efficiency is best seen in the condition of the streets since he took charge. Mr. Maag is a thirty-second degree member of the Scottish Rite Masons and a Noble of the Mystic Shrine. He is also a member of the Benevolent and Protective Order of Elks. Although not a member of any religious denomination he attends the German Lutheran church.

JOSEPH B. COWEN, M.D., a promising young physician of Cincinnati, O., was born in that city Feb. 5, 1876, and is a son of James and Catherine (Foley) Cowen, who were the parents of seven boys and four girls. The Cowen family is of Scotch-Irish extraction, James Cowen being a native of the North of Ireland. For many years he was engaged in the wholesale shoe business in Cincinnati, and died there in 1886. Doctor Cowen was educated at St. Xavier's college, at Cincinnati, afterward graduating from the medical department of the University of Cincinnati in 1897. Shortly after receiving his degree he located at Oxford, O., where he practiced until early in the year 1904, when he came to Cincinnati. Here he has succeeded beyond his expectations, considering the short time he has been established in his native city. Doctor Cowen is fully alive to the progress of his profession and is not the last to avail himself of new discoveries in the practice of medicine. In July, 1900, he led to the altar Miss Elizabeth Gentry, the daughter of Gilbert Gentry, of Indiana. To this union there have been born two daughters, Marie Louise and Elizabeth.

WILLIAM JAMES BREED, of the Crane-Breed Manufacturing Company, Cincinnati, O., is a son of Abel D. and Bethiah G. Breed, and was born at Fairhaven, Mass., in the year 1835. He received his education in the Hughes high school and the Phillips academy, at Andover, Mass., and in 1852 came to Cincinnati, where he was one of the founders of the Crane-Breed Company eight years later. This company manufactures hearses, metallic caskets, undertakers' supplies of various kinds, and is one of the best known concerns of its kind in the country. Their trade extends over a large territory, their goods going to almost every part of the continent where Christian burial is vouchsafed the remains of the dead. Mr. Breed's mother died in 1877 and his father on Dec. 24, 1888. Both were of that sturdy New England stock that believes in a high standard of morals and died as they had lived, true to their ideals, and respected by all who knew them. Mr. Breed was married in 1868 to Miss Laura Adams of Boston, who is as popular in social life as her husband is in commercial circles.

HOWELL LEWIS LOVELL, a retired manufacturer of Covington, Ky., was born in what is now the State of West Virginia, July 9, 1824. He is a son of Joseph and Bettie (Washington) Lovell, and through Betty Lewis, a sister of George Washington, the family are related to the first president of the United States. At the age of sixteen years Mr. Lovell began life on his own account and at the age of twenty-two he was successfully operating a salt manufactory on the Kanawha river, a short distance from the city of Charleston, the present capital of West Virginia. The discovery of gold in California attracted thither thousands of young men from the East and in 1852 young Lovell joined a party bound for the new El Dorado. They crossed the plains with ox teams and after a long and tedious trip of four months arrived at the gold fields, only to find that their expectations were not likely to be realized. After a short time in the placer mines Mr. Lovell returned to the States, bought a large number of milch cows, organized a party of men and returned to California, via Nicaragua, and disposed of his cattle, receiving in many instances $150 for a cow. He remained in California until 1864, when he returned east. Four years later he located in Covington and in 1871 engaged in the manufacture of smoking and fine cut chewing tobaccos, his factory being located on Second street, in Cincinnati. In 1875 the business was removed across the river to Covington and Mr. Lovell remained actively connected with it until 1892, when he retired to enjoy the fruits of his industry of former years, the treasures of his well-selected library, and the associations of his many friends. On April 21, 1856, Mr. Lovell was married to Miss Emma A., daughter of F. G. and Frances Buhring, and four children were born to this union: Mary L., wife of James W. Sayre, of Lexington, Ky.; Fannie B.; Virginia L., wife of John T. Hodge, of Newport, Ky., and Howell Lewis, Jr., who made his home in the Adirondacks, of New York, until his death. He married Miss Mary Fallis Rogers, a granddaughter of the late John F. Fallis, of Cincinnati, for many years president of the Merchants' National bank of that city.

T. J. SMITH, of Covington, Ky., is a Kentuckian, born in Henry county, July 31, 1838, and removed to Covington with his widowed mother, in 1846, where he has since lived, but conducts his printing and publishing business in Cincinnati. When little more than a child Mr. Smith became an apprentice in a printing establishment, and having an alert, receptive mind, soon mastered the details of the trade, at which he wrought as a journeyman for some years. In 1860 he started the Cincinnati *Dramatic Review,* which venture succeeded, and his business finally developed into an extensive book and job printing concern. In 1868 he projected and established the *Merchant and Manufacturer,* which publication was the first to suggest and advocate the series of industrial expositions—an enterprise that during its course did more to advertise and render Cincinnati famous on both sides of the Atlantic than any or all other agencies. Since then Mr. Smith has engaged in several other journalistic ventures, among them the *A. O. U. W. Bulletin,* for years the national organ of Ancient Order of United Workmen; the *Shoe and Leather Age,* the *Jobber and Retail Grocer,* and the *Knights' Journal,* organ of the Knights of the Golden Rule, of which order he was one of the founders, and for which he wrote the ritual and shared in preparing its constitution and general laws. For fourteen years Mr. Smith held the office of supreme secretary of the order, and was devoted to its welfare. The papers submitted by him to the supreme commandery are models of their kind and stamp him as a clear, logical and original thinker, and a thoroughly equipped authority on subjects pertaining to beneficial orders, having for many years given to them his best thought and most energetic efforts. Mr. Smith ranks with the oldest and most popular citizens of Covington, whose people he has faithfully served in various positions of trust and honor, in the school board, in the city council, where he was for two terms president, and one term as the president of the board of aldermen. The esteem and respect of his fellow towns-men he enjoys in an unusual degree—the reward of a life of moral, personal and political cleanliness and prob:ty, and the faithful discharge of every public duty imposed upon him. Having no offspring of his own, Mr. Smith has reared and educated several orphan children. Be-sides, his love of the little ones is so well known that half the children in his neighborhood greet him as "uncle." He is no bigot, but, with charity and tolerance for all, he is a consistent and liberal member and supporter of the church of his preference.

THOMAS W. GRAYDON, M.D., an eminent physician of Cincin-nati, O., and a citizen who has been closely interwoven with the official life of the city for several years, was born in Ireland in the year 1850. In his youth he was a diligent student, but at the age of fifteen his eyes began failing and he was compelled to forego the pleasant associations of his books to prevent total blindness. When he was eighteen he came to America, where for a year or two he was employed in farm work in the State of Illinois. The outdoor life and the continued abstention from reading so strengthened his eyes that in 1871 he entered Griswold college, at Davenport, Ia., and graduated from that institution with an honorable standing. Next he received a degree from the Iowa State university, and while a student there he was elected as the Iowa repre-sentative to the interstate oratorical contest, at Indianapolis, where he was awarded the second prize. In 1876 Dr. Graydon located in Cin-cinnati, which city has ever since been his home. Here he soon suc-ceeded in building up a lucrative practice, in which he commands the respect of his brother physicians and enjoys the confidence of his patients. Politically Dr. Graydon is a Republican, but his opponents give him the credit of being a fair fighter. His interest in public matters led to his being elected to represent Hamilton county in the state legislature in 1885-86, and he was offered the nomination for a second term, but declined in order to attend to his practice. In 1888 Governor Foraker appointed him a member of the old board of public affairs, upon which he continued to serve until 1890, when it was abol-ished, the board of city affairs taking its place. The mayor of the city appointed Dr. Graydon a member of the new board, where he served for some time, always being in favor of every measure that had for its purpose the upbuilding of his adopted city. For many years he was an earnest and persistent advocate of new water works, but failed to secure the support and co-operation of the people. Dr. Graydon has a wife and an interesting family of five sons and four daughters. Their home in Clifton is one of the coziest in that section of the city and is always open to their friends.

LOUIS BARDES, storekeeper, or county stationer, of Hamilton county, O., was born in the city of Cincinnati, Aug. 14, 1856. He is the second son of Christian and Lisette Bardes, both of whom were natives of the province of Bavaria, Germany. Christian Bardes was born at Anweiler, in March, 1827. He was educated in the public schools of the Fatherland, afterward learning the trade of butcher. When he was about twenty years of age he came to America, settled in Cincinnati, and there followed the butcher business until 1869, when he purchased a tannery which he conducted until his death, July 16, 1878. During his life he was one of the prominent figures in the city, taking considerable interest in politics as a Republican. He was a member of the Lutheran church. Louis Bardes was educated in the Cincinnati public schools, learned the trade of his father and followed the same until 1879. After the death of his father he became associated with his brothers in the management of the tannery, until 1896, when he sold his stock to his brothers to engage in other business. In 1898 he received the appointment of deputy clerk of the Hamilton circuit court, holding the position until August, 1900, when he was appointed to his present position by the county commissioners. Politically, Mr. Bardes has always been an unswerving Republican and ready to defend his opinions against all comers. He is a prominent member of the Masonic order, belonging to lodge, chapter, commandery, Scottish Rite and the Mystic Shrine. He is also a Knight of Pythias, a Knight of the Maccabees, a member of the Royal Arcanum, and is supreme eminent ruler of "Ye Ancient Order of Why-not." On Oct. 21, 1878, Mr. Bardes was married to Miss Flora Belle Houk, and to this union there have been born the following children: Florence and Lulu, twins, born Nov. 21, 1879; Henrietta, June 2, 1881; Christian H., Aug. 7, 1883, and Fred. L., Jan. 10, 1885. The family live at 2402 Jefferson ave., South Norwood, where Mr. Bardes owns a beautiful residence. It is believed that the Bardes family are descendants of the old Bardes family of Italy. On the reaches of the Appenines there still remains the ancient seat of the Bardes, bearing the name "Alto Mena." The early ancestors were the Bardes who loaned to Edward III. the money to marshal his hosts that fought the battle of Crecy, and on the walls of Alto Mena hangs an old parchment pledging the crown of England to repay the loan, but the pledge has not been kept. After Crecy the Black Prince, the first Prince of Wales, to prove his admiration for the valor of the blind king of Bohemia, adopted from his insignia the three plumes and the motto, "Ich Dien," for his own crest.

JACOB BASCHANG, whose portrait appears at the head of this sketch, is a descendant of the good, old, conservative German element that has been such a potent factor in building up the city of Cincinnati. His parents, George Fred and Elizabeth Baschang, were natives of Germany. The father learned the trade of carpet weaver in the Fatherland and while still a young man came to America. Settling in Cincinnati he continued to follow his trade until the Civil war broke out, when he enlisted in the One Hundred and Sixth regiment, Ohio volunteer infantry, and remained in the service of his adopted country until his death, in 1865. He was an ardent Republican in his life, and a member of the German Lutheran church. The mother, left a widow with four children, managed to rear and educate them by her own labors and the assistance of a pension received from the government. One of these children is the subject of this sketch. He was born in the city of Cincinnati, June 3, 1859. After receiving a common school education he began life in the Pape Bros. picture frame works. Later he went with the Mosler-Baumann safe and lock works. Here he began as a drill boy, gradually working his way up until he had charge of the intricate machines used for cutting out the steel for safe doors. He remained with this company until 1887, when he was appointed janitor in the county auditor's office. After six years in this position he was made night watchman in the treasurer's office, and in 1896 was appointed Dow tax collector, which office he still holds. In all the positions that Mr. Baschang has filled in the public service, his appointment has been made as a Republican, and it is no exaggeration to say that he is one of the party's most active workers in Hamilton county. He holds membership in a number of secret societies, in which he is popular because of his genial disposition. On Feb. 8, 1882, Mr. Baschang was married to Josephine Miller, daughter of Frederick and Magdalena Miller, of Cincinnati. Her father came from Germany about 1850 and settled in Cincinnati, where he reared a family of seven children, Josephine being next to the eldest. He died in 1883 and his remains rest in the Vine St. Hill cemetery. Mr. and Mrs. Baschang have four children living, viz.: Ida, born July 18, 1883; Edward, March 28, 1885; Albert, Aug. 22, 1888, and Elsie, Dec. 18, 1892.

J. HENRY HUELSMANN, a prominent undertaker and funeral director of Cincinnati, O., was born Dec. 17, 1858, at Cincinnati. His father was Ferdinand Huelsmann, who was born in Germany, coming to America in 1852 and settling in Cincinnati, where he followed the trade of blacksmith. His mother was Mary (Roettinghouse) Huelsmann. Mr. Huelsmann's early education was received in the Cincinnati public schools, after leaving which, at the age of thirteen, he entered the furniture factory of Henshaw & Sons in 1871, and continued in their service until 1895. By constant application to his duties and an earnest endeavor to forge ahead he was made foreman of the factory at the age of nineteen years. In 1895 he entered the undertaking business and connected himself with Henry Dusterberg under the firm name of Dusterberg & Huelsmann, which association continued until 1901, when Mr. Huelsmann purchased the interest of his partner and has since been conducting the business alone. In 1895 he graduated from Clarke's school of embalming at Cincinnati. He was married in 1881 to Louise Schmidt of Cincinnati and they have had four children, the following of whom are living: Mary, Gertrude and Alfonse. Mr. Huelsmann is a member of St. Paul's Roman Catholic church.

WILLIAM RIEDLIN, president of the Bavarian Brewing Company, of Covington, Ky., is a native of Germany, having been born at the town of Mulheim, in the province of Baden, Nov. 20, 1850. In 1870 he came to America, landing on July 1, and three days later he was in Cincinnati. There he learned the blacksmith trade with John Aulls, who had a shop on Central avenue, near Findlay street, and after learning the trade was for many years in the employ of McNeil & Urban. On the twenty-first day of June, 1877, he opened a grocery at the corner of Elm and Greene streets and continued in that business for some time, afterward becoming the manager of Tivoli Hall. In 1882 he came to Covington and became associated with John Mayer in the brewing business. This undertaking developed into the Bavarian Brewing Company, one of the distinct features of Covington and one of the largest concerns of its kind in the country. Mr. Mayer retired from the business in 1890. In addition to the brewery proper, the company is largely interested in the manufacture of ice, having one of the largest and most complete plants to be found anywhere. Mr. Riedlin is a man of enterprise and public spirit, and for the last fifteen years has been regarded as one of Covington's most valued citizens, always contributing with his money and influence toward the best interests of the municipality. From October, 1891, to January, 1897, he was a member of the city legislature as an alderman, and while in that position he aided in the introduction of many needed reforms, which have contributed in no small degree to the city's growth. Mr. Riedlin is one of the directors of the German National bank and is prominently connected with other public institutions of Covington. He is a Republican in his political views, but his broad-mindedness has won for him a host of Democratic friends. On Aug. 2, 1877, he was married to Miss Emma, daughter of Samuel and Maria Hoffman, of Riesenburg, Prussia. To this union there have been born eight children, four of whom are living. They are William F., born July 19, 1881; Walter, born Oct. 31, 1888; Mary, born March 24, 1883; and Louisa, born June 2, 1890. William was married on Nov. 9, 1903, to Norma, daughter of August Wittgenfelt, of Cincinnati, and is now associated with his father in business. Carl, Emma, Edward and Charles are deceased.

JAMES COLLINS (deceased), for many years a familiar figure in the business world of Cincinnati, O., was born in Mason county, Ky., March 17, 1835, and died at his home on Mount Auburn, Cincinnati, Dec. 15, 1903. When he was but five years of age his father, Levi Collins, came to Cincinnati, where James began his business career, while still in his boyhood, as an employe of the United States Express Company. Later he was with the National Union and still later with the American Express Company, where he had charge of all the eastern shipping up to a short time before his death. This company thought so well of him as a man, and so highly appreciated his services as one of its trusted employes, that for several years prior to his death he drew a pension from the company, being unable to perform his duties on account of failing health. Mr. Collins was a modest, unassuming man, whose highest aim was to subserve the interest of his employers by a courteous treatment of all the company's patrons and a close application to the business entrusted to his care. He was a man of steady habits and a member of Kilwinning Lodge of Free and Accepted Masons, in which he had a high standing. Mr. Collins was united in marriage to Miss Isabella, daughter of Jonathan Wilson and Elizabeth (Ashton) Bendle. She was born in Liverpool, England, but came in early life with her parents to America. To this marriage there were born the following children: Albert Henry, Emma B., Clifford Frederick, Ella Ashton, Jennie Shaw and Harry Stanley. These children with their mother still survive. Albert Henry married Marie Brady of Cincinnati, on Nov. 2, 1897. She died on Nov. 2, 1901, leaving one son, Robert Wilson, born Nov. 30, 1898. Clifford F. married Miss Lottie Beal of Cincinnati, and they have four children: Dorothy, Glenn, Marjory and Clifford. Ella Ashton married Edward Schoenbaum, superintendent of the Otto Marmet Coal Company, of Cincinnati. Jennie Shaw married Frank Butler and resides in Philadelphia, Pa. Harry Stanley is unmarried and is with the Fairweather & La Due Company, of Chicago.

JOHN COFFEY (deceased), for many years the senior member of the law firm of Coffey, Mallon, Mills & Vandenbury, of Cincinnati, O., was a native of the Emerald Isle, having been born in Dunnamore parish, County Cork, Ireland, Jan. 6, 1844. He died on May 8, 1904. When he was ten years of age he came with his father to this country and for about five years lived in the city of Boston. In 1859 he came west and finally located at Cincinnati. When the Civil war broke out he enlisted in the Thirty-fourth Ohio infantry and, although but little more than a boy, he was made sergeant of his company. Young Coffey remained with the regiment until the expiration of the war, when he worked some time as a book agent, studying law in the meantime as opportunity offered, until he was able to pass a satisfactory examination and secure his admission to the bar. Early in the seventies he was admitted to practice and soon afterward formed a partnership with the late Patrick Mallon, whose son was later a member of the firm, and in a short time he acquired a wide reputation as a criminal lawyer. Mr. Coffey soon came to be recognized as the wit of the local bar, and many a time this wit has helped him out of a tight place. As an after dinner speaker he was hard to excel. His proverbial wit was always made to do duty on such occasions and the guests at social functions were always glad to observe his name on the programme for a response.

In 1887 he was nominated by the Democracy of Cincinnati for the office of judge of the probate court, but the city at that time was hopelessly Republican and he was defeated with the rest of his party ticket. On Aug. 25, 1877, Mr. Coffey was united in marriage to Miss Mary Bolger, daughter of Captain Bolger, of Cincinnati. To this union there were born ten children, seven of whom are still living. They are Guy, John F., Edward, Clarence, Albert, Ruth and Marguerite. Mrs. Coffey preceded her husband to the tomb. Mr. Coffey was a member of the Church of the Guardian Angel, Mount Washington, and was a consistent practitioner of the precepts of his religion. His death was the result of disease incurred while serving in the army during the war. He has left to posterity a clean record as a lawyer, a citizen, and as a man. He was a strict observer of the ethics of the legal profession and avoided everything like pettifogging; he was a law abiding and patriotic citizen; his wit was always refined and free from sting, and his charity was of the kind that lets not the left hand know what the right hand doeth.

EZRA W. VAN DUSEN, of the Buckeye Bell and Brass Foundry, of Cincinnati, O., is one of the oldest, if not the oldest active business man in that city at the present time. He was born Aug. 20, 1824, at the southwest corner of Elm and Water streets, his parents being Abraham and Johanna (Kellog) Van Dusen, who were among the early settlers of Cincinnati. His grandfather, Matthew Van Dusen, was born on June 15, 1761, died in Cincinnati, Aug. 6, 1820, and was buried in the rear of the old stone church on the site now occupied by the Wesley Chapel, on Fifth street. Abraham Van Dusen and Johanna Kellog were married on April 9, 1809. Ezra Van Dusen received his early education, which was somewhat limited, by attending the common schools and night schools. At the age of twelve, he went to work in the glass works of Parker, Cummings & Alexander, on East Front street. In April, 1838, he went to the Buckeye Bell and Brass Foundry, his first duty being that of running the engine. Next he got to making cores and finally became the boss coremaker, thus laying the foundation for acquiring a thorough knowledge of the brass foundry business. In 1856 he became a partner in the concern with which he had been employed for eighteen years, the other members of the firm being G. W. Coffin and C. T. Tift. Some six years before this Mr. Van Dusen had purchased the scales of Francis Meyer for the manufacture of chime bells. In 1865 Mr. Coffin retired from the company and upon the death of Mr. Tift, in 1894, Mr. Van Dusen purchased his interest from the estate. Since then he has been the sole owner and proprietor of the works. About a year after this Mr. Van Dusen cast the largest swinging bell on this continent. It was cast on Oct. 30, 1895, and hangs in the belfry of St. Francis de Sales church, East Walnut Hills, Cincinnati. The contract called for a bell weighing thirty thousand pounds, with a tone of D sharp or D natural, and so perfect was the work done that it requires the most expert musicians to detect its tone lacking vibrations. The bell is nine feet in diameter at the rim, five feet at the crown, seven feet in height, and the sounding board is nine inches in thickness. The only bell on the Western Continent that approaches it in size is the one in the Notre Dame Cathedral, Montreal, Canada, the weight of that bell being twenty-eight thousand pounds. Notwithstanding his fourscore years Mr. Van Dusen is active in his business, takes great pride in turning out good work, and rarely uses glasses to assist his sight. He was married on Oct. 16, 1844, to Miss Annie Eliza Dowds; and to this union there have been born the following children: Henrietta Elizabeth, married William P. Mounts, of Morrow, O.; Ezra W., married Annie Rogers, of Branch Hill, O.; Rhoda; Annie, married Dr. M. F. Baldwin, of Blanchester, O.; George W., married Grace Julian; Charles Alser; Martha W.; Cora, married J. F. Dye, of Newport, Ky.; Frank E., married Carrie Cullom, of Mainville, O., and now resides at Loveland in the same state. Mr. Van Dusen is a member of Christ Episcopal church, is a strong temperance advocate, and never takes any active part in political contests. The best efforts of his life have been given to building up a business in which he stands at the head in the United States, and when he shall have laid down the burden of life the world will be the better for his having lived in it.

ROBERT J. BONSER, of Cincinnati, O., one of the largest wholesale carpet dealers in the United States, was born in London, Canada, March 5, 1863, his parents being Edward E. and Sarah (Potter) Bonser. His mother, a daughter of Col. Robert Potter, of the English army, was born in the West Indies while her father was stationed there on military duty. In the early sixties Edward Bonser came with his family to Cincinnati, where he followed the vocation of painter and paper-hanger. In 1872 he went to Lafayette, Ind., and established himself in the wall paper business, later becoming a member of the firm of Ward & Co., of that city. Returning to Cincinnati in 1877 he remained there until 1884, when he removed to Topeka, Kan.; went to Tacoma, Wash., in 1884, and subsequently returned to Cincinnati, where he still lives. Robert J. Bonser was educated in the public schools of Cincinnati and in 1879 began his business career as a salesman in the collar and cuff department of C. R. Mabley. After a short time in this department his superb qualifications as a salesman began to be made manifest and he was transferred to the men's clothing department, where he remained for nine years, rising from one important position to another until he had charge of the department. Other mercantile establishments noted his ability as a salesman and his services were sought after by some of the best houses in the city. Early in July, 1889, Mr. Bonser purchased an interest in the wholesale and retail carpet house of Lowry & Goebel, and although he had never handled that line of goods, within a month he educated himself in all the details of the business, took the road as a salesman, with the result that from the start his orders compared favorably with the old veterans. In 1897 he severed his connection with this house and established himself at No. 21 West Pearl St., under the name of Robert J. Bonser, as a wholesale dealer in carpets, mattings and linoleums exclusively. The first year the volume of business amounted to three hundred and fifty thousand dollars, and this has steadily grown until now the house does a business amounting to a million and a quarter of dollars annually. A corps of efficient and energetic traveling salesmen represent Mr. Bonser in the States of Ohio, Indiana, Michigan, West Virginia, Kentucky, Tennessee, Alabama, Georgia and the eastern portion of Illinois. The growth of the business necessitated larger quarters and early in 1904 Mr. Bonser leased the adjoining building at No. 23 West Pearl St., having previously established a large warehouse at No. 26 West Second St. He also uses the storage warehouse of the Big Four railway. The marvelous growth of this house is due chiefly to the energy, ability and personal magnetism of Mr. Bonser. Added to this is the good taste shown in the selection of stock, designs, etc., which, with the prompt payment of bills, gives the concern a reputation second to none in the country and makes Mr. Bonser the acknowledged monarch of the carpet trade in the territory where his house is known. Mr. Bonser is a prominent figure in fraternal circles in Cincinnati and vicinity. He is a Thirty-second degree Mason in the Cincinnati Consistory, and has also taken the York Rite of the Order, being a member of Willia Chapter, Royal Arch Masons, and Trinity Commandery, Knights Templars. For a number of years he has been a Knight of Pythias. In political matters he is a Republican, keeps well informed on public questions, but is not an active politician, and in religion he is a Presbyterian. Mr. Bonser was married on March 5, 1884, to Miss Ella, daughter of Philip and Mary Metzger, of Cincinnati, and to this union there have been born two children: Horace and Isabella.

HON. ALBERT S. BERRY, an attorney and prominent citizen of Newport, Ky., is a descendant of one of the oldest and most highly connected families of Campbell county. His grandfather, Washington Berry, was a native of Virginia, but came to Kentucky at an early date, where he was one of the trustees that laid out the city of Newport and was the first judge of Campbell county. He married Miss Alice Taylor, daughter of Gen. James Taylor, a soldier of the war of 1812 and one of the largest land owners of Kentucky. James T. Berry, a son of this marriage, was born in 1806. He was one of the largest farmers and land owners in Campbell county and was one of the leading citizens. His wife was Miss Virginia Wise, a daughter of Nathaniel Wise, a prominent attorney of Washington, D. C., where he died in 1826. Her mother was a Miss McKeney. James T. and Virginia Berry were the parents of the following children: Washington N., who died in the Confederate service during the Civil war; Albert S., the subject of this sketch; Virginia, wife of Philip B. Spence, of Nashville, Tenn.; Jane, who died as the wife of Taylor Williams; Mildred W. and Betty, both of whom died unmarried; and James T. and Edmund F., also deceased. Albert S. Berry was born on his father's farm in Campbell county, in 1837, and has always claimed that county as his home. He was educated at the Miami university, Oxford, O., after which he attended the Cincinnati law school and in due course of time was admitted to the bar. He began the practice of his profession at Newport, where he has had a successful career ever since, being in continuous practice except what time he served in the army during the war, and by his elections to various official positions. In 1851 he was chosen superintendent of public instruction; city attorney in 1858; served as president of the school board for some time; mayor of the city for four terms; two terms in the state senate; was nominated by his party for governor in 1887, but was defeated by a chain of circumstances over which he had no control; was elected to Congress from the Sixth Kentucky district in 1892 and was three times re-elected, serving four consecutive terms, and in January, 1904, he was appointed by Governor Beckham to the position of circuit judge of Campbell county, to fill the vacancy caused by the death of Judge Newman. At the outbreak of the Civil war Mr. Berry enlisted in Company A, Fifth Kentucky Confederate cavalry, and served four years. Some time after his enlistment he was made adjutant in the signal service and served as such for about a year. He was then promoted to the rank of lieutenant in the marine service and ordered to Charleston Harbor. After the march of Sherman to the sea the marine force with which he was stationed was sent to Richmond to join Lee's army. Three days before the final surrender at Appomattox he was captured and held a prisoner at Johnston's Island for two months when he was released and returned to Newport with the rank of captain. Mr. Berry was married in 1867 to Miss Annie Shaler, daughter of Nathaniel B. and Ann (Southgate) Shaler, the former a native of New York and the latter of Newport. To this union there have been born five children, viz.: Alice, wife of William H. Nunn, Portland, Ore.; Shaler, a practicing physician at Newport; Anna, at home; Albert S., Jr., a graduate of the Cincinnati law school and in practice at Newport; and Robert L., who served as a cadet from the third class at Annapolis on the San Francisco during the Spanish-American war. The vessel was shot through by a Spanish gun near Morro Castle at Havana. After the war he returned to Annapolis, completed his course, graduated with the class of 1899, and is now an ensign on the United States torpedo boat destroyer, "Hull."

HUBBARD SCHWARTZ, of Newport, Ky., circuit court clerk of Campbell county and a well-known newspaper man, was born in Newport, April 15, 1868. His grandfather, John Frederick Schwartz, was a native of Hamburg, Germany. During the political agitation there in 1831 he expressed his sympathy for the opponents of the existing state of affairs, incurred by this course the displeasure of the authorities, and fled with his family to America. After a voyage of thirty-one days they landed at Baltimore, but fearing that he would be captured and sent back, Mr. Schwartz made his way with his family overland to Wheeling. On this journey they suffered much discomfort from the melting of the heavy snows, which caused the great flood of the early spring of 1832, the second greatest in the history of the Ohio river. The grandfather died at Wheeling and in 1838 his widow with her children floated down the river on a barge to Cincinnati, where she lived for several years, and finally died in Grant's Lick, Campbell county. Her three sons were John,

Henry and Herman. The first two are deceased and Herman left Cincinnati for Texas, since which time all trace of him has been lost. John Schwartz, the eldest son, was born in Hamburg in 1825. Upon the death of his father he became the main assistance to his widowed mother. Soon after coming to Cincinnati, in 1838, he was apprenticed to a rope maker for a year, his wages going to his mother to help toward the support of the family. He continued to work at the business until he was eighteen years old, when the family removed to Jamestown, now a part of Dayton, Ky. For several years he operated a rope-walk in what is now Isabella street, one of the principal thoroughfares of Newport. John Schwartz was the first mayor of Jamestown and also the last one before it was consolidated with Brooklyn to form the city of Dayton. He was also president of the board of education for some time. In 1864 he was elected sheriff of the county on the Democratic ticket and at the close of his term was re-elected. Upon retiring from the sheriff's office he farmed for five years in Grant's Lick precinct, where he had bought a farm, and at the end of that time returned to Newport, residing there while operating rope factories at Paris and Nicholasville, Ky. In 1875, he was elected city jailer and held the office for six years, when he retired from both business and politics. He died in 1889. Owing to the death of his father, already mentioned, his opportunities to secure an education were such that he never attended school a day in his life. However, by self study he learned to read and write, and ultimately became a well-informed man. He married Wilhelmina Bandermann, a native of Salzburg, Germany, who, when she came to America, made the trip from Baltimore to Cincinnati on the first regular passenger train between those two cities. She died in 1891. The children of John and Wilhelmina Schwartz are: John, now living on the old homestead at Grant's Lick; Cornelia, widow of Jeremiah Lane, of Ashmore, Ill.; Henry, with the Filley Stave Company, of St. Louis; Anna, wife of John Ludewig, of Newport; Lettie, wife of Fred Wahle, of Newport; William, with the Langdon Grocery Company, of Cincinnati, and Hubbard, the subject of this sketch. Hubbard Schwartz obtained his primary education in the public schools of Newport, afterward taking the complete course in the Nelson Business college, of Cincinnati, in half the allotted time; from 1885 to 1890 he was a professional baseball player in various league clubs; then became connected with the daily and weekly *Commonwealth*, of Covington, as a reporter; remained with that paper about three years; started a paper in Dayton and Bellevue, called the *Day Bell;* sold his

interest to his partner in a few months to become a staff correspond-
ent of the *Toledo Bee;* later, went to the Cincinnati *Enquirer* as the
Campbell county reporter; in that capacity reported all the details
of the famous Jackson and Walling case, for the murder of Pearl
Bryan; became connected with the *Times-Star* in April, 1897, as reporter and later as assistant managing editor, and still later as telegraph editor, remaining with that paper until January, 1904. In 1903
he received the Democratic nomination for clerk of the circuit court
and although the county is normally Republican by about 600 majority he was elected by 560, which tells the story of his personal
popularity better than words. In his canvass he received the warmest
endorsements from the Democratic press of the States of Ohio and
Kentucky, while the Republican papers had little or nothing to say
in opposition. Mr. Schwartz is well known in fraternal circles, being
an Odd Fellow, an Elk, a Knight of Pythias, a Modern Woodman,
and a member of the Royal Circle and the Tribe of Ben Hur. He
was married on Nov. 21, 1893, to Miss Belle Taft McArthur, daughter of Peter McArthur, a member of one of the old pioneer families
of Campbell county. Mr. and Mrs. Schwartz have one daughter,
Vivian Leanor, aged eight years. Both parents are members of the
Baptist church.

WILLIAM F. LOHSTROH, assessor
of Campbell county, Ky., was born in the
city of Newport, where he now lives and
has his office, April 7, 1861. His father,
Henry Lohstroh, was a native of Hanover, Germany, where he was born, June
21, 1827. When Henry was about fifteen
years of age, his father having died, leaving himself and one brother, he came to
America and soon after his arrival in this
country located in Newport, where he
passed the remainder of his life. What
schooling he had was obtained in his
native land. His first position in Newport was that of hostler for
Gen. James Taylor and later he had charge of the livery stable of
Horatio T. Harris, a son-in-law of General Taylor. After some time
in this place he went into business for himself, running a number of
drays and express wagons, and doing a general transfer business, which
he continued to follow as long as he lived. During the Civil war he

was a member of the home guards and took part in the movement to resist General Morgan in his great raid. In 1853 he was married to Miss Louise Wuelner, a native of Germany. He died on Jan. 21, 1869, and his widow survived him until 1896, when she too entered her final rest. They had nine children, viz.: J. Henry, in the commission business in Cincinnati, but lives in Newport; Louis, died in infancy; Mary, wife of Charles Heiler of Price Hill, Cincinnati; John F., in the grocery business in Mt. Auburn, Cincinnati; William F., the subject of this sketch; Anna and Charles, both died in infancy; Edward, who runs a grocery in Newport, and Emma, who died in childhood. William F. Lohstroh received his education in the Newport public schools. While still in his teens he entered the employ of W. M. Spencer & Son, preserve makers, of Cincinnati, and remained with the firm for twenty-five years, filling every position from office boy to general foreman. During this time he served three terms as councilman from the Sixth ward in the city council of Newport, and in 1901 he was nominated by the Republicans for the office of county assessor. At the ensuing election he was victorious by a handsome majority and is now holding the office for a term of four years. Mr. Lohstroh is a prominent figure in fraternal circles, being a member of the Free and Accepted Masons, the Independent Order of Odd Fellows; the Knights of Pythias; the Benevolent and Protective Order of Elks; the Junior Order of American Mechanics; the Sons of Young Pioneers; the Knights of the Maccabees; and belongs to the Eastern Star and Rebekah degrees of Masonry and Odd Fellowship. He is also a member of the Brotherhood of Stationary Engineers, No. 18, of Cincinnati, and is affiliated with the Federation of Labor. He is president of the Newport Building and Loan Association, No. 1, and is a director in the Kentucky Building and Loan Association, the largest in Newport. On Jan. 24, 1884, Mr. Lohstroh was married to Miss Mary Jaeger, a native of Germany, and they have had five children. William Henry, Leslie John and Elsie Marie are deceased; Stanley Otto and Pearl are at home with their parents, the son now being a student in the Newport high school. He was born Sept. 11, 1886, and Pearl was born July 8, 1888.

PETER McARTHUR, a retired citizen of Dayton, Ky., is a member of a family that has been long and prominently identified with the history of Campbell county, Ky. His grandfather, whose name was also Peter, was born in Argyleshire, Scotland, in 1764. When he was about twenty years of age he came to America, having for his traveling companion on the voyage his cousin, Duncan McArthur, who rose to the rank of general in the war of 1812 and was the eighth governor of the State of Ohio. Peter McArthur came to Kentucky, located near Georgetown, and soon afterward found employment as a surveyor, following that occupation for several years in Central Kentucky and Southern Ohio, locating land warrants for the soldiers who served in the Revolutionary war. In 1815 he settled in Newport, where he engaged in the hotel business, and lived there until his death in July, 1828. On Dec. 26, 1800, he married Mrs. Mary Tompkins, *nee* Michie, a native of Louisa county, Va., but of Irish extraction. She died Sept. 1, 1853, and was buried by the side of her husband in Evergreen Cemetery at Newport. Their children were Augustus E., Thomas Jefferson, Gilbert, Nancy, and James Madison, all now deceased. James Madison, the youngest of the family, was born near Georgtown, Jan. 31, 1810, and was five years old when his parents removed to Newport. There he attended private schools until he was fifteen years of age, when he entered Center college, at Danville, and studied for one year, which completed his schooling. Upon reaching manhood he became an extensive dealer in real estate, at one time owning over one-third of the land in Campbell county. He then turned his attention to the improvement of Newport; opened the first street in the city; invested large sums of capital in the building of houses for residence and business purposes; sold much of his property on long time to assist others in getting homes; established the Newport Safety Fund bank, and was its president from 1852 to 1856; in company with James T. Berry and Henry Walker he laid out the town of Dayton; spent both time and money in building up the new town; built the street railway between Dayton and Newport; owned it for nine years, after which he sold it and turned his attention to other lines of business. Mr. McArthur was also active in politics. For ten years he was president of the Newport city council; was twice elected to the legislature, in 1846 and in 1873; introduced and secured the passage of the "Cemetery Act;" the act levying tax on real estate to aid in the establishment of common schools; the mechanics' lien law; and various other important acts of legislation. In 1837 he was married to Miss Mary J., daughter of Charles Stricker, of Philadelphia. She died on April 6, 1893, and he on Feb. 11, 1900. They had seven children, viz.: Peter, born May 28, 1838, the subject of this sketch; Mary, born April 10, 1840, and died June 1, 1865; Alice, born March 4, 1842, now the widow of Henry M. Rand; Annie, born Sept. 30, 1844, now Mrs. T. J. Haggard, of Dayton, Ky.; Charles, born Jan. 8, 1847, connected with the Savannah,

Florida & Western railway, at Jacksonville, Fla.; Ida, born June 1, 1850, and died March 17, 1894; William W., born Oct. 23, 1858, and died Jan. 3, 1903. Peter McArthur, the eldest child of the family, has always claimed Campbell county as his home. He was educated in the public schools of Dayton and finished his education with a course at College Hill, O. After leaving school he engaged in mercantile pursuits at Carthage and continued in that business until the war broke out. During the war he did all he could do to advance the cause of the Confederacy. After the war he went to Missouri, where he followed merchandizing for about two years, when he returned to Newport and was superintendent of the Newport and Dayton street railroad until 1875. For some time succeeding this he was the proprietor of a line of steamboats running between Memphis, Tenn., and points on the Black and White rivers in Arkansas. In 1902 he sold out his interests in this business and since then has lived retired at Dayton. Mr. McArthur has always taken an active interest in politics; served as deputy sheriff for a number of years; was once nominated for sheriff but was defeated by a combination of circumstances; and is always ready to do his part to advance the interests of his party. He is a member of the Masonic fraternity and the Independent Order of Odd Fellows. On May 18, 1865, he was married to Miss Calista E., daughter of Dr. Willard F. Taft, a distant relative of the family from which comes W. H. Taft, the present secretary of war. Mr. and Mrs. McArthur have five children: Mame is the wife of Charles Auspaugh, of Dayton; Ida Lee is deceased; Jesse is in the laundry business at Dayton; Belle is now Mrs. Hubbard Schwartz (see sketch); and Calista is at home with her parents. Mrs. McArthur and the children belong to the Baptist church.

SAMUEL F. WRIGHT, a well-known farmer of Campbell county, Ky., residing near Alexandria, was born on the old homestead, where he now lives, Aug. 15, 1851. He is the next to the youngest of ten children born to Samuel and Elizabeth (Baker) Wright, and a grandson of that Joseph Wright who came from Bracken county in 1818 and settled near Alexandria. (For a complete account of the ancestry see the sketch of Joseph F. Wright.) Samuel F. Wright has lived all his life in Campbell county. He received a good, practical education in the common schools and upon attaining his majority he adopted the life of a tiller of the soil, which has been his vocation ever since. He does a general farming business and is regarded as one of the successful men of his neighborhood. In 1871 Mr. Wright was married to Miss

Anna Riggall, a daughter of Richard Riggall, who came from England and settled in Campbell county several years ago. Mr. and Mrs. Wright have the following children: Alice, now the wife of John Hully, of Avondale, O.; Fannie, at home with her parents; Walter, who lives at Hamilton, O.; and Albert, Edna and Eva at home. Mr. Wright is a man of domestic tastes and spends most of his time with his family. He is a member of the Independent Order of Odd Fellows and an occasional evening at the lodge-room is one of the causes for his being away from home after nightfall. As a citizen he has the confidence and respect of his neighbors and acquaintances, and as a farmer he is looked upon as one of the most progressive in his locality.

DANIEL RIEDEL, of Newport, Ky., sheriff of Campbell county, was born in the city of Cincinnati, July 2, 1849, and is the oldest child of Christian and Margaret Riedel, both natives of Bavaria, Germany. In 1858 his parents moved to Zanesville, Ohio, and started in the bakery business, and in 1863 his father lost his life by the falling of the market house, caused by the weight of a heavy snow on the roof. His mother is living, now residing in Newport. Daniel was not quite sixteen years of age when he left home and began life for himself. Going to Cincinnati he found employment as a deck-sweeper on one of the river steamers and for the next nine years he was on the Ohio, Mississippi and Missouri rivers, and their tributaries, filling various positions of trust and responsibility in the river trade. Upon leaving the river he located in Newport and since 1875 he has been engaged in the business of moving household goods, etc., having one of the best equipped lines of furniture vans about the three cities. Mr. Riedel has always taken an interest in political affairs. He served five years as a member of the Newport city council with credit to himself and to the entire satisfaction of his constituents. In the campaign of 1901 he was nominated by the Republicans for the office of sheriff and although the county is comparatively close, the Democrats electing part of the ticket, Mr. Riedel's majority was 1,195, the largest ever given to a candidate for sheriff in the political history of the county. His term expires Jan. 1, 1906. Mr. Riedel is a member of the Junior Order United American Mechanics, the Knights of the Ancient Essenic Order, and the St. Paul Lutheran church. He was married in April, 1875, and has two sons, John C., a draughtsman and designer, now in San Francisco, Cal., and Daniel, Jr., an electrical engineer in charge of the construction department of the Cincinnati and Columbus Traction Company.

JAMES TAYLOR THORNTON, city attorney of Newport, Ky., was born in that city, Jan. 3, 1879, and is the eldest son of Reuben Taylor and Maggie L. (Sinclair) Thornton. The family came originally from England. In 1849 Thomas Griffin Thornton, a native of Caroline county, Va., crossed the mountains with his family and half a dozen slaves and settled in Campbell county, Ky., where he was engaged in the ice business the remainder of his life. His wife was Sarah J. Thornton, a first cousin, her father being Henry Thornton and her mother, a sister of Gen. James Taylor. She is still living in Newport, at the advanced age of eighty-nine years. Their children were Louis B., Mary Moss, James B., Edmund Taylor, Reuben Taylor, John H., Horatio Harris, Thomas Griffin, and Bettie. Those living are John H., who is in the ice business in Newport; Horatio H., a railroad man, also lives in Newport; and Bettie, wife of Col. J. Taylor Williams, of Highlands, near that city. Thomas Griffin died in Washington, D. C., in 1898, where he was chief clerk of the geological survey. Reuben Taylor, the fifth of the family, was born in Caroline county, Va., in 1847. He received his education in the Newport public schools and in a private institution conducted by Rev. Father Guilfoil. After arriving at manhood's estate he continued in the ice business for some years, at the same time serving as agent of the Gen. James Taylor estate. In June, 1885, he was appointed gauger for the United States government and continued to act in that capacity until his death, Feb. 26, 1890. In 1870 he was married to Maggie L. Sinclair, a daughter of John L. Sinclair, of Prince William county, Va., and a cousin. The following are the children born to this marriage: Lucy Taylor, Mrs. C. H. Murdock, of Cincinnati; Mary Moss, wife of Albert Collins, also of Cincinnati; James Taylor, the subject of this sketch; John Sinclair, bookkeeper for the Big Four railroad company; Sarah Virginia, at home, and Walter Crail, employed in a broker's office at Cincinnati. James T. Thornton graduated from the Newport high school with the class of 1897; read law with Aubrey Barbour, his cousin, of Newport; entered the law department of the McDonald Institute of Cincinnati in September, 1898; graduated in June, 1901, having been elected orator of his class; and was admitted to the bar in Campbell county in September, 1900, before his graduation. Upon leaving school he entered upon the practice of his chosen profession in Newport and is regarded as one of the rising young barristers of that city. In August, 1903, he was nominated by the Democracy for the office of city attorney and in November following was elected by a majority of 110 votes, though the city usually goes about 500 Republican. Mr. Thornton is the youngest man ever elected to the position, but his youth and ambition are rather in his favor, and is a guarantee that the city's interests will be zealously guarded during his term of office. During his first year in office he has been sustained by the court of appeals in his advice to the general council, and he has never been beaten in a jury case of any kind. In June, 1902, he formed a partnership with A. T. Root, which was dissolved when he entered upon the duties of his office, on his twenty-fifth birthday, Jan. 3, 1904.

WILLIAM HARTMAN, postmaster at Alexandria, Ky., was born in Hanover, Germany, in 1842. When he was about three years of age he came with his parents, Henry and Diena Hartman, in 1845, to America. Henry Hartman was a wagonmaker by trade, having learned that occupation in his native land, but after coming to America he purchased a farm about three miles east of Alexandria, Campbell county, Ky., and followed farming until his death in 1858. His wife survived him until 1884, when she, too, passed away. They had three children. One died in infancy, the other two being William, the subject of this sketch, and Elizabeth, wife of Christopher Pfender, of Campbell county. William Hartman grew to manhood in Campbell county, received his education in the public schools there, and at the age of fifteen started to learn the carpenters' trade. He continued to work at this until he was about twenty years old, when he went to Cincinnati, where he entered an undertaking establment and served an apprenticeship. In 1863 he located at Alexandria, where he has since followed the business of an undertaker. Mr. Hartman has served as one of the town trustees for a number of years and was also bridge commissioner of Campbell county for several years. He has in addition to the above held the position of secretary and manager of the Alexandria cemetery company from 1875 to the present time. In April, 1904, he received the appointment of postmaster at Alexandria and now holds that position. In both public position and private life Mr. Hartman is distinguished by his careful, conscientious methods of doing business—methods that have won the confidence of all who know him. He is a member of the Knights of Pythias and has served master of the exchequer of Jewel Lodge, No. 44, at Alexandria, ever since the lodge was organized in 1895. About the time he embarked in business at Alexandria he was married to Miss Mary Jane Parker, daughter of Thomas Parker, an old and honored resident of Campbell county. To this marriage there were born the following children: Charles, who died at the age of eight years; Rose, now the wife of Edward M. Reiley, at Alexandria; and Ella, who lives at home with her father, since the death of her mother, which occurred in 1901.

JOSEPH F. WRIGHT, a fruit grower residing at Alexandria, Campbell county, Ky., is a descendant of one of the old pioneer families of the state. The Wrights are of English extraction, the family traditions being that they originally came from Lancashire. About the close of the eighteenth century three brothers, Joseph, John and Robert Wright, came to Kentucky, and located in Bracken county, then part of Mason county. John afterward removed to Owen county, where he became one of the leading citizens, and later went to Missouri, located near Independence, and some of his descendants are still to be found in that locality. Robert left Bracken county after a few years and went to Louisville, where he passed his last days and where some of his descendants are still living. In 1818 Joseph Wright left Bracken county, came to Campbell and bought four hundred acres of land in the Brush Creek neighborhood near Alexandria. There he lived and followed farming until his death in 1848. He was twice married, both times in Bracken county. His first wife was Mary King and to this union there were born three children: John, Robert and Mary, all now deceased. The second wife was Miss Esther Potts (originally spelled Putts), a native of Pennsylvania. To this marriage there were born twelve children, all of whom are now deceased. Joseph went to Missouri, and although a man of over sixty years of age, was drafted into the Confederate army under Price, and died of disease in the hospital at Cape

Girardeau; Elizabeth married Jacob Manning; Patience married Pollard Gosney; William lived and died in Campbell county; Thompson also passed his whole life in the county; Evaline married Greenberry Gosney; Andrew Jackson lived in Campbell county; Emily married Jonathan White; David went to Missouri and died near Independence, that state; Jane married William Harris, a resident of Campbell county; Elston died in his youth, and Samuel was the father of the subject of this sketch. Samuel was born in Bracken county in 1807 and came with his parents to Campbell county when he was about eleven years of age. As a boy he attended such schools as that early day offered and upon reaching manhood adopted the life of a farmer, which was his occupation through life. He took an interest in the development of the country and held several local offices. He was united in marriage to Elizabeth Baker, daughter of Nicholas Baker, one of the pioneers, and to this marriage there were born the following children: William J., now living in Newport; Joseph F., the subject; Sarah, deceased; Nicholas E., a farmer of Campbell county; Susan H., now living in Alexandria; Emma, now in Newport; John W., sexton of Grace Church, Newport; Thomas J., in Missouri; Samuel F., residing in Campbell county; and James F., a grocer at Perry, Ia. The father of these children died in March, 1885, and the mother in 1890. Joseph F. Wright, the second son of the family, was born on the old homestead in Campbell county, Sept. 17, 1836. His early life was not much different from that of all farmer boys. He received an academic education and engaged in farming until 1863, when he came to Alexandria and for the succeeding fourteen years was in the business of merchandizing. He then returned to farming and has since that time devoted much of his time and attention to fruit growing, in which he has been quite successful. Mr. Wright studies his business and goes at anything intelligently. It is to this patient, systematic way of doing things that he owes his success in the fruit growing industry. While other men conduct their business by "guess-work" he has reduced the business to a science and operates with a certainty. Mr. Wright was married in 1862 to Miss Mary A., daughter of Solomon Todd, a native of England. She died in 1879, without issue, and in 1881 Mr. Wright was married to Miss Emma J. Ripley, of Indianapolis. To this union there have been born the following children: Ethel B., born May 25, 1884, now a student at Oxford college in Ohio; Elsie R., born Jan. 9, 1887, and a student at the same college; Grace R., born Aug. 25, 1889, and J. Donald, born July 13, 1892.

JAMES H. GOSNEY, senior member of the firm of J. & R. Gosney, dealers in general merchandise, Alexandria, Ky., is a native of that county and is a descendant of one of the very oldest of the pioneer families. About 1750 two brothers, Richard and Henry Gosney, came from England to America. The vessel upon which they took passage landed near the mouth of the James river, where the brothers disembarked and proceeded inland until they reached Culpeper county, where they settled upon land belonging to the old Lord Fairfax grant. There they reared large families, a son of Richard dying in the Colonial army a short time before the surrender of Lord Cornwallis. Henry Gosney was twice married. By his first wife he had the following children: Richard, Frederick, John, William, Benjamin, Polly and Betsy. The children of his second marriage were Nimrod, Peter, James, Harry, Fanny and Polly. Two sons of the first marriage, Henry and John, removed to Ohio and Marshall counties in Western Virginia, and Frederick, William and Benjamin, with the four sons of the second marriage, came to Kentucky about 1780 and settled in Campbell county. Peter afterward went to Missouri, where some of his descendants still reside. Benjamin Gosney operated the salt mills at Grant's Lick, Campbell county, for many years after coming from Virginia. He was twice married. By the first wife his children were John and Millie and by the second Armstead, Oliver, Pollard, Benjamin, Zacharias, and Peggy, all now deceased. Zacharias Gosney, the youngest son, was a native of Campbell county, where he followed farming all his life. He was married twice, first to Mildred Lovelace, a native of Pendleton county, Ky., and second to a Miss Gosney, a distant relative. The children of his first wife were Harkie, Francis M., Henry C., and William, and of his second wife Benjamin, John, Eliza, Margaret, and Jane. None of these children are living except Henry C., who resides at Indianapolis, Ind., and Benjamin and John, who live in Pendleton county. Francis Marion, the oldest son of Zacharias Gosney, was born in Campbell county, Feb. 22, 1833. After a common school education he started in to learn the blacksmiths' trade, but after a short time he engaged in the business of teaming with headquarters at Newport. Later he became the proprietor of the omnibus lines running from Newport to Alexandria and Grant's Lick. For more than thirty years he continued to operate these lines and since his death, on Jan. 8, 1904, his heirs have incorporated the business as the F. M. Gosney transfer company. He was married on Aug. 20, 1857, to Miss Sarah M. Yelton, daughter of Daniel Yelton, an old resident of Campbell county. She died on Jan. 1, 1901. They were the parents of the following children: the first born, a daughter, died in infancy; Thomas W., born Oct. 21, 1859, now lives in Campbell county; Carrie B., born Dec. 12, 1860, now the wife of Julius Plummer,. of Newport; Louis N., born May 7, 1862, married Miss Libbie, daughter of Robert Grizzel, and is a rectifier and compounder of spirits at Newport; Sarah J., born Sept. 29, 1864, now the wife of M. L. Christian, of Cloverport, Ky.; James H., the subject of this sketch; Edward H., born May 5, 1868, married Miss Anna Walker and is manager of the "Old '76" Distilling Company, of Campbell county; Daniel B., born Feb. 27, 1870, married Miss Lucy Taylor, and is a driver of one of the omnibuses between Newport and Alexandria; Lambert M., born Oct. 20, 1872, married Miss Lulu Anderson, and is an agent for the New York life insurance company; Della I., born June 5, 1877, now the wife of Charles T. Lawson, agent for the Metropolitan life insurance company at Newport. Julius Plummer was the sheriff of Campbell county who officiated at the execution of Jackson and Walling, the murderers of Miss Pearl Bryan. James H. Gosney was born July 7, 1866; received a common school education, drove the Grant's Lick 'bus for about twelve years; then engaged in the business of merchandizing at Claryville until July, 1900; sold out and again became connected with the 'bus line; came to Alexandria in October, 1901, and opened a general ,store as the senior member of the firm of J. H. & R. Gosney, and has been in this business since. He is a member of the Alexandria Lodge of Masons, and Jewel Lodge, No. 44, Knights of Pythias, in which he holds the office of chancellor commander. He is also a member of the Baptist church. On Oct. 8, 1890, he was married to Miss Emma K., daughter of John H. Byrd, an old resident of Campbell county. She died on Dec. 16, 1899, leaving two children: Clifford B., born Feb. 1, 1893, and Anna, born Aug. 4, 1896. Mr. Gosney was married on March 13, 1904, to Miss Merta Jenner, daughter of James Jenner, an old and honored resident of the county.

MARTIN CLAUSE, market master, weigher, and official sealer of weights and measures of Newport, Ky., was born in Allegheny county, Pa., in 1844. His father, John Henry Clause, was a native of Germany, born in Hanover about the year 1810. He received a common school education in his native land, learned the trade of baker, and served five years in the German army. While still living in Germany he married and in 1842 came to America, locating in Allegheny county, where his wife died, leaving the following children: Mary, deceased; Godfrey, deceased; John, now a city employe in Cincinnati; Andrew, deceased; Henry, an engineer at McDonald, W. Va.; and William, deceased. He married Sarah Sauer, of Allegheny county, some time after the death of his first wife, and to this marriage there were born five children: David and Aaron are both dead; Sarah is the wife of William Latham, of Pawnee, Ill.; Lena is dead, and Martin, who is the oldest of the family, is the subject of this sketch. The family came from Pennsylvania to Dearborn county, Ind., about 1845, where the father followed farming until his death in 1869. The mother died in Newport in 1884. Martin Clause received a limited education in the district schools of Dearborn county. In 1861 he enlisted in Company D, Fifth Ohio cavalry, but after about four months' service his father secured his discharge on account of youth. Martin then worked on the farm until the fall of 1864, when he joined a bridge building crew, working for the government, and passed the winter in the South. In 1866 he went to Cincinnati and secured employment in a wood working establishment, remaining in that line of work for twenty-nine years. In 1874 he took up his residence in Newport and has lived in that city ever since. In 1895 he gave up the wood working business, having some time prior to that date become interested in the grocery business, and since then has continued in that line until his election to his present position in 1896. He was elected to this office by the city council and has been annually re-elected ever since first taking the place. Mr. Clause is a member of the Mystic Circle and the Independent Order of Odd Fellows. In 1867 he was married to Miss Mary Miller, of Dearborn county who died in 1873, leaving one son, Arthur Edward, now a grocer in Newport. In 1875 Mr. Clause married Mary Elizabeth, daughter of Edward Biltz, of Newport, and to this marriage there were born four children, William, Florence, Alma and Walter. William is a printer in the Methodist Book Concern of Cincinnati; Florence and Alma are at home, and Walter is a drug clerk in Cincinnati. In his present position Mr. Clause has fearlessly, impartially and conscientiously discharged his duties and his annual re-election to the office has been in response to a popular demand for one who is both fair and prompt in the enforcement of law.

THOMAS A. ALFORD, a well known farmer, living near Alexandria, Campbell county, Ky., was born in Hancock county, Ind., in the year 1844. His father, John William Alford, was a native of Lancashire, England, where he grew to manhood, received a good education, and learned the trade of iron molder. He was also a fine vocalist and sang in the churches in his early life. Soon after attaining his majority he came to America, locating in Ohio. After a few years he returned to

England and married Miss Sarah Cooper, and after returning to this country they lived for a time in Hancock county, Ind. Their children were Elizabeth, John Ellis, James H., Richard B., Rebecca, William, Thomas A., Ellen A., Susie, Missouri B., Charles T., Robert, and George. Those living are Elizabeth, wife of William Davis, of Campbell county; James H., of Alexandria; Richard B., Thomas A., Charles T., Robert and George, all living in Campbell county; and Ellen A., wife of John Wilson, of San Francisco, Cal. When Thomas A. Alford was about three years of age his parents came to Campbell county and there he grew to manhood, received a common school education and learned the trade of cooper. Later he abandoned this occupation for the life of a farmer and he is today one of the most prosperous in the county, and one of the leading citizens. He takes a deep interest in everything having a tendency to better the conditions in his county, is well informed, and while not a politician is ready to do his part to secure good government and good institutions. He was married on Dec. 5, 1867, to Miss Mary Jane, daughter of Joseph Shaw, an old and respected resident of Campbell county, and they have the following children: Matilda Ann, wife of Coleman Moore, living near Alexandria; Edward Osborn, a farmer in Benton county, Ind.; Joseph, also a farmer there; Thomas W., at home; David, a farmer in Campbell county; Lucy Emily, wife of Edward Droege, of Cincinnati; John William, who lives in Benton county, Ind.; Grover Byron, and Charles Robert, at home. Mr. and Mrs. Alford are both consistent members of the Baptist church.

RICHARD T. PARKER, a well-known farmer, living near Oneonta, Campbell county, Ky., was born in that county, Nov. 16, 1862. He is a son of the late Thomas Parker, a native of the same county, and who spent his entire life there, with the exception of a short time he lived in Illinois. Thomas Parker was a farmer and in his day was one of the best known men in the eastern portion of Campbell county. He was married three times. His first wife was Miss Sallie Parker, of Ohio, and by this union he had the following children: John, who died in childhood; Sarah Jane, who married William Hartman and died as his wife; Susan, who lives in Alexandria; George and Joseph, both in Cincinnati; Louise, deceased;

James, a resident of Dayton, Ky.; and Richard T., the subject of this sketch. The mother of these children died in 1875. The second wife was a Mrs. Eckel, who died without issue, and the third wife was Mrs. Hannah Clark, *nee* Gaskins, of Campbell county. No children were born to this marriage. Thomas Parker died on Sept. 1, 1901, his wife having preceded him to the tomb. Richard T. Parker has always lived in Campbell county. He received a common school education and has followed farming for a livelihood all his active business life. In this vocation he has been measurably successful, owing to his industrious habits and his painstaking way of conducting his farming operations. In 1880 Mr. Parker was united in marriage to Miss Elizabeth, daughter of David Truesdell, who was the fourth son of Solomon and Mary Truesdell. His parents left Pennsylvania in 1791, to seek their fortunes in Kentucky, which was at that time an unbroken wilderness. On December 22 of that year they landed where the little town of Columbia now stands, in Hamilton county, O., but were driven across to the Kentucky side by the Indians, who, elated by the defeat of General St. Clair, had become very troublesome to the early settlers or those about to settle in the Ohio Valley. Not far from where the Newport waterworks now stands Solomon Truesdell and another pioneer built a cabin, and it was in this cabin that David Truesdell was born on Oct. 23, 1792. It is said that he was the first white male child born in what is now Campbell county. On Nov. 12, 1820, David Truesdell and Nancy, daughter of Thomas and Sarah Griffey, were united in marriage. She was born Oct. 23, 1800, and died Oct. 23, 1879. To this marriage there were born three sons and three daughters. David Truesdell was stricken with total blindness in 1862, and about five years before his death he became unable to walk. He died on Aug. 18, 1877. He and his wife were consistent members of the Methodist Episcopal church. A short time before his death he was asked if he thought he would recognize his four children who had passed away. To this he replied: "No, for when I get to that land of glory, in the fulness of joy, all will be alike to me." His death was calm and peaceful. Mr. and Mrs. Parker are both members of the Methodist Episcopal church and interested in promoting its good works. They have no children.

CHRISTOPHER PFENDER, a farmer living near Alexandria, Ky., was born on March 15, 1846, and is a son of Christopher Frederick and Anna M. (Walter) Pfender, both natives of Wittenburg, Germany, where the father was educated in the local schools and learned the tailor's trade, at which he worked for some time before coming to this country. Upon coming to the United States he landed at New Orleans, was there married, and after a short period in that city came to Alexandria, where he followed the occupation of tailor until his death, with the exception of the time he served in the Federal army during the Civil war. In 1862 he enlisted as a private in Company D, Twenty-third Kentucky infantry, and served until the close of the war, taking part in all the operations in which his command was engaged. His widow is still living in Alexandria. They had eight children, viz.: Christopher, the subject of this sketch; Frederick, a farmer in Kansas; Caroline, wife of Harvey Hasey, of Columbus, O.; Kate, widow of August Beeilerin, of Covington, Ky.; Henrietta, residing at Alexandria; Henry, living at Newport; Mary, wife of Martin Seimer, of Covington; and George, deceased. Chris Pfender, as he is familiarly called, grew to manhood in Campbell county, received a common school education, and learned the tailor's trade with his father, but never followed it. In July, 1863, he enlisted in the Union army as a private in Company H, Thirty-seventh Kentucky mounted infantry, and served until the early spring of 1865, when he was discharged, his term of enlistment having expired. He immediately re-enlisted, however, as a member of Company F, One Hundred and Ninety-fifth Ohio volunteer infantry, and served in that organization until the final surrender. Among the engagements in which this regiment took part was the raid on the salt works near Richmond. After the war Mr. Pfender returned to Campbell county and took up the life of a farmer. He now owns one of the best farms in the county, well improved and in a good state of cultivation. He is a member of the Grand Army of the Republic and is commander of William T. Sherman Post, No. 102, at Alexandria. Mr. Pfender was married in 1870 to Miss Elizabeth Hartman, a daughter of Henry Hartman, and sister of William Hartman, the postmaster at Alexandria (see sketch). Mr. and Mrs. Pfender have had born to them the following children: Dena, deceased; William, Joseph, and Charles, all living in Campbell county; George, a grocer in Newport; Mary, Albert, August and Chris., Jr., at home. Both parents are members of the Lutheran church. Chris. Pfender is a fine type of the German-American citizen. Industrious, frugal but not stingy, he has accumulated what he has by his own efforts, relying at all times on his own resources. While he loves the traditions of the "Faderland" he is none the less a loyal American, as may be seen in his record as a soldier, when he fought to preserve the institutions and the destinies of his adopted country.

GEORGE HENRY MILLER, a farmer, near Trace, Campbell county, Ky., was born at Shoenan, Germany, Oct. 8, 1829. His father, Christian Miller, was a native of Alsace, now a German province, where he was born in 1787. His opportunities to secure an education were very limited, but he made the best of such as presented themselves and managed to pick up a fair rudimentary knowledge of the common branches. In early life he learned the trade of blacksmith and locksmith, at which his family had worked for several generations. In 1837, being at the time fifty years old, he came with his family to America and located in Brown county, O., where he purchased a farm and followed farming until his death in June, 1845. He was married in 1811 to Miss Barbara Beyder, a native of Germany, who survived her husband for several years, finally entering her rest in October, 1863. Their children were Christian, who died at the age of four years; Frederick, died at the age of thirty-two; Margaret, now the widow of Wendell Gwiner, of Campbell county; Barbara, Laura, and Elizabeth, all deceased; George H., the subject of this sketch, and Charles Lewis, now a farmer in Franklin township, Brown county, O. George H. Miller came with his parents to America when he was about eight years of age. He grew to manhood in Brown county, where he received a limited education, which he has improved by general reading and self-culture. Upon reaching his majority he went to Cincinnati, but after about two years there he came to Campbell county and purchased the farm adjoining the one upon which he now lives. That was in 1852 and since then Mr. Miller has been closely identified with the development of many of Campbell county's institutions. Although not a politician he was once nominated for representative to the legislature, but was defeated, his party being in the minority. He owns a large tract of land and is one of the fore-handed farmers of the county. In February, 1856, Mr. Miller was united in marriage to Miss Julia Schwartz, a native of Germany, and to this union there have been born eleven children. Elizabeth, Barbara, Christian, Frederika and Julia K. all died in early childhood. Those living are John, a carriage maker in Dayton, Ky.; Henry, at home with his parents; Charles, also at home; Eliza, wife of Frank Wiley, of Campbell county; Frederick, a resident of the same county; and Emma K., now Mrs. Melvin H. Boots. All the children have grown up to be useful members of society, the training of their parents being such as to inculcate moral and industrious habits. Mr. Miller and his wife enjoy the full confidence and friendship of their neighbors and acquaintances and few men have a higher standing in the business or social life of Campbell county than Mr. Miller.

FRANK SPILLMAN THATCHER, farmer and fruit grower, near Alexandria, Ky., was born on the farm where he now resides, April 28, 1856, and has passed his whole life in Campbell county. His father, John Thatcher, was born in the same county, March 14, 1809. Upon reaching man's estate he was married to Miss Margaret Spillman, daughter of one of the old residents. They had six children, viz.: Daniel, Mary, Henry, Rose, Maria and Frank. Daniel is deceased; Mary died in girlhood; Henry died in early manhood; Rose is the wife of George T. Youtsey, of Newport; Maria is now Mrs. Edward Harmer, of Cold Springs, Campbell county; and Frank S. is the subject of this sketch and the youngest child of the family. Frank S. Thatcher was educated in the schools of his native county and has been engaged in agricultural pursuits all his life. For the past twenty-five years the production of small fruits has commanded a great deal of his time and attention and in this line he has been quite successful. In more recent years he has given considerable attention to raising and dealing in fine saddle horses, an occupation which he has found both congenial and profitable. Politically Mr. Thatcher is a Democrat of the kind that it is always safe to place in the advance guard. He is a member of Jewel Lodge, No. 44, Knights of Pythias, at Alexandria, and is always a welcome attendant at the meetings of the lodge. He was married, in 1882, to Miss Mary E. Grant, of Kenton county, Ky., and five children have come to bless the union, viz.: Mary, Edith, Fannie, Ruth and Jack. All are living except Mary, who died at the age of thirteen years.

CLAYTON WHITTEMORE SHAW, M.D., of Alexandria, Ky., one of the leading physicians of Campbell county, was born near California, in that county, Aug. 10, 1871, and is the eldest son of James Fremont and Lura (Reed) Shaw. His father is a prominent citizen of the county and has served with distinction in the legislature. (See sketch of James F. Shaw.) Dr. Shaw grew to manhood on his father's farm and received his primary education in the common schools at Cal-

T. M'D. HILL.

ifornia. In 1891 he entered the Medical College of Ohio, at Cincinnati, and graduated with the class of 1894. For about a year after his graduation he practiced at Dayton, Ky., and in January, 1896, he located at Alexandria, where he has a lucrative practice and stands high in his profession, both with his brother practitioners and the general public. Believing in association as a means of progress and advancement Dr. Shaw is a member of the State Medical association of Kentucky and the Medical Society of Campbell county. He keeps in close touch with the new discoveries in the field of medical science and is regarded as one of the progressive physicians of his section of the state. In fraternal circles Dr. Shaw is a member of Jewel Lodge, No. 44, Knights of Pythias, at Alexandria, and of Alexandria Lodge, No. 121, Independent Order of Odd Fellows. On Nov. 12, 1901, Dr. Shaw was united in marriage to Miss Fay Fern, daughter of the late Hon. Theodore McDonald Hill, a prominent citizen of Campbell county, whose widow now lives with her daughter, Mrs. Dr. Shaw. Dr. Shaw and his wife have one son, named Hill McDonald Shaw. The doctor is a member of the Baptist church and outside of his profession is one of the leading citizens of the community in which he lives.

WILLIAM HILL, the first of this family to come to America, was born in County Antrim, Ireland, about 1730. A few years before the American Revolution he came to this country, settled in Western Pennsylvania, and served in the Continental army during the Revolutionary war. In the spring of 1794 he came with his family on a flatboat down the Ohio river, landing at Fort Washington, now Cincinnati, on May 25. Here he was for many years proprietor of the old-time tavern known as the "Black Bear" on what is now Sycamore street, near Ninth. For a time he lived in the "Black Bottoms" of the Miami Valley, but returned to Cincinnati and died there Dec. 9, 1828. His wife was Jane McDonald, of the Isle of Skye, and a cousin. Both husband and wife were cousins to the famous Scotch beauty, Flora Macdonald, an account of whom may be found in "Chambers' Miscellany." Jane Hill died on May 2, 1834, near Cincinnati, the mother of a large family. One of the sons was William Hill, Jr., who was born at Cincinnati, May 25, 1794, the night after the family landed there. When the war of 1812 began he ran away from home and enlisted under General Scott, fighting at River Raisin, Fort Meigs, the Thames, Chippewa and Lundy's Lane. He also served under Scott in the Mexican war. His chief occupation through life was that of stonemason. He died near Alexandria, Ky., Sept. 16, 1872. He married Elizabeth, daughter of Joel and Mary (Albright) Nation, the former of English and the latter of German descent, but both natives of North Carolina. William and Elizabeth Hill settled in Campbell county, near the little village of California on the Ohio river, twenty-three miles above Cincinnati, in the early forties. There their only son, Theodore McDonald, was born on July 4, 1842. When he was about a year old his mother died and he was reared to manhood by foster parents, Mr. and Mrs. Samuel Thompson. In his boyhood Theodore attended the common schools of his native county, went to Indianapolis, Ind., with the Thompson family, and there finished his education at Butler university, but did not graduate. When the Civil war broke out he returned to Kentucky and enlisted in Company D, Fourth Kentucky Confederate cavalry, and served with that command until the end of the war. For about a year he was a prisoner of war at Rock Island. After the war he decided to study law and entered the office of R. T. Baker, a prominent attorney of Alexandria, and one of the leaders of the Republican party in Kentucky, and on Feb. 22, 1871, was admitted to the bar. In 1872 he was elected police judge of Alexandria, and to the legislature in 1877 and again in 1879. From 1871 until 1888 he practiced his profession at Alexandria, where he acquired a high reputation as a jurist. In 1888 he was appointed by the board of county magistrates to fill the vacancy in the county judgeship, caused by the death of Judge McKibben, and he removed to Newport. Two years later he was elected by the people to succeed himself, and was re-elected in 1894. In 1895 he was nominated by the Democracy of Campbell county for state senator, but was defeated by the Republican wave of that year, along with the rest of the ticket. In 1899 he was again nominated for state senator and this time was triumphantly elected, but before entering upon the duties of the office his death occurred, May 4, 1900. Mr. Hill was married to Miss

Isaphine White, daughter of Henry E. White, an old resident of the county, and their children were Rhea Rhodes, died at the age of eight years; Malcolm Macdonald, died in infancy; Fay Fern, now Mrs. Dr. Shaw of Alexandria; and Pearl Pauline and Roy Raymond, both of whom died in infancy.

MICHAEL KINSTLER, a well-known farmer living near Alexandria, Ky., was born in Hamilton county, O., Aug. 14, 1857, his parents being Adam and Elizabeth (Orr) Kinstler, both natives of Germany. Adam Kinstler was born in the duchy of Berne, near Oldenburg, Nov. 11, 1827. He received a good education in his native land and followed various occupations there until 1855, when he came to America and located at Cincinnati. There he learned the coopers' trade, at which he worked until 1859, when he purchased a farm of thirty-two acres near Alexandria and removed to it. Although he worked some at his trade after this his principal occupation was farming. Shortly after his arrival in this country he was married at Cincinnati to Miss Elizabeth Orr, a native of Hesse Darmstadt, and a daughter of Conrad Orr, who died comparatively young in his native land. Elizabeth Kinstler died on May 21, 1894, and Adam Kinstler on Jan. 25, 1895. They had two sons: Michael, the subject of this sketch, and John, a machinist in Newport, Ky. Michael Kinstler was less than two years old when his parents located in Campbell county. Since that time he has always lived in the county. His schooling was limited to eighteen months in the common schools, but by close application he has obtained a fair education at home. From his father he learned the trade of cooper, at which he has worked some, but the greater part of his attention has been given to his farming interests. He is one of the directors of the Bank of Alexandria, and is a man of affairs in his neighborhood. He believes in good government, good roads, etc., and is always willing to do his share to secure them. On Nov. 11, 1880, Mr. Kinstler was married to Miss Katherine Schuster, daughter of Louis Schuster, an old resident of Campbell county, and to this marriage there have been born eleven children. Anna died at the age of one year, and the others, Catherine, Mary, Frank, John, Adam, Elizabeth, Emma, George, Hubert and Genevieve, are all living at home with their parents. Mr. Kinstler is a member of the Ancient Order of United Workmen and he and his family belong to the Catholic church at Alexandria.

JOSEPH FREDERICK LEOPOLD, a farmer near Ten Mile, Campbell county, Ky., and the oldest living son of Frederick and Louise (Kessler) Leopold, was born near Alexandria, in the county where he now lives, Nov. 23, 1856. His grandfather, Charles Leopold, was the first of the family to come to America. He was a native of Germany, and there grew to manhood and married. While a young man he served his time in the German army and about 1835 came to this country, located on the upper branch of Tuck Fork in Campbell county, and there followed farming until his death in 1879. At the time the family came to America Frederick Leopold, the father of Joseph, was about ten years of age. He grew to manhood and received a common school education in Campbell county. Upon reaching his majority he became a farmer and followed that occupation until the fall of 1902, when he removed to Cullman, Ala., where he now resides. During the Civil war he was a member of the home guards. In 1855 he was married to Miss Louise Kessler, of Cincinnati, and to this marriage there have been born nineteen children, six of whom died young. Charles, Henry, George and Louis died later in life and those living are: Frederick, the subject of this sketch; John C., who enlisted in the Eleventh United States infantry in the Spanish-American war and is now supposed to be in Porto Rico; Frank, William, and Valentine, now in Newport; Edward, who lives in Georgia; Ernest resides in Campbell county; Hannah, now the wife of William Kulel, of Campbell county, and Lizzie, now Mrs. William Perry, of Fort Thomas. Joseph F. Leopold received a moderate education in the common schools of his native county and upon arriving at manhood took up the calling of a farmer, which has been his occupation through life and in which he has been successful. On April 20, 1880, he was united in marriage to Miss Francisco Mary Knack, a daughter of John Knack, a native of Germany, but an old resident of Campbell county. To this marriage there have been born the following children, together with the dates of their birth: Charles, March 25, 1881; John, March 21, 1883; Anna, March 7, 1885; Louisa, Aug. 7, 1887; Lena, May 12, 1890; Katrina, June 30, 1892; and Lizzie, Dec. 18, 1898. Charles is employed in Newport and the others are all at home. The family are members of the Lutheran church.

EDWARD C. FOX, recorder of Dearborn county, Ind., was born at Greendale in that county, Jan. 10, 1872. He is descended from one of the oldest and most worthy German families of the county. His grandfather, Nicholas Fox, came from Germany in 1817 and settled in Lawrenceburg, where he conducted a meat market until 1884. He died in Dearborn county in 1891. His son, also named Nicholas, the father of the subject of this sketch, was born in Lawrenceburg, in April, 1843, and for the last forty-three years has been in the meat business in his native city. Edward C. Fox, after attending the public schools of Greendale and Lawrenceburg, graduated in 1893 from Nelson's business college in Cincinnati. For awhile after leaving school he was engaged as bookkeeper for a coal company at Lawrenceburg. He was then appointed truant officer for Dearborn county, serving in that capacity until elected recorder in 1902. At the age of twenty-one he was elected to the council in the town of Greendale, to which office he was re-elected for four terms; serving in all seven years, after which he was elected marshal for one term. Mr. Fox is a Democrat and is always ready to do battle for his political convictions. His term as recorder expires in 1908. He was reared and educated in the faith of the German Lutheran church and is now a member of that denomination. In 1899 he was married to Miss Susie E., daughter of the late John Mahoney, and they have two sons and one daughter, viz.: Leslie M., Lorena C., and Nicholas H.

JOHN LEAP, a farmer on the Licking river, near Alexandria, Ky., was born in Bavaria, one of the States of the German Empire, Feb. 15, 1841. When he was about six months old his parents, Casper and Barbara (Smith) Leap, (German Leoöp), came to America, and soon after their arrival in this country they located at Cincinnati, where both the parents died. They had five children. The eldest son, whose name was also John, died in Cincinnati; Susan is the wife of Adam Guyman of Campbell county, Ky.; John is the subject of this sketch; and Frank and Carrie are both deceased. John Leap lived in Cincinnati until he reached his majority and was educated in the public schools of that city. In 1862 he enlisted in Company E, Eighth Kentucky Federal cavalry, for a term of one year, and during that time was in all the operations of his regiment, among which was the pursuit and capture of Gen. John Morgan, the famous raider. After the war Mr. Leap became a farmer in Campbell county and since 1881 has occupied his present farm, which is one of the best in the county. He is a member of the Grand Army post at Alexandria and is one of the most respected citizens of his neighborhood. In 1871 he was married to Miss Anna Seibert, a native of Germany. She died in 1895, the mother of the following children: John, Jr., is a resident of Campbell county; Anna is dead; Joseph works in a paper mill at Middletown, O.; Josephine is the wife of William Weinel, of Cumberland, O.; Augustus is at home; Peter, Leo, Mary, Frank and William are all deceased, and Katy is at home with her father.

JAMES F. SHAW, a farmer living about one mile east of California, Ky., was born near New Richmond, Clermont county, Ohio, Jan. 5, 1847. He is a son of John and Ida (Webb) Shaw, both natives of Ohio, the former having been born in Clermont county, April 1, 1810, and the latter in Hamilton county, Sept. 17, 1812. Five children were born to this union, viz.: Nancy, now Mrs. Frank Bettle, of Ohio; Clayton, enlisted at the beginning of the Civil war in the Fifth Ohio cavalry and died at Pittsburg Landing soon after the battle; James F., the subject of this sketch; John C., a farmer in Clermont county; Viola, now Mrs. E. M. Reed, of Detroit, Mich. Mr. Shaw's ancestry has figured prominently in the affairs of the Ohio valley for several generations. His maternal great-grandfather, John Morin, fought in the American army during the Revolution. After the independence of the United States was established his family in Virginia wanted him to become a slaveholder. This he refused to do and came to Kentucky. He never went back to Virginia and some of the old estate there is still unclaimed by his heirs. The paternal grandfather of Mr. Shaw came to Mason county, Ky., about the year 1790, and later settled in Campbell county. He served in the militia during the Revolution. Both of Mr. Shaw's grandfathers served several terms in the Ohio legislature—being members at the same time—and a brother of his father fought with Sam Houston for Texan independence. One of Mr. Shaw's uncles was wounded in a skirmish with the Indians while with a surveying party in Texas, and afterward fought in the Mexican war. James F. Shaw was educated at Parker's academy, in Clermont county, and at Antioch college, at Yellow Springs, Ohio. For several years after leaving school he was engaged in teaching, after which he turned his attention to farming. For the past thirty-three years he has resided upon the farm where he now lives. This is a beautiful farm of 170 acres, overlooking the Ohio river. In politics Mr. Shaw is an unswerving Democrat and takes a keen interest in all public questions. In 1883-84 he represented Campbell county in the legislature. While a member of that body he was a member of the committee on education, and championed the bill revising the school laws of the state. This bill became a law and remained in force until the adoption of the new constitution in 1889, when its leading features were incorporated in the organic law. On Sept. 29, 1870, Mr. Shaw was married to Miss Lura, daughter of Whittemore and Almira Reed, who came from New Hampshire and settled in Meigs county, Ohio, and later in Clermont county. One of Mrs. Shaw's uncles graduated from West Point at the head of his class, received a commission as first lieutenant, and served in the regular army until his death, which occurred in 1859. To Mr. and Mrs. Shaw have been born the following children: Clayton W., a physician at Alexandria, Ky.; Frederick, living at Fort Thomas, Ky.; Elwood R., graduate of the Ohio normal school in the class of 1902, now at home; George A., merchant in Chicago; and Ida, Carl and Alice, at home. Mr. Shaw is a member of Mayo Lodge, No. 198, Free and Accepted Masons, at California. His wife is a Presbyterian, the eldest son is a Baptist, and all the other children are members of the Christian church.

JACOB ANDERSON, a farmer near Carthage, Campbell county, Ky., was born on the farm where he now lives, June 5, 1827. His parents were John and Elizabeth (Carmack) Anderson, the former coming to Kentucky from Virginia with his parents when he was but nine years of age. The Carmacks originally came from Scotland. Jacob is one of a family of ten children, only three of whom are now living. George lives in Campbell county, Ky. He is nearly eighty years of age and is almost blind. America, now Mrs. Wesley White, lives near Carthage. Mr. Anderson's opportunities to acquire an education were extremely limited. In his boyhood he attended private or "subscription" schools for a few months and this constituted his schooling. This he has supplemented by reading until he is one of the best informed men in his neighborhood. He is particularly fond of reading the Scriptures and few men know more of the Book of Life than he. His farm, which consists of about 100 acres, is directly opposite New Richmond, O. From a point near the house one can see up the beautiful Ohio for fifteen miles, and down the river for about ten miles, while opposite the city of New Richmond, with its surrounding hills, forms a gorgeous panorama. The farm is also widely known for a fine spring of water. This Mr. Anderson has utilized for keeping milk and butter, dairy products being the principal output of the farm. Along the side of the farm next to the Ohio river runs the Chesapeake and Ohio railway. Before the war Mr. Anderson was a Whig. Since then he has been a Democrat, though he takes no active part in politics. On July 4, 1848, he was married to Mary Hester, daughter of James and Margaret (Dicken) White, both of whom were natives of Campbell county. Mrs. Anderson's mother was a distant relative of Charles Dickens, the celebrated English novelist, though for some reason the American branch of the family dropped the final letter of the name. Mrs. Anderson was born at Alexandria, Ky., May 25, 1830, and received her education in the schools of her native town. Mr. and Mrs. Anderson are the parents of eight children, viz.: John, died at the age of eighteen months; Martha, married Robert Mell and died at the age of twenty-six years. A daughter of this marriage, Miss Birdie Mell, a bright and amiable young lady, now lives with her grandparents. Joseph Wesley, now a farmer living near Winnebago City, Minn.; Millard Fillmore, who died near New Richmond, O., in 1902; Margaret Lizzie, now Mrs. Zeno Barker, living near Carthage; Mary Jessie, now Mrs. William Madden, of Mount Washington, O.; Jacob, a farmer near Carthage; and Esther Holmes, wife of Thornton Painter, a farmer near Carthage. Mr. and Mrs. Anderson are both members of the Baptist church and are firm believers in the faith of that denomination. They practice the teachings of their religion, are charitable to the unfortunate, and their home is one of the most hospitable in Campbell county.

GEORGE W. HENDERSON, pilot on the steam ferry boat operated by the Chesapeake & Ohio railroad, at New Richmond, was born in Campbell county, Ky., Oct. 26, 1861. His paternal grandfather, John Henderson, was a native of Ireland, but came to America while still a young man, settling in Pennsylvania. There he married Abigail Livingston and about 1810 or 1811 came to Cincinnati, which was then a small village. A year or two later he removed to Campbell county, where, after serving in the war of 1812, he died when about forty years of age. His widow married Henry Martin, a wealthy farmer and large land owner of Campbell county. Two sons of John and Abigail Henderson are still living, John and Asa, and four sons and two daughters are deceased. One of those was George W., the father of the subject of this sketch. He was born after the family settled in Kentucky and was for the greater part of his life employed on the river, most of the time in the lower trade. During the Civil war he and his brother

Alva were the first and second mates on the steamer *"Prima Donna"* and were captured by the Confederates and held as prisoners of war for about four months. He married Nancy Bruce, a native of Campbell county. Her parents came from Pennsylvania and were among the pioneers of the settlement about Carthage. George W. and Nancy Henderson had three children. Alice is now Mrs. T. J. Tarvin, of Carthage; Ella is the widow of Solomon Anderson and at present lives in New Richmond, O., and George W. Mr. Henderson received a good common school education, after which he, like his father, found employment in the steamboat trade of the Ohio. For more than thirteen years he has followed the river, the greater part of that time in his present position. He owns a fine farm of seventy acres on the Kentucky side, opposite the ferry, and when not engaged upon the boat devotes his time to fruit growing. In October, 1885, Mr. Henderson led to the altar Miss Lucy, the daughter of Oliver and Mary Moore, old and honored residents of Campbell county. Her father is dead and her maternal grandfather, whose name was Boots, was a soldier in the American army during the Revolution. Mr. and Mrs. Henderson have five children: Mary, aged eighteen; Roger, fifteen; Raymond, twelve; Daisy, five; and Delpha, two. Both parents and the eldest daughter are members of the Methodist Church South at Carthage.

HON. WILLIAM H. O'BRIEN, president of the Citizens National bank, of Lawrenceburg, is one of the best known and most popular men in Southeastern Indiana. His father, Cornelius O'Brien, a native of Callan, Ireland, landed in Dearborn county in 1835, fresh from the Emerald Isle. He has been described as genial, energetic and quick-witted, and the son has inherited these characteristics in a marked degree. About 1847 Cornelius O'Brien was elected county treasurer and shortly after the expiration of his term he was appointed to fill out an unexpired term in the county clerk's office. At the next election he was chosen to succeed himself in that office and from that time until his death he was an influential factor in the Democratic politics of his state. In 1856 he was a delegate to the national convention that nominated James Buchanan, and was the same year elected to the state senate. In 1860 he was a candidate for clerk

of the supreme court. He married Harriet Hunter, daughter of James
W. Hunter, and they had two sons, Robert Emmett and William H.
William H. O'Brien received his primary education in the Lawrenceburg schools, and later attended Asbury—now DePauw—university,
for two years. His old schoolmates speak of him as a quick-minded,
mischief-loving youngster, yet his love of fair play was so well known
that he was frequently called upon to act as umpire or referee in games
of different kinds. Upon leaving college he became deputy clerk of
his county for a short time, and in 1877, in company with Dr. W. D. H.
Hunter, purchased the Lawrenceburg *Register*. They published the
paper until 1894, when they sold out. The latter part of that time Mr.
O'Brien had practically full control of the paper, Dr. Hunter having
been appointed collector of internal revenue for the old Sixth district,
in 1885. That year Mr. O'Brien was elected mayor of Lawrenceburg
and was re-elected at each succeeding election until 1894, when he declined a renomination. As mayor he played an important part in the
construction of the levee to protect Lawrenceburg from the Ohio river
in times of flood. Besides securing government aid to the amount of
$60,000 he recommended the issuance of bonds to the amount of $50,-
000 by the city. The benefits derived from the construction of the levee
are seen in the appreciated values of all city property. In 1898 a peti-
tion, signed by a majority of the business men, was presented to Mr.
O'Brien asking him to again consent to the use of his name as a candidate for mayor. He reluctantly consented and was elected by the largest
majority ever given any one for the office. In 1890 he was one of the
principal organizers of the Citizens National bank, and after serving for
some time as vice-president and cashier he was elected president, which
office he has held ever since his first election. He was also one of the
organizers of the Lawrenceburg Fair Association and was secretary for
several years. Governor Matthews appointed Mr. O'Brien a trustee of
Purdue university, and he has been reappointed by two subsequent
governors. He has also served as trustee of Moores Hill college for a
long period. Mr. O'Brien has been active in political work outside of
local offices and affairs. From 1880 to 1886 he was secretary and from
1888 to 1902 chairman of the county committee. This brought him
in contact with party leaders from all over the state and gave him a
chance to increase the scope of his political usefulness. From 1890
to 1896 he was a member of the state central committee, and during the
campaigns of 1896 and 1898 served on the state executive committee.
In 1900 he was a delegate to the national convention, and was the
Indiana member of the committee appointed to notify Mr. Bryan of his

nomination. In January, 1902, he was elected chairman of the state central committee, and was re-elected in 1904. He was nominated for state senator in 1902 and triumphantly elected from the district composed of Dearborn, Ohio and Franklin counties. He was a delegate-at-large to the Democratic national convention at St. Louis in 1904 and was the Indiana member of the committee to notify Judge Parker of his nomination. Mr. O'Brien is a member of Lawrenceburg Lodge, No. 4, Free and Accepted Masons; Aurora Commandery, No. 56, Knights Templars; and a thirty-second degree member of the Scottish Rite. He is also a Knight of Pythias, a member of the Phi Gamma Delta fraternity; and of the Methodist Episcopal church. Mr. O'Brien was married in 1882 to Miss Harriet, daughter of his old partner, Dr. W. D. H. Hunter. They have six children living. Cornelius, cashier Citizens National bank; Frances, a graduate of Glendale female college; Robert Emmett, a cadet at the United States Military academy, West Point, N. Y.; William H., Elizabeth and Harriet. The youngest daughter, Ruth, died in August, 1900, aged eighteen months.

JACOB M. BAUER, president of the Bauer Cooperage Company, and director in the Citizens National bank, Lawrenceburg, Ind., was born in Cincinnati, O., in the old Flat Iron ward, Feb. 12, 1858. His father was a native of Stuttgart, and his mother a native of Munich, Germany. They both came to America in 1850. His father was an old time boniface of Cincinnati, well known to all the old timers as the proprietor of the Washington hotel in the East End, which was so well known all over the country during its day, and especially during the war. He died in 1885, but the mother is still living; also a sister, Mrs. H. E. Ruigel, of Cleveland. Jacob M. Bauer attended the public schools in Cincinnati, but left school at an early age to take up study of law. Not finding this to his liking he abandoned it and entered into the employ of Jeffras, Seeley & Co., first as clerk and then as traveling salesman. During this time he and his brother, John G., made an extensive tour of the European countries. In 1879, in company with his brother, they started the cooperage business so well known the world over as The Bauer Cooperage Company, of Cincinnati.

In 1882, they removed their plant to Lawrenceburg and consolidated with James Walsh & Sons, retaining the old established name of The Bauer Cooperage Company. In 1894 the Bauer interest bought out the Walsh interest. These works employ two hundred and twenty-five people and have a capacity of twelve hundred whiskey barrels per day, this being their specialty. Nine mills are scattered through West Virginia, Kentucky and Tennessee to supply the staves necessary for the company's demand. These mills give labor to thousands of men. Politically Jacob M. Bauer is a Republican, dyed in the wool, and was chosen as a delegate to the national convention of 1904, which nominated Roosevelt and Fairbanks. He stands high in Masonic rank, being a thirty-second degree member of the Scottish Rite, a Knight Templar, and a Noble of the Mystic Shrine. He is also a member of the Knights of Pythias; several clubs at Cincinnati; the German Lutheran church; and is a contributor to all other churches. He was married in 1885 to Evangeline, daughter of Col. Ezra G. Hayes, the well-known capitalist and distiller of Dearborn county, Ind., and four children have come to bless this union. Two, a son and daughter, are now dead, and two daughters, Laura H. and Catherine E., are now attending the Bartholomew Ely school at Clifton, Ohio. Mr. and Mrs. Bauer have hosts of friends and their beautiful home is well known for its hospitality and social functions.

AMBROSE E. NOWLIN, collector of internal revenue for the Sixth district of Indiana, with offices at Lawrenceburg, was born in Dearborn county, Ind., in the year 1843, and has been a resident of the county all his life. His father, Jerry Nowlin, was born in Kentucky in 1806, but came with his father to Indiana while still in his boyhood. He passed his life as a farmer in Dearborn county and died there in 1873. Ambrose received his early education in the common schools, afterward graduating in the scientific course from Miami university, at Oxford, Ohio. From college he returned home and took up farming as an occupation, which he has followed ever since. In 1890 he was one of the five supervisors of the census in Indiana, and in 1894 was elected auditor of the county.

Notwithstanding Dearborn county is generally Democratic by a majority of seven or eight hundred he was elected by a plurality of three hundred. After serving two years as auditor he resigned to accept his present position, having received the appointment from President McKinley in 1897. Mr. Nowlin is a director in the People's bank, which he helped to organize twenty-two years ago. He is a Knight of Pythias and a member of Lawrenceburg Lodge, No. 4, Free and Accepted Masons. In 1870 he was married to Flora B., daughter of W. H. Baker, of Dearborn county. They have one daughter, Margaret, now the wife of M. W. Fisk. Their son, Oakey, after completing his education and becoming established in business with bright prospects for a successful career, was stricken with typhoid fever and died just as he was entering the twenty-second year of his life.

GEORGE C. COLUMBIA, vice-president of the Citizens National bank, of Lawrenceburg, Ind., is of English extraction. A few years before the beginning of the Revolutionary war his great-grandfather, John Columbia, came with two of his brothers to America, and all three fought in the Continental army during the war for independence. After the war he settled in Maryland, where his son, William, the grandfather of the subject, was born. For a time he lived in Pennsylvania, but died in Hamilton county, Ohio, in 1826. John Columbia, the father of George C., was born in Pennsylvania in 1799. When he was about a year old he went with his parents to Columbia, Ohio, and in 1819 came to Dearborn county. There he passed his life as a farmer and died in 1890. George C. Columbia was born in Dearborn county, Jan. 30, 1835. He passed his youth and early manhood in farm work, attending the country schools during the winter months. In September, 1861, he enlisted in the Seventh regiment Indiana volunteer infantry as a private, but in the following February was made a sergeant. He was with his regiment in some of the hardest fought battles of the war, among them being Winchester, Port Republic, Cedar Mountain, Second Bull Run, Fredericksburg, Chancellorsville, Gettysburg, Mine Run, The Wilderness, Spottsylvania C. H., North Anna River, Cold Harbor,

Petersburg and Weldon R. R. He was wounded once slightly and at
Second Bull Run was taken prisoner. Three days later he was paroled
and sent home, rejoining his regiment in December, 1862. From June
to August, 1864, he was under fire every day before Petersburg, and
was in the two days' fight at Weldon railroad in August of that year.
In September, 1864, he was discharged, returned home, and for the
next sixteen years was engaged in farming and teaching school. In
1867 he was elected assessor of his township, holding the office three
years. In 1873 he was made superintendent of the county schools for
two years and at the close of his term was re-elected. At the close of
the first year of his second term he resigned. He served eight years as
recorder of the county, being elected in 1878 and again in 1882, each
time without opposition, and was for three years a member of the
Lawrenceburg school board. In August, 1884, he was appointed postmaster at Lawrenceburg and held the office for four years. Upon retiring from the postoffice he also retired from active business pursuits
but in January, 1899, he was elected vice-president of the Citizens
National bank, in which he had long been a stockholder. In all the
positions Mr. Columbia has held he has been noted for his careful,
conscientious conduct of affairs and no man stands higher in the estimation of his neighbors. Mr. Columbia is a member of the Methodist
Episcopal church, the Independent Order of Odd Fellows, and is a
Royal Arch Mason. Mr. Columbia was first married to Ann J.,
daughter of Julius C. Churchill. She died Oct. 26, 1881, leaving one
daughter, Emma. On Dec. 29, 1887, he was married to Margaret M.,
daughter of Samuel Martin, and at the time of her marriage to Mr.
Columbia the widow of William J. Fitch, by whom she had one son,
Charles W. Fitch, now in the drug business at Lawrenceburg.

EDWIN M. LEE, mayor of Lawrenceburg, Ind., and one of the
popular merchants of that city, was born in Switzerland county, Ind.,
in 1867. He is a son of Rev. Charles W. Lee, one of the best known
Methodist ministers in the state. The early life of the subject of this
sketch was passed in various localities as his father removed from one
church to another. The greater part of his education was obtained
in the public schools of Edinburg and at Moores Hill college. In
1887 he became connected with the G. Y. Roots Co. (now the Lawrenceburg Roller Mills Co.), and eight years later was made assignee of
the company. After four years in this capacity the company was reorganized and Mr. Lee went to Muncie, Ind., where he engaged in merchandizing for one year, when he returned to Lawrenceburg. There

he opened a mercantile establishment, which he has conducted ever since. Politically Mr. Lee is a Republican and has always taken a lively interest in political contests. In 1892 he was elected to the Lawrenceburg council from the Third ward, serving for three years. He was a member of the city school board for three years and in May, 1904, was elected to the office of mayor. He is also president of the Commercial club, a thirty-second degree Mason and a Knight Templar, and a member of the Methodist Episcopal church. In church, lodge, and the community Mr. Lee has a deservedly high standing, owing to his genial disposition, his progressive notions, and his regard for his fellow-man.

CHARLES M. BEINKAMP, of Aurora, Ind., auditor of Dearborn county, was born at Cochran, in that county, April 21, 1861. At the age of nineteen years he was graduated from the Aurora high school and entered the offices of the Crescent Brewing Company of that city as shipping clerk. After about six months in this position he met with an accident that disabled him for some time, and upon his recovery he went into the dry goods department of Robert Maybin's mercantile establishment at Aurora, where he remained for eighteen months. He then went to Johnson City, Mo., and took charge of the general store of Dr. J. W. Wheeler for a year. One of the customers of this store was the famous outlaw, Cole Younger. After a year in Johnson City Mr. Beinkamp returned to Aurora and engaged in the grocery business, which he successfully conducted for about nine years, when he and two of his wife's brothers, Selwyn and William Mitchell, embarked in the manufacture of brick, under the firm name of the Mitchell Brick Company, in which he is still interested. The company maintains and operates two factories, one at Lawrenceburg, Ind., and the other at Delhi, O. Ever since he became a voter Mr. Beinkamp has taken a keen interest in political matters, being a Jeffersonian Democrat "on both sides of the house," as he expresses it. For some time he served as a member of the Aurora city council, and in 1898 he was elected to the office of auditor of Dearborn county. In 1902, at the close of his first four years' term, he was triumphantly re-elected, leading the county ticket by a majority of 250 votes, being the first auditor in more than thirty years to succeed himself. His re-election in the face of this long one term precedent tells the story of his personal and political popularity, as well as his efficient discharge of official duties during his first term. In October, 1884, Mr. Beinkamp and Miss Maggie Mitchell, of Lawrenceburg, were united in marriage and they have one daughter, Harriet.

JOHN T. SHERRIFF, manager of the roller mills, Lawrenceburg, Ind., is a native of Toledo, Ohio. While still in his childhood his parents removed to North Dakota, settling at the town of Mandan. Here the subject of this sketch was reared and received the greater part of his education, though he attended school in the East for some time. He began his business career in the employ of the Mandan Roller Mills Company, with which he served for six years, learning the miller's trade in all its branches. In 1897 he came to Lawrenceburg as assistant manager of the Lawrenceburg Roller Mills, the largest mills in Indiana, with a capacity of eighteen hundred barrels daily. After one year as assistant Mr. Sherriff was made manager and under his control the mills have had a prosperous career, the products finding their way into a constantly widening market. As a miller and manager Mr. Sherriff has few equals. His training has been thorough and his natural adaptability for the work has enabled him to take a high rank among the leading millers of the country. He is member of the Masonic fraternity and of the Episcopal church.

R. H. COLT, attorney at law, Lawrenceburg, Ind., was born in that city May 21, 1860. At the age of seventeen he graduated from the high school and was the valedictorian of his class. From that time until he was twenty-eight he was employed as a clerk in a store or as a traveling salesman. During the last two years of that time he studied short-hand and in the fall of 1868 he attended a short-hand school, increasing his speed from sixty-five to one hundred and eighty-five words a minute. He was appointed court stenographer, and held that position through the year 1889, his teacher making the statement that he was the only one who ever left the school and immediately became a court reporter. In the meantime Mr. Colt had commenced the study of law with John K. Thompson, of Lawrenceburg, and in 1890 was admitted to the bar. In 1892 he formed a partnership with his old preceptor which lasted until the death of Mr. Thompson in 1898. Mr. Colt has always been an enthusiastic Republican and in 1898 he was elected chairman of the central committee of Dearborn county. His management of the campaign of that year was so satisfactory to his party associates that he has been continued as chairman ever since. He is a member of the Dearborn County Bar Association and was for ten years treasurer of the organization. He is a stockholder in the Greendale Cemetery association, one of the finest and best kept cemeteries in the state, and has for years been prominent in its affairs. At the age of nine years he joined the Presbyterian church, in which he has served as deacon, elder and treasurer. In 1890 he was married to Miss Carrie G. Walters, daughter of Dr. Carl G. Walters, of Lawrenceburg, and they have two children: Carl Thompson and Helen J.

GEORGE M. ROBERTS, of the law firm of Roberts & Johnston, Lawrenceburg, Ind., was born in Ripley county, Ind., in March, 1843. When he was about eleven years of age his parents removed to Quincy, Ill., and while living in that city he acquired his primary education in the common schools. In 1863 he graduated from Knox college, Galesburg, Ill., and for about a year afterward was a clerk in the Chicago, Burlington & Quincy Railroad Company's offices at Quincy. In May, 1864, he went into Company A, One Hundred and Thirty-seventh regiment Illinois volunteer infantry, as first lieutenant, serving five months and taking part in the fight with General Forrest, at Memphis, Tenn., in October, 1864. Upon leaving the army he entered the Albany, N. Y., law school and graduated from that institution in June, 1865. He first located at Omaha, Neb., and remained there for about four years, coming to Lawrenceburg in January, 1870. Here he has continued practice ever since and few lawyers in Southeastern Indiana have a higher standing at the bar. Mr. Roberts is a Republican and one of the kind that never hesitates to defend his party's position on all public questions. While living in Omaha he served one term as mayor and since coming to Lawrenceburg has served as mayor of that city three terms. In law, politics, official or private life he is recognized as a just and fearless individual, one who ever tries to be on the side of the right, and by his courageous course he has won the esteem of his fellow-men. Mr. Roberts is a Royal Arch Mason and a member of the Methodist Episcopal church, and in both organizations he is an influential factor in shaping their policy.

ARCHIBALD SHAW, postmaster at Lawrenceburg, Ind., was born in Switzerland county, Ind., Aug. 8, 1847. His paternal grandfather, John Shaw, and his father, William Shaw, were both natives of Paisley,

Scotland. The father, John Shaw, and all his family came to America in 1816 and after a few months in Philadelphia came to Switzerland county. In 1825 he married Linda Rous, who was born in Yorkshire, England, but came with her parents to this country in 1812, on the merchant vessel *"Packet."* The war of 1812 then being in progress and the *"Packet"* being an American vessel it was captured by a British man of war and crew and passengers carried to Nova Scotia as prisoners. There their passports were examined and being found lawfully executed they were released and came on to the United States. William Shaw was for many years engaged in trading on the river, making a number of trips to New Orleans, after which he engaged in merchandizing. He died in 1873 and his wife in 1892. The early years of Archibald Shaw were spent on a farm in Switzerland county, where he attended the common schools, afterward taking a four years' course at Asbury—now DePauw—university. From the time of his leaving college until 1898 he was engaged in various business enterprises. Ever since becoming a voter he has taken an active interest in politics, using all his influence to promote the success of the Republican party. For eight years he has been chairman of the central committee of Dearborn county; has served as city school trustee; and in 1898 was appointed postmaster by President McKinley. Mr. Shaw is a member of Lawrenceburg Lodge, No. 4, Free and Accepted Masons; Dearborn Lodge, No. 49, Knights of Pythias, and is secretary of the official board of the Methodist Episcopal church. He has three brothers and three sisters living, one brother, Lucien, being one of the supreme judges of California. In 1873 he was married to Miss Hannah V. Fitch, daughter of De Witt C. Fitch, who was a well known resident of Lawrenceburg. To this marriage there have been born eight children: Ida C., Cora L., and William De Witt are deceased. Those living are Harris F., Edward R., John A., Ella M., and De Witt C.

ORVILLE S. JAQUITH, M.D., one of the best known physicians of Lawrenceburg, Ind., is a native of Dearborn county, having been born at Wright's Corners, Sept. 27, 1872. His father, Edwin L. Jaquith, also born at Wright's Corners, was in business there for many years, and died there in April, 1904. The family is of French extraction, the doctor's grandfather having been a native of France. Dr. Jaquith's mother was a Miss Anna E. Howard. In his boyhood he attended the common schools, where he received a good rudimentary education, and in the spring of 1897 was graduated from the Miami Medical college, of Cincinnati, with the degree of M.D.

Shortly afterward he began practice at Lawrenceburg, where he has ever since continued, being associated with Dr. House part of the time. Dr. Jaquith was not content with merely receiving a diploma from a medical college. He wanted to know more of his chosen profession. Hence in 1898 and again in 1903 he took post graduate courses in the Chicago Polyclinic Institute, thus keeping in touch with medical progress, and placing his name on the roll of progressive physicians of the country. Dr. Jaquith is a member and one of the trustees of the Christian church. In June, 1900, he was united in marriage to Miss Maud Rinaman, daughter of Victor Rinaman. To this marriage there have been born two children: Mildred and Maurine.

GEORGE SUTTON, late of Aurora, Ind., was born in London, England, June 16, 1812. His parents emigrated to America in 1819 and located in Cincinnati, Ohio, from which city they removed to Whitewater Valley, Franklin county, Ind. After he had spent several years at Miami university he began the study of medicine in Cincinnati under the instruction of Prof. John Eberle and afterwards under that of Prof. S. D. Gross, a distinguished authority on medicine. After attending three full courses of lectures at the medical college of Ohio he graduated from that institution in 1836. Two of his sons have since received diplomas from that celebrated school. Locating at Aurora, he practiced his profession in his home city for fifty years, building up a large and profitable business. Doctor Sutton was a close and observing student and all of his writings are replete with original and valuable ideas. He contributed largely to both medical and scientific literature, his articles having been extensively copied in various journals of the country. In the winter and spring of 1843 he wrote a series of papers on epidemic erysipelas, popularly known as "black tongue," a disease then prevalent in Aurora and the surrounding country, and these papers were published in full in "Copland's Medical Dictionary," and "Numerly on Erysipelas," both standard English works. He gave much attention to microscopic study, and made valuable discoveries in regard to trichina and trichinosis, showing that from three to ten per cent. of the hogs in Southeastern Indiana are affected with trichina, and that the disease may assume various forms hitherto unnoticed by the profession. "His method of reducing dislocations of the hip joint," says Professor Pooley of Columbus, Ohio, "is a beautiful, original and practical piece of surgery, and one sure to be adopted by the profession." In 1867 he was elected president of the Indiana State Medical society, an honor highly appreciated by him because he was not present at that meeting and had not sought the office. In 1877 he was chosen president of the board of trustees of the college of physicians and surgeons of Indiana and served in that capacity for several years, delivering the annual address to the graduating classes. As president of the Rocky Mountain Medical association he delivered a masterly adress before that body at its meeting in New Orleans, May 6, 1885. Although engaged in active practice in the different branches of his profession, he devoted a portion of his time to geology, meteorology and archæology, directing his special attention to the antiquities of the neighborhood. He made collections of fossils and geological specimens, and formed a cabinet of many thousand specimens, unsurpassed by another in this portion of Indiana, and valuable for their local interest. Among the subjects upon which Doctor Sutton has written are the following: Cholera, erysipelas, trichina, scarlatina, placenta praevia, parasites, dislocation of the hip joint, epidemics of Southeastern Indiana, hog cholera, glacial deposits, formation of storms and causes of the great floods in the Ohio valley. Doctor Sutton was a man remarkable for independence of thought and action, and enjoyed the confidence of his fellow-men for over half a century. He took an active part in whatever was for the good of the city; was elected mayor of Aurora for three successive terms; was a member of the board of school trustees for more than sixteen years, being instrumental in the establishment of the graded school system and the erection of the handsome school building in the southern part of the city. On June 7, 1838, he married Miss Sarah Forlbre and by her had five children, four sons and one daughter, of which number only one son and the daughter are living. At the time of his death Doctor Sutton was a member of the International Medical congress; the American and Indiana State Medical associations; the Dearborn County Medical society, which he helped to found and which is now one of the foremost in the state; the American Association for the Advancement of Science; the Archaeological Association of Indiana; the Natural History societies of Cincinnati and Dearborn county, being president of the latter, and an honorary member of numerous other societies of similar character.

HARLEY H. SUTTON, M.D., of Aurora, Ind., was born in that city, Dec. 24, 1852. His father, Dr. George Sutton, a sketch of whose life appears in this work, was of English descent, and his mother, Sarah Folbre Sutton, was a daughter of Charles and Phoebe Folbre, who were among the early settlers of Southeastern Indiana. Dr. H. H. Sutton is the youngest of five children, three of whom are now deceased. His early life was spent in his native town where he received his elementary education, graduating from the Aurora high school in 1870, under Prof. Edward Clark. He then entered the Indiana State university at Bloomington, where he took a special two years' course preparatory to the study of medicine. In 1873 he began the study of medicine under his father and during the first year rendered valuable assistance with the microscope, especially in the examinations of pork for trichina, which subject his father was making a special study at that time. In 1874 he entered the medical college of Ohio at Cincinnati, and graduated in the spring of 1876. In the fall of that year he entered Jefferson Medical college at Philadelphia, and graduated from that institution the following spring, the subject of his thesis being "The reduction of the dislocation of the hip joint by means of a fulcrum placed in the groin." This thesis was mainly the description of a new method of reducing dislocation of the hip joint, originated by his father, with a history of a case of three months' standing under the care of Prof. William Pancoast, the reduction having been made by Dr. George Sutton at Blockly hospital in Philadelphia. His health being somewhat impaired by his close application to study Dr. Sutton decided to take a rest before seeking a location for the practice of his profession, but the serious illness of his brother, Dr. W. E. Sutton, then engaged in practice with their father, made it necessary for him to take his brother's place in their father's office at Aurora. Dr. W. E. Sutton never regained his health, but died in 1878, and Dr. H. H. Sutton continued to practice with his father until the latter's death in 1886, and today he is a busy practitioner in his old home. He has won an enviable reputation as a diagnostician, and for the careful and painstaking way in which he handles his cases. Being fortunate enough to be able to eliminate from his practice certain features which were irksome, he is enabled to devote more time to other branches of his profession, and diseases of children is one which he has given special attention. Dr. Sutton believes in home institutions, and that more benefit is to be derived from local organizations than from the larger bodies. He has therefore devoted a great deal of his time to the upbuilding of the county medical society; has been honored many times as the representative of the society in both the State and National associations, and has filled all the offices of the society. He is a member of the American Medical association, the Indiana State and Mississippi Valley Medical societies. For years he has been the surgeon for the Big Four Railway company; was for a long time health officer of Aurora; and in 1896 took a post-graduate course in the New York polyclinic. He has written many papers on various subjects, but mainly pertaining to his profession, and the county medical society always gets the benefit of these productions. In addition to his profession Dr. Sutton is a director and vice-president of the Aurora Coffin Company, the Aurora Lumber Company, and the Aurora Chair Company, and is a director of the River View Cemetery association, besides belonging to various clubs and other organizations. Dr. Sutton inherited many of his father's traits. He is especially fond of out-door sports, particularly hunting and fishing, consequently he has visited the wilds of the Rocky mountains and the swamps of Louisiana, Missouri and Texas in quest of game, and has spent several seasons among the lakes of Michigan with his rod and net. Nearly every season finds him in some new spot, where the country is wild and game is plentiful, for a vacation. In 1887 he married Miss Mary, eldest daughter of Mr. and Mrs. W. R. Duchemin, of Aurora, and to this union there have been born two daughters and a son. Only the son is now living. He is in his twelfth year and bears the name of his grandfather, George Sutton. Dr. Sutton lives at the old homestead on the hill south of town, and he has so improved the place that with its natural beauty, it is one of the most attractive on the Ohio.

RICHARD CLAYTON BOND, M.D., late of Aurora, Ind., was at the time of his death one of the oldest physicians in that section of the state. He was born in Wood county, W. Va., March 22, 1822, his parents being Lewis and Lydia (John) Bond, the former a native of Maryland and the latter of Pennsylvania. The paternal ancestors came from England, while the mother was of Welsh descent. Dr. Bond was educated in the schools of Fayette county, Pa., after which he began the study of medicine with Dr. Stevenson, of Greensboro, in that county. While prosecuting his medical studies he taught school at intervals in Fayette and Green counties and in 1847 was licensed to practice. At that time the great West offered promising inducements to young men and soon after receiving his license he came to Lawrenceburg, Ind. After practicing there for a short time he went to Ripley county for about eighteen months and then located at Aurora, where he ever afterward remained. In 1857 he received the degree of M.D. from the Miami Medical college, of Cincinnati, and was one of the members of the alumni association of that institution. When the Civil war began he was appointed surgeon of the Fifteenth Indiana infantry, commanded by Colonel Geo. D. Wagner. He was with his regiment in several engagements, among them being Rich Mountain, Garrick's Ford, Green Brier and Shiloh. After a service of one and a half years he was compelled to resign on account of his health. Dr. Bond was always active in every movement for the upbuilding of Aurora and served as a member of the town council. He was a member and also an ordained minister of the Baptist church. In addition to his work as a physician he preached for ten years at various points in Southern -Indiana. In 1846 he was married to Miss Eliza Bevan, daughter of Thomas Bevan, a Cincinnati manufacturer. To this marriage there were born three sons and three daughters. One son, Marc L., adopted his father's profession. He was born at Aurora, March 12, 1859; educated in the public schools of Dearborn county; and graduated from the Ohio Medical college in 1882. For about a year he practiced at Louisville, Ky., but failing health compelled him to abandon his practice, and for three years he was practically an invalid. At the end of that time he became associated with his father, which association continued until the latter's death, June 30, 1904, since which time he has practiced alone. He is a member of the Dearborn County Medical society and of the State Medical association. In 1896 he was honored with the presidency of the county society, which shows the esteem in which he is held by his brother physicians. Dr. Bond was married on Nov. 29, 1893, to Lyda Trulock, of Aurora.

WILL H. CONWAY, a well-known citizen of Aurora, Ind., was born in Dearborn county, June 14, 1853. The Conways were among the earliest settlers of that county, and have been prominently identified with its progress. John L. Conway, the father of the subject of this sketch, was a steamboat man all his business life. During the

Civil war he was in the government service as pilot of a transport, of which his brother Daniel was captain. Among the exciting experiences he encountered in those stirring times was that of running the blockade at Vicksburg. He married Emily Shaddock, whose father came from Maine to Dearborn county at an early date. His death occurred at his home in Dearborn county in 1878. Will H. Conway was educated in the public schools and began his business career as a merchant, in which line he was engaged for a number of years. For the past twelve years he has been connected with the Aurora Gas Company. Politically Mr. Conway is a Republican and takes a lively interest in political contests. In 1900 he was elected township trustee, overcoming an adverse majority of 220. Several times he has acted as chairman of the Republican township committee. He is a member of the Aurora Masonic lodge, the Independent Order of Odd Fellows, and the Royal Arcanum. In 1884 he was married to Miss Emma, daughter of William Green, an old and highly esteemed citizen of Dearborn county. They have two children, Charles L. and Mabel E.

EDWIN SMITH, M.D., of Aurora, Ind., was born at Conway, Franklin county, Mass., April 29, 1832, his parents being Rufus and Polly (Foskett) Smith, the former of an old Massachusetts family and the latter of Welsh descent. During his early boyhood Doctor Smith attended the local public schools, but the death of his father occurring, when he was but eleven years of age, made it incumbent upon him to assist in the support of the family. When he was eighteen years old he took private instruction in literary and scientific branches from his pastor with a view to studying medicine. Then for several years he was engaged in the life insurance business and in 1852 located in Cleveland, where he started in business for himself. After a short time he retired on account of his health and for several years was engaged in teaching. Through all these years he never gave up the idea of becoming a physician. While studying some of the old school text-books he became interested in the subject of Homeopathy. Purchasing Dr. Pulte's handbook and a case of medicines he began treating himself and a few of his friends. The results made a favorable impression on his mind, he gave up teaching, entered the Pulte Medical college, of Cincinnati, and graduated in May, 1877. Besides the regular course he made a special study of diseases of the eye and ear and gynecology, in which he received a special diploma. At the time of his graduation he received a prize for his thesis on the eye and ear. In July, 1877, he located at Aurora, where he has built up a large practice. He has one of the best equipped offices in the country, in the way of scientific appliances, and a large and well-selected library. He is a great believer in electricity as a therapeutic agent and regards it as being indispensable in the treatment of certain diseases. He is a member of the Pulte Medical association, of Hamilton county, Ohio; the Indiana State Medical association; and the American Institute of Homeopathy. Dr. Smith is active in church work as a member of the Baptist denomination, having served as secretary of the Canton, O., congregation, the Wooster association, the Sabbath school convention, and has been a contributor to religious journals. He has been married three times. His first wife was Miss Mary Andrews, daughter of Hon. Luther Andrews of Warren county, N. Y. She died on Jan. 11, 1861, leaving an infant son Edwin R., Jr. In 1867 the doctor married Miss Cornelia Whitmore, daughter of Russell Whitmore, of Georgetown, N. Y. Her death occurred on New Year's day, 1877. His third wife was Teresa Sheurmann, daughter of Martin Sheurmann, of Dearborn county.

CHARLES DAVIS WEBBER, treasurer of the city of Aurora, Ind., is a descendant of one of the oldest families in America, the records showing that the first of the family in this country came over in the Mayflower. His paternal grandfather was one of the first settlers of Aurora, where William Webber, father of the subject of this sketch, was born soon after the family's arrival. They came from Massachusetts and William is said to have been the second white child born in Aurora. He was a man of high moral character and was greatly respected by his neighbors. During his life he was engaged in a number of business enterprises,—publishing a newspaper, flat boating, merchandizing, etc. In later years he was manager for Chambers, Stevens & Co.'s grocery department. In 1852 he was married to Miss Mary Jane Davis, of Mississippi, and Charles D. is the oldest son born to that marriage. He was born at Aurora, Aug. 13, 1853, was educated in the public schools and began life in 1869 as a clerk in the First National bank of Aurora. Two years later he went to Cincinnati as teller in the First National bank of that city, where he remained until failing health compelled him to resign the position. Regaining his health he took a position with T. & J. W. Gaff with whom he has remained ever since, filling various positions of trust. In political matters Mr. Webber is a Republican and prominent in the affairs of his party. In May, 1904, he was elected treasurer of the city on the Citizens' ticket, receiving more votes than any other man on the ticket. Besides his official duties he is inspector of the local board of underwriters and occupies several other important positions, among them deacon and clerk of the First Baptist church, of which he is an active member. In June, 1878, Mr. Webber was married to Miss Julia Lane, whose father, the late G. W. Lane, was one of the most prominent men in Southeastern Indiana. He was a native of Burlington, Ky., but came to Dearborn county in his childhood. In 1835 he became a resident of Aurora and did much to build up the town. He built the first bridge over Hogan's creek, thus connecting Lawrenceburg and Aurora; was the first auditor of the county; was twice elected to the legislature; served as superintendent of the Denver mint, and was for eight years assistant treasurer of the United States. In 1850 he acquired the ownership of the Lawrenceburg *Register,* which he published for some time. While in the legislature he secured charters for several turnpike companies, as well as for the Ohio & Mississippi Railroad Company, of which he was one of the directors. He was also a director in the old Lawrenceburg & Indianapolis Railroad Company. Although a Democrat his broad ideas commanded the respect of his political opponents. He was deeply interested in the early history of the county and went to the trouble to preserve records of many interesting incidents of the early days. Mr. and Mrs. Webber have five children: Bessie, Harris B., Lane D., Alma, and Jean.

HENRY J. SMITH, justice of the peace, Aurora, Ind., was born in Hanover, Germany, April 10, 1834. While still in his boyhood he came with his parents and five other children to America. The family settled in Dearborn county, Ind., where the father farmed for two years, and where Henry attended school for three months, the only schooling he received after coming to this country. In 1847 they removed to Ripley county, the father buying a farm there and becoming one of the first settlers in the neighborhood where it was located. Later they returned to Dearborn county, where the father, whose name was Henry J. Smith, died in his ninetieth year. He was twice married and had seven children by each wife. As the subject of this sketch grew up he worked on the farm with his father and by the month for other farmers. After becoming of age he lived with his oldest brother until the Civil war broke out, when he enlisted in Company E, Seventh Indiana infantry, the first company that left Aurora. The regiment was commanded by Colonel, afterward General, Dumont, and took part in the battle of Phillippi, the first real engagement of the war. Later it was at Carrick's Ford, where General Garnett, commander of the Confederate forces, was killed and his entire command captured. At the expiration of his term Mr. Smith re-enlisted and served for three years in General Shields' command, participating in all the battles in which it was engaged. He was captured on Jan. 9, 1862, and held for some time as a prisoner at Lynchburg and Belle Island. After the war he returned to Aurora, where he has lived ever since. In 1888 he was elected a justice of the peace and has held the office by re-election continuously since that time. Mr. Smith is a Knight of Pythias, belonging to Union Lodge, No. 34, and is a member of J. A. Platter Post No. 82, Grand Army of the Republic. He has been twice married. His first wife was Caroline F. Stegemueller, to whom he was married in November, 1865. Her death occurred on Jan. 6, 1867, and in August of the succeeding year he was married to Miss Elizabeth Kuhlman. By this marriage he has three children living and one deceased. One daughter, Emma, is the wife of Martin L. Dove, of Aurora. He is in the service of the national government.

WILLIAM H. GREENE, a farmer living two miles west of Dillsboro, Ind., is a descendant of the same family as Gen. Nathaniel Greene of Revolutionary fame. His grandparents, William and Mary (Cochrine) Greene were natives of Culpeper county, Va., but at an early date emigrated to Kentucky, settling first in Fayette county and later at Split Rock, opposite Aurora, Ind. Still later they removed to Bellevue, Boone county, where they passed the remainder of their lives. Their children were John C., Edward, Reuben C., Sylvester, Morton, Helena and Mary. The first named was the father of the subject of this sketch. He was born near Bellevue in 1802 and died there in August, 1858. In 1825 he was married to Sallie Stowe Greene, who, although of the same name, was no known relation. She was a native of Connecticut and a daughter of Joseph and Nancy (Mallory) Greene. Her father was a sea captain and a relative of General Greene, and her mother was a sister of Daniel Mallory, the historian. John C. and Sallie S. Greene had six children. Joseph learned the trade of blacksmith, served in the Mexican war under General Breckenridge, and was first lieutenant in Company A, Twenty-third Kentucky infantry, in the Civil war. He died in 1876, in the fiftieth year of his age. He never married, and at the time of his death was living with his brother, William, near Dillsboro. Martha is now living in Kansas City, Mo., as the widow of John T. Ross; Elizabeth married Louis Clinkenbeard, and died in February, 1900; George M. was wounded at the battle of Stone River and died about two weeks later at Nashville, Tenn. He was in the same company as his brother, Joseph. John died at the age of nine years. William H. Greene was born on a farm in Boone county, Ky., Feb. 27, 1833, and is next to the youngest child of the family. His entire life has been spent on the farm, much of his time in later years being devoted to stock raising. In 1864 his brother, Joseph, was appointed deputy provost marshal for Boone county. At that time feeling ran high in that section of Kentucky, and in the discharge of his duties he aroused the enmity of some of the citizens who were opposed to the war. This led William to come to Indiana, and in December of that year he located on the farm where he now lives, his brother Joseph coming with him. Mr. Greene has been a member of the Patrons of Husbandry ever since the order was founded. Before the war he was a Whig, in 1868 he voted for General Grant, and since that time he has affiliated with the Democratic party. He never held an elective office, but when the law was passed creating the county council he was appointed a member of that body in Dearborn county to serve until the next regular election, his appointment being asked by members of all political parties. Although his early education was somewhat limited he has been a great reader and keeps well informed as to the world's progress. On Nov. 10, 1858, Mr. Greene was married to Miss Susan Durham, a daughter of John and Mary (Field) Durham, both natives of Kentucky, the former of Perryville and the latter of Danville, though later they lived in Montgomery county, Ind. Their children were Henry C., who died in May, 1903; John, now a resident of Hendricks county, Ind., where he has a large farm. He has two sons in Indianapolis, one an attorney and the other a physician. Mary F., now Mrs. G. H. Adams, of Junction City, Kan.; James W., a farmer, near Council Bluffs, Ia. Mrs. Greene is the third child of the family. Her mother died in 1846, and her father married Sarah Stubbins, of Kentucky, and to this marriage were born eight children. Mr. and Mrs. Greene have four children: Joseph was born Sept. 10, 1863, before his parents came to Indiana. He attended the Aurora high school, graduated from the normal department of Moore's Hill college, and for eleven years taught in the common schools. He is now the electrician for the Southeastern Indiana Telephone Company and one of the stockholders in the Dillsboro Natural Gas Company that recently found gas near his father's farm. He lives at home with his parents. Minnie M. was born Sept. 10, 1865. She is now Mrs. Hansel E. Gray of Brace, Tenn., where her husband is a planter. Sallie Stowe was born Aug. 28, 1871, and lives at home. Harry D. was born Oct. 1, 1874. He attended the Northern Indiana Normal college for three years, and one term at Moore's Hill college. Since leaving school he has been engaged in teaching. He also lives with his parents. Mr. Greene owns a well improved farm of 155 acres and is recognized as one of the most progressive farmers of Dearborn county.

JAMES POE COULTER, one of the leading merchants of Aurora, Ind., was born in the city of Philadelphia, May 29, 1835. He is a son of James and Jane (Moore) Coulter, both natives of County Tyrone, Ireland, but came to America shortly after their marriage. They first settled in Philadelphia but when James was about three years old the family removed to Columbiana county, Ohio, where the father died. Upon leaving school Mr. Coulter worked for some time at general carpenter work and then found employment as a bridge builder for the C. & A. Railroad Company. His industry and regular habits commended him to the company's officials and he was called to take charge of a division, a position he held for several years. Leaving this company he went into the car works at Bloomington, Ill., where he remained for ten years, the last six of which he was assistant foreman of the shops. In 1872 he was appointed master car builder for the Springfield division of the B. & O. S. W., holding that position for about four years, when he was made superintendent of the car department of the same company with headquarters at Aurora. Twelve years later he resigned the place and went into the dry goods business, and for the last nine years has been one of the most prominent merchants of Aurora. It has been a rule of his life to do whatever came in his way to the best of his ability. His promotions in the railroad service and his success as a merchant are unquestionably due to this trait of character. In 1855 he was married to Catherine Ann Roan, daughter of John and Catherine Roan, of Stark county, Ohio. To this union were born five children, two dying in infancy. Mrs. Coulter died in 1900, leaving a husband and three daughters. He married Ella Cadwell, of Aurora, in June, 1901, and has two children by his second marriage. He is a member of the Methodist Episcopal church, and is prominent in Masonic circles, being a member of Aurora Lodge No. 51; Royal Arch Chapter No. 13; Aurora Commandery No. 17, Knights Templars; Indianapolis Consistory, Scottish Rite, in which he holds the thirty-second degree; and the Supreme Council, where he has received the thirty-third degree, the highest in the order.

CHARLES H. CONAWAY, attorney at law, Dillsboro, Ind., was born in Dearborn county, Ind., March 28, 1864. He is a son of Hamilton and Elizabeth (Harper) Conaway. Hamilton Conaway came with his father from Virginia, the family being among the pioneers of Dearborn county. He was a lawyer by profession, beginning practice as early as 1838, and served three terms as trustee of Clay township. His death occurred on March 17, 1899. Charles H. Conaway was educated in the public schools of Dearborn county and then took up the study of law with his father. When the latter retired the son succeeded to the practice, having been admitted to the bar in 1884, and since 1887 he has been in active practice, making his headquarters at Dillsboro. In 1902 he was elected to the lower house of the legislature, as the joint representative of Dearborn and Ohio counties, for a term of two years. Mr. Conaway is a modest, unassuming gentleman who devotes most of his time to his business or in quiet social intercourse with his friends. He is one of the charter members of Dillsboro Lodge No. 333, Knights of Pythias, the only society in which he claims membership. In 1890 Mr. Conaway was married to Miss Annie B. Weaver, daughter of Joseph Weaver, one of the old residents of the county. They have one son, Carl C.

JOHN W. GRIMES, a farmer near Dillsboro, Ind., is a native of the Hoosier state, having been born in Ripley county, Oct. 18, 1832. His parents were John and Mary (McDaniel) Grimes, both natives of Nicholas county, Ky. They came to Indiana during the territorial days, traveling on horseback, and settled in what is now Ripley county. Of their nine children Thomas was the only one born in Kentucky and was a mere babe at the time the family crossed the Ohio. He was a farmer and Free-will Baptist minister and lived to be more than seventy years of age. Rachel married Jacob Green, a carpenter of Ripley county. Henry passed his whole life as a Ripley county farmer. James was also a farmer in the same county. His death occurred in 1903. Elizabeth married Thornton Rogers, a farmer and bricklayer. Both she and her husband are deceased. Joseph Grimes was a farmer in Ripley county, and died in 1880. John W. is the seventh and only surviving member of the family. Samuel followed the occupation of farming and teaching during the winter months. A few years ago he went to Kansas, where his death occurred in 1902. Mary A. died at the age of sixteen years. Mr. Grimes' paternal grandparents were natives of Ireland. His grandfather came to this country in childhood, fought in the Revolutionary war, and afterward immigrated to Kentucky. He died in Ripley county, Ind. But little can be learned of his relatives in Ireland. The maternal grandparents of Mr. Grimes, Joseph and Rachel McDaniel, were of Scotch descent. Their early lives were passed in Maryland, but after their marriage they came by boat down the Kanawha and Ohio rivers and settled at Maysville, Ky. Joseph McDaniel was a soldier in the Revolution and was engaged in numerous skirmishes with the Indians. He came to Indiana and died at the age of ninety-seven years. Mr. Grimes' great-grandfather McDaniel was captured by a band of Indians and was killed while running the gauntlet. Mr. Grimes' father fought with Gen. W. H. Harrison in the war of 1812, and when nearly seventy-five years old received a land warrant for his services. He and his wife each lived to be eighty years of age. The opportunities to secure an education were very meager in the days of Mr. Grimes' boyhood. He had to assist in the support of the family, but by self-study and reading he has managed to acquire a practical education. He has been a member of the Independent Order of Odd Fellows for over fifty years, joining the order while living at Elrod in Ripley county, though he now belongs to Chapman Lodge, No. 78, of Dillsboro. He has passed through the chairs and has represented his lodge in the Grand Lodge. Mr. Grimes has been twice married. His first wife was Miss Jeannette Hartley, whose parents were natives of Kentucky. One child, Francisco, was born to this marriage, but it died at a tender age. His first wife died in 1852, and two years later he was married to Miss Nancy J. Hartley, a cousin to his first wife. To them five children have been born. Clark died at the age of six years. Jeannette and Eva were twins. The former died at the age of three years, and the latter is living at home with her parents. Walter attended Moore's Hill college, where he studied for the ministry. He is at this time about forty years of age, is a member of the Indiana Methodist Episcopal conference, and is located at Utica, in Clark county. He married Miss Ada Lenover of Dillsboro. Ella, the youngest of the family, is at home. Mr. and Mrs. Grimes and all their children are members of the Methodist Episcopal church.

HENRY BULTHAUP, president of the State bank, Dillsboro, Ind., was born in the city of Cincinnati, Feb. 22, 1845. His parents were Rudolph and Louisa (Westmire) Bulthaup, both natives of Germany. While still a young man Rudolph Bulthaup, with three of his wife's brothers, came to Dearborn county, bought a tract of land in Cesar Creek township, and there lived for a number of years. Subsequently he bought another farm, which is now the property of the subject of this sketch, who has been a farmer even since he was old enough to work for himself. Henry Bulthaup has been interested in a number of business enterprises, however, besides his farming interests. When the Dillsboro State bank was organized in 1901 he was elected president, which office he has since held, and under his management the bank has attained a marked degree of success and usefulness. In politics he is a Democrat and has several times been elected to office, his personal popularity bringing him numerous votes from the opposing party. He has filled the offices of township trustee, township asesssor, and county commissioner with signal ability and fidelity. In 1892 he was elected sheriff of the county and two years later was re-elected, each time leading the ticket. Mr. Bulthaup is a member and past master of Hopeville Lodge No. 80, Free and Accepted Masons, and of the Bear Creek Baptist church, located at Friendship in Ripley county. In 1870 Miss Margaret Connell, daughter of Joseph Connell, one of the oldest settlers in the county, became Mrs. Henry Bulthaup. They have one daughter, Luella.

WILLIAM C. WULBER, cashier of the First National bank, Dillsboro, Ind., is a native of Dearborn county, having been born in Cesar Creek township, Jan. 6, 1847. His parents, John Frederick and Louise (Ellerman) Wulber, were natives of Germany but were married at Cincinnati. In 1845 they removed to Dearborn county, where the father engaged in farming until his death, March 16, 1880. His wife survived until Dec. 1, 1894, when she, too, passed away. William C. Wulber received his education in the public schools and at Moore's Hill college. Since leaving college he has been prominently identified with the affairs of his county. From 1884 to 1888 he was trustee of Clay township. In 1894 he was elected treasurer of Dearborn county and was re-elected in 1896. A remarkable thing connected with his election to the treasurer's office was that he had no opposition at either time he was a candidate, something that never happened in the county before nor since. About 1894 the First National bank, which had previously been operating as a private bank, was organized and Mr. Wulber was elected president. He has maintained his connection with the institution ever since, now holding the position of cashier. In addition to his banking interests he owns a fine farm near Dillsboro, upon which he resides. He was married on Nov. 23, 1868, to Miss Sophia Pruss, daughter of Frederick Pruss, of Dearborn county, and five children have been born to the union. Emma L. and Amelia D. are deceased. Those living are Theodore J., Laura L., and Louisa D. Theodore is an attorney at law. In 1902 he was elected prosecuting attorney for the circuit composed of Dearborn and Ohio counties. During his term several important cases came into his hands, the most notable being the famous Gillespie murder case, at Rising Sun, which attracted wide attention. He makes his headquarters at Dillsboro, is a member of the Benevolent and Protective Order of Elks and is looked upon as one of the most promising young lawyers in Southeastern Indiana.

PROF. TECUMSEH H. MEEK, superintendent of the public schools, Lawrenceburg, Ind., was born in that city, March 22, 1866. He is descended from an old English family, and is the sixth generation from Adam Meek, of Lincolnshire, the oldest known member of the family. The succeeding generations are traced in an unbroken line to Professor Meek, through Jacob, Nathan, Samuel, and Willis Meek, the last named being Professor Meek's father. During his boyhood Tecumseh attended the common schools of his native town, graduating from the high school at the age of fifteen. Before he reached his sixteenth birthday he had received a license to teach, and he has been engaged in school work ever since, either as a teacher, superintendent, or student at the State university at Bloomington. In 1884 he took charge of the public schools of Aurora, in the south district, holding the position for three years. In the fall of 1887 he was made principal of the Lawrenceburg high school, remaining there until 1891. He then retired from school work for a year, but in the fall of 1892 he was made principal at Ludlow, Ky. During the years 1893-94-95 he was a student at the State university, taking his old place as principal of the Lawrenceburg high school in the fall of 1895. In 1898 he was appointed superintendent of the city schools and held the position till the end of the school year in 1904, when he resigned his position to continue his work in the University of Indiana, from which institution he received his degree of Bachelor of Arts in 1904, and will receive the degree of Master of Arts in 1905. Professor Meek is a Republican in politics but he is not active in political work. His highest aim is to be a school man, and under his management the schools of Lawrenceburg have kept pace with any city of like size in the country. He is a member of the Masonic fraternity, having received the Royal Arch degree; the Modern Woodmen of America; the Junior Order of United American

Mechanics; and the Methodist Episcopal church, in which he is superintendent of the Sunday school. He was married Dec. 26, 1895, to Miss Nannie B., daughter of Ransom P. Meek, of Morton, Ill., and one son has come to bless the union: Harold T., born June 30, 1897.

FRANK B. SHUTTS, a popular attorney of Aurora, Ind., was born at Moore's Hill, Dearborn county, Ind., Sept. 11, 1870. He was reared and received his primary education at Cochran, Ind., and in 1887 graduated from the Aurora high school, winning the Wabash college scholarship as a prize. At the age of eighteen years he was appointed deputy prosecuting attorney of Dearborn county and served eighteen months. In 1890 he entered the law department of De Pauw university, Greencastle, Ind., and on Sept. 11, 1891, was formally admitted to the bar of his native county. In June of that year he formed a partnership, before he had attained his majority, with George E. Downey, now judge of the Seventh judicial circuit. In June, 1892, Mr. Shutts was graduated from the law department of De Pauw university by special dispensation owing to his failure to attend the sessions of that year. Two years later he was admitted to practice in the State supreme court and in the United States district and circuit courts. In 1894 he was the candidate for prosecuting attorney in the circuit composed of Dearborn, Ohio, and Switzerland counties, and although the normal Democratic majority was about twelve hundred, he was defeated by only fifty-three votes. In 1900 he was a candidate before the Republican State convention for the office of lieutenant-governor, and, as he says, "narrowly escaped nomination." Mr. Shutts is a prominent figure in the Knights of Pythias, and is also a member of the Royal Arcanum and of the Methodist Episcopal church.

JAMES WALKER ISHERWOOD, superintendent of the gas company, Lawrenceburg, Ind., was born in that city in the year 1855. His father, John Isherwood, was born at Bolton, Lancashire, England, in 1820, and there grew to manhood. Soon after attaining his majority he married and in 1847 came with his wife to America.

After two years in Lawrence, Mass., and two in Cincinnati, they located at Lawrenceburg. While in Cincinnati the father worked at his trade of machinist, but after coming to Lawrenceburg he established himself in the grocery business and followed that vocation until his death in April, 1897. He also acted as agent for the Cincinnati newspapers for many years. His widow is still living. James W. is the only surviving child of this couple. After the customary training in the schools of his native city he attended the National Normal school at Lebanon, Ohio. Shortly after leaving school he became associated with the Lawrenceburg Gas Company and in a little while was made superintendent, a position he has held ever since. In addition to his duties with the gas company Mr. Isherwood does considerable business as an underwriter. He is an enthusiastic Republican in political matters, is a Knight of Pythias, and a member of the Methodist Episcopal church. In 1880 Miss Sadie P., daughter of Benjamin Eversole, of Lawrenceburg, became Mrs. J. W. Isherwood, and they have one daughter, Lucy K.

EDWARD J. EMMERT, M.D., a popular surgeon of Lawrenceburg, Ind., is a native of that city, having been born there in 1871. After a primary training in the public and high schools he attended DePauw university at Greencastle, Ind., and later Johns Hopkins university at Baltimore, Md. Having finished his collegiate education he took up the study of medicine and in 1895 was graduated from the Miami Medical college, at Cincinnati. During the two years following his graduation he served as interne and house surgeon in the Western Pennsylvania, Pittsburg hospital, after which he spent another year in post-graduate study in hospitals of Philadelphia and New York. In the month of February, 1898, he returned to Lawrenceburg and began the practice of his profession in his native city. Since that time he has practiced continuously in Lawrenceburg and Cincinnati. But little more than six years have elapsed since Dr. Emmert began to establish himself in his chosen calling, yet in that time he has demonstrated his professional skill in a way that has won the admiration of his brother physicians and the confidence of the public. Dr. Emmert belongs to the Dearborn County Medical society; American Medical association; Phi Kappa Psi literary fraternity; Sigma Nu medical fraternity; is surgeon to the Big Four Railroad Company; medical examiner for the New York Mutual, Philadelphia Fidelity, Illinois, and New York security trust and life insurance companies.

SAMUEL H. COLLINS, MD., of Lawrenceburg, Ind., was born at Plymouth, Mass., in 1851. During his childhood and youth he lived in Taunton and Fitchburg, Mass., and Somersworth, N. H., there attending the public schools. In 1873 he graduated from Dennison college, Granville, O., with the degree of A.B. He next entered Miami medical college, Cincinnati, and graduated in 1876. For the next year he was an interne in the Cincinnati hospital and then practiced in Cincinnati until 1878, when he took charge of a corps of six physicians and two druggists to go to Memphis to assist in fighting the yellow fever epidemic there. In three weeks after their arrival in Memphis Dr. Collins was the only survivor of the expedition. He had the fever but recovered, and received a testimonial from the Howard Society for his services—the only one in the State of Indiana. In 1879 he was made secretary of the Memphis board of health, and in August of that year the national board of health appointed him as surgeon and inspector-general. For a time he was stationed in Memphis and Shelby county, being there when the second scourge of yellow fever came. In April, 1880, he was transferred to New Orleans as port officer. In September he was sent to Vicksburg to take charge of the quarantine there, and in November he was transferred to Ship Island, in the Gulf of Mexico, to look after the quarantine stations along the Gulf Coast. He remained at Ship Island until June, 1881, when he went back to Memphis to superintend the erection of a hospital boat, and in November following located at Lawrenceburg. Few physicians have had a wider or more varied experience than Dr. Collins, yet in all the trying situations to which he has been subjected he has proven equal to the demands. He is a member of the Indiana and Tennessee State Medical associations and the Dearborn County Medical society, and served on the board of pension examiners during the administration of President Harrison. Politically he is a Republican and has served three terms in the Lawrenceburg city council, twice carrying a Democratic ward. He is a Knight Templar Mason, a member of the Knights of Pythias, and in 1895 was elected surgeon of the Third regiment, Indiana Uniform Rank, with the rank of major.

CAPT. ALEXANDER B. PATTERSON, cashier of the Aurora National bank, Aurora, Ind., was born in the city of Cincinnati, May 20, 1835. When he was about two years of age the family removed to Aurora, where he was reared and educated. Qualifying himself for the work of a civil engineer he went west in 1857 and remained there for three years in that line of employment. In the fall of 1860 he returned home and in the following April he enlisted in Company E, Seventh Indiana infantry, being the first man in Aurora to offer his services to his country. He went out as second lieutenant of the company and when the regiment was reorganized in September, 1861, he was made first lieutenant. Six months later he was promoted to the captaincy and served in that capacity until the close of the war. He was in all the engagements in which the army of the Potomac participated, except in the Peninsular campaign under McClellan, and was twice wounded. After the war he returned to Aurora, where for some time he was engaged in the drug business. From 1869 to 1878 he was in the internal revenue service. He then served as county auditor for four years and upon leaving the auditor's office he was elected cashier of the bank, which position he has held since. Besides his banking interests Captain Patterson is president of the Cemetery and Public Library associations of Aurora, as well as of the Aurora Chair Company, and is secretary of the Aurora Tool Works. The only civic organization of which he is a member is the Grand Army of the Republic. In 1864 he was married to Miss Elizabeth C., daughter of Dr. W. T. S. Cornett. They have two daughters, both of whom are married. Anna G. is the wife of F. D. Cobb, and Alexina is the wife of Dr. E. L. Haring, of Aurora.

RANDALL J. WYMOND, manager of the Samuel Wymond Cooperage Company, of Aurora, Ind., was born at Dillsboro, Dearborn county, Ind., Jan. 8, 1857. His father, Samuel Wymond, was born in Cornwall, England, but came to America in early life and located at Dillsboro, Ind., where he lived until 1865, when he removed to Aurora. There he founded the cooperage business that still bears his name and was also engaged in merchandizing. He died in 1884, leaving four children. His father, William Wymond, lived and died in Cornwall. Randall was educated in the town schools, graduating from the high school in 1873. Two years later he graduated from the Chickering institute (now extinct), of Cincinnati, and entered the law department of the Michigan university at Ann Arbor. After studying law for two years he left school and went into his father's office as a clerk, remaining there for nine years. In 1887, three years after the death of his father, he was one of the incorporators of the company and was elected secretary, treasurer and general manager. Mr. Wymond is a director in the First National bank and is spoken of as one of the most reliable business men of Aurora. He is a thirty-second degree Mason and a Knight Templar, and belongs to the Episcopal church. He was married June 11, 1884, to Miss Mabel Criswell, daughter of Robert Criswell, and they have one daughter, named Jean C.

HENRY P. SPAETH, the head of the hardware firm of H. P. Spaeth & Co., Aurora, Ind., was born in Wurtemberg, Germany, Dec. 25, 1838. When he was about seven years old his father, Christopher Spaeth, came with his family to America, settling in Cincinnati, where he was in the grocery business until 1849, when he died of cholera during the epidemic of that year, leaving five children. The death of his father made it necessary for the subject of this sketch to quit school and begin life for himself. He went to work in a little paper box factory at the munificent wage of one dollar a week. After two years in this factory he went into a chair factory, where he learned the trade of wood turner and worked there until the beginning of the Civil war. He cast his first vote for president in 1860 and was an ardent Lincoln man in that campaign. In April, 1861, he enlisted as a private in Company D, Ninth Ohio infantry, and served until June, 1864, when he was discharged as first lieutenant of Company C, of the same regiment. During his service he was in the West Virginia campaign and with the army of the Cumberland. He was in the battles of Chickamauga, Mission Ridge, and was on the campaign from Dalton to Kingston, Ga., receiving some slight wounds. When he received his discharge he returned to Cincinnati and began clerking in a store, remaining there until December, 1867, when he came to Aurora and bought a tin shop. Four years later he added a stock of hardware, which was the beginning of the present firm. Besides his hardware business Mr. Spaeth is president of the Aurora Furniture Company; vice-president of the Aurora National bank; a director in the Aurora Coffin Company and the Aurora Chair Company; and has been president of the Aurora Tool Works. Ever since 1860 he has been a Republican, but the only office he ever held was that of member of the Aurora school board, which came to him unsolicited and which he held for six years. He is a member of the Independent Order of Odd Fellows, the Masonic fraternity, and the Presbyterian church. Mr. Spaeth has been twice married. In 1871 he was married to Miss Sophie Kastner. She died in 1874, leaving two children, Julia A. and Fred K. On Feb. 8, 1880, he was married to Mary E. Smith, of Aurora.

E. H. NIEBAUM, postmaster, Aurora, Ind., was born in Hanover, Germany, Dec. 27, 1839. In 1845 he came with his parents to America, settling in Dearborn county, Ind. From that time until he was twelve years of age he worked on the farm, attending the common schools a few months each winter. When he was twelve years old he went to Cincinnati, where for over two years he worked in a job printing office. In the meantime his parents had removed to Ohio county, Ind. He left the printing office, went back home and remained on the farm for two years, when he came to Aurora as a clerk in a dry goods store. He continued in this line of work until 1878, when he went into business for himself, operating a dry goods store in company with Joseph McCreay. The partnership was dissolved by the death of Mr. McCreay, but Mr. Niebaum continued the business for several years afterward. In 1898 he was appointed postmaster by the late President McKinley and was reappointed by President Roosevelt. During the Civil war Mr. Niebaum served about four months as a private in Company E, Seventh Indiana volunteer infantry. He was in the battles of Philippi and Carrick's Ford, but when the regiment was reorganized he did not enter the new organization. He is a member of the Grand Army of the Republic and of the German Lutheran church. In 1862 Mr. Niebaum was married to Miss Clara E. Rieman. They have three children, viz.: Frank W., Charles H., and William E.

E. J. LIBBERT, M.D., a prominent physician and surgeon of Aurora, Ind., was born in Dearborn county, Ind., Sept. 8, 1868. His father, Charles Libbert, was born in the same county in 1844. During the Civil war he served in Company A, Seventh Indiana volunteer infantry. He lost his left arm and was severely wounded in the chest, dying in 1882 from the effects of these injuries. Seven of his children—four sons and three daughters—are still living. Dr. Libbert received his general education in the schools of his native county. In 1889 he graduated from the Cincinnati College of Medicine and Surgery, receiving the degree of M. D. He began practice in the little village of Farmers Retreat, Dearborn county, and remained there until September, 1898, when he located in Aurora. Here he has built up a lucrative practice and stands well both with the profession and the public. He is a member of the American Medical association, the Indiana Medical association, and the Dearborn County Medical society. In fraternal circles Dr. Libbert is well and favorably known. He is a member of the Independent Order of Odd Fellows, the Improved Order of Red Men, the Modern Woodmen of America, and is a Royal Arch Mason. He is also a member of the Methodist Episcopal church. In April, 1891, Dr. Libbert was married to Miss Clara M., daughter of Cornelius Buchanan, of Dearborn county, and they have three children: Marshall S., Cornelius H., and Edwin L.

JOSEPH H. WILDER, superintendent of the Royer Wheel Works, of Aurora, Ind., was born at Holliston, Mass., in the year 1844. His father, Joseph M. Wilder, was born at Lancaster, Mass., in 1811, and when he grew to manhood became a manufacturer of horn combs. In 1862 both father and son came West, locating at Fort Wayne, Ind. There the father conducted a shoe factory for a number of years, but finally returned East and died at Holliston in 1896. The son found employment at Fort Wayne as a clerk in a carriage manufactory and wood working establishment, and remained with the concern for thirty years. In 1892 he came to the Royer Wheel Company, then located in Cincinnati, as superintendent. In 1901 the manufacturing department of the company was removed to Aurora, Mr. Wilder coming with it as superintendent and also a director. Mr. Wilder is a fine example of what can be accomplished by energy and perseverance. While other young men have been lamenting their lack of opportunities he has gone steadily upward, filling positions of trust with satisfaction to his employers and with profit to himself.

He is a Republican in opinions but is not an active politician, and is a member of the Episcopal church. In 1867 Mr. Wilder was married to Miss Jennie L. Leland, daughter of Alden Leland, of Holliston, and they have one daughter, Constance L.

WILLIAM E. STARK, vice-president and general manager of the Cochran Chair Company, Cochran, Ind., was born at Versailles, Ripley county, Ind., Oct. 29, 1866. He was reared and educated in his native town, living there until he was eighteen years old, except three years at Sedalia, Mo. Leaving school at the age of fourteen years he began life as a drug clerk. For four years he worked in drug and grocery stores, and then came to Cochran, where he was employed for six years in a general store. At the end of that time he became bookkeeper for the Cochran Chair factory, and when the company was incorporated in 1899 he was elected to his present position. Mr. Stark is a member of the Methodist Episcopal church. He was married in 1891 to Miss Sarah E., daughter of George Smith, of Augusta, Ky., and they have two sons, Leland W. and Harold L. The family resides in Aurora. Mr. Stark's father, Silas Stark, was born in Versailles in 1844, and died in Sedalia, Mo., Feb. 14, 1876. He was a farmer all his life. He married Margaret E. Johnson and of the five children born to them three are still living: Luella, wife of William Radspinner; William E., and Ambrose E. The Stark family came originally from Virginia, though the paternal grandfather of William E. Stark was born near Paris, Ky., July 4, 1811, and came to Versailles about 1828. His name was Elijah Stark. He went to Grant City, Mo., in 1890 and died there ten years later.

JOSIAH C. WRIGHT, senior member of the firm of J. C. Wright & Son, dealers in lumber and builders' supplies, Aurora, Ind., was born in Dearborn county, Ind., Jan. 5, 1850. His paternal grandfather, Ira Wright, was born in Pennsylvania in 1789, came to Dearborn county in his early manhood, entered land there, and died a farmer in 1876. His son, Henry F., father of the subject of this sketch, was born in Dearborn county in 1826. He served in the Third, and later in the Seventh Indiana cavalry, during the Civil war, holding the rank of captain and acting major. He died of disease at Memphis in 1864, having had command of his regiment for three months prior to his death. Of his family Josiah and three sisters are living. Josiah C. Wright attended the public schools of the country districts and the town of Aurora until he was sixteen years of age. He then stayed on the farm until he was twenty-two, when he went into the Ohio & Mississippi (now the Baltimore & Ohio Southwestern) car shops at Cochran, Ind. After two years in the shops he went West, working as a carpenter in Lincoln, Neb., and Wichita, Kan. Returning home he began the business of contracting on a small scale, which has gradually grown. In 1901 he opened a lumber yard and is today the largest contractor in Aurora. Mr. Wright belongs to no secret order or religious denomination, yet he is the publisher of a religious paper called *Alpha and Omega,* which is now in its seventh year. Politically he is a Prohibitionist and by precept and example teaches the doctrines of doing right for the sake of the right. He was married in 1871 to Miss Mary E. Echels, of Aurora, and they have seven children: Harley E., Emma, now Mrs. Cumback; John W., Ralph, Oran, Mabel, and Naomi.

ANDREW P. DAUGHTERS, M.D., of Moores Hill, Ind., has practiced medicine in that vicinity for almost half a century. He was born in Dearborn county, Ind., Aug. 12, 1831. His paternal grandfather, Hudson Daughters, was a native of Wales. He came to America in the latter part of the eighteenth century and settled in Delaware, where James Daughters, father of the doctor, was born in 1799. He came to Dearborn county, where he followed farming for many years and died there in 1856. Dr. Daughters received his early education in the public schools, afterward attending Asbury— now De Pauw—university during the sessions of 1849-50. He then taught for two years, read medicine, and in 1855 was graduated from the Miami Medical college of Cincinnati. He located at Moore's Hill, where he has practiced ever since, except what time he was in the army. In June, 1861, he enlisted in the Eighteenth Indiana volunteer infantry, as first lieutenant of Company A, but two months later was made assistant surgeon and shortly afterward surgeon of the regiment. He was with his regiment in the engagements at Bentonville, Mo., Elk Horn Tavern, Pea Ridge, Wilson's Creek, Pilot Knob, Port Gibson, Champion Hills, and a number of others. At the siege of Vicksburg the demands upon him were so great that he was completely exhausted. He remained at his post, however, until the city capitulated, when he resigned and came home. For some months prior to that time he had held the position of staff physician on the staff of Brig.-Gen. H. D. Washburn. Dr. Daughters is a member of the Dearborn County Medical society and since 1896 has been president of the pension examining board. He is a member and one of the trustees of the Methodist Episcopal church; has been an Odd Fellow since 1853, and has taken all the degrees of the order; and is a Royal Arch Mason. He was married in 1860 to Althea A. Justis, and of the nine children born to them six survive, viz.: Deborah J., Andrew N., Peter B., Sarah B., James E., and Pearl. Mrs. Daughters died in 1884.

HARRIS FITCH, hardware merchant and dealer in farm implements and vehicles, was born in Lawrenceburg, Ind., March 26, 1859. After attending the city schools he was a student at old Asbury university (De Pauw) and Nelson's Business college in Cincinnati. His first position was as a clerk in the First National bank. He went into the livery and implement business in 1878. In 1888 he sold out the livery and in 1892 added a line of general hardware to his implement trade. His business is the largest of the kind in this part of the state. His house has a popular standing, it having been said he keeps everything "from a needle to a threshing machine." He is a Methodist. In politics he is a Republican.

The Fitch family is one of the oldest and most prominent in this part of the country, tracing its ancestry back more than three hundred years, when Thomas Fitch near the close of the sixteenth century became, by descent, the proprietor of an estate near Braintree, Essex county, England, and after an honest and peaceful life died, leaving a widow and five sons. Shortly thereafter, these descendants with their mother emigrated to New England, about 1638. These five sons, Thomas, James, Samuel, Joseph, and John, make it easy to account for the great number by the name in New England and New York, and the part they took in their colonial history. For a descendant of one of these numerous branches, Fitchburg, Mass., was named. Another, Thomas, was governor of Connecticut under George II. John Fitch, the inventor of the steamboat was the great-grandson of the first Joseph in this country, who made a large purchase of land in Windsor, Hartford county, Conn. James, the second of the five American Fitches, was born at Bocking, Essex county, England, Dec. 24, 1622. After removing to New England in 1638 he studied seven years for the ministry under the distinguished ministers, Hooker and Stone. He became pastor of the First Church (Congregational) in Saybrook, 1646. After a service of fourteen years, he, in 1659, with Captain John Mason and a company of thirty-five followed along the banks of the Thames river to a picturesque spot between the Yantic and Shetucket rivers and founded the town of Norwich, which Dr. Holmes justly described as "a town of supreme, audacious, Alpine loveliness." He was a large land owner in Norwich, Windham, and Lebanon and interested in the settlement of these towns. He learned the language of the Mohegan Indians, and was popular among them, preaching to them in their own tongue, sharing his land with them, and teaching them agriculture. Rev. James Fitch in 1664 married as his second wife Priscilla Mason, daughter of John Mason. He died at Lebanon, Conn., Nov. 18, 1702. Joseph, their son, was born in Norwich in November, 1681. On Dec. 29, 1721, Joseph married as his second wife Annie Whiting, eldest daughter of Samuel Whiting. Joseph died at Lebanon, May 9, 1741. Their son, Capt. Azel Fitch, was born in Lebanon, Nov. 7, 1728. He married Rhoda Collins, daughter of Rev. Timothy Collins, 1767. He was her third husband. Azel Fitch died at Albany, N. Y., about 1767. Their son, Joseph, was born at Lebanon, Conn., in June, 1768. In 1784 he married Elizabeth Harris, born in Cornwall, Conn., May 7, 1765. They went to Amena, Dutchess county, N. Y. There the first son, Azel, was born, Nov. 25, 1790. From here they moved to Kingsbury, Washington county, where were born Collins, May 13, 1793, Harris, March 13, 1796, and Clarissa, June 1, 1798. The fifth, Alonzo, was born at Queensbury, Warren county, and Morgan and Lewin born at Scipio, Cayuga county, June 13, 1806. Shortly after the death of his sister, Harris, the grandfather of the present Harris, together with his parents and brothers except the eldest, came to Lawrenceburg. When he was grown he engaged in the then great traffic on the river. In those early times when every man must almost of necessity be jack-of-all-trades, he was more—in fact, master of at least six. His garden with its fine fruit, of his own grafting, its great variety of vegetables, the beds bordered with flowers and walks laid with tanbark, was the wonder and admiration of the town and the delight of his family. For years he was proprietor of the Fitch House, which he built. In 1821 he married Hannah Biggs. To them were born eight children. Three died in infancy. The others were George, De Witt Clinton (father of Harris), Jane (Mrs. Gazlay), William, and Virginia. De Witt Clinton Fitch, like his father, engaged in trade on the Ohio and Mississippi rivers, selling cargoes of hay and potatoes in New Orleans. Later he was engaged in farming, then in the grocery business. From 1862 to 1883 he was president of the First National and City National banks. On Aug. 20, 1850, he married Leah Hayes. To them nine children were born, Harris being the fourth. All are living. He was always an active and public spirited man.

THOMAS B. COTTINGHAM, one of the leading farmers and stock raisers of Dearborn county, Ind., was born near Logan's Cross Roads in that county, April 3, 1846, and is a son of Thomas and Sarah (Stohms) Cottingham. His father was born in Baltimore, Md. From there he came to Cincinnati, where he learned the blacksmith trade, after which he located at Logan's Cross Roads, and there followed that trade for many years. The last years of his life were spent with his children and he died at the home of one of his daughters, a Mrs. Liddle, in 1897. His wife, the mother of the subject of this sketch, died in 1852. Thomas B. is the seventh of nine children. Two died in childhood, two passed away later, and five are living, all useful members of society. At the age of sixteen Thomas began business for himself, working out for a while and saving his money until he had enough to engage in the business of merchandizing, when he opened a store at Bright, Ind. Later he sold out and since then has been a tiller of the soil. In 1892 he sold his first farm and bought the 160 acres known as the "Langdale Farm." He raises some of the best bred stock in Dearborn county and had the only corn from the county on exhibition at the World's Fair at St. Louis in 1904, for which he received a medal. In 1874 Mr. Cottingham was married to Miss Louisa Langdale, a native of Dearborn county, and a daughter of R. H. Langdale, one of its prominent citizens. To this marriage there were born three children: Stanley, who was accidently killed while duck hunting,

March 15, 1900; Howard, who lives at home with his parents; and Edna, now the wife of John Moore, of Indianapolis. Mr. Cottingham is a Democrat, is a man of intelligence, high moral character, and integrity, and both himself and wife are members of the Christian church.

JOHN H. JACKSON, a well-known farmer of Dearborn county, Ind., is a native of that county and was born May 15, 1854, his parents being Reuben C. and Isabelle Jackson, old and honored residents of the county. The paternal grandfather came to Indiana during the territorial days, cleared a farm and lived here all his subsequent life. He met his death by drowning in Tanner's creek. John H., who bears his grandfather's name, is the tenth of a family of thirteen children born to his parents. He received a common school education and after leaving school married and took charge of the home farm, which he now owns. It is a farm of two hundred acres of fine land and he carries on a successful business as a general farmer. His mother, whose maiden name was Isabelle Langdale, was a native of England but came with her parents to the United States when she was twelve years of age. Mr. Jackson is a solid Republican though not altogether a politician. He is a member of the Bright Lodge, Woodmen of the World. He was married in 1887 to Miss Mary E. Smith, a daughter of Jacob and Ann Smith, of Dearborn county, where her father is a successful farmer. To Mr. and Mrs. Jackson there were born two children, Clyde A. and Floyd S., both well educated and both living at home, though Clyde is married. His wife keeps house for the family since the death of Mrs. Jackson, which occurred on August 29, 1902. Mr. Jackson is a man who enjoys the respect and esteem of his neighbors and has the confidence of all who know him as a man of unimpeachable integrity.

DAVID E. JOHNSTON, M.D., of Moore's Hill, Ind., is one of the most popular and efficient physicians of the younger school in Southeastern Indiana. His paternal grandfather was a native of Virginia but came at an early date to Dearborn county, Ind., where James Johnston, father of the doctor, was born in 1831. There he followed farming and teaching in the common schools until he was about thirty years of age, when he removed to Indianapolis and engaged in the real estate business. He died there in 1903. Dr. D. E. Johnston was born in Indianapolis, Jan. 27, 1873. When he was about seven years old his mother died and he was sent to relatives in Dearborn county to find a home. There he grew to manhood, receiving a good education in the common schools and at Moore's Hill college. For three years he taught in the Dearborn county schools, after which he took up the study of medicine and in 1900 graduated from the Medical College of Indiana, located at Indianapolis. For a year after receiving his degree he was an interne in the Protestant Deaconess hospital of Indianapolis, and he then was engaged in general practice in that city for another year. In 1902 he located at Moore's Hill, where he soon built up a fine practice, in which he has demonstrated his skill as a physician of the highest order. Without disparagement to other physicians of the place it can be said that he is the leading doctor of Moore's Hill. Dr. Johnston is a member of the Masonic fraternity; the Independent Order of Odd Fellows; the Baptist church; the State Medical association; the Dearborn County Medical society, and is a Democrat but not a politician.

JOHN SHANKS (deceased) was born in Dearborn county, Ind., in the year 1800. His father, Michael Shanks, came to Kentucky in a very early day, and there his parents and all his brothers and sisters were killed by the Indians, except one sister, who was carried into captivity and was never heard of afterwards. In the latter part of the eighteenth century Michael Shanks came to Indiana, entered the land now owned by his grandson, and there passed the remainder of his days. During the war of 1812 he served with distinction under Gen. William H. Harrison. John Shanks grew to manhood in Dearborn country. He was the only son in a family of five children. For nearly a quarter of a century he followed flatboating on the Ohio and Mississippi rivers. He died in 1876 and his wife in 1893. They had a family of eleven children, viz.: William, now residing in Illinois; Eliza J., deceased; Ezra F., deceased; Oliver, now living in Terre Haute, Ind.; Isaac, Sarah and Nancy, all deceased; Margaret E., at home; John F., married and living at Sullivan, Ind.; Van, who runs the old home farm, and Harry M., who tills his allotted portion, located on the pike between Guilford and Lawrenceburg. All had a common school education and all became useful citizens. The old homestead, entered by Michael Shanks, on which the primitive log cabin has been replaced by a substantial three story frame dwelling, and which is now occupied by Van Shanks, is one of the oldest farms in Dearborn county, as well as one of the best. Harry M. Shanks has 147 acres of good land which he rents to tenants. In politics he is an unswerving Democrat, and as a farmer he is thoroughly up-to-date, living on one of the rural free delivery routes and having telephone communication with Lawrenceburg and Cincinnati. The old log house, in which he lived until the summer of 1904, was one of the oldest in that section and was the place of the first postoffice in Dearborn county.

ROBERT J. NOWLIN, one of the most prosperous and progressive farmers of Dearborn county, Ind., was born in Miller township of that county, Aug. 26, 1865, and is a son of Enoch B. and Jane H. (Langdale) Nowlin, both natives of the township. The paternal grandfather, Jeremiah Nowlin, was one of the early settlers of the county and was a typical pioneer. He lived and died in Miller township where he was a successful farmer and a man that was universally respected. Enoch B. Nowlin was a well educated man and in his early life taught for several years. He then bought a farm and followed that vocation throughout the remainder of his life. He died on June 17, 1900, his wife having departed this life on July 10, 1884. The Langdale family is one of the oldest and most highly respected in Dearborn county. Enoch and Jane Nowlin had four children: H. L. is a farmer in Miller township and resides at Greendale; Mary P. died at the age of four years; Robert is the subject of this sketch, and Annie died in 1893, a graduate of the Wesleyan college of Cincinnati. Robert J. Nowlin received a high school education and attended one year at college. At the age of nineteen he rented land in Kansas and began farming. After five years in that state he returned to Indiana and for two years was in the hardware business in Lawrenceburg. He was then on the farm until 1893, when he went to Cincinnati and engaged in the live stock commission business for three years. Returning to the farm he devoted his attention to raising thoroughbred stock, particularly full-blooded Berkshire hogs, in which he has been very successful. He has a farm of 425 acres, well improved, and the greater part of it under cultivation. In 1901 he rebuilt and has one of the finest and best equipped residences in the state. Modern heating and ventilating; hot and cold water in every room; telephone connections; rural free delivery, etc. Barns in keeping with the house mark him as one of the men who know how to get the greatest comfort out of farm life. On April 4, 1885, he was married to Miss Catherine Russell, daughter of P. J. Russell, a prominent farmer of Eureka Springs, Ark. She died on Dec. 15, 1889, and on May 5, 1891, Mr. Nowlin was married to Gertrude V. Gore, a native of Brown county, O., and a daughter of Charles H. and Hester B. Gore, her father being a civil engineer. The second Mrs. Nowlin died on Jan. 5, 1897, and Mr. Nowlin was married a third time on Nov. 19, 1899. His third wife was Margery E. Gore, a sister to his second wife. Mr. Nowlin has five children: Enoch R., is at home; Carrie O., is also at home; Robert L.; Margery, died in infancy, and Gilbert S. The two first named are the children of his first wife and the others by his second. All the children are attendants at school and the daughters are also paying considerable attention to music. Mr. Nowlin is a Republican politically and well informed on the public questions of the day. On matters relating to farming and stock growing he is an authority, and few men are more earnest or energetic in what they undertake. It is to this trait of his character that he owes the greater part of his success.

ROBERT F. HUDDLESTON, farmer, merchant and postmaster at Guilford, Dearborn county, Ind., was born in that county, Oct. 31, 1842. His parents, John and Hannah Huddleston, were both natives of England. His paternal grandparents came from England to the United States in 1837 and settled in Dearborn county, where the grandfather, whose name was Thomas, followed farming until his death. John Huddleston, Robert's father, was also a farmer. During his life he was a Whig until after the dissolution of that party, when he became a Democrat. He died in 1866 and his wife survived him for twenty years, dying in 1886. Robert is the eldest of five children, the others being, William, deceased; John, a farmer in York township, Dearborn county; Frank, who is a farmer living near Nokomis, Ill.; and Wilson, who also lives near the same place. Robert F. Huddleston received his education in the public schools and soon after reaching his majority went to work for the government as a civil employe, remaining in the government service for over two years. For the next twenty-nine years, and over, he was employed as a bridge builder by different railroads, being nine years with the Big Four and ten years with the Cleveland & Marietta, and for some time with the Chesapeake & Ohio, part of the time as foreman and the remainder as superintendent. During his service as a bridge builder he was in four disastrous wrecks and two collisions.

In 1895 he embarked in the mercantile line of business at Guilford and has been thus engaged since. He owns a farm of eighty acres adjoining the town, which he rents. Soon after President McKinley was inaugurated in 1897 he was appointed postmaster at Guilford and has held the office by reappointment until the present time. In politics he is an unwavering Republican; is a member of the Free and Accepted Masons; and both himself and wife belong to the Methodist Episcopal church. Mr. Huddleston was married in April, 1873, to Miss Mary, daughter of William and Eveline (Rawling) Lazenby.

JOHN F. MEYER, one of the best known farmers in Dearborn county, Ind., was born in the neighborhood where he now resides, Dec. 24, 1854. His father, also named John F., came from Germany in 1848, at the age of nineteen. At the time of his arrival in this country he had nothing and could not speak sufficient English to make himself understood. He went to work for seven dollars a month, saving enough to bring his parents to America, and later bought two hundred acres of land from a railroad company. This he cleared and improved and by industry, energy, and frugality added to it until at the time of his death, in April, 1900, he was the owner of over 1,300 acres of good land. He married Mary Basker, a native of the Fatherland, who came to America when six years of age and they had a family of eight children. Annie S. married Leonard Randall, a farmer of Dearborn county; John F. is the subject of this sketch; Henry J. and William are both farmers in Dearborn county; Dora married Henry Kiser, a farmer in Ohio county, Ind.; Frederick is the owner of a farm of 245 acres, which he is conducting; George lives on the old homestead, and Mary died in 1899. With that filial affection and unity of purpose which characterize the German family, the boys all stayed with their father, helping him to accumulate what he had. In turn the father, before his death, gave each of them a farm. At the time of his death the father had reached the age of seventy-two years. He died at what is known as the Three Mile House, where he passed the last years of his life in retirement from active business cares. He and his wife were both devout Lutherans and during his life he helped to build several churches and schoolhouses. His widow is still living and makes her home with her children. John F. Meyer, the son, grew up on his father's farm, obtained a good common school education, and at the age of twenty-three years he rented part of his father's land and began life on his own account. At the death of his father he inherited 145 acres, to which he has added until he now owns about 350 acres. He carries on general farming and is generally recognized as one of the successful farmers of his community. In 1879 he was married to Margaret Behlmer, the daughter of Court Behlmer, a Ripley county farmer, and to this marriage there have been born four children: Charles F., Lena, Clara, and Maggie. All are at home with their parents. Mr. and Mrs. Meyer are both members of the Lutheran church. In political matters he is a rock-ribbed Democrat, takes an active interest in the political situation, and is now serving his second term as a member of the county council. He is interested in good roads and for thirteen years has held the office of road supervisor. He lives on one of the rural free delivery mail routes, keeps in touch with what is going on in the world, and is one of the most practical and progressive men in his township.

GEORGE W. NEVITT (deceased) was born at Lawrenceburg, Dearborn county, Ind., April 13, 1829, and during his day was one of the leading farmers of the county. His parents, David and Eliza (French) Nevitt, came from Pennsylvania some time in the twenties and settled at Lawrenceburg, where the father for some time followed his trade of hatter, but in later years engaged in farming. George W. grew to manhood in Dearborn county, obtaining his education in the old-fashioned log schoolhouse, and at the age of twenty-six years bought a farm of his own. To this first purchase he added from time to time until at the time of his death he owned 370 acres of good land, well improved and in a fine state of cultivation. On Jan. 27, 1857, he was married to Ann M. Stewart, a daughter of Silas and Mary (Hendricks) Stewart, who were also immigrants from Pennsylvania. Thomas Hendricks, the father of Mrs. Nevitt, came from Pennsylvania at an early date and was the founder of the city of Greensburg, Ind., where he passed his last days. George W. and Mary Nevitt were the parents of four children. The youngest died in infancy; Stewart S. and his brother John D., the second and third of the family, live upon the old homestead; and David L. died in childhood. The father of these children died on June 27, 1886. Since the death of the father the two sons have added to the homestead until they now own about 600 acres of as good land as there is in Dearborn county, and are numbered among the progressive and successful farmers of Southeastern Indiana. They are on one of the rural free delivery routes, have telephone connection, etc., and get about all the comforts out of life that are possible. Both are Republicans in political matters though neither is particularly active in political work.

JOHN E. HEUSTIS, a farmer of Manchester township, Dearborn county, Ind., was born in that county, Aug. 14, 1839, and is a son of Elias and Sarah (Ellis) Heustis, the former a native of New York and the latter of Pennsylvania. They came to Indiana some time in the twenties, located in Dearborn county, bought a tract of eighty acres of wild land, and lived the life of the pioneers until their death. Elias Heustis at the time of his death in 1896 was 'the owner of 450 acres of good land. He was a Quaker and was one of the best men in the county. He was twice married, having one child by his first wife and a family of eight children by his second wife. Rhoda, the daughter of the first wife, married Absalom Hall and since his death makes her home with relatives. Of the second wife's children Lavinia is the widow of Sanford Mendell; Benjamin is deceased; William is a farmer of Dearborn county; John E. is the fourth child and the subject of this sketch; Hannah married Jeremiah Watkins, now deceased, and lives in Kansas; Abigail married Thomas Johnston, a farmer of Dearborn county; Mary is the widow of T. T. Annis, who died in 1904, and lives in Lawrenceburg, and Oliver resides at Wilmington, Dearborn county. John E. Heustis has in his possession an old Bible, printed in 1793, which was the property of his paternal grandfather, and from the record it contains it can be learned that Elias was the fourth child in a family of eleven children born to William and Rhoda Heustis. The names and birth dates of the family are as follows: Oliver, Oct. 11, 1793, Jesse, Nov. 22, 1794; Major, Aug. 24, 1796; Elias, May 27, 1798; James, March 6, 1800; Amy, Dec. 28, 1801; Sarah, Oct. 6, 1803; Henry, Nov. 11, 1805; George, April 22, 1809; Martha, March 12, 1811; and Hannah, Feb. 18, 1814. Mr. Heustis also owns a copy of an old newspaper containing an account of the death of Gen. George Washington. Elias Heustis was a soldier in the war of 1812. John E. Heustis is one of the wide-awake farmers of his community. He is a member of the Methodist Episcopal church, as is also his wife, and he belongs to the Modern Woodmen of the World. In politics he is a Democrat and takes an active interest in furthering the interests of his party. Since 1902 he has been a member of the board of county commissioners of Dearborn county. On Oct. 14, 1869, he was married to Sara E. Walser, a native of Dearborn county and a daughter of James and Mary (Bailey) Walser, also natives of the county. For many years her father was engaged in flatboating on the Ohio river, but in later years turned his attention to agricultural pursuits and became one of the leading farmers of the county. Mr. and Mrs. Heustis have had born to them five children. Mary, the eldest, is now Mrs. M. I. Butterfield, and resides at Muncie, Ind.; Myrtle is at home with her parents; Pearl is attending the Indianapolis Business university; John is married and lives in Indianapolis; and Scott is at home. Mr. Heustis is a believer in education and has practiced what he preaches by sending his children to school, thus giving them a good start toward solving the problems of life.

DAVID A. ANNIS, farmer, near Lawrenceburg, Ind., was born in Dearborn county, of that state, Jan. 9, 1829, his parents being Thomas D. and Rhoda Annis, the former a native of New York and the latter of Massachusetts. The maternal ancestry can be traced back to Jonathan Fayerbanke, who came from England in 1633 and settled at Dedham, Mass. Thomas and Rhoda Annis came to Indiana in 1821 and settled at Lawrenceburg. The father was a carpenter by trade and followed it for a short time, then entered a tract of land in Miller township, cleared and improved it, and followed farming for the remainder of life. They had a family of seven children, three of whom died in infancy and four grew to maturity. Thomas T. died in later life at Lawrenceburg, and the subject of this sketch is the only one now living. David A. Annis received a good practical education in the Lawrenceburg schools, took up the work of a surveyor and followed it for some time in his early life. In the fall of 1850 he went to Iowa, where for a few months he engaged in teaching school. Subsequently he returned to Indiana, and in 1862 bought a farm of 120 acres, part of the old homestead, in Dearborn county. In February of that year he was married to Mary E. Pearson, a daughter of Joseph A. Pearson, a farmer of Indiana, and they had a family of seven children, five of whom, grown to manhood and womanhood, are now living. The mother died Dec. 25, 1903. Mr. Annis has been a successful farmer, not that he has amassed wealth, but that he has cultivated a farm on the hills of the Ohio river near Lawrenceburg for forty-five years, and this farm today is more productive, in better condition and a higher state of cultivation than ever before. This is what he calls successful farming. The subject of this sketch is unassuming, charitable in disposition, and well respected by his neighbors.

WILLIAM ALONZO COTTINGHAM, a member of the firm of Cottingham & Ingham, dealers in general merchandise, at Bright, Dearborn county, Ind., was born in that county, Feb. 3, 1840. His parents were Thomas and Sarah Mills Stohms Cottingham and his paternal grandfather was George Cottingham, a member of one of the old families which came from England and settled in Maryland. He lived and died in that state, there married a woman of German descent, who, after his death, came with the family, consisting of three sons and a daughter to Cincinnati. At that time the city consisted of a few scattering houses and the widow Cottingham found herself upon what seemed to be the outermost edge of civilization. After a few years in Cincinnati the family came to Dearborn county, locating near Logan creek, where two of the sons, Thomas and William, opened up a farm. The third son, George, went to Illinois and there farmed until his death. William also went to Illinois and in later life to Kansas where he died in 1902, at the age of ninety-four years. Thomas remained in Dearborn county, where he was one of the typical pioneers. He died March 31, 1897, aged eighty-six years. Game was abundant. Mr. Cottingham saw bears chased by hounds, and wolves preyed upon the live stock of the early settlers. He received his education in the little log schoolhouse, with the huge fire place and puncheon floor. In addition to pulling stumps and driving oxen on the farm he learned the trade of blacksmith, which he followed for many years with a marked degree of success. In politics he was a Jackson Democrat. He and his wife were both members of the Christian church and were active in promoting its good works. They had the following children: Eliza, who married William Liddle and now lives a widow at Bright; Charlotte, deceased; William A., the subject of this sketch; Sarah, now Mrs. Joseph Haddock, lives at Harrison, O.; Jacob, deceased; Thomas B., whose sketch appears on another page of this work; Matilda, now Mrs. W. S. Fagaly, of Lawrenceburg; Louisa, who died in girlhood; and two children who died in infancy. William A. Cottingham began life for himself at the age of sixteen years. Commencing at the bottom of the ladder as a farm hand at small wages he saved his money until he had accumulated a few hundred dollars, when he married and rented a farm. He prospered from the very beginning and after three years he bought ninety acres in Miller township, of Dearborn county, upon which he lived for four years, when he sold it to a good advantage and bought sixty acres adjoining the village of Bright. Shortly afterward he embarked in the mercantile line by purchasing a half interest in a general store at Bright, which he sold after four years. Some years later he formed a partnership with Robert Ingham, and they are now conducting a general store at Bright, Mr. Cottingham also managing his farm. In political matters Mr. Cottingham has followed in the footsteps of his honored father and votes the Democratic ticket. He has been elected township trustee, serving with credit to himself and greatly to the advantage of the township. He has also held other minor offices. He and his family are members of the Methodist Episcopal church. In September, 1863, Mr. Cottingham was united in marriage to Miss Jane Haddock, daughter of Robert and Jane (Hargitt) Haddock. Both the Haddock and Hargitt families were among the pioneers of Dearborn county. Mrs. Cottingham's parents were born and married in England; came to America in 1821, after a tedious voyage of seven weeks on a sailing vessel, and located in Dearborn county. During their long and tedious voyage a fellow-passenger declared he would agree to eat the engine of the first steamer that ventured to cross the ocean, supposing that to be an utter impossibility, though Fulton's steamboat had been plying in the waters of the Hudson river for several years. Robert Haddock was a man of fine education and native ability as a teacher and in his day was a local preacher of considerable renown in the Methodist Episcopal church. To Mr. and Mrs. Cottingham there have been born the following children: Belle, wife of B. R. White, agent of the Canadian Pacific railway, and resides in Cincinnati; Daisy, wife of M. L. Rechenbach, residing at Harrison, O.; Hattie, at home; and Clyde H., who lives in Cincinnati. Mrs. Cottingham died on Aug. 21, 1902.

FRANCIS SWALES, retired farmer and veterinary surgeon of Dearborn county, Ind., was born near London, England, May 6, 1822. His parents were George and Mary Swales, both natives of England. His father, after years of study, graduated in medicine, veterinary surgery and chemistry, and in his day was regarded as an authority on all questions relating to live stock. In 1831 the family came to America on a sailing vessel, the voyage lasting nine weeks. They landed in Canada and from that country came to the State of New York, later descending the Ohio river on a steamboat to Lawrenceburg, Ind. Locating in Harrison township, Dearborn county, the father there practiced medicine and followed farming until he met his death by drowning in the Whitewater river. Both parents were members of the Presbyterian church. Francis studied veterinary surgery under his father; learned both the cooper and blacksmithing trades, and followed these occupations for a time, when he bought eighty acres of land and began farming. At one time he owned over 600 acres of improved land, but has given each of his children a farm. Since 1845 he has devoted the greater part of his time to the work of veterinary surgery, though in 1856 he put up a saw mill, which he operated for several years. Mr. Swales was married in 1845 to Miss Hannah Grubbs, a daughter of James Grubbs, and they had a family of four children: Sarah is now Mrs. Edward Judson; David is a farmer in Kansas; Eveline died as the wife of William Haddock; and William has a farm, that his father gave him, near the village of Bright. He is also a veterinary surgeon, making the third generation of the family to follow that calling. Mr. Swales and his family are members of the Presbyterian church. In politics he is a Democrat of the Andrew Jackson type, and is one of the best informed men in his township. He is a member of the Masonic fraternity and although past the age of four score still takes an interest in the work of the order. He is still hale and hearty for one of his age and believing that the laborer is worthy of his hire never asks his hired man to do unreasonable tasks. In this he shows the spirit of justice that has been his ruling motive through life, and which thas won for him the confidence and regard of his neighbors and acquaintances.

THOMAS HARGITT, a farmer of Logan township, Dearborn county, Ind., was born in that county, Jan. 22, 1825, and is a descendant of one of the pioneer families. His father and grandfather, both of whom were named Thomas, were natives of Yorkshire, England. The father of the subject of this sketch came to this country in 1820 and the grandfather came a year later with his family. They located in Dearborn county, where the elder Hargitt bought government land for himself and sons. His wife was a Miss Jarvis, a member of one of the old English families. Thomas Hargitt, the father of the subject, married Ann Sutton, *nee* Mason, whose husband died on the voyage to America. She was also a native of Yorkshire. Thomas Hargitt, the subject of the sketch, attended such schools as they had in those days and by self-study, by associating with educated people at every opportunity, secured a good, practical education. His early life was passed as a farm hand or at work in a saw mill. In 1850 he purchased forty acres of land and began farming. Three years later he sold that farm and bought seventy-two acres in Logan township, to which he has added fifty-eight acres. Starting from the log cabin he has today one of the best improved farms in the county, comfortable residence, good barns and outbuildings, all telling the story of his industry and prosperity. He was married on Sept. 8, 1850, to Mary Lynas. To this marriage there were born seven children. The eldest died young; Charles W. is now vice-president of the Syracuse university, Syracuse, N. Y.; Sarah is the wife of John Bonham, a Dearborn county farmer; George is a cattle raiser in Kansas; Elmer is a farmer in Jackson county, Ind.; R. N. is engaged in teaching; Jane is the wife of Howard Liddle, a Methodist minister. Mrs. Hargitt died on Oct. 20, 1870, and Mr. Hargitt married a second time, the second wife being Mrs. Sarah E. Dunn, *nee* Sweet, a daughter of W. P. Sweet of Butler county, O., and the widow of Dr. John G. Dunn, who died in 1885. By the second marriage his children are: Victor B., a graduate of Moore's Hill college and a minister of the Methodist church. In August, 1904, he started for India as a missionary. Romania, married and now living in Kansas City, Mo. Mr. and Mrs. Hargitt are both members of the Methodist Episcopal church, and for twenty-five years he has been superintendent of the Sunday school. In politics he is a Republican and is in every way a model citizen.

JAMES BOWTON, a well known farmer of Miller township, Dearborn county, Ind., was born in that township, Aug. 19, 1844, his parents being Charles and Nancy (Craig) Bowton. The paternal grandfather, Mack Bowton, came to the United States, with his family, consisting of a wife, four sons and one daughter, in 1832. He located in Dearborn county, where he bought a tract of wild land, which he improved and cultivated, and there lived the life common to the pioneers of Southern Indiana. He was a cabinet maker by trade and died at the age of thirty-five years of cholera. All the boys had to make their own way in the world and at the age of nineteen Charles Bowton, the father of James, left home and began life for himself. First he rented land for a few years, then bought 350 acres of his own. Later he bought land in the State of Illinois and at the time of his death owned about 500 acres in the two states. Two of his brothers still live in Illinois. Charles and Nancy Bowton had a family of five children: James, Mary J., Sarah, Elizabeth and W. W. Sarah and Elizabeth are deceased. The others are all married and are useful members of society. The father died July 15, 1902, his wife having passed away in 1888. Both were members of the Presbyterian church. James Bowton lived at home with his parents until he reached the age of thirty years, when he took charge of 100 acres of land, formerly belonging to his father, and to this he has added 50 acres more, giving him one of the best improved farms in the county. He carries on a general farming business and is regarded as one of the progressive men of his township. In politics he has followed in the footsteps of his honored father and is a Democrat. He keeps informed on the questions of the hour and votes intelligently on whatever proposition may be submitted to the electors of the country. He was married in 1875 to Miss Ella Reese, a daughter of Jacob and Barbara Reese of Dearborn county. To this union there have been born two children: Reese C., aged twenty-eight, and Elma T., who died in 1903 at the age of twenty-four. Both were well educated, the daughter being proficient in music, and the son has taught in the public schools. Mr. Bowton is a self-made man and all his success has come through his industry, his intelligence, and his habit of keeping fully in touch with the progress of the world, which enables him to take advantage of any emergency that is likely to arise.

CHARLES WHITFIELD NOWLIN, a farmer in Miller township, Dearborn county, Ind., was born near where he now lives, Sept. 16, 1855, and is the son of Silas and Martha (Hargitt) Nowlin. The father was born in Kentucky but came with his parents to Indiana when a small boy, grew to maturity in Dearborn county, and there passed his entire life as a farmer and flatboatman on the Ohio river, following the latter occupation for a number of years when he was a young man. After giving all his attention to farming he became quite successful, but met with reverses in later life. He was twice married and reared a family of seventeen children —seven by his first and ten by his second wife—Charles W. being the fourth child by the second marriage. Both parents died in the spring of 1891, the father on March 26, and the mother on May 17. Charles W. Nowlin attended the common schools during his boyhood days, there receiving the major portion of his education. He remained on the farm with his father until he was twenty-four years of age, when he bought the farm in Miller township where he now lives. This he has improved until he has one of the nicest and most productive farms in that part of the county. On Feb. 11, 1880, soon after purchasing this farm, he was married to Miss Anna Judd, a daughter of Orin and Mary J. (Cook) Judd, both natives of Dearborn county, where Mrs. Nowlin's grandfather, Job Judd, was one of the pioneers. Mr. and Mrs. Nowlin have four children: Guy L., born on Nov. 11, 1881, is now married, his wife having been Maude Boxell; Lulu B., born April 19, 1884; Clinton Otis, born Dec. 20, 1885; and Eva L., born May 27, 1886. The three younger children are at home with their parents. All have good educations and Eva is proficient in music. Both parents are members of the Methodist Episcopal church. Mr. Nowlin believes in the farmer having some of the good things of this life as well as his city cousins. He has therefore managed to have many of the modern conveniences introduced into his home. He lives on one of the rural free delivery mail routes, giving him an opportunity, which he is not slow to improve, to read the daily papers and thus keep in touch with the outside world.

ROBERT DUCK (deceased), formerly a prominent citizen of Dearborn county, Ind., was born in Lancashire, England, Dec. 11, 1827. His father, whose name was also Robert, was a wealthy farmer of Lancashire. In 1829 he came with his wife and son to America; located at first at Cincinnati, but after six months they came to Dearborn county and bought a farm of one hundred and sixty acres in Miller township. Here he improved his farm until it was the best in the neighborhood, and died there in 1841. Robert took charge of the farm after the death of his father, although but fourteen years old, and continued to manage it until 1862, when he removed to Lawrenceburg and embarked in the grocery and ice business, which he continued for several years. He then retired to his summer home, two and a half miles from Lawrenceburg, and lived there for some time when he again took up his residence in the city and died there in 1887. On April 2, 1860, he was married to Catherine Ann, daughter of David and Catherine (Balte) Perine, of Yorkville, Dearborn county. Her father was a native of New York and her mother of New Jersey. Robert and Catherine Duck had four children, all daughters, viz.: Jennie K., Nettie A., Ella May, and Lilly Belle. All received good educations by governess and later in the Lawrenceburg schools, Nettie being a graduate of the high school. They were all somewhat proficient and Jennie, who is the only one now living, studied art. In his day Robert Duck was considered one of the substantial men of his county. In politics he was a Democrat and he and his wife were both members of the Methodist Episcopal church. She died June 22, 1903, and her death was sincerely mourned by a large circle of friends.

FREDERICK J. WALDO, editor and proprietor of the *Rising Sun Recorder,* Rising Sun, Ind., was born at Vevay, Switzerland county, of that state, Jan. 25, 1831. He is son of Otis and Sarah (Smith) Waldo, the former a native of Ohio and the latter of New York. The Waldos originally came from England. Otis Waldo was a son of Frederick Waldo, of Connecticut, and in 1814 the father and son both came to Indiana, located at Vevay, where they ran a general store for a number of years. Two years later the maternal grandparents located in the same neighborhood. Otis and Sarah Waldo had three children. Otis S., deceased; Frederick J., the subject of this sketch; and Lois, who died in infancy. After attending the common schools until he was fourteen years old Frederick was apprenticed to the printers' trade at Vevay, and from that time he has been connected with the newspaper business, in almost every capacity from "devil" to editor and proprietor.   In 1853, when he was but twenty-two years of age, he bought the *Ohio Valley Gazette,* at Vevay, and changed the name to that of the *Vevay Reveille,* which it has ever since retained. Mr. Waldo continued to conduct this publication for ten years, when he sold out and was postmaster at Vevay for over two years.   He was then for six years assistant assessor of internal revenue at Vevay. In 1873 he came to Rising Sun and bought the *Recorder,* of which he is still the owner and manager.   Ever since he became a voter Mr. Waldo has been a consistent and intelligent Republican.   His paper has always stood up for the principles of his party.   A half century has elapsed since he made his first venture into the field of journalism and he is today one of the oldest and best known newspaper men in Southern Indiana.   In 1852 Mr. Waldo led to the altar Miss Martha, daughter of Benjamin and Margaret Egelston, of Covington, Ky. Her father was a farmer in early life but later removed to the city of Covington, Ky., where for years he held the office of justice of the peace.   Mr. and Mrs. Waldo have had born to them ten children, viz.: Emerson G., now associated with his father in business; John F., deceased; Martha; Io, deceased; William W.; Otis B.; Sarah; Jessie; Mary and Margaret E., both of whom died in infancy.   All the boys are practical printers.   Both parents and all the children are members of the Universalist church.

W. P. NEWMAN, of Ironton, Ohio, proprietor of the Great American Water Shows, was born at Ironton, March 27, 1872.   For many years his father was engaged in the business of operating a saw mill, but now lives retired. He reared a family of seven children, the subject being the fifth.   At the age of fourteen the subject of this sketch left home, having acquired a high school education, and for a while trimmed windows in stores, flower wagons, etc., in different cities. He then engaged in the dry goods business at New Martinsville, W. Va., for about eighteen months, but sold out his business there and in 1901 built and equipped the traveling exhibition of which he is still proprietor and manager.   His outfit consists of a large barge, covered with a tent and containing two circus rings and seats for two thousand people.   This barge is towed from place to place by a steamboat, the show exhibiting at all the principal towns on the Ohio and Mississippi rivers.   Mr. Newman carries with his show forty-two people, nineteen trained ponies, twenty-two acting dogs, and in 1904 bought out the W. W. Colshaw circus.   He is the pioneer in the water show business and has the only circus traveling by and giving exhibitions on the water. Wherever he has been his show has been well received and he is laying the foundation for a fortune and a reputation as great as that of P. T. Barnum. Many of the river towns have no railroad connection, and this gives him practically a monopoly of the show business in a profitable field. But Mr. Newman aims to retain that monopoly by the excellence and high toned character of his performances. He trains all his animals himself and in his shows can be seen many features not to be found elsewhere. On Nov. 25, 1896, Mr. Newman was united in marriage to Miss Carrie Haller, of Bucyrus, O. She is a lady of many attainments and travels with her husband as the cashier of the shows.

JAMES W. CORSON, auditor of Ohio county, Rising Sun, Ind., was born in that county, Oct. 18, 1877, his parents being John K. and Sarah E. (Pate) Corson, both natives of Ohio county. The paternal great-grandfather came with his family from Massachusetts to Indiana at an early day, settled in Ohio county, where he bought a place and lived there until his death. The grandfather, Albert Corson, continued to live on the place until the flood of 1840, when they were drowned out. In trying to save their effects the father of James came near losing his life by falling from the raft into the water, he being an infant at the time. All their household goods were lost and they had to start over again. But Albert Corson was a man of great pluck and industry and at the time of his death was worth several thousand dollars. John K. Corson grew up in Ohio county; followed farming and has been engaged in various other business enterprises; owns property at Indianapolis, Marion, Ind., and other places; served as a member of the city council; prominent in Masonry and Odd Fellowship, having taken all the degrees in the latter order; also a member of the Methodist church, to which his wife, who died Oct. 6, 1899, also belonged, and now lives a retired life at Rising Sun, The maternal grandparents were Peter S. and Elizabeth (Crandall) Pate, and the great-grandfather, George B. Pate came to Ohio county in 1818, fording the Ohio river with his teams; bought 400 acres of wild land and built one of the first stone houses in the county. He owned 500 acres of land at the time of his death, which land is still owned by his great-grandchildren. Peter S. Pate died in 1880, owning 700 acres and was estimated to be worth $25,000. In his time he held several local offices and was prominent in the affairs of his township and county. He helped to start the national bank at Rising Sun, was elected the first president, and at the time of his death owned two-fifths of the capital stock.   John K. and Sarah E. Corson had a family of four children: John P. married Marion Hunt and is now manager of the home, farm.   For awhile he lived in Indianapolis, where he was assistant secretary of the board of trade, and later was in the wall paper business in that city for five years.   James W. is the subject of this sketch; Albert T. is a dentist in Indianapolis, in the office formerly occupied by his brother, and Elizabeth is at home with her father.   James W. Corson received a high school education at Rising Sun; entered the Indiana dental college at Indianapolis in 1896 and graduated in 1899; took charge of a dental office in Indianapolis the fall before he graduated; practiced there until 1901; turned over the office to his brother Albert and came to Rising Sun to look after his father's interests there while the latter was in California; elected auditor in the fall of 1902 and took the office Jan. 1, 1904.   Mr. Corson has always taken an active interest in political affairs and is one of the leading Democrats of his county.   He is prominent in Odd Fellowship, being a member of Capital Lodge, No. 124; Metropolitan Encampment, No. 5; and Olive Branch Lodge, No. 10, Daughters of Rebekah.   In Masonry he is a member of Rising Sun Lodge, No. 6; Aurora Chapter, Royal Arch Masons, No. 13; Aurora Commandery, Knights Templars; and the Indianapolis Consistory of the Scottish Rite.   He is always active in lodge work and is a popular member of the different bodies named.   Mr. Corson was married, Nov. 7, 1900, to Miss Annie Carson, at Indianapolis.   She is a daughter of Aquilla Carson of Dearborn county and was attending business college at the time of her marriage.   Mr. and Mrs. Corson are members of the Methodist church and are identified with the social life of Rising Sun.

WYMOND G. SINK, recorder of Ohio county, Rising Sun, Ind., is a descendant of some of the pioneer families of that section of the state.   His paternal grandfather, Bright Sink, was a farmer and road builder there in an early day.   Later he went South and there he passed the remainder of his days.   The paternal grandfather was William Loder, one of the first physicians in Rising Sun, but afterward went to Indianapolis, where he married Sophronia Fisher, a native of that city, though her parents came from Stafford, Vt.   William Sink, the father of Wymond, married Rebecca Loder and lived in Rising Sun, where he was prominent in politics as a Republican, serving as city marshal for some time, and was also well known in Odd Fellowship.   He died at Rising Sun in August, 1898.   His widow still lives in Rising Sun. They had four children: Rebecca married Charles Berkshire, a Kentucky farmer; Jennie married Alfred Neal and lives in Rising Sun; Daisy is at home with her mother, and Wymond is the subject of this sketch. He was born at Rising Sun, April 20, 1879, and lived in his native town, until 1896, obtaining an education in the public schools. He then went to Chicago, where he learned the trade of sign painter, and was for two years with the R. J. Gunning company, traveling over the country and painting advertising signs. In that time he visited every state in the Union and Canada. After leaving this company Mr. Sink was for a short time in the employ of the Illinois Central Railroad Company. On July 20, 1899, he enlisted in the United States hospital corps and served three years in China and the Philippines, being discharged as a hospital steward. In August, 1902, he came back to Rising Sun and at the election in November of that year was elected recorder of the county, taking the office on the first of January, 1903, for a term of four years. Mr. Sink is a Democrat politically and is a member of East Bend Lodge, No. 114, Knights of Pythias.

HENRY RUMP, better known as "Harry," sheriff of Ohio county, Rising Sun, Ind., was born in that county, Sept. 1, 1873, and is a son of Henry and Clara (Selmire) Rump, the former a native of Dearborn county, Ind., and the latter of Germany. The paternal grandfather, Frederick Rump, came from Germany at an early date and settled in Dearborn county, where he followed farming all his life. There his son Henry grew to manhood, married Clara Selmire, and in 1863 removed to Ohio county, where he bought a farm of about 100 acres and reared a family of twelve children, three of whom are now dead. Of the nine living children all but one are married and have comfortable homes. All the children received a good education. Henry attended the common schools until he was about sixteen years of age, when he left school and learned the blacksmith trade. Later he bought a small farm near Rising Sun, where he combined farm work with his trade. From the time he became a voter Mr. Rump has taken an active part in political affairs as a Democrat, always standing ready to help his party to win a victory. In 1902 he received the nomination of his party for the office of sheriff, was triumphantly elected the following November, and took the office on the first day of January, 1904. Mr. Rump's name will go down in history as the sheriff connected with the famous "Gillespie case," one of the most noted murder trials of Ohio county, and in fact of the state. In that case Mr. Rump won the approbation of the bench, bar, jury and spectators by his careful attention to his duty, and his readiness to minister to the comfort of the court, the attorneys and the visitors to the court room during the long and somewhat tedious trial. He is a Knight of Pythias, which is the only fraternal organization to claim his membership. Mr. Rump was married on May 8, 1895, to Miss Elizabeth, daughter of Ernest Detner, of Ohio county. Like her husband, Mrs. Rump is of German extraction. They have one son, Paul H., born Dec. 3, 1898. Both Mr. and Mrs. Rump are members of the German Reformed church.

HOWARD J. NORTH, clerk of the circuit court of Ohio county, Rising Sun, Ind., was born in that county, May 24, 1871. He is a son of Ernest C. and Tobitha E. North, the former a native of Switzerland and the latter of Ohio county, Ind. The Norths are of English extraction. Royal North, the grandfather of Howard, came from New York to Indiana at an early date and settled in Switzerland county, where he followed farming until his death. Ernest North lived in Switzerland county until after his marriage, when he removed to Ohio county and embarked in the produce business at North's Landing. When the Civil war broke out he enlisted in Company C, Eighty-third Indiana infantry, as a corporal and served through the war. He was wounded in action three times and for his gallant conduct was promoted to the position of first lieutenant. He is still living, takes an active interest in politics as a Republican of the old school and in the affairs of the Grand Army of the Republic, of which he is an honored member. Ernest and Tobitha North had a family of two children: Nellie A. graduated from the Rising Sun high school, attended the State normal at Terre Haute, and has been a teacher for eleven years. She lives at home. Howard also received a high school education and took up the work of a teacher, but after one term in Kentucky and three in his native county he turned his attention to other lines of employment. In 1898 he was nominated by the Republicans of his county for the office of clerk and was elected, taking the office in 1900 for a term of four years. He is a member of the Sons of Veterans, the Modern Woodmen, and the Knights of Pythias, and has held all the offices in the different lodges to which he belongs. Mr. North has a farm of about seventy acres three miles from Rising Sun. This he rents out while he is in the clerk's office, and as an evidence of his progressive notions it is worth noticing that he has this farm connected with the outside world by telephone, thus keeping in touch with his tenant and giving the latter the advantages of such an arrangement.

ANDREW WALLACE DARLING, postmaster at Carrollton, Ky., was born in that city Nov. 29, 1864. He is of Scotch descent, his grandfather, Thomas Darling, having been born in the county of Haddington, or East Lothian, a few miles east of the city of Edinburg, and there grew to manhood. He married Jannet Wallace, whose ancestry can be traced back to Robert Bruce. In 1819 they came to the United States with their family, consisting of five sons and two daughters, viz.: Thomas, Adam, Andrew W., William, James, Isabella, and Jane, and settled in Wood county, in what is now West Virginia. Andrew W. Darling, the father of the subject of this sketch, was born near Edinburg, Scotland, Aug. 12, 1816, and was therefore but three years of age when his parents came to this country. He was naturalized with his father and brothers in Wood county in 1829, and while still a mere boy worked as time keeper on the first railroad that was built west of the Alleghany Mountains. In 1834, in company with his two brothers, Thomas and Adam, he went to Kentucky and assisted in building Cedar lock on the Kentucky river. After this he was for some time engaged in flatboating on the Ohio and Mississippi rivers. He then bought a farm in Carroll county and started the Darling distillery. He sold his interest in this concern before his death and spent the last years of his life in retirement. He married Eliza J. Troutman, a daughter of Peter and Katherine (Giltner) Troutman, the former born near Hagerstown, Md., and the latter in Bourbon county, Ky. Katherine Giltner's ancestry can be traced back to William, King of Holland. The children of Peter and Katherine Troutman were Elijah, Frank, Jacob, Barney, Thomas, John, Mary A. E., Eliza J., Nancy, and Katherine. Eliza J., the mother of the subject, was born in Bourbon county, Ky., Nov. 12, 1826, and now resides in Carrollton. Andrew W. Darling, the subject of this sketch, is one of eight children born to his father's second marriage, two children having been born to a previous union. He was educated in the public schools and after passing through the high school attended for some time the State university at Lexington. Upon leaving school he started life as a grocer's clerk. In 1886 he entered the employ of the Carrollton Furniture Manufacturing Company and a year later became a traveling salesman for the company. He remained on the road until 1895, when he resigned his position to engage in other pursuits. Always an active Republican he found favor with the national administration and in 1902 was appointed postmaster. In this position his long business training as a traveling salesman and his general qualities as a

mixer have made him a popular and efficient official. He has introduced numerous little reforms in the service that have met the approval of the public and which have facilitated the handling of mails,
giving better service to the patrons of the office. Mr. Darling is a
Knight of Pythias and a Royal Arch Mason. In both orders he is
popular because of his genial disposition and his readiness to assist
in every worthy charity undertaken by his lodges. He lives at home
in Carrollton, with his mother, one brother and two sisters.

WILLIAM O. PROTSMAN, postmaster at Vevay, Ind., and one of the
Republican leaders in Switzerland county,
was born at Moorefield, in that county,
April 2, 1875. His parents, John W. and
Lottie A. (Ogle) Protsman, were both
natives of the county. The paternal
grandfather was named William, and the
great-grandfather, John Protsman, came
from Maryland in a very early day, being
one of the first settlers in Switzerland
county. On the maternal side the grandparents were Hiram and Charlotte
(Tague) Ogle, both of whom were born in the county. The great-
grandfather on this side was Hiram Ogle, who came from Maryland
in 1808, though he was a native of Virginia. He built the first jail in
Switzerland county and was the first mail carrier between Vevay and
Versailles. John W. and Lottie A. Protsman had four children: William is the subject of this sketch; Edward died at the age of seven years;
Grace married Festus Flinn and lives at Georgetown, Ky.; and Mabel
is at home. William received a high school education and for three
years taught in the common schools. He was then in agricultural pursuits until 1902, when the *Vevay Reveille* company, which had been
formed the preceding year, elected him secretary and treasurer. This
company had purchased the *Vevay Reveille,* one of the oldest newspapers
in Southern Indiana, of W. J. Baird, who had conducted it for thirty-
eight years. Since taking charge of the paper in 1902 Mr. Protsman has
doubled the circulation and made the paper more aggressive in its
political sentiments, as well as more complete in its news departments.
Ever since he attained his majority Mr. Protsman has been an earnest
and active Republican. In 1900 he was chosen chairman of the county
central committee, and although he was but twenty-five years of age he

demonstrated in that campaign his ability as an organizer and a political strategist. During the legislative session of 1901 he was a clerk in the Indiana state senate, and on Feb. 4, 1902, he assumed the duties of post-master at Vevay. Mr. Protsman is a member of the Vevay Lodge, No. 149, Knights of Pythias, and Switzerland Lodge, No. 122, Free and Accepted Masons. He was married, Feb. 18, 1896, to Miss Leo C., daughter of Albert G. Bakes, a well known Switzerland county farmer, and they have two children: Helen, born April 24, 1897, and Merriam, born Oct. 27, 1899. Mr. Protsman occupies one of the coziest homes in Vevay and he and his estimable wife are prominent in the social life of the little city.

ANDREW J. BRUCE, clerk of Carroll county, Carrollton, Ky., was born at Warsaw, Gallatin county, of that state, Dec. 7, 1842, and is a son of Henry and Sarah (Jackson) Bruce. His father was born at Aurora, Ind., and was a son of Henry Bruce, who came from Virginia in the early part of the nineteenth century, being one of the first three white men to settle at Aurora. Andrew's father grew to manhood at Aurora, but removed to Gallatin county, Ky., in 1835 to take charge of the farm formerly owned by his father-in-law. He continued to live on this farm until 1890, when he sold out and came to Carrollton, where he died in 1892. His wife died in 1886. He was a Baptist and she was a member of the Christian church. They had a family of six boys and four girls, of which Andrew was the third child and the eldest son. Andrew obtained a good education in the public schools and by self-study. He commenced teaching at the age of eighteen and followed that occupation until 1884. He was in love with his work and was one of the most successful teachers in Kentucky, as may be seen from the fact that he taught for twelve years in one precinct. In 1880 he came to Carroll county, which has ever since been his home. In 1867, while living in Gallatin county, he was elected county assessor and held the office for two terms. In 1892 he went into the marble business, in which he was successful, at the same time taking an active part in shaping the affairs of the Democratic party, as he had done ever since becoming a voter. His activity in this line and his well established qualifications marked him out as a suitable candidate for the office of county clerk, and in 1897 he was nominated and elected, taking the office the following year. In 1902 he was again elected by a handsome majority, attesting his popularity and efficiency. Mr. Bruce was married on June 14, 1894, to Felicia C. Hopwood, *nee* McGee, a native of Trimble county, Ky. To this union there have been born two children: Hester, born Aug. 27, 1896, and Jessie, born April 28, 1898. The latter died in August, 1900. Mr. and Mrs. Bruce are both members of the Christian church and take a commendable interest in its good works.

FRANK H. GAINES, M.D., a well known physician and surgeon of Carrollton, Ky., was born in Washington county, Va., Nov. 4, 1834. His father was Samuel Dalton Gaines, a son of Ambrose and Mary (Moore) Gaines. Ambrose Gaines was a soldier in the American army during the Revolutionary war, and was a cousin to Gen. Edmund P. Gaines who was connected with the arrest of Aaron Burr, and who rose to the rank of brigadier-general in the war of 1812. Mary Moore, Dr. Gaines' grandmother, was a sister to Gabriel Moore, who was the fifth governor of Alabama after its admission as a state. After the Revolution Ambrose Gaines settled in Tennessee, where for many years he followed the profession of teaching. On the other side Dr. Gaines' mother, whose maiden name was Sarah E. Gaines, was a daughter of James, a veteran of the Revolution and a brother to Gen. Edmund P. Gaines above mentioned. Among the relics of the Revolutionary period in the possession of James Gaines was the Jacob's staff used by George Washington while surveying. Samuel Dalton Gaines grew to manhood in Tennessee, inherited the old homestead, and was for many years a minister of the Methodist church. After the war he went to Arkansas and later came to Kentucky. He died at Bristol, Tenn., while on a visit, Nov. 20, 1887. His wife died May 4, 1878. Both were members of the Methodist church. Dr. F. H. Gaines is the eldest in a family of nine children. Elizabeth is now Mrs. J. H. Dorman, of Owenton, Ky.; Margaret is the widow of John Grace and lives in Arkansas; one of her sons, Frank, grew up in the family of Dr. Gaines and is now a physician in Alabama; Letitia died as the wife of Lot. Pence; Sarah married Dr. N. C. Brown, of Ghent, Ky., and died as his wife; Ambrose died at the age of fourteen years; John still lives in Kentucky; Fannie is deceased; George is a graduate of the Louisville Medical college and engaged in practice at Milton, Ky. After obtaining a common school education in Virginia Dr. F. H. Gaines attended high school at Blountsville, Tenn.; read medicine under one of the leading physicians there; took a course of lectures at Louisville; graduated from the Nashville university in 1855; received the degree of M. D. from Jefferson Medical college of Philadelphia in 1861, and took a post-graduate course at Bellevue Hospital college in New York in 1880. During the war he served four years as surgeon of a battalion in the Third Tennessee cavalry, being engaged in active service the whole time. After the war he located in Gallatin county, Ky.; removed to Ghent in 1869; practiced there until 1888, when he removed to Carrollton. He is a member and ex-president of the Carroll County Medical society, the American, the Kentucky State and the Mississippi Valley Medical associations. Dr. Gaines was married on Oct. 15, 1856, to Elmira, daughter of John and Harriet (Rice) McFarland, the former a native of Tennessee and the latter of Connecticut. They were married at Marble Hall near Rodgersville, Tenn. Mrs. Gaines died in 1881 and the following year Dr. Gaines married Mrs. Priscilla Fisher, *nee* Linsley, a daughter of Gen. Jesse Linsley who came from Virginia to Kentucky in pioneer days. Dr. Gaines has had eight children. Lillian M. is deceased; S. Fisher married W. T. Sebree and resides in Carrollton; Harriet is the wife of L. G. Lawrence of Chicago; Roxanna died in infancy; Francis died young; Frank McFarland, born Jan. 30, 1870, is associated with his father in the practice of medicine; Samuel Sherman is in business in Louisville. Dr. Frank M. Gaines is one of the rising young physicians of Carroll and adjoining counties. He graduated from the Kentucky School of Medicine, at Louisville, in 1893, and since then has been associated with his father, profiting by his long experience and assisting him in the large practice that they enjoy. He is a member of the Carroll County, Kentucky State, and Eagle Valley Medical societies. The elder doctor is a member of the Masonic fraternity and the Odd Fellows, and the son belongs to the Knights of Pythias and is a Royal Arch Mason. The father and all his sons are unswerving Democrats, and all the family belong to the Christian church. Frank M. Gaines married Daisy B. Jemison, of Henry county, Ky.

JOSEPH S. LEHMANN, M.D., a prominent homeopathic physician of Carrollton, Ky. was born at Midway, Woodford county, in that state, and is a son of David W. and Elizabeth (Marsh) Lehmann, the former a native of Wurtemberg, Germany, and the latter of New York City. David Lehmann came to the United States with his two brothers, William and John, and for a time they remained in the city of New York. Later William went to Florida and John to Georgia. David was a cabinet maker in his early life. After leaving New York he came to Kentucky, settling first at Lexington and later at Midway, where he embarked in the furniture and undertaking business.

Subsequently he took two of his sons into partnership, under the firm name of D. Lehmann & Sons, and added lumber to his trade. David and his wife are members of the Presbyterian church, and he and all of his sons are Democrats. There were seven children in the family. John died in infancy; Alice married F. D. Carpenter and resides at Lexington; Annie married John Freml and also lives in Lexington; David lives at Midway and is a traveling salesman for the Springfield Coffin and Casket Company; William and Harris are associated with their father in business at Midway; and Joseph is the subject of this sketch. All the children attended the private academy of Prof. J. R. Hammond. After attending this school Doctor Lehmann spent one year in the Central university, at Richmond, Ky. In 1894 he entered the Cleveland Medical college and graduated in 1896. For a year he practiced at Lexington, after which he located at Carrollton, where he has built up a lucrative business and ranks high as a physician. He possesses to a large degree that analytical turn of mind, that love for patient research and ambition to succeed that has made the physicians of Germany the greatest on earth. Less than a decade has elapsed since he received his degree yet these traits of character have won for him a name in the medical profession and the future holds out bright prospects for greater achievements.

COL. FRANK P. SEBREE, planter, stock dealer, tobacco buyer, and a prominent Democrat of Carroll county, Ky., was born near Ghent in that county, Dec. 16, 1856. For more than a century his family have been identified with Kentucky, its growth, its development, and its politics. In the latter part of the eighteenth century his paternal grandfather came from Virginia and settled near Frankfort. There Richard W. Sebree, the father of Colonel Sebree, was born in 1799. Before attaining his majority he was interested in keelboating on the Kentucky river, conveying hay from Carrollton to Frankfort. In 1835 he went to Owen county and in 1847 he came to Carroll, locating near Ghent, where he passed the remainder of his life as a successful farmer. He was a first cousin to Col. Dick Johnson, so well known in the annals of Kentucky. Richard W. Sebree married Emily Poindexter, and to this union were born ten children, nine of whom lived to maturity. Frank is the youngest of the seven sons. He received a high school education and when he was nineteen years of age the farm was turned over to his management. In 1888 he went to Louisville, where for ten years he was a familiar figure in the tobacco market, buying and rehandling, and in which he was successful because of his keen foresight and untiring industry. Coming back to Carroll county in 1898, he bought a farm of 220 acres, on the west side of the Kentucky river, within half a mile of Carrollton. His farm is about equally divided between valley and hill lands and is nearly all in a high state of cultivation. Fine buildings add to its appearance and the whole place bears witness to the thrift of its owner. In politics Colonel Sebree has followed in the footsteps of his worthy sire and is a potent factor in the councils of the Democratic party. Imbued with the righteousness of that fundamental principle of Democracy—"majority rule"—he is always found working for its advancement and perpetuation. He was a personal friend and an ardent supporter of the late lamented Governor Goebel, and in June, 1900, he was appointed on the staff of Governor Beckham with the rank of colonel. This appointment was an act of wisdom on the part of the governor and was duly appreciated by Colonel Sebree's many friends. In 1904 Colonel Sebree was nominated for representative to the state legislature by the Democracy of Carroll county, another evidence of the esteem in which he is held by his fellow citizens. He is prominent in Masonic circles, being a member of the lodge at Worthville and the Royal Arch Chapter at Ghent. Colonel Sebree was married on Oct. 1, 1881, to Miss Susan P., daughter of George P. and Maria Gullion, of Carrollton. Mr. and Mrs. Sebree have two daughters, Frankie and Ruth Lester. Both parents are members of the Baptist church, to the good work of which Colonel Sebree is a liberal contributor.

RALPH M. BARKER, one of the leading citizens of Carrollton, Ky., was born at Covington in that state, Nov. 22, 1875, and is a son of M. I. and Virginia A. (Clark) Barker, the former born at Penn Yan, N. Y., and the latter in the city of Philadelphia, Pa. They were married in St. Louis; removed to Cincinnati in 1876; and in 1879 the father built the first tobacco factory in Carrollton. After several years in the tobacco business, during which he was the largest broker in that staple in Cincinnati, he came to Carroll county, where he has ever since been engaged in that business. He also bought a fine farm, erected the finest farm house in the county and turned his attention to raising fine horses. Among the fast horses bred and reared at the Barker farm may be mentioned Navy Bean, 2:11½; Nellie B., 2:14½; Gentry's Treasure, 2:10, and a host of others. In this work Ralph has been intimately associated with his father and is one of the best trainers in the country. He knows all about pedigrees and understands all the intricate points in the combinations of blood to produce the best possible horse. In 1898 Ralph M. Barker secured a franchise and built telephone lines connecting Carrollton with all the surrounding towns and cities, using about five hundred miles of wire for the purpose and giving the people of these towns and cities an excellent local service. In 1903 he sold out his telephone interests and built the canning factory at Carrollton, which gives the farmers a home market for their fruits and vegetables at the best possible prices. He also built and equipped a steam laundry and in 1904 organized the firm of R. M. Barker & Co., wholesale liquor dealers. He is also treasurer of the Barker Packing Company; secretary of the Carrollton & Prestonville Bridge Company; director in both the above corporations and also in the Ohio Valley Traction Company. The name of Richlawn stock farm, of which Mr. Barker is the proprietor, is becoming known to horsemen all over the country, for the excellent stock that has been bred there, and it is in this enterprise that Mr. Barker finds his greatest delight. In all his business undertakings Mr. Barker has been guided by quick decision, cool judgment, undaunted courage, confidence in his ability, firmness, and above all an unflinching honesty and a strict adherence to correct business principles. While he has worked for his own financial benefit he has not been unmindful of the public welfare, and Carroll county can boast no more public spirited citizen, no one more interested in the general prosperity than Ralph M. Barker. In political matters he is actuated by the desire to promote the public weal and votes for the man that his judgment leads him to believe is the best for the place. Consequently he is not wedded to his party idols but exercises the right of suffrage as a freeman should—candidly, fearlessly and intelligently. Mr. Barker was elected mayor of Carrollton in 1901, more upon his merits as a man than upon his record as a politician. Under his administration the interests of the city were guarded with the same care and the same success that direct and attend his private business. In fraternal circles he is a member of Louisville Lodge, No. 8, Benevolent and Protective Order of Elks. On Dec. 14, 1899, Mr. Barker was united in marriage to Miss Nellie Gill Long, a daughter of Capt. E. E. and Kate Gill Long, of Vevay, Ind. Her father is a well known steamboat captain. Mr. and Mrs. Barker have one son: M. I., born June 19, 1901. Mrs. Barker is a member of the Presbyterian church.

CAPT. ALBERT N. JETT, United States storekeeper, residing at Carrollton, Ky., was born in Carroll county, Ky., Oct. 27, 1840, his parents being R. H. V. and Elizabeth (Bradley) Jett, the former a native of Virginia and the latter of Delaware. William Jett, his grandfather, was a member of one of the old Virginia families, came to Kentucky in the early teens and located in Carroll county. R. H. V., the father of Albert N. Jett, moved to Carrollton, in 1844. In politics he was, until 1860, an Old Line Whig and upon the nomination of Abraham Lincoln for President, he espoused that cause, remaining a Republican until his death, which was in 1872. Of the ten children born to the parents of Albert N. Jett, William is dead; Mary Jane married and is now a widow; Richard Henry is a planter and merchant in Gregory, Ark.; Kate is the wife of William Langstaff of Indianapolis, Ind.; John B. served in the Union army in the Thirtieth Kentucky infantry and died in 1881; Albert N. is the subject of this sketch. Joseph S. Jett is a distiller in Peoria, Ill.; a second son, named William, died in 1847; James F. and Joseph S. Jett are the proprietors of the Richland distillery, the opera house, and several other large interests in Carrollton; and George W. is engaged at Jett Bros.' distillery. All received good educations and became good, useful citizens. In September, 1861, at the age of twenty, Albert N. Jett and his brother, Joseph S., enlisted in the Federal army in Company K, Thirteenth Kentucky volunteer infantry. He was soon promoted from first duty sergeant to first lieutenant and when mustered out of service at Louisville, Ky., in January, 1865, he was captain of his company. During his service in the army, he was in some of the fiercest battles of the war, among them being Shiloh, Corinth, Iuka, and the operations in East Tennessee. He was wounded in the battle of Huff's Ferry near London, Tenn., and participated in many of the battles of the Atlanta campaign. After the war was over he returned to Carrollton. In 1867 he moved to Harrison county, Ky., where he was engaged as distiller until 1872, when he received the appointment of United States storekeeper, which he held until 1881, when he moved to Carrollton, and with his brothers, Joseph S., James F. and George W., built and operated a distillery until 1888. Then he and George W. sold their interest in the distillery to Joseph S.

and James F. Jett, at which time he was appointed deputy collector, which he held for one year, and was again appointed United States storekeeper, which he held until Cleveland's second term as president. He resigned in August, 1893, and again entered the distillery with his brothers, but in February, 1898, he again sold his interest in the distillery and accepted another appointment as United States storekeeper, which place he still holds and says that he will hold it until a Democratic president is elected or death removes him. Captain Jett is an uncompromising Republican and takes an active part with his party. He attends most all congressional and state conventions and as chairman of the Republican county committee helped to bring the party in Kentucky up to the election of a Republican governor and once to give her electoral vote to McKinley. He was married in 1867 to Miss Sarah B. Price, of Harrison county, Ky., and to this marriage were born the following children: Minnie C., wife of Charles E. Heinrich, of Cincinnati; John B., a resident of Harrison county, Ky.; Bettie M., now the wife of Charles Radcliff, of London, Ky.; Richard and Henry Mc., both of whom died in infancy. Mrs. Jett died in 1875 and Mr. Jett subsequently married Mary Morgan, of Covington, Ky. She died in 1889. To this second marriage there were born David H., now married and living in Carrollton; Grace F., at home; Mabel, wife of Ernest Lewellyn, county superintendent of schools of Carroll county, and Joseph at home. On Sept. 21, 1890, Captain Jett was married to his present wife, who was Miss Sallie B. Tate, of Bourbon county, Ky., this marriage taking place at Paris, Ky. The children of the third wife are Daisy, aged twelve years, and Katie, aged six, at home with their parents; and James F., the second child, who died in infancy. Captain Jett and his family have always been strong and consistent members of the Christian church.

L. P. HOLZHAUER, government storekeeper and gauger, Newport, Ky., was born in that city in 1873. His father was a native of Wurtemberg, Germany, and his mother of Cincinnati. The father came to this country at the age of sixteen, located at Newport and there followed the vocation of druggist until his death in 1895, being one of the oldest and best known druggists in the city. The mother is still living in Newport. Of their four children L. P. is the subject of this sketch; Edna is the widow of Frank Meadowcroft and resides in Newport; Iona is Mrs. Milton S. Smith, of Newport; Clara is an actress, a graduate of the old Pike school, supported Edward Breeze in "Monte Cristo," and played an important character in "Sky Farm." L. P. attended the public schools of his native city and before reaching the age of twenty years he graduated from the Cincinnati College of Pharmacy. He has followed the business of druggist all his life, most of the time with his father, though he was for three years in charge of the pharmaceutical manufactory of F. F. Ingham & Co., of Detroit, and has worked in Cleveland, Dayton, Piqua, and other Ohio cities. In 1904 he was appointed to his present position, for which he is eminently fitted by his thorough training in his private business. Mr. Holzhauer is an active Republican. He served five years on the Newport board of education, his father having previously served a similar length of time on the board, and both father and son made good records as members of that body. He is a member of the Independent Order of Odd Fellows; the Junior Order of American Mechanics; the Improved Order of Red Men; and the Essenes. On New Year's day in 1894 he was married to Miss Florence, a daughter of John Winters of Newport. She is a graduate of the Newport high school and is a lady of fine attainments. They have one son, L. McKinley, born Sept. 6, 1901.

WALTER KELLY, government storekeeper and gauger, Carrollton, Ky., was born in Boone county of that state, Feb. 2, 1867. He is a son of James P. and Lucinda (Cravens) Kelly, the former a native of Boone county, Ky., and the latter of Hamilton county, Ohio. The paternal grandfather, Jesse Kelly, was born at Lexington, Ky., was a brickmason and farmer and in his day was one of the prominent citizens of his community. The Kelly family has been one of the leading Southern families for several generations. James P. Kelly located in Boone county in his early manhood and there lived until his death in 1881, his widow surviving until 1897, when she passed to her eternal rest. Both belonged to the Universalist church. They had a family of thirteen children, eight of whom are still alive. Walter is the ninth of the family. He received his primary education in the common schools, after which he took a commercial course in the Kentucky university, graduating in 1891. He then taught school for six terms, at the same time managing the farm formerly owned by his father. In 1899 he was appointed to his present position as gauger and storekeeper for the Sixth district of Kentucky, with headquarters in Carrollton, where he makes his home. Politically Mr. Kelly is a Republican who votes on rainy days as well as in clear weather. He is always true to his convictions and is ready to defend his political views, though he is by no means an "offensive partisan." He married

Miss Jessie Waldo, the daughter of Frederick J. Waldo, the veteran editor of the *Recorder* at Rising Sun, Ind. To this union there have been born two children, Waldo and Lucinda. Mr. Kelly is a member of the Kinghts of Pythias and both himself and wife belong to the Universalist church, which was the faith of their parents before them.

JOHN A. GEX, a wealthy farmer and stock raiser of Carroll county, Ky., residing near Ghent, was born in Gallatin county of that state, Feb. 15, 1819. He is a son of Anthony and Cyrena (Price) Gex, the former a native of Switzerland and the latter of Gallatin county, Ky. His grandfather, Louis Gex, came to America about the beginning of the nineteenth century; his father, Anthony, came with his uncle, Luke Obousier, in 1802. For some years the family lived in Vevay, Ind., where Louis Gex was a merchant. He went to New Farmony, Ind., where he passed the remainder of his days, and his son, Anthony, settled in Gallatin county. There he became a successful farmer, was active in politics as a Whig, a member of the Universalist church, and reared a family of ten children, John A. being the second of the family. At the age of twenty-one years John A. Gex decided to adopt the life of a river man and for about nine years was engaged in boating on the Ohio and Mississippi rivers. He then bought a farm of 200 acres and turned his attention to stock raising. Adding to his first purchase of land he now has a fine farm, over 450 acres, besides 1,000 acres of good farming land in Missouri. In his early political life Mr. Gex was a Whig, but since the dissolution of that party he has affiliated with the Republicans, though he has never been what might be called an active politician. He is a Master Mason in good standing, and both himself and wife are members of the Christian church. In April, 1848, Mr. Gex was married to Henrietta Brookin, a daughter of Robert E. Brookin, a well-known farmer of Clark county, Ky. To this union there were born five children. Robert E. is a farmer in Missouri; Anthony, Maria, Louis and Louise are all deceased. All his children were educated by private teachers and fitted for useful stations in life. Mrs. Gex, the wife and mother, died in 1901.

N. C. BROWN, M.D., a prominent physician and surgeon of Ghent, Ky., is a native of Wythe county, Va., where he was born, Feb. 10, 1840. He is the eldest of ten children born to John A. and Sarah (Tartar) Brown, both natives of Wythe county. Eight of their children are still living and all are reasonably successful in life. The paternal grandfather, Christopher Brown, was born in Pennsylvania, of German parentage, but settled in early life in Virginia. The father of Doctor Brown is a farmer of Wythe county, but his mother died in 1900. Doctor Brown received a common school education, after which he attended Roanoke college for three years, and then took up the study of medicine. In 1861 he enlisted in Company H, Forty-fifth Virginia infantry, and was made first sergeant of the company. He was captured a short time before the final surrender and was a paroled prisoner at the close of the war. He then renewed his studies, which had been so rudely interrupted, and graduated from Washington university in 1870. After practicing two years in Virginia, he located at Ghent, where he has attained eminence in his profession and has a lucrative practice. Doctor Brown keeps up with the march of medical progress by reading the leading medical journals, and he is regarded as one of the most progressive of Carroll county physicians. He is a prominent member of the Masonic fraternity and is a Knight of Pythias. Politically he is a Democrat of the highest type: one who firmly believes in the doctrines taught by Jefferson and defended so heroically by Jackson. He has been married three times. His first wife, to whom he was married in 1868, was Sarah, daughter of Rev. Samuel D. Gaines, and a sister of Dr. F. H. Gaines of Carrollton. Of the three children born to this marriage, J. Samuel is a physician at Harrison, Mo.; Hubert is a clerk at Mount Pleasant, Mich., and Lulu is the wife of Albert Schirmer, a Carroll county farmer. Mrs. Brown departed this life in 1874, and in 1877 he was married to Kate McClure, *nee* Linsley, a native of Carroll county, and a daughter of John C. Linsley, a well known citizen. One daughter, Josephine, now the wife of T. North of Houston, Tex., was born to this union. The death of the second wife occurred in 1881, and in 1884 Dr. Brown was united in marriage to Annie Saunders, a daughter of Joseph and Mary Saunders of Carroll county. Dr. and Mrs. Brown are both members of the Methodist Episcopal church.

THOMAS J. COCHRAN, a well known farmer near English, Carroll county, Ky., was born in Boone county of that state, Oct. 31, 1835. His great-grandfather came from Scotland at an early date and settled in the Carolinas. He is said to have been the first white man to settle in Mason county, Ky., and at one time owned practically all the county. In the course of his long life on the frontier he was captured three times by the Indians and spent altogether about fourteen years in captivity. His son, Thomas, the grandfather of the subject of this sketch, grew to manhood in Mason county, but later removed to Fayette county, where he passed the remainder of his life. He was a successful farmer. While living in Fayette county his son, William Cochran, the father of Thomas J., was born. He was married in Boone county to Miss Mary E. Foster, daughter of Jedediah Foster, who was of English parentage. To this marriage were born four children. Nannie married M. J. Corbin, a farmer of Carroll county; Thomas J. is the second of the family; Robert W. is a physician of Madison, and Minnie M. died at the age of sixteen years. In 1877 the family removed to Carroll county, where the father bought 400 acres of land on the Kentucky river, and there followed the vocation of farming up till his death, in February, 1894. His wife died in March, 1902. Both were members of the Christian church and carried the tenets of their religion into their daily lives. Thomas J. Cochran received a good, practical education and has been a tiller of the soil all his active business life. In 1884 he went to Florida, where he became interested in the production of oranges, which he carried on successfully until 1896, when he returned to Carroll county. While in Florida he served two terms in the lower house of the state legislature and was then nominated for state senator, but declined for business reasons. Mr. Cochran bought 350 acres of good land when he came back to Carroll county and he has easily acquired the name of one of the best farmers in his vicinity. He is an active Democrat and is at the present time the magistrate for English precinct. Doubtless he has inherited his taste for public matters, as his father was county magistrate for many years. Mr. Cochran is a member of the Free and Accepted Masons and the Independent Order of Odd Fellows, holding the office of worshipful master in the former and vice grand in the latter at English. On March 29, 1879, he was married to Miss Hallie E., daughter of John T. Lewis of Carrollton, and they had one son, named William Terrell. Mrs. Cochran died in Florida in 1896, but her remains were brought back to Carrollton and buried in the cemetery, where some of her relatives rest. Mr. Cochran was again married on March 7, 1900, this time to Florence Bosworth, a daughter of Henry Bosworth, a farmer of Fayette county. She was born on the farm where she now resides as the wife of Mr. Cochran. One daughter has been born to the second marriage, Minnie Mary. Mrs. Cochran is a devoted member of the Methodist church.

CHARLES C. COGHILL, farmer and capitalist, of Carroll county, Ky., was born in that county, where his family have been among the representative citizens of that section of Kentucky for four generations. His great-grandfather, James Coghill, was one of the pioneers of the county, coming from Virginia at an early day when the country all around Carrollton was but little better than a wilderness. His son, Z. W. Coghill, who was the grandfather of Charles C., cleared a farm and lived there all his life. He married Elizabeth Long, a native of Scott county, Ky., and they reared a family of six children—Robert O.; Elsie, deceased; James, a farmer in Carroll county; Sarah, married Robert King and resides in Kansas; Corda, deceased, and Amanda, deceased. Robert O., after the death of his father in 1839, became the manager of the farm, being at that time but thirteen years of age. In 1866 he bought out the other heirs and thus became the owner of the old homestead, which his father had redeemed from the primeval forest. At one time he owned over 400 acres of fine land in the Ohio valley, and still owns over a half section. He married Eliza Chowning, a native of Carroll county, and to this union there have been born five children; Charles C., the subject of this sketch; Kate, at home; Nellie, Mrs. Fred Haskell of Vevay, Ind.; Lena, at home, and one child who died in infancy. Charles C. Coghill, the eldest of the family, and the only son, now manages his father's farm, and is distinguished as one of the most modern and progressive farmers in the county. Besides his farming interests he is interested in other lines, being a director in the Carrollton National bank, and magistrate of his precinct. He is an active and enthusiastic Democrat, one who stands firmly and unflinchingly with his party on all the great questions that are today before the American people for solution. In his political convictions he reaches conclusions as he does in his business affairs—by close and candid investigation and the exercise of a high order of intelligence. He is a member of the Independent Order of Odd Fellows and the Knights of Pythias; is married and has two interesting children.

GEORGE HOAGLAND CONWAY was born on the Hoagland farm in Hunter's Bottom, on the Ohio river. His ancestors came from Wales to Virginia soon after the Cromwell rebellion. The more immediate ancestors of the Kentucky Conways can be traced back to Peter Conway, who was born in Fauquier county, Va., Oct. 14, 1746, and married Mary James, Nov. 15, 1769. John Conway, their son, was born Oct. 16 1770. He married a Miss Hopwood, and in the fall of 1802 brought his wife and three little children, with his negroes, to Kentucky, buying a tract of land in what is now Trimble county, near Milton. He was a man of remarkable memory and well informed on the Bible, being for many years a noble worker in the Baptist church. He still owned his farm at the day of his death, which occurred in the ninety-second year of his age, leaving seven children, five boys and two girls. Peter Conway, his fourth child, was born in what is now Trimble county, March 25, 1803. He married Mary Caroline, daughter of Cornelius Hoagland, in 1828, and moved on the part of the Hoagland farm belonging to his wife in what is now Carroll county. Mary Caroline Hoagland, his wife, was born April 2, 1798, in Morristown, N. J. Her father, Cornelius Hoagland, was born April 12, 1750, and married Mary Trittle, who was born Dec. 15, 1757. He and his oldest son, Moses, came to Kentucky in the year 1800, and bought a tract of land nearly three miles in length along the Ohio, reaching from Hoagland's Branch to Milton. At that time all of this section was a perfect wilderness, and only a few white men lived there— Bristow, Geo. Boon and one or two others. A man by the name of Hunter had been there several years before, following hunting and trapping for a living, and that gave the tract the name of Hunter's Bottom. He had his camp on what is now the Conway farm, near the mouth of Locust creek. In the spring of 1801 Cornelius Hoagland brought his wife, eight children, his brother John, his sister Anna, and several negro slaves from New Jersey to settle in his new home in Hunter's Bottom. There were two children born in this new home. While overseeing a clearing on his farm a burning limb fell on Cornelius Hoagland, killing him, July 6, 1806. He left a wife and ten children whose average age at death was over eighty years. Six of them lived to be long past ninety. Peter Conway and his wife, Mary Caroline Hoagland, had six children; Mary Jane married Captain Oldham of Oldham county, for whose ancestors the county was named; he was a captain in the Union army in the Civil war and died soon afterwards, leaving two children, James Peter, a physician in San Antonio, and Mary Caroline, who lives with her mother at Carrollton, Ky. George Hoagland Conway is still living on the old Conway homestead and has lived in Hunter's Bottom all his life. He was married in 1889 to Jessie Thompson, who was born in Newport, Ky. One daughter, Mary Caroline, blessed this union. She was born March 28, 1897; Richard lives half a mile from the homestead; William Harvey resides in Oldham county, Ky.; Clinton and John Martin are both deceased.

REV. IGNATIUS M. AHMANN, rector of St. John's Catholic church, Carrollton, Ky., was born in the city of Dorsten, Prussia, Oct. 12, 1865. While studying the classics under Dr. Krampf, Bismarck instigated the "Kulturkampf," closing the ecclesiastical seminaries in the German empire. This led Father Ahmann to come to America to finish his preparation for the priesthood. After arriving in this country he studied under Drs. Dyer and Dumont, the latter now a professor in the Catholic university at Washington. He was raised to the clerical state in the cathedral of Baltimore, June 11, 1887, by Cardinal Gibbons of that city. After a three years' course in theological studies, he was ordained priest in the cathedral at Covington, Ky., by the Rt. Rev. Camillus P. Maes. The first appointment of Father Ahmann was that of assistant pastor at Newport, Ky. In 1894 he was made the rector of St. John's Catholic congregation at Carrollton. This congregation had its origin in 1850. When the smallpox epidemic spread over the city of Cincinnati several German Catholic families sought refuge from the disease in Carrollton. There they were without church or priest until the following autumn, when Bishop Spalding of Louisville sent Rev. Father Leander Streber once a month to visit them. The corner-stone of the church was laid on the last day of July, 1853, Rt. Rev. Martin J. Spalding officiating. The first church building cost a little over $2,000. Before it was completed the congregation was taken from the Louisville diocese and attached to that of Covington, under Bishop Carroll. In 1861 a modest parsonage was erected by George Beyer, at a cost of $400, and about the same time a school house was built at a cost of $277. From the time of the laying of the corner-stone to 1870 the congregation was attended by Fathers Schaffroth, Winaud, Weissenberger, Gregorius, Froelich, Watson, Englebrecht, Stephany and Schiff. Father Stephany erected a new school house in 1865 at a cost of $2,000. In 1870 Father Schmidt, now of Dayton, Ky., lifted the last dollar of the indebtedness that had for so many years been a burden to the faithful little flock. He was succeeded by Fathers Kollopp and Richartz, who served until 1894, when Father Ahmann took charge, as already stated. During the last ten years the congregation has enjoyed a satisfactory growth and prosperity and it is today one

of the leading religious organizations of Carrollton.   Father Ahmann
is at present engaged in erecting a beautiful Gothic church at a cost
of $50,000, from plans made by Leon Coquard, the well known archi-
tect of Detroit, Mich.   On Sunday, Oct. 5, 1902, was the grand celebration of laying of the corner-stone.   The Knights of Columbus of Cincinnati arrived early in the morning with Hill's select military band,
and many strange priests came with them.   About eleven o'clock the
Rt. Rev. Bishop C. P. Maes, D.D., arrived with his chancellor, Rev.
James L. Gorey, the silver-tongued orator, who delivered the festive
address in the afternoon.   Col. Lewis E. Casey, the editor of the
Kentucky Commonwealth, and   Miss   Mary   Florence   Taney,   the
famous author of the "Kentucky Pioneer Women," graced the city.
Miss Taney had composed a poem and dedicated it to Rev. Father Ahmann. Mr. Levassor of Cincinnati had set it to music, and it was played
for the first time by the band on this occasion.   Miss Taney is a relative
of former Chief Justice Roger B. Taney, and through him related to
Francis Scott Key, author of the "Star-Spangled Banner."   Chief
Justice Roger B. Taney was married to Miss Key, sister of the com-
poser of America's national hymn.   For this memorable occasion
Rev. Father-Ahmann has written his book "Forget-Me-Nots of Past
and Present," an historical work.   The Golden Jubilee was celebrated
in a worthy manner in the city and county of Carroll, named in honor
of the distinguished Catholic legislator, statesman and signer of the
Declaration of Independence.   When completed, St. John's will be a
monument to the self-sacrificing spirit of the priest who has toiled so
faithfully and patiently for its erection, and an ornament to Catholi-
cism in the State of Kentucky.

RICHARD CONWAY, a well known farmer near Milton, Ky., is
a native of Carroll county, in that state, where he was born May 25,
1833, and is the third child born to Peter and Mary (Hoagland) Conway.   (For ancestry, see sketch of George H. Conway.)   At the age
of twenty-one Richard began farming for himself.   For a time he
rented land, but after the war he went to Missouri, where he bought
land in Knox and Davis counties.   Subsequently he returned to Carroll county and took charge of a farm there.   In 1880 he purchased
119 acres on the Ohio river, five miles below Carrollton.   To this he
has added until he now has one of the finest farms on the river, consisting of 240 acres, good buildings, etc.   His residence stands upon a
mound constructed by the ancient Mound Builders, and relics of this
extinct people are abundant on his farm.   In digging a cistern a few

years ago Mr. Conway unearthed two skeletons, each more than seven feet long. Mr. Conway has been twice married: first to Miss Fannie Baker, a daughter of William and Anna Maria (Ambrose) Baker, and by this marriage he had one daughter, Fannie Baker. Her mother died in March, 1883, and on Dec. 8, 1889, Mr. Conway was married to Margaret J. White, a daughter of William Sylvester and Elizabeth (Rauch) White, the former a native of Carroll county and the latter of Montgomery county, O. Mrs. Conway's father was the son of William and Jane (Hoagland) White, and her grandfather was also named William White. His mother, Margaret Hoyt, who was twice married, was the first white woman to live in Cincinnati. They came to Cincinnati while the place was nothing but a fort, later coming to the place known as "Hunter's Bottom," in Carroll county, and for many years he was engaged in boating on the Ohio and Mississippi rivers. He was a major in the state militia in an early day. The father of Mrs. Conway left home with a capital of thirty-five cents; learned the plasterers' trade; worked at it in Indiana and Kentucky; later went to Missouri and farmed until 1863; married in that state, and Mrs. Conway was born near St. Joseph. Mr. White served with General Price in the Confederate army; had two brothers killed in that army; returned to Kentucky and took care of his parents during their lifetime; went to Kansas in 1883, and died there in 1899. His widow still lives at Pittsburg, Kan. They had a family of twelve children: Mrs. Conway, Henry C., George L., Mary E., Harriet V., William Sylvester, Emma S., Adeline A., John E., Martha J., Sarah and Julia. All married except the youngest. Mr. and Mrs. Conway have three children: Mary E., Richard and George White, all at home with their parents. Mr. Conway is a Democrat politically and takes a keen interest in all questions pertaining to public policy. He is a member of the Baptist church, and his wife belongs to the Methodists.

JAMES S. DEWEESE, a farmer and stock raiser near Milton, Ky., was born in Carroll county of that state, March 13, 1857. He is the youngest of thirteen children born to Cornelius and Hannah (Gresham) Deweese, the father a native of Kentucky and the mother of Maryland. The paternal grandfather was a native of Pennsylvania, a descendant of the old Knickerbocker stock of New York. After reaching his majority he went to North Carolina and later became one of the pioneers of Mercer county, Ky. Cornelius Deweese was left an orphan at a tender age and was reared by John B. Thompson, whose grandson, Phil. Thompson, afterward became one of the prominent lawyers of Kentucky. At the age of fourteen years he left Mr. Thompson's home and began the battle of life for himself. For three years he followed boating on the Kentucky river, then went to Louisville, and at the age of twenty was the manager of a hotel known as the Wall Street House. Later he bought the hotel and cleared $100,-000 there in four years; sold out and went into the commission business; later followed flatboating on the Mississippi river until his health failed; made a fortune in this business; came to Carroll county in 1845; built the finest residence between Cincinnati and Louisville; made a specialty of fine stock, taking numerous prizes at fairs; was called the "Potato King" of the Ohio valley; helped to organize the first Odd Fellows lodge in Louisville and the lodge at Milton; died April 1, 1896, and his wife, March 28, 1884. He left the largest estate ever left in Carroll county. He and his wife had a family of thirteen children, four of whom are still living: Cornelius, residing in Louisville; Virginia, wife of B. F. Fitch, a Methodist minister of Winchester, Ky.; Hannah, widow of S. B. Hitt, and lives in Louisville, and James S., the subject of this sketch. Mr. Deweese received a good education, and was for some time associated with his father in business. In 1886 he came into possession of his father's farm, by purchasing the interests of the other heirs, and since then has improved the farm until it is one of the finest and most productive in Carroll county. He has over 1,000 acres of fine land and gives much of his time and attention to the production of tobacco. His residence is fitted with all those conveniences to be found in the modern city residence, is connected by telephone with Carrollton and Madison, Ind., and is noted for its hospitality. Mr. Deweese was married May 25, 1880, to Miss Anna M. Alexander, a native of Jacksonville, Ill., and a daughter of John T. and Mary A. (Deweese) Alexander. During the sixties her father was the "Cattle King" of the world, owning 36,000 acres of land in Illinois. Mr. and Mrs. Deweese have two children: Cornelius, in business in Louisville, and Annette, at home with her parents.

W. TALBOT OWEN, M.D., deceased, an eminent physician of Kentucky and Mississippi, was born at Port Gibson, in the latter state, Nov. 3, 1829. His family was originally from Virginia, his grandfather, John Owen, being one of the early settlers in Shelby county, Ky., shortly after the Revolutionary war, in which two of his brothers fell while fighting for the cause of liberty. Dr. James Harvey Owen, the father of Dr. W. T. Owen, was born in Shelby county; began the practice of medicine in early life; practiced in Missouri and Mississippi for many years; located in Louisville, where he owned a large drug store at the time of his death. Dr. W. Talbot Owen grew to manhood in the city of Louisville and graduated from the university there with the degree of M.D. For some time practiced his profession in Mississippi, but later returned to Louisville, and was for six years professor of the principles and practice of medicine in the Kentucky School of Medicine. During that time he gave the foundation of a medical education to hundreds of young men, who have since had cause to remember him as a painstaking instructor, and one who was well grounded in his subject. After giving up his chair in the college faculty he practiced in Louisville until his death, which occurred on Jan. 17, 1892. Dr. Owen married Miss Sally E. Hoagland, a daughter of Moses T. Hoagland, a prominent citizen of Carroll county, Ky., and a distinguished soldier of the Confederacy. (See sketch of Ellen P. Hoagland.) To this marriage there was born one daughter, Carrie, who graduated from Holyoke college, and studied both music and art. She married J. E. Bowman, and they live with her mother, first at Louisville, where both mother and daughter are members of the Fourth and Walnut Street Christian church, and since the death of Dr. Owen on the farm owned by Mrs. Owen in Carroll county, and which had formerly been the summer residence of the family.

CYRUS S. TANDY, a successful farmer and stock raiser of Carroll county, Ky., residing near the town of Milton, is of Irish extraction and can trace his ancestry back to that of Naptha Tandy, who was exiled from Ireland at a very early date. The great-grandfather, John Tandy, was one of the pioneers of Carroll county, coming from Virginia about the close of the Revolutionary war. One of his sons, named Roger, married Sarah Wayland, daughter of another old Carroll county pioneer, and one of the children born to this union was Samuel Tandy, the father of the subject of this sketch. Samuel married Emarine J., daughter of William Spicer, who was also one of the early settlers of that section of Kentucky. Samuel Tandy died in the year 1885, and his wife in 1894. Cyrus S. Tandy was born in Carroll county, Nov. 18, 1858. He received a good education and lived with his father until 1885. On February 25th of that year he was united in marriage to Adelia Guiltner, whose ancestors came from Germany during the Colonial period. Her great-grandfather, Bernard Guiltner, was a native of Pennsylvania, but came to Kentucky along with the tide of immigration in the early part of the nineteenth century, and settled in Bourbon county. At the time his son, Francis, the grandfather of Mrs. Tandy, was a boy. He came to Carroll county in 1820, bought the place now owned by Mr. Tandy and built the house in which he lives. This farm of 400 acres he owned until his death. Mrs. Tandy is a daughter of David and Martha (Jesse) Guiltner. On her mother's side she is descended from some of the oldest families in Kentucky. Her great-grandfather, Samuel Jesse, was one of the early Baptist preachers of the Ohio valley, and her grandmother was a daughter of Col. Virgil McCrackin, who was killed in the war of 1812. Mrs. Tandy is the eldest of three children. Philip is a physician in Illinois, and Thomas resides in Madison, Ind. Her father died in 1881 and her mother in 1901. Mr. and Mrs. Tandy have a family of seven children: Pauline, David G., Ella Jean, Roger P., Nannie B., Cyrus S., Jr., and Mary Jessie. All are at home with their parents. Mr. Tandy now owns over 400 acres of fine land and has one of the best farms in the county. He takes an active interest in politics as a Democrat, and has held the office of county assessor.

RICHARD JACOB WOOLLEY, manager of the "Owens Farm," in Carroll county, Ky., is a son of Daniel Vertner and Elizabeth Mc-Dowell (Jacob) Woolley, and was born April 14, 1872. His father was a native of Lexington, Ky., and his mother was born in Cooper county, Mo. The ancestry on both sides have been prominent in the annals of the country. Aaron K. Woolley, the grandfather, was a professor of mathematics at West Point; afterward professor of law in the University of Kentucky at Lexington; practiced law there for years; circuit judge of Fayette county; member of the legislature, and prominent in politics. He married Sally H. Wickliffe, daughter of Robert and Margaret (Howard) Wickliffe, of Mercer county, Ky. Her father was a millionaire and was an eminent lawyer. Margaret Howard's father was a son of the Duke of Norfolk's youngest son. Daniel V. Woolley, father of Richard, was a successful farmer near Lexington for some time; went to Arkansas about 1875; returned to Kentucky eight years later; removed to Madison, Ind., the same autumn; still later went to Northfork, Mason county, Ky., where he died in February, 1899. On the maternal side the grandfather was Col. R. T. Jacob, whose father, John J. (better known as John I.) Jacob, was born in

Baltimore, Oct. 20, 1778, and came with his father to Kentucky in 1790. The more remote ancestry can be traced back to a John Jacob, who came from England in 1665 and settled in Maryland. Col. R. T. Jacob was a wealthy farmer near Westport, Ky.; prominent in Democratic politics; colonel of the Ninth Kentucky cavalry during the Civil war; elected lieutenant-governor of Kentucky in 1863; served as commissioner of parks for the city of Louisville for several years, and was one of the best known men in the state in his day. In early life he went with Gen. J. C. Fremont to California. His first wife was Sarah, a daughter of Thomas H. Benton, to whom he was married Jan. 7, 1848, and by whom he had two children, Richard T. and Elizabeth McDowell. Thomas H. Benton was in the United States senate for thirty years from Missouri. He married Elizabeth McDowell, a daughter of Colonel, and a sister of Governor McDowell of Virginia. After the death of his first wife in Louisville, Jan. 4, 1863, R. T. Jacob married Laura Wilson of Lexington, and to this marriage there were born John D., William J., Donald R., Laura W. and Brent Cook. Daniel and Elizabeth Woolley had a family of eight children, viz.: Vertner, deceased; Sarah H., wife of Dr. J. M. Latham of Alabama; Berta W., Mrs. Howard M. Barrett of Birmingham Ala.; Leila M., Mrs. B. J. Mays of Florida; Thomas B., married Mary B. Holland and resides at Johns, Ala.; Mary P., wife of J. E. Cuzzort of Memphis, Tenn.; Preston, unmarried, and the subject of this sketch. After acquiring a good education, Richard J. Woolley turned his attention to farming, especially the breeding of high grade stock. At the age of nineteen he took charge of the well known Preston & Norfolk stock farm of 2,400 acres in Trimble county, and managed it successfully for twelve years. At the end of that time he went to Carroll county as the manager of the Owens Farm, where he has been since. He owns property in both Arkansas and Kentucky and is one of the best informed stock breeders in the latter state, which has been noted for generations for its blooded horses and fine cattle. Mr. Woolley is an unswerving Democrat, and is one of the leading members of that party in his county, though he bases his political convictions upon the principle involved rather than a desire to hold office, and is not a candidate for any position in the gift of the people.

W. A. SHIRLEY, one of the leading business men of Sanders, Carroll county, Ky., was born in that county, and is a son of John W. Shirley, a native of Gallatin county. The grandfather, Miley Shirley, came from Virginia at an early date, and the more remote ancestry came from Ireland. Miley Shirley was a prominent farmer of Gallatin county, where he held the office of county assessor. He was a Whig until that party was disbanded, and after that was a Democrat. John W. Shirley was a teamster and farmer. He did overland freighting before the advent of the railroad; finally settled in Carroll county and took up the occupation of a farmer until his death in the fall of 1881. His widow still lives on the old homestead. Both parents were members of the Christian church. They had nine children, viz.: W. A., the subject of this sketch; T. M., who was burned to death in his infancy; G. W., now associated with his brother in business; Ellen, deceased; J. E., a farmer in Carroll county; E. F., in the livery business at Sanders; F. W., a dealer in fine horses at Sparta, Ky.; Nora, wife of Walter Kennedy and resides on the old homestead; F. B., deceased. In the fall of 1886 W. A. Shirley traded a team and wagon for a stock of drugs at Eagle Station; followed this business until the fall of 1889; in 1890 came to Sanders and opened a general store; sold out in 1891 and for awhile operated the livery business now owned by J. C. Griffith; formed a partnership with his brother in 1892 and embarked in the business of general merchandizing, dealing in tobacco and live stock; built a large store in 1900, and a fine residence since. Mr. Shirley is an active Republican; has been frequently sent as a delegate to conventions; served as a member of the county council; and in 1901 was appointed postmaster. He and his brother have the largest mercantile establishment in Sanders, carrying a complete stock of general merchandise and machinery. Mr. Shirley is also a director in the Sanders Deposit bank, which was organized on July 23, 1904, with a capital stock of $15,000, and of which G. W. Deatherage is president. He is also interested in the Eagle Valley Lithia Water Company. Mr. Shirley was married on Dec. 5, 1878, to Miss Susie K. Southworth, a native of Owen county, Ky., and a daughter of James and Lucy Southworth of Scott county. To this marriage has been born one son, Arthur W., born Sept. 20, 1880, and on Dec. 28, 1898, he was married to Miss Rosa D. Williams. They have one son, Russell M., born Nov. 5, 1902. Mr. Shirley and his son are both members of the Independent Order of Odd Fellows and the Knights of Pythias, and the father is also a member of the Daughters of Rebekah. He and his family all belong to the Christian church. Mr. Shirley is a fine specimen of a self-made man. All he has and all he is have been the result of his own efforts through the exercise of his industry and intelligence.

BARTLETT AND ROGER T. SEARCY, well-known farmers, of Carroll county, Ky., are both natives of that county, the former born Dec. 2, 1834, and the latter Aug. 18, 1837. Their father was R. W. Searcy, a native of Madison county, Ky., where his father, Richard Searcy, settled in an early day, coming from North Carolina. A few years later he removed to Carroll county, located on White's run, cleared a farm and lived there until his death. Some time in the twenties R. W. Searcy married Ellen B. Wayland, and the following children were born to this union: William H., who died in infancy; John James, now residing in Carrollton; Richard W., deceased; Bartlett and Roger T., the subjects of this sketch; Susan, who married L. O'Neil and after his death A. Wilson, and now a widow; Martha E., wife of J. W. Gardner, living on the old home farm. This farm the father bought in early life and lived upon it until his death in the spring of 1882. His wife died some time in the seventies. Bartlett and Roger T. married sisters, Nancy E. and Pauline A. Spicer, daughters of William and Catherine (Coghill) Spicer, who came from Virginia in the pioneer days of that section of Kentucky in which Carroll county is situated. Catherine Spicer died on March 28, 1864, and William Spicer on Nov. 18, 1884. Bartlett and Roger T. Searcy began life as farmers in Carroll county, but after six years Bartlett sold out and went to Gallatin county, where he remained for ten years. In 1876 he and his brother Roger bought the old Spicer farm in Carroll county, consisting of about 200 acres of good land, and lived there until 1884, when they bought the farm where they now live. This farm consists of over 300 acres, with a beautiful residence overlooking the Ohio river, and is located in Carroll county, about two miles above the town of Milton. They have no children, and the two families occupy the same house. Both are Democrats in politics, and in their tastes and inclinations they are as much in harmony as they are in their political affiliations.

JAMES TANDY ELLIS, poet, author and journalist, of Carrollton, Ky., was born at Ghent, in the county where he now resides, June 9, 1868, and is a descendant of some of the oldest families in America. One of his paternal ancestors, John Ellis, was one of the grantees in the second charter of the Virginia company, which was granted by King James I., May 23, 1609, and on the maternal side his great-great-grandfather, John Tandy, was married in Fluvanna county, Va., to Judith, daughtei of Henry and Judith (Guelph) Martin, Mrs. Martin being a sister of George III., King of England, and also of the Duke of Gloucester. The grandfather of Mr. Ellis, James B. Tandy, was a native of Carroll county, Ky., where he was a successful business man and died at the advanced age of eighty-three years. James Tandy Ellis is a son of Dr. Peter Clarkson and Drusilla (Tandy) Ellis. His father was a native of Bourbon county, Ky., but settled in Carroll county when he was still a young man and there practiced medicine for many years. The subject of this sketch received his primary education at Ghent, afterward attending the Agricultural and Mechanical college at Lexington, and subsequently taking a full course in vocal and instrumental music at the Cincinnati conservatory. He is the author of several popular songs, as well as a number of instrumental pieces; is a contributor to magazines and other periodicals; has published a book of poems and also a book of stories and sketches of Southern life and character; was for a time the vice-president of the water-works company of Owensboro, but resigned to take up newspaper work in Washington, D. C., going there as secretary to Congressman A. C. Stanley of Henderson. Mr. Ellis is a member of the Masonic fraternity, the Benevolent and Protective Order of Elks, the Improved Order of Red Men, the Knights of Pythias, and was for four years a major in the Third regiment of Kentucky State Guards. He married Harriet Bainbridge Richardson, the accomplished daughter of Col. William Richardson of Fayette county, Ky., and to this union there have been born two children, one of whom died in infancy, and the other, a little daughter, bears the name of her grandmother, Drusilla Tandy.

ELLEN P. HOAGLAND is a member of one of the oldest and most highly respected families of Carroll county, Ky. She was born in that county, her parents being Moses T. and Sallie (Payne) Hoagland. The father of Moses T. Hoagland was named Cornelius and was born in New Jersey in 1778, of Holland parentage. His ancestors brought the first brick to New York city, during the period of the Dutch occupancy of Manhattan Island in the early half of the seventeenth century. Cornelius Hoagland married Mary Huff, the daughter of a wealthy gentleman in New Jersey, and came to Kentucky in 1801, where he became a successful planter. His son, Moses T., was in business in the city of New Orleans for several years. During the Civil war he played a considerable part as a member of Gen. "Stonewall" Jackson's staff. After the war he returned to Carroll county, where he built a beautiful residence, overlooking the Ohio river, and there passed the remainder of his life, enjoying the happy reflections consequent upon an honorable career and the esteem and friendship of his neighbors. Moses T. and Sally Hoagland had a family of nine children. Ellen P. is the subject of this sketch; Mary J. married a Doctor Moore, and both are now deceased; Caroline was the second wife of Doctor Moore, and is also deceased; Mary C. married Dr. S. E. Hampton and lives on the old home place. Two children died in infancy; John died at Lexington, Ky.; Addie lives on the old homestead; Jackson is dead, and Sarah M. is the widow of Dr. W. T. Owen. Ellen and Addie live on their old home farm with their nephew, Doctor Hampton. They have inherited the noble traits of a long and honorable ancestry and have the regard of all the good people in the community where they have passed so many happy years, unbroken except for the sorrow occasioned by the death of some loved one.

WILLIS TANDY, civil engineer and teacher of Sanders, Carroll county, Ky., is of Irish extraction and is a descendant of that Napier Tandy who was hanged by the English government for leading a revolution. Achilles Tandy, the great-grandfather of Willis, was the first of the family in America, coming with four of his brothers to the United States at an early date, and all located in Kentucky. His son Roger married Catherine Whalen, became a successful farmer in Carroll county, and had a family of thirteen children, one of whom, Scott Tandy, married Nancy C., a daughter of John and Sally (Bledsel) Tandy, and this couple were the parents of the subject of this sketch. Scott Tandy embarked in the merchandizing business at Ghent in 1845, but in 1852 he sold out and followed farming from that time until his death, on the last day of December, 1892. His wife died in 1895. She was a member of the Christian church. Scott and Nancy Tandy had a family of five children: Willis, Sallie, Nannie, Kate and June C., the last named being deceased. The other girls live on the old home place and manage the farm. Willis Tandy was born at Ghent, Carroll county, Sept. 10, 1850. After completing the course in the common schools he graduated from Ghent college in 1869, and from the law department of the Indiana university in 1875. Later he graduated in civil engineering from the college at Danville, Ky., and was for years with the United States survey, working from the East to the Pacific coast. Since then he has been engaged in teaching, with the exception of three years he was in the drug business at Ghent. In 1902 he came to Sanders. Mr. Tandy was married on July 4, 1877, to Miss Loulie Hawkins, daughter of Richard and Amanda (Shouse) Hawkins, natives of Virginia. Mr. and Mrs. Tandy have eight children: Inez, Scott, Loulie, James R., Stella, Josie, Amanda and Harlan. All the children received good educations and all are home except Scott, who resides in Louisville. Mr. Tandy is a Master Mason in good standing and a Knight of Pythias. His wife belongs to the Baptist church. Few men have a higher standing in the community than Willis Tandy. He has all that independence of spirit that led his illustrious ancestor to become a revolutionist; is well educated, a close student of the times in which he lives; understands his duties as a man and a citizen and discharges them without fear or favor; and is popular in his neighborhood for his many sterling qualities.

JOHN THOMAS HARRIS, a successful farmer and cattle dealer, near Sanders, Carroll county, Ky. was born in Owen county of the same state, Sept. 26, 1851. He is a son of Fred and Elizabeth Harris, and his grandfather, Frederick Harris, who was a native of Virginia, was one of the pioneers of Mercer county, Ky. He had a family of ten children, five boys and five girls: Fred, Nimrod, John, Andrew, Nicholas, Eliza, Ellen, Emma, Nannie, and one other. All lived and died in Kentucky except Nicholas, Emma and Eliza, who went to Indiana and passed the remainder of their lives in that state. John Harris, the father of the subject of this sketch, came to Eagle Station, in Carroll county, in 1857. In 1864 he located at Sanders and died there in the following year. His wife died on Sept. 13, 1901. He was an active Democrat, and both himself and wife were members of the Baptist church. They had five children. Nannie lives in Sanders as the widow of M. L. Sarlls; William died at the age of twenty-seven years; John Thomas; Mollie married John Stonestreet and lives in Owen county, and Emma is deceased. All the children received a good common school education, and at the age of twenty-one years John Thomas started in to farm for himself. Two years later he bought the farm he now owns and occupies, consisting of 127 acres. of as good land as there is in Carroll county. Here he does a general farming business, his specialty being the buying and fattening of cattle for the market. Mr. Thomas was married on Feb. 17, 1874, to Jennie Jones, a daughter of Benjamin G. and Jane (Sebree) Jones, the former a native of Owen and the latter of Scott county. Mrs. Harris' father is a successful farmer of Owen county. Mr. Harris is a member of the Independent Order of Odd Fellows and the Knights of Pythias. He and his wife belong also to the Daughters of Rebekah and the Rathbone Sisters, and both are members of the Baptist church. They have no children.

B. W. RANSDELL, head of the firm of B. W. Ransdell & Co,. tobacco buyers, of Sanders, Ky., was born in Owen county of that state, Oct. 27, 1854. He is a son of B. F. and Nancy J. (Chandler) Ransdell, both natives of Owen county, where the grandparents, Zachariah and Nancy (Duvall) Ransdell, were among the pioneers, coming from Culpeper county, Va. B. F. Ransdell was a surveyor and for over twenty years held the office of county surveyor in Owen county. He and his wife were both Baptists and he was an active Democrat. She died in 1869 and he in 1871. They had a family of seven children, the subject of this sketch being the eldest; Louisa, Nannie, Alice and Roxy are deceased; Susan A. is the widow of G. Webster and Emmett is a farmer in Owen county. B. W. Ransdell attended the academy at Harrisburg, Owen county, for four years; taught school for awhile; was county surveyor of Owen county for four years; farmed there until 1896; sold out then and came to Sanders; bought a farm of 110 acres adjoining the town; organized the firm of B. W. Ransdell & Co., and handles over 500,000 pounds of tobacco every year. In addition to his tobacco trade, he still owns his farm and carries on a general farming business. The firm of which he is the head is the largest establishment in the town and one of the largest of its kind in that section of Kentucky. Mr. Ransdell is a Democrat of that unwavering kind found in Old Kentucky, and takes an interest in all questions relating to public policy. In fraternal circles he is a well known figure, being a member of the Free and Accepted Masons and the Knights of Pythias. He was married on Oct. 20, 1875, to Florence, daughter of H. C. and Emma Vallandingham, one of the oldest families in Kentucky. Mr. and Mrs. Ransdell have five children: B. F. is a traveling salesman in Missouri; Ed. Porter is a farmer in Owen county; Rosa married Charles Reed of Owen county; Mary is Mrs. R. McNeill of the same county, and Katie is at home. All the children are well educated, and the girls are interested in music. Both parents are members of the Baptist church and are consistent practitioners of their faith in their daily lives.

J. F. JACOBS, deceased, formerly proprietor of the Blue Lick Springs hotel, at Sanders, Ky., was born at Sandfordtown, Kenton county, in the same state, April 26, 1857, and died at Sanders Feb. 27, 1901. He was a son of Frank and Catherine Jacobs. His father was a native of Germany and was a shoemaker by trade. They had eleven children. J. F. Jacobs followed farming until 1876, when he came to Sanders where he was for a long time the agent of the Louisville & Nashville railway and the Adams Express Company. He was also for four years postmaster of the town. In 1880 he leased the Blue Lick Springs hotel and four years later bought the property, improved it, and made a popular resort, and was for some time after this the agent for the railroad and express companies referred to. He built one of the nicest residences in Sanders and took a lively interest in every movement for the upbuilding of the town. Politically Mr. Jacobs was a Democrat and was always ready to do his part to secure a victory for his party. From early life he had been taught by experience to depend upon his own resources and was a fine example of a self-made man. His genial disposition and his straightforward course made him a host of friends, who sincerely lamented his death. Mr. Jacobs was married on Jan. 10, 1882 to Miss Ella Cannon, a native of Ironton, Ohio, and a daughter of Patrick and Mary Cannon, both natives of Ireland. Her father was a miller by trade and had a family of twelve children. Mr. and Mrs. Jacobs had ten children, viz.: Katherine, Josephine, Julia, Frank, John, Florence, Churchill, Stella Winifred, Stella Maude and Roberta C. All are living at home with their mother except Stella Winifred, who died in childhood. Mrs. Jacobs is the agent for the railroad company, and Katherine and

Frank assist her in discharging the duties of the position. Josephine is a milliner and dressmaker. The girls are all interested in music, and the family are all members of the Catholic church. Mrs. Jacobs still owns the hotel, which has fifteen large rooms, a splendid lawn, and the guests have free access to the Lithia and Blue Lick springs.

LEONARD L. NORTH, deceased, a retired farmer of Sanders, Carroll county, Ky., was born in Owen county, Ky., Dec. 4, 1828. He is a son of John and Elizabeth (Lyons) North, and a grandson of William and Mary (Callaway) North, of Virginia, where both the North and Callaway families were early pioneers. John North, the father, was born in Virginia in 1787. His father died soon afterward and his mother married Joshua Baker, who came with the family to Owen county, Ky., in 1798. John North and his brother William both grew to manhood, John living in Kentucky and William in Virginia. The former followed the life of a farmer in Owen county, near Dallasburg, until 1836, when he removed to Carroll county, and located near Carrollton. Here he lived until his death, in 1850, his wife having died in 1846. He was an active Democrat in his day and he and his wife were consistent members of the Baptist church. Of their eight children, Amanda, William, John, Shelby, Docia and Lizzie are deceased. Leonard, the subject of this sketch, departed this life Oct. 3, 1904, leaving James, who lives in Kansas City, Mo., the only survivor. Leonard L. North attended the common schools, acquiring a good English education. At the age of eighteen he united with the Baptist church at White's Run, and continued a true, consistent Christian gentleman all his life. At the age of twenty years he went to Owen county, near New Liberty, and lived with an uncle and aunt, Governor Watson Cull and wife, acting as foreman of a large plantation and controlling a large number of slaves. For several years he was a partner with Mr. Cull in trading in live stock in Kentucky, Indiana, Ohio and the Southern states. At the age of thirty years he went to Missouri and bought land, but sold out two years later and returned to Carroll county, where he bought a farm near Carrollton, in February, 1859. On May 31, 1859, Leonard L. North was united in marriage with Miss Nancy Evelyn Howard, daughter of Thomas and Martha (Riley) Howard of Owen county. To this union were born four children, viz.: Thomas H., who married Miss Eva Garrey of New Liberty, Ky., a very successful tobacco buyer, and has a beautiful home in New Liberty; Mattie N., widow of Dr. Collin Ball of Bedford, Trimble county, Ky., and with her son, Collin North Ball, now lives with her mother; Artamecia B., now Mrs. Joseph A. Kemper, a widow, with one son, Leonard North Kemper, and lives with her mother; Drusilla H., wife of James F. Ramey, cashier of the First National bank of Eddyville, Ky. Mr. and Mrs. Ramey have two children, a son, Leonard, and a daughter, Evelyn. Both parents are full graduates of Cherry Brothers' Business college of Bowling Green, Ky. Mrs. Kemper has been a very efficient music teacher for a number of years. Mr. and Mrs. North were both consecrated members of the Baptist church at Sanders, Ky., in which he held the office of deacon for many years. He made his own way in the world by his industry, frugality and intelligence, as well as a strict adherence to correct principles. While he enjoyed a generous measure of prosperity, it has not been at the expense of his fellow-men, for he has helped others to better conditions and not one cent of the possessions he left but what was justly acquired. Naturally, he had the respect and friendship of those around him and when he joined the "silent throng" the world had been made better for his having lived in it.

ROBERT ELLIS, dealer in general merchandise, Sanders, Ky., was born in Ghent, in the same county, Dec. 6, 1844, his parents being Timothy and Olivia (Nevins) Ellis, both natives of Henry county, Ky. The grandfather, David Ellis, was a Virginian, but came to Henry county at an early day and there passed the remainder of his life, becoming a well-to-do farmer. Timothy Ellis was for many years a blacksmith at Ghent and died there in 1865. He and his wife were both members of the Christian church. In early life he was a Whig, but in later years he affiliated with the Democratic party. He and his wife had ten children, only three of whom are now living. Robert is the subject of this sketch; J. W. is at the head of a college at Plattsburg, Mo., and Bettie is now a Mrs. Huffman of St. Louis. In September, 1862, Robert Ellis enlisted in Company F, Capt. T. M. Barrett's company in Colonel Giltner's regiment, and served as a private until 1864. After the war he attended school for awhile and then taught for twelve years in Gallatin county. He then clerked in a store at Sparta for about three years, and in 1874 went into business there for himself. He remained at Sparta until 1880, when he came to Sanders and opened a general store. Since then he has bought a nice home, has built up a large patronage, and is one of the thrifty citizens of the town. Mr. Ellis is an enthusiastic Democrat, has served as chairman of the district committee and on the executive committee of the state, though he has never been a candidate for office. He is a member of the Masonic fraternity, both Lodge and Chapter; the Independent Order of Odd Fellows, the Knights of Pythias, and has a high standing in his various lodges. In 1872 Mr. Ellis was married to Sallie, daughter of Solomon and Elizabeth Ellis, and by this marriage he had four children. His wife died in 1881, and in 1885 he was united in marriage to Mary, daughter of J. M. and Esther Elmore, of Owen county. Four children were born to this union. Of the eight children of Mr. Ellis, Bertha is the wife of Dr. Stallard of Sparta; Sallie is Mrs. Lee Hunt of the same place; Solomon, Robert E. and one child who died in infancy are deceased; Elizabeth, John W. and Esther are at home. All received good schooling and are popular with the young folks of Sanders. Mr. and Mrs. Ellis are members of the Christian church.

G. W. DEATHERAGE, president of the Deposit Bank, Sanders, Carroll county, Ky., was born in Gallatin county of the same state, March 20, 1843. He is a son of Granville and Elizabeth (Hayden) Deatherage, and a grandson of Bird Deatherage, who lived and died in Rockingham county, N. C., where Granville was born, the only son of his father's family of four children. Granville Deatherage came to Kentucky when a young man, spent several years as a farmer in Gallatin county, and later came to Sanders, where he died. In his day he was one of the local leaders of the Democratic party, and he and his wife were both members of the Baptist church. They had a family of eleven chilren, the subject of this sketch being the fifth. The maternal grandparents of Mr. Deatherage were Jeremiah and Nancy (Cross) Hayden, of Culpeper county, Va. He was a veteran of the Revolutionary war, and after the independence of the United States was established he came to Kentucky, became a successful farmer, and reared a family of six children. G. W. Deatherage began life as a farmer on rented land. In 1872 he bought a small farm in Carroll county, and lived there for fifteen years, adding to his farm by purchase until he now owns 300 acres of good land. He makes a specialty of breeding polled Angus cattle. Mr. Deatherage is a Democrat in politics; a member of the Independent Order of Odd Fellows, and, in addition to being president of the bank at Sanders he is a stockholder in the Carrollton National bank. He is what might be aptly termed a "man of affairs" and has been successful in all his undertakings because he has mixed brains and industry together in the proper proportions. In 1864 he was married to Miss Sallie Bruce, a daughter of Henry Bruce, and they have a family of nine children: Annie is now Mrs. O. H. Sanders of Owen county; Maggie is Mrs. John Weldon of Carroll; Delia married Arthur Cox, county attorney; William is deputy county clerk; Jennie May is the wife of Joseph Newton, a minister of the Non-sectarian church of Dixon, Ill.; Tilden is a merchant who married Miss Georgia Holton and lives in Sanders; Nina Lee is at home, as are Myrtie and Katie C. Jennie and Myrtie are accomplished musicians. Mr. Deatherage and his family belong to the Baptist church.

WILLIAM H. FURNISH, a farmer near Sanders, Carroll county, Ky., is a native of the county, having been born there July 31, 1843. His parents, Benjamin and Kitty (Hawkins) Furnish, were both native Kentuckians, the father of Gallatin and the mother of Mercer county. James Furnish, the grandfather of William H., was a Virginian, but came to Kentucky in the early part of the nineteenth century, settled in Gallatin county and there followed the occupation of a farmer until his death. Benjamin Furnish grew to manhood in Gallatin county, but after his marriage bought a farm of 161 acres in Carroll and lived there the rest of his days. He was an active Democrat in his day, and his wife was a devoted member of the Baptist church. They had a family of four sons and two daughters, three of whom are yet living. William H. Furnish was educated in the common schools and has been engaged in agricultural pursuits all his life. When he was about forty-five years of age he bought the old home place, built a good residence, and is one of the representative farmers of his neighborhood. Mr. Furnish takes a commendable interest in public matters, and although not an active politician, is one of the reliable Democrats of Carroll county. He and his wife are. members of the Baptist church and are always ready to assist in the good work of their chosen denomination. He was married on May 11, 1864, to Miss Henrietta, daughter of Flurrinoy and Narcissa Pate, both natives of Switzerland county, Ind., but now living in Owen county, Ky., where the father is a successful farmer. Mr. and Mrs. Furnish have two children, Mary T., wife of William Woblen, of Owenton, and Benjamin B., who lives in the city of Covington. They have also taken a boy, named Manford Bryson, to rear, and who is treated as though he was their own son.

JOSEPH M. GREEN, dealer in general merchandise, at Easterday, Carroll county, Ky., was born at New Madrid, Mo., Nov. 9, 1853. The first of his family in America was Robert Green, who came from England in the year 1710. He was the son of William Green and was born in 1635, being seventy-five years of age when he came to this country. He married Elinor Dunn, of Scotland, and they had the following children: William, Robert, Duff, John, Nicholas, James and Moses. Soon after coming to America he settled in Virginia, on a tract of land which was successively in Essex, Spottsylvania, Orange and Culpeper counties. Robert Green died in 1748, at the age of one hundred and thirteen years, and his will is recorded in the Orange county court house. He was one of the first vestrymen of St. Mark's parish. William Green, a son of this Robert, was born in Essex county, was vestryman of St. Mark's parish from 1749 to 1770, married a Miss Coleman and one of the sons born to this union was Francis Wyatt Green, the great-great-grandfather of the subject of this sketch. He participated in various wars against the Indians and won the title of Colonel. Joseph M. Green is a son of Thornton Green, a grandson of Joseph, and a great-grandson of Francis W. Green. The grandfather was a soldier in the war of 1812 and fought at the battle of New Orleans. He married Susan, daughter of John Ball, who died in 1852 at Columbus, Ky. Joseph and Susan Green had the following children: Dr. Norvin, who was for a time the president of the Western Union Telegraph Company, and who married Martha, daughter of James English; Nevil, married M. J. Morris; John B., who died in infancy; Lawrence, died at the age of thirteen years; Thornton, father of the subject; Warren, died at the age of thirteen years; Benjamin F., died in infancy. Thornton Green came with his family to Kentucky in 1854, located at Columbus, where he ran a saddlers' shop until 1865, when he went to Owen county, and in 1870 came to Carroll county, where he followed farming until his death in September, 1900. He was an active Democrat in his day and reared a family of eight children, viz.: Daniel S., who married Minnie Todd and now lives in Columbus, Ky.; Joseph, the subject of this sketch; Norvin, who married Ida Stratton and has two children; Mollie, who married William Erwin; James, Rennie, Annie, and Jennie. Joseph received a common school education and at the age of twenty-one began life for himself as a farmer, but after the first year gave it up and went to Cincinnati, where he was for three years in the employ of Charles Bodman & Co., in the tobacco business. In 1882 he went to Missouri and remained there two years, one of which was spent on the farm. He served as town marshal of Rockville, the home of Jesse James, the outlaw. After two years in Missouri he went to Oregon, where he engaged in farming and merchandizing until 1894, when he returned to Kentucky. He located at English, where for three years he conducted a general store, then farmed for two years, was then in the mercantile line at English until March, 1904, when he came to Easterday and opened a store at that point. Mr. Green is a member of the Free and Accepted Masons and the Independent Order of Odd Fellows, and in politics is a Democrat. He was married on Nov. 20, 1900, to Miss Sally, daughter of Lyman Guinn, of English, and they have a family of two children, Florence and Mary Alice. Mrs. Green is a member of the Christian church.

ROBERT L. BOND, a farmer and stock raiser, living near Ghent, Ky., was born in Carroll county of that state, Aug. 18, 1836. His grandfather, John Bond, came to Kentucky from the State of Virginia in 1803 and located in Owen county, where he became a successful farmer. His son William, the father of Robert, was born Sept. 9, 1793, before they came to Kentucky. He married Harriett Scott, who was born May 1, 1798, the daughter of Rev. John Scott, a Baptist minister, born in Ireland, and who married Jane Sneid. After his marriage, William Bond located in Carroll county, took up a homestead of wild land near Ghent and died there Jan. 12, 1863. He was a soldier of the war of 1812, in Col. Dick Johnson's regiment. His wife died only six days later. They were both members of the Baptist church and had a family of seven children: Samuel, John C., Mary J., James A., Julia F., Benjamin F. and Robert L., the last named being the only surviving member of the family. William Bond was a Whig in his early life but later became a Democrat. Robert L. Bond has been a tiller of the soil all his life, except what time he was in the Confederate army during the war. In September, 1862, he enlisted in Company B, Fourth Kentucky cavalry, under Capt. John G. Scott, and served until the final surrender as sergeant of his company. He was one of forty who would not surrender on Kentucky soil but surrendered at Woodstock, Ga., the latter part of May, 1865. They were permitted to retain their horses and side arms and Mr. Bond rode home on the same horse that he furnished at the time of his enlistment, and which was with him through the entire time of his service. After the war he bought a farm in Carroll county and settled down to farming. Mr. Bond does a general farming business, his specialties being Shorthorn cattle, fine roadsters and saddle horses and fox dogs. He was one of the organizers of the American National Saddle Horse association. He is fond of fox chasing, and in 1867 won a dog collar made of Mexican silver dollars, for the best fox dog of Kentucky. He married Martha J., daughter of Richard and Priscilla (Magruder) Ramey, of Henry county, Ky., and they have a family of five children: Maynie, Margaret, Julia, James D. and Frank. Mr. and Mrs. Bond are members of the Baptist church and he is one of the best Southern Democrats in Carroll county. He is also interested in good schools and is a friend of education.

WESLEY HAINES, deceased, a well known farmer near Eagle Station, Carroll county, Ky., in his day, was born in that county in 1813, and died there on March 17, 1887. His parents, Abraham and Eleanor (Dean) Haines, came from Pennsylvania to Carroll county in an early day and started life in the woods. They lived the typical pioneer life of the log cabin but conquered all the hardships of frontier life and became successful. Wesley grew to manhood in Carroll county and upon the death of his father took charge of the old farm, where he had been born and reared. Later he bought out the other heirs and lived upon the old homestead until his death. He was one of the leading local Democrats for many years and was a consistent member of the Methodist Episcopal church. On Oct. 22, 1859, Mr. Haines was united in marriage to Jane E. Williams, a daughter of Elisha and Zerelda (Scott) Williams, of Trimble county. William Williams, the grandfather of Mrs. Haines, came from Virginia and was one of the early settlers of Trimble county, where he passed the rest of his life as a prosperous farmer. Wesley and Jane Haines had three children. Lulu married James M. Driscoll, and Bertie married Russell Craig, both of whom are Carroll county farmers. Bertie has a family of seven children. Jessie, the third daughter, graduated from the kindergarten training school and taught in the kindergarten schools of Carrollton for three years, and for four years in the state of Tennessee. All three of the children were given a good education, and all are more or less proficient in music. Mrs. Haines still lives on the farm, which she rents out. She has 150 acres of good land, all in a high state of cultivation. During his life Mr. Haines was a man of domestic habits and spent most of his time with his family. He was a Methodist. His wife belongs to the Baptist church, and the family enjoyed the esteem and friendship of their neighbors.

WILLIAM F. PEAK, president of the Bedford Loan and Deposit bank, Bedford, Ky., was born in that portion of Henry county, Ky., now constituting the county of Trimble, Dec. 1, 1829. He is a son of Thomas and Harriet (Walker) Peak, the former a native of Virginia and the latter of South Carolina. The grandfather, W. A. Peak, came to Kentucky in 1809 and located in Scott county, but a year later settled in Henry, where he lived the rest of his life. An old spring house that he built on his farm is still standing. He was a soldier in the war of 1812, as one of the famous "Kentucky Rifles." Thomas Peak was a carpenter by trade, and also followed farming. He was a Democrat prior to 1896, but that year, and again in 1900, he voted for McKinley. He died in March, 1902, his wife having died in 1889. Of their children George W. is a merchant at Bedford; William F. is the subject of this sketch; Lucretia married Bart Nixon and lives at Jeffersonville, Ind.; Elizabeth is now Mrs. W. B. Averitt, of Trimble county; Lafayette died in Indiana; Mary, Martha, and Thomas are deceased. W. F. Peak received his education in the private or subscription schools and at the age of twenty years began his business career as a clerk in a store at Bedford; served four years in this capacity; kept hotel for two years; was elected county coroner and served four years; then elected sheriff and served two years in that office; elected both county and circuit court clerk; held the two offices for seven years; was then circuit clerk for seventeen years; was master commissioner ten years of that time; served as member of the legislature in 1883-84 and again in 1891-92-93. Since 1891 he has been interested in banking business. In November of that year he was one of the organizers of the Loan and Deposit bank, and in 1893 he was elected to the presidency, holding the office ever since by re-election. Mr. Peak is a part of the warp and woof of Trimble county. He is public spirited, in favor of good government and public improvements, and his judgment is of such a character that he is frequently consulted by his acquaintances and his advice sought in matters of importance. Besides his banking interests he owns four fine farms in the county and has an interest in several others. He lives in one of the most handsome residences in the town and is universally respected. Politically he is a Democrat and is one of the best informed men in the county on the political questions of the day. The only fraternal organization to claim him as a member was the Independent Order of Odd Fellows, to which he belonged until the outbreak of the Civil war, when his lodge was broken up. In 1854 Mr. Peak was united in marriage to Miss Margaret A. Willett, daughter of David and Margaret (Beebe) Willett, of Covington, Ky., where her father followed the trade of cooper. Of the children born to Mr. and Mrs. Peak, George W. is an undertaker at Bedford, is also an attorney and master commissioner of the Trimble circuit court, and is married and has seven children; Lottie J., married Jack Garriott and lives at Danville, Ill., the mother of three children; Robert F. is judge of the circuit court of the twelfth judicial district and resides at Shelbyville, Ky., a graduate of the Louisville Medical college, practiced two years, then studied law, was commonwealth attorney two years, is married and has five children; Hallie married Fall Mahoney, lives at Lexington, and has seven children; Elizabeth married L. F. Zerfoss of Ashland, Ky., and has three boys; D. H. is at home and is the cashier of the bank. Mrs. Peak and all the children are members of the Methodist Episcopal church.

NANNIE S. TANDY, one of three sisters who manage a large farm near Eagle Station, Carroll county, Ky., is a daughter of Scott and Nancy C. Tandy, and is a descendant of some of the first families of Kentucky. The grandfather, Roger M. Tandy, was born on Christmas day, 1786, and came to Kentucky in his early manhood, where he reared a family of thirteen children, viz.: Scott, the father of the subject of this sketch, born Dec. 22, 1813; Richard, born Feb. 21, 1815; Catherine, Aug. 5, 1816; Nancy, Nov. 7, 1818; Russell H., March 18, 1821; Samuel S., Oct. 15, 1822; Martha, Aug. 24, 1824; Whalen, July 9, 1827; Daniel B., May 9, 1831; Mary E., March 9, 1833; Lucy J., Nov. 1, 1834; Seany, March 16, 1836; and Robert S., May 8, 1838. Richard, Seany, and Lucy died in infancy. (For family ancestry see sketch of Willis Tandy.) Scott and Nancy Tandy had the following children: Willis,

now living at Sanders; Sally, one of the girls on the farm; Julius, who
died in 1888; Nannie S., the subject of this sketch, and Kate A., who
lives with her sisters and.assists in the management of the farm.   The
Tandy farm consists of 214 acres of highly improved land.   The sisters
pay considerable attention to raising Shorthorn cattle, as well as to the
production of general crops.   All three attended the college at Ghent,
are well educated, have studied music and art, and are ladies of culture
and refinement.   Their home is one of the most hospitable in that part
of the county and they have a large circle of friends, who esteem them
for their many womanly graces.

JOSEPH P. POWELL, a farmer and tobacco buyer, living near
Bedford, Trimble county, Ky., was born in that county, Nov. 25, 1849.
His grandfather, Lindsay Powell, was one of the early settlers of that
section of Kentucky, and his parents, Wyatt and Adeline (Law) Powell,
were both native Kentuckians.   The father was born in Oldham county,
Dec. 14, 1829, and the mother in Trimble county, Nov. 30, 1830.   Both
died in Trimble, the former on Sep. 26, 1878, and the latter on Oct. 31,
1888.   They had the following children: Joseph P., the subject of this
sketch; John, George, and Homer, farmers of Trimble county; Lucy,
wife of M. C. Rowlett, a Trimble county farmer; Eva, who married
M. O. Rowlett, and is now deceased; James, deceased, and one child that
died in infancy.   After leaving school Joseph started in to farm for
himself.   Starting with no money, he rented land until the spring of
1874, when he bought sixty-five acres of his own.   To this he has added
by subsequent purchases until he now owns 240 acres of good land.
He carries on a general farming business and does quite a business in
buying and shipping tobacco.   In political matters Mr. Powell has followed in the footsteps of his father and is a Democrat of the uncompromising type.   He is always ready to do his part toward achieving
a Democratic victory and in 1901 he was elected sheriff of the county.
He is a member of the Independent Order of Odd Fellows and is always
ready to assist in the benevolent work of the order.   Mr. Powell was
married in 1869 to Miss Nannie Adcock, whose grandfather, Joseph
Adcock, was a veteran of the war of 1812, and a pioneer settler of Kentucky.   To this marriage there have been born the following children:
George, a farmer and deputy sheriff of Trimble county; Robert, a
farmer; Amanda, Mrs. Warner Ford, of Oldham county; Rosa, wife of
William Baxter and resides in Scott county, Ind., and William, who is
at home with his parents.   Mr. Powell and all his family are members of
the Baptist church, as his parents were before him.

LOUIS G. CONTRI, M.D., a well-known physician and surgeon of Winona, Ky., was born at Rome, Italy, Dec. 24, 1840, his parents being Evandro and Elvira (Crump) Contri, the mother being the daughter of a distinguished surgeon. The Contri family is one of considerable prominence in Italy, the father of Dr. Contri having been a member of the diplomatic corps, and the grandfather, Michael Angelo Contri, marquis of San Gemignano, was, a general of artillery in the Italian army. Dr. Contri was educated at the Collegio Tolomei, and graduated in medicine from the University of Pisa, the second oldest medical school in the world. In May, 1860, he was one of the thousand, who, under General Garibaldi, landed at Marsala, under the eyes of the navy of the king of Naples, and fought at Marsala, Catalafini, Palermo, St. Angelo and Caserta. In the last named engagement he was wounded and received the honors of knighthood for capturing a flag of the enemy's. In 1861 he came to America, being attracted hither by our constitutional form of government. Embarking on a sailing vessel he was shipwrecked off Gibraltar, but finally reached Sidney, Nova Scotia, made his way by stage to Halifax, and from there came to Boston. Endorsing the doctrine of secession, he joined the Confederate army, and being an expert swordsman was appointed drill master of the Sixth Virginia cavalry, commanded by Col. Julian Harrison. Later he was stationed at Jackson's hospital as assistant surgeon and was still later attached to Witcher's battalion. He was in charge of the provisory Confederate hospital at Hagerstown, Md., during the battle of Gettysburg. On Sunday, July 12, 1863, he was captured by General Kilpatrick's cavalry, but escaped the same night while marching from Hagerstown to Frederick city. He was recaptured the next night while crossing the Potomac, being dressed in citizen's clothes, was treated as a spy, imprisoned in Fort McHenry, near Baltimore, and sentenced by a court martial to be shot on the second day of November. On Sunday, September 27, he again made his escape, through the influence of Free Masonry, and reached Richmond on the very day his sentence was to have been executed. He then served until the close of the war and was mustered out as captain. When the Fenian troubles broke out in Canada he organized a regiment of twelve companies in Massachusetts, raised the money to equip and transport his men and went to

Canada to fight against the English. Dr. Contri was made colonel of the regiment, which was attached to General Spear's command. They entered Canada about the first of June, 1866, and fought the British soldiery at Pigeon Hill and Slab City, when the United States government interfered and ordered the men to return to their homes. Dr. Contri's father having died in the meantime, he went to Europe to settle some of his affairs, and upon returning to this country in 1868, after about a year abroad, he located in Wyoming and for some time practiced in the West. Later he went to Jay county, Ind., and from there to Kentucky, where he has since remained. Dr. Contri is a member of the American and Kentucky State Medical associations; is secretary and treasurer of the Trimble County Medical society; secretary of the board of health of the same county, and belongs to the society of the medical officers of the Confederate army and navy. He joined the Masonic fraternity is his native land and is a thirty-second degree member of the order. Although reared a Catholic he is now a member of the Baptist church. As a physician he has a high standing, is a successful practitioner, and has the good will and confidence of his patients.

CLARENCE R. DRAKE, clerk of the circuit court in Switzerland county, Ind., was born in that county, June 3, 1852. The Drake family is of English origin. Robert Drake, the paternal grandfather of the subject of this sketch, came from England at an early date, settling first in Louisiana and later near Boonesborough, Ky., where he became acquainted with and shared many hardships of the celebrated Daniel Boone. From Boonesborough he came to Switzerland county, sacrificing all his property en route to save his life from the Indians. He died, June 19, 1845, and is buried in the old Drake graveyard in Switzerland county. Clarence R. Drake is a son of Dillard R. and Hevila (Hawkins) Drake, the former a native of Ohio and the latter of Switzerland county. Dillard Drake was twice married, Clarence being the eldest child by the second marriage. The children of the first wife were Benjamin F., Mary J., and Flavius J. Those of the second wife, besides the subject of this sketch, were Robert B., born Feb. 11, 1854; Sarah E., born Dec. 20, 1856; Claretta F., born Jan. 1, 1860; Lulu E., born Nov. 24, 1863; Elmer D., born in December,

1866; and Oscar M. and Hattie, both of whom died in infancy. Mr. Drake's mother was born, Oct. 9, 1822, and is still living at the advanced age of eighty-two years. Her father, Jonathan Hawkins, was a native of New York, and her mother, Sarah Hawkins, of Connecticut. Cretia Drake, an aunt of the subject of the sketch, was the first white child born in Switzerland county. Clarence R. Drake received his education in the common schools and has successfully fought his way upward until today he occupies one of the most important offices in his county. He was elected clerk by a majority of ninety-five votes. This in a county where the majorities rarely run over ten was certainly a victory of which any man might be proud. It tells the story better than words of his popularity, and of the confidence reposed in him by his friends and neighbors who know him best. Since coming into the office he has conducted it in the interests of the people who elected him and all who come in contact with him in his official capacity find courteous treatment. Mr. Drake married Miss Amanda Chittenden, and they have three children: Chester, born Aug. 9, 1878, is in charge of the Vevay electric light plant; Josie, born April 11, 1880, is at home with her parents; Clyde, born Feb. 23, 1882, occupies an important position at Newport, Ky.

CAPT. J. L. GRAHAM, familiarly known as "Captain Jack," captain and manager of the steam ferry between Vevay, Ind., and Ghent, Ky., was born at Vevay, Oct. 28, 1869, his parents being Robert T. and Mattie (Lester) Graham. Robert Graham was born in Ghent, in 1834, and died at Vevay in 1903. He was a son of Timothy and Martha Graham, both natives of Virginia, and his wife was born at Jacksonville, Ind., in 1840. She is still living. Capt. Robert Graham founded the ferry between Vevay and Ghent and operated it for more than forty years. At first he had a skiff for persons and a hand flatboat for horses and vehicles. This was succeeded by the horse power transfer boat, which in turn gave way to the modern steam ferry boat. The present steamer is named the *Eva Everett*, after the twin brother and sister of Capt. J. L. Graham. Everett is now assistant engineer on the boat. The Graham family have been brought up to the business, and it is worthy of note that Miss Juna Graham, a sister of the subject of this sketch, is a successful pilot, probably the only female pilot in the United States. The *Eva Everett* runs from early in the morning until late at night every day in the year except when the ferry is obstructed by ice. The distance from landing to landing is about one mile, yet the little boat covers it in six minutes. Both boat and proprietor are popular with the patrons. Captain Graham and his father have both made an enviable record as life savers. During the old flatboating days the father saved a number from a watery grave, and the son has fourteen lives to his credit. Such a record speaks well for his bravery and shows that in times of danger or emergency his presence of mind can be relied on to master the situation. Captain Graham has never married, preferring to live with his mother, to whom he has always been a dutiful son. He takes a great interest in Free Masonry, being the only Knight Templar in Switzerland county, and is a member of the Christian church.

CAPT. A. J. SCHENCK, of Vevay, Ind., is of Swiss descent, his ancestors being among the first settlers of Switzerland county. His great-grandparents were Philip Jacob and Marianne (Gras) Schenck, the former a native of Worms and the latter of Canton Berne, Switzerland. Philip J. Schenck died in Switzerland county, Dec. 15, 1819, his wife having died on the voyage over and was buried at sea. One of their sons, John James Philip Schenck, was born in Locte, Switzerland, Feb. 16, 1788, and died in Switzerland county in 1873. He married Mary Julia Jacot, a native of Champdismitien, where she was born April 3, 1788, and this couple were the grandparents of Captain Schenck. His grandmother died on a farm near Vevay, Feb. 6, 1864. Coming down to the next generation, Captain Schenck's father was Ulysses P. Schenck, born in Canton Neuchatel, Switzerland, May 16, 1811. He came with his family to America in the early part of the nineteenth century and in later years was one of the busiest and most prominent men of the Lower Ohio Valley. For many years he was engaged in the river trade, being the owner of several steamers. The large amount of hay he shipped to Southern markets gave to him the title of "The Hay King." He organized the First National bank of Vevay, and was its president for more than twenty years, and contributed more than one-half the cost of the First Baptist church building. He married Justine Thiebaud, born in Canton Neuchatel, May 29, 1809, and to them were born eleven children: Harriet, born at Louisville, Ky., Oct. 16, 1831, and died at Ghent, Ky., Aug. 4, 1884; George W., born at Louisville Feb. 19, 1833, and died at New Orleans, Aug. 9, 1855; Benjamin F., born at Louisville, Nov. 3, 1834, died at Jacksonville, Fla., April 24, 1877; Thomas J., born at Louisville, May 30, 1836, died at Vevay, July 3 1837; Josephine L., born at Vevay, May 7, 1838, died there July 30, 1862; Emily L., born at Vevay, April 24, 1840, died there Sept. 23, 1862. Andrew J., the subject of this sketch and the only survivor, born at Vevay, Dec. 28, 1842; Justine A., born May 4, 1845, at Vevay, and died there Oct. 7, of the same year. Julia A., born Aug. 19, 1846, died Feb. 16, 1861; Alice, born Feb. 15, 1849, died March 28, 1850; Ulysses P., born Oct. 12, 1851, died April 30, 1892. Captain Andrew J. Schenck received his education in the common schools and Franklin college, after which he was associated with his father, from whom he received a thorough business training. In July, 1864, he became his father's partner, but subsequently became prominently identified with river shipping. His first experience was as a steward on the steamer *Argosa*. In 1866 he was licensed captain and pilot of the same vessel, plying between Louisville and Cincinnati. Later he commanded the steamers *Sam J. Hale, H. Clay Wilson* and *U. P. Schenck,* and was for several years a director in the Southern Transportation Company. In 1875 Captain Schenck retired from active service on the river to look after his father's large and growing business. He was taken into full partnership under the firm name of U. P. Schenck & Son, which continued until his father's death, Nov. 16, 1884. Some years later he retired from mercantile pursuits, though he is still actively interested in a number of Vevay's leading business institutions. He is director of the First National bank; the Vevay Furniture Company; and the Vevay Woolen Mills; is president of the Moorefield Turnpike Company, and a stockholder in the Vevay Ice Company, besides holding large farming interests. He is a leading member of the First Baptist church and is an enthusiastic Mason. On Nov. 5, 1889, he was married to Miss Letitia Craig, of Kansas City, Mo. Her parents, Lewis E. and Letitia (Tandy) Craig, were natives of Carroll county, Ky., where the former was born, in July, 1819, and the latter in November, 1821. Lewis E. Craig died in Chicot county. Ark., and his wife at Tipton, Mo.

HON. HIRAM FRANCISCO, a prominent attorney, of Madison, Ind., and at the present time judge of the circuit court, was born in Jefferson county, Ind., Jan. 28, 1851. He is a son of Hiram and Mary (McNutt) Francisco, the former a native of the State of New York and the latter of Switzerland county, Ind. The Francisco family is of Spanish origin. The McNutts came from Pennsylvania early in the nineteenth century. Judge Francisco's father settled in Jefferson county in 1840. He soon became identified with nearly every movement that had for its object the advancement of the county's welfare and was noted for his enterprise and public spirit. Although he did not seek office he was chosen to represent the county in the state senate during the sessions of 1873-75, and while a member of the legislature the interests of his constituents were carefully guarded. He died in 1895. Of the six children born to Hiram and Mary Francisco four are still living. Oliver is a farmer; Anna F. married a nephew of Senator Jesse D. Bright; George is a farmer; and Hiram is the subject of this sketch. Judge Francisco's life was passed on a farm until his fifteenth year, attending the common schools during the winter seasons. At the age of fifteen he entered a private institution in Shelby county, Ky., where he spent two years, finishing his education. He then went into the law office of Harrington & Korbly as a student and in 1872 was admitted to the bar. For one year he was in partnership with his old preceptor, Henry W. Harrington, at Indianapolis, after which he returned to the farm for two years and then began practice at Madison. In 1878 he formed a partnership with Edwin G. Leland, which lasted until 1881, when he became associated with Capt. A. D. Vanosdol, a veteran of the Civil war. The firm enjoyed a large and lucrative practice until 1902, when Mr. Francisco's merits as an attorney recommended him to the Democracy of the Fifth judicial circuit, composed of Jefferson asd Switzerland counties, for the nomination of circuit judge. At the ensuing election he was elected by a large majority and entered upon the duties of the office on Oct. 23, 1903. This office he still holds, his record as judge giving abundant evidence that no mistake was made in selecting him for the position. Judge Francisco is a charter member of Syracuse Lodge, No. 104, Knights of Pythias, and as a member of the Commercial club is active in promoting the interests of the city of Madison. He was married, Feb. 11, 1877, to Miss Louisa Otto, whose parents, Henry and Mary Otto, were natives of Germany. To this marriage there have been born seven children: Mary, Helen, Louise, Martha, Georgia, Graham and Van Edwin. Mary is the wife of Warren Francisco, general freight agent of the Seaboard Air Line, at Montgomery, Ala. Louise is the wife of Charles Horuff, of Madison, and Martha is the wife of Hon. Edward S. Roberts, private secretary of Comptroller R. J. Tracewell, Washington, D. C. The family are members of the Catholic church.

HON. JOHN M. CISCO, mayor of Madison, Ind., was born in that city, Oct. 8, 1859. He is a son of Calvin and Ann (Scholl) Cisco, the former a native of Ohio and the latter of Indiana. They were early settlers at Madison, where they reared a family of ten children, five of whom are still living. For many years Calvin Cisco was one of the leading butchers and meat dealers of Madison. He served in the Mexican war, was for twelve years marshal of the city, and is still living at the advanced age of seventy-nine years. John M. Cisco was educated in the Madison public schools and after leaving school became associated with his father in business. In 1882 he embarked in business for himself and by square dealing has built up a large patronage. He recently erected one of the most substantial business blocks in the city, a building of modern design, where he handles all kinds of meats. Mr. Cisco takes great interest in all matters pertaining to the welfare of the city. This led to his election as councilman from the sixth ward in 1898, and at the next election, three years later, he was re-elected. At the close of his second term he was elected mayor, on May 3, 1904, over John G. Moore, who was a candidate for re-election. The success which Mr. Cisco has attained, both is business and politics, is due to his energy and sterling integrity and he may feel justly proud of his career. On April 4, 1880, he was married to Miss Christiana Miller, an estimable young lady of Madison, and to this marriage there have been born three children: William H., Blanche and John Calvin. All of Mr. Cisco's family except himself are members of the Catholic church.

JOHN J. YOUNG, one of the leading farmers of Trimble county, Ky., residing near Bedford, was born in the neighborhood where he now lives, June 11, 1833. His grandparents on the paternal side were James L. and Frances (Whitaker) Young, early settlers of Bedford, where the grandfather ran the first store and hotel in the town. He was a veteran of the war of 1812 and came from Maryland. Frances Whitaker was a daughter of Col. Aquilla Whitaker, commander of Whitaker's Station in pioneer times, and a sister of Gen. Walter C. Whitaker, who died in Louisville. In 1830 James L. Young bought the farm upon which the subject of this sketch now lives. The parents of John J. Young were James F. and Fannie M. (Hunter) Young, both natives of Kentucky. James F. was born in Shelby county in December, 1812, and is one of a family of four children. R. H., John J., Mary M., and Adeline K. Mary is married and lives in Bedford, and Adeline is the wife of Capt. Thomas English, of the Fourth Kentucky cavalry during the Civil war. James F. Young was a Whig in his early life but in later years became a Democrat. He was a member of the Catholic church and his wife was a Baptist. John J. Young enlisted in the Union army in 1863 as a private in Captain Harris's company of the Thirty-fourth Kentucky infantry. About a year later he was transferred to Company L, Fifth Kentucky cavalry, and served until the end of the war. After the war he returned home and has ever since followed farming. He owns 400 acres of fine land and is regarded as one of the prosperous and up-to-date farmers of his community. In politics he is a solid Republican and is always ready to defend his political principles. Mr. Young was married in 1877, to Georgia M., daughter of Dr. Robert Foster of Bowling Green, Ky. She was born in Allen county, Ky., was a member of the Methodist church, and died in April, 1899. On Jan. 1, 1901, he was married to Cora Brewington, a native of Aurora, Ind., though they were married in Kansas. Mr. Young has one son, Robert, who is a farmer in Trimble county. Mrs. Young is a member of the Methodist Episcopal church.

CAPT. ARGUS D. VANOSDOL, one of the leading attorneys of Madison, Ind., was born in Jefferson county, Ind., Sept. 18, 1839, and is a son of Thomas J. and Charlotte (Eastwood) Vanosdol, the former a native of Kentucky and the latter of Ohio. His paternal grandfather, Jacob B. Vanosdol, was a Kentucky Ranger during the Indian troubles in the Northwest Indiana Territory in 1810 and the succeeding years, serving under Maj. Zachary Taylor in the defense of Fort Harrison. After the close of hostilities he returned to his home in Mercer county,

Ky., married a Miss Susanna Smith, and in 1818 came with his family to Indiana, settling in Switzerland county. Twenty years later the family removed to Jefferson county, where the grandparents passed the remainder of their lives. The maternal grandfather was also a soldier in the war of 1812. Thomas J. Vanosdol learned the trade of stone cutter and was for many years engaged as a contractor in the towns of Vevay and Madison. The later years of his life were passed in retirement on a farm in Switzerland county, where he died in 1887. Captain Vanosdol was educated in the public schools and at the Indiana State university at Bloomington. On July 4, 1861, he enlisted in Company A, Third Indiana cavalry, and was appointed sergeant-major of the regiment. In the following February he was promoted to the rank of captain and transferred to Company I of the same regiment, and on March 9, took command of the company at Nashville, Tenn. He served in the Department of the Cumberland until May 13, 1863, when he was discharged on account of disabilities incurred in the Kentucky campaign, and at the battle of Stone River. In the meantime he had married, in August, 1862, Miss Mary Henry, daughter of Hon. David Henry, of Pleasant, Switzerland county. In the spring of 1865 his health was sufficiently recovered to enable him to again enter the service and he enlisted in the One Hundred and Fifty-sixth Indiana battalion. He was soon promoted to the rank of first lieutenant and served with his command until August, 1865, when he was mustered out with his battalion. His only brother, Christopher G. Vanosdol, was mortally wounded in Wilson's raid near Richmond, Va., in 1864, and after being wounded was captured by the Confederates and died in their hands. His grave is one of those marked "Unknown" at Poplar Lawn, Va. After the war Captain Vanosdol's health was such that he took up his residence on a farm, occasionally teaching in the common schools, until the summer of 1870, when he had so far regained his health that he entered the law department of the State university and graduated in March, 1871. He then located at Madison in the practice of law, where he has continued ever since. For nearly twenty-three years he was the senior member of the firm of Vanosdol & Francisco, the partnership being dissolved by Mr. Francisco's election to the position of judge of the circuit court. For four years Captain Vanosdol was prosecuting attorney of the Fifth circuit, his administration characterizing him as an able, conscientious and fearless official. He is well known in the political life of Indiana; is a stanch Republican; has served as county chairman in several campaigns, and as a member of the state central committee. He is also prominent in the Grand Army of the Republic.

During the years 1886-87 he was inspector general on the staff of Commander-in-chief S. S. Burdett, and in 1888 he was department commander of the Department of Indiana, G. A. R. For four years he was one of the board of control for the Reform School for Boys, at Plainfield, Ind., and for sixteen years was colonel of the Fourth regiment, Uniform Rank, Knights of Pythias. He has received many souvenirs and testimonials from his comrades and associates in token of their appreciation, which he prizes very highly.

RICHARD JOHNSON, one of the most progressive business men of Madison, Ind., was born in Belfast, Ireland, Jan. 11, 1829. His parents, John and Margaret (Warring) Johnson, passed their entire lives on the Emerald Isle, where the father was a manufacturer of soap and candles, at Belfast. They had eight children, only two of whom survive; Richard, the subject of this sketch, and Bella, who lives in Belfast. Richard was educated in the private schools of his native town and upon leaving school served his time with the pork packing firm of O'Neilly, Bayly & Co., of Belfast. He then engaged in the butter business for himself but after one year sold out and came to America, landing in New York city on St. Patrick's day, 1849. He came directly to Madison, where he entered the branch house of the firm with which he had served his apprenticeship in his native land. He remained with this firm until their failure, which resulted from their embarking in the business of making starch, after which Mr. Johnson began the manufacture of starch on his own account. His venture was successful and he continued in that line until 1890, when he, with twenty other concerns, sold out to the trust. At that time the Madison starch works employed about one hundred and fifty people. Mr. Johnson then purchased the Eagle cotton mills, which had twice failed, and by his energy and tact built up a successful business, the mills now running every day in the year with a force of some four hundred operatives. In 1900 he established the R. Johnson yarn and cordage mills, which has also proved to be a paying industry, employing about one hundred and fifty people the year round. Besides his manufacturing interests Mr. Johnson owns one of the best farms in Jefferson county, consisting of 300 acres, though he resides in the city.

He is also president of the First National bank, a position he has held for several years; president of the Firemen's and Mechanics' Insurance Company, the No. 3 fire company, and the Madison Chautauqua assembly. Few men have done so much to advance the social and industrial interests of Madison as Mr. Johnson, and none have done more. He came to Madison a poor boy and his business standing has been acquired by diligence, and a strict adherence to correct principles. He has two sons and two daughters, David, William J., Margaret and Anna, all of whom have been brought up to become useful members of society. David is the superintendent of the Eagle cotton mills; William J. is manager of the yarn and cordage mills; and Margaret is the wife of Manly D. Wilson, the bookkeeper of the Eagle mills. Since coming to America Mr. Johnson has crossed the Atlantic Ocean fifteen times on visits to his old home in Ireland, which is still dear to his memory.

CURTIS MARSHALL, a rising young lawyer of Madison, Ind., was born in Gallatin county, Ky., March 10, 1868. When he was six months old his parents removed to Jefferson county, Ind., where they both died before the subject of this sketch was three years old. He was adopted by a kindly old couple, and by them carefully and conscientiously reared to manhood. They were not very well to do, and consequently young Curtis was compelled to rely, to a great extent, upon his own efforts to make his way in the world. He attended the common schools, and afterwards the private academy of Prof. A. W. Blinn at Paris, near his home. He also attended a teachers' normal school at Lancaster, Ind., one term. Until he was twenty-five years old he continued to reside in the country, teaching in the common schools during the winter months, and working on the farm during the summer. He taught in all eight schools, and in 1893 went to the city of Madison, where he entered the law office of Judge John R. Cravens, one of the ablest lawyers in Southern Indiana. In September, 1895, he was admitted to the bar, and entered upon the practice of law at once, remaining in the office of his preceptor, and upon the death of Judge Cravens in 1899, he succeeded to the greater part of that eminent lawyer's business. He has built up a leading and lucrative practice in all branches of the profession, and is noted as being especially strong in real estate, commercial and probate law. At the present time he is the city attorney for Madison, and has had to deal with a number of very knotty legal problems since assuming the duties of that office, particularly in the matter of the renewal of a lighting contract with the city, which carried with it a contract to operate a street railway within the city, and to build and operate an electric interurban road from the city to the town of Hanover, some few miles distant. This contract necessitated the granting of certain privileges and franchises, and called for an unusual degree of care and legal skill on the part of the city attorney, but Mr. Marshall measured up fully to all expectations. Another very important matter which confronted him was the defalcation of a city treasurer, and the refusal of his bondsmen to make good a shortage of more than eighteen thousand dollars. This matter is pending yet, but there is entire confidence on the part of the citizens that the city's interests will be taken care of by the city attorney. Mr. Marshall is an influential and enthusiastic Democrat. Before reaching his majority he acquired quite a local reputation as a public speaker, and in every campaign in the past sixteen years he has either been on the stump in behalf of his party, or else has been engaged in the management of the campaign as chairman of his party committee. During the campaigns of 1902 and 1904 he was chairman of the Jefferson county Democratic central committee, and, although the county is normally Republican by 800 majority, he succeeded in cutting that majority down very materially upon the general ticket in both years, and in the former year over half the Democratic county ticket was elected—the first time a Democrat had been elected in the county for twenty-six years—and in the latter year a small part of the county ticket was elected, the county being one of the only two counties in the State of Indiana that showed a gain for the Democratic party over the vote of 1900. Mr. Marshall was also chairman of the Democratic city central committee during the city campaign in the spring of 1904. and, although Madison is normally Republican by 250 majority, yet almost the entire Democratic ticket was elected by good majorities. He was elected a member of the school board of the city of Madison in 1897 and served as a member and president of the board for a term of three years, his knowledge of school affairs, acquired by teaching in his earlier years, enabling him to fulfill the duties of that office most acceptably to the general public. In fraternal circles Mr. Marshall stands high. He is a Knight Templar Mason, and he filled the position of Worshipful Master of Union Lodge, No. 2, during the years of 1903 and 1904; is a member of Juniata Tribe, No. 24, Improved Order of Red Men; a charter member of Clifty Falls Camp, No. 5751, Modern Woodmen of America, and its first Venerable Consul; has a reputation extending all over the state as a leading Odd Fellow, being a member of Madison Lodge, No. 72, of the subordinate branch of that order; of Wildey Encampment, No. 2; La Belle Reviere Rebekah Lodge, No. 624; is a Past Grand of his local lodge; is nearly always a member of one of the important committees in the Grand Lodge; is at the present time the District Deputy Grand Master for District No. 39, consisting of Jefferson county, and is ever alert in the interests of that great order, whose motto is Friendship, Love and Truth. Although he was brought up in the Christian church, Mr. Marshall belongs to no religious denomination, yet his conduct is governed by high ideas of morality and charity toward his fellow-men. He is unmarried, and is devoted to his profession, his lodges and his party work.

LOUIS SULZER, proprietor of the firm of Sulzer Bros., wholesale dealers in crude drugs, Madison, Ind., was born in that city, Oct. 10, 1862. His parents, Raphael and Rachael (Heimerdinger) Sulzer, were natives of Alsace, Germany, but came to this country in 1854, locating at Madison, where the father founded the business that has since grown to large proportions. He is still living at the advanced age of eighty-five years. The mother died at the age of seventy. Two sons and two daughters of the children born to them are still living. Louis Sulzer was educated in the Madison public schools, and upon completing his education he became associated with his father in the business of buying up roots and herbs for the manufacturing chemists over the country. In time he became the manager of the firm's affairs, and he has conducted it so successfully that today it is the largest concern of the kind in the world. Foremost among the crude materials handled by the firm are golden seal, mandrake, blood root, wahoo, slippery elm, etc., the annual volume of business running from $175,000 to $250,000. Mr. Sulzer is known to all the pharmaceutical chemists of the United

States and throughout Europe, most of whom he supplies with the raw materials for the preparation of their various remedies. Although he never studied botany, he can readily give the scientific name of any root or herb and give its medicinal properties. Besides the office of the firm, at 318 Mulberry street, two large buildings are occupied at the corner of Second and West streets. The firm also handles thousands of dollars worth of raw furs every year. In addition to his large interests in this line, Mr. Sulzer is also connected with several other important enterprises. He is secretary and general manager of the Root-Herba Company, manufacturers of Houz's blood purifier, and a number of other remedies. He is also secretary and general manager of the Ohio Valley Shell and Pearl Company, dealers in pearls and manufacturers of pearl button blanks, with a factory at Madison. In March, 1903, he organized the People's bank and served as vice-president of the institution until May, 1904, when he resigned. He is a member of the Independent Order of Odd Fellows, Knights of Pythias, the Independent Order of Bnai Brith, of which he is president, and is the treasurer of the Adath Israel congregation, of which he was also president for several years. On June 8, 1892, he was married to Miss Rose Lefly of Cincinnati. They have two children: Helen, aged eleven, and Rachael, aged seven, both of whom are in school.

JOHN W. THOMAS, manufacturer of spokes and barrels, Madison, Ind., was born in Jefferson county, Ind., Oct. 30, 1849, his parents being Joseph and Amanda A. (Remley) Thomas. About a century ago his paternal grandfather, John Thomas, came down the Ohio river on a flatboat from Pennsylvania and settled about two miles from Madison, where he built a two-room log house. At that time the Indians were quite troublesome in Southern Indiana and the portholes left in the walls may be seen in the old building, which is still standing, and which is now used as a gristmill. He lived upon the land he entered from the government until his death. The maternal grandfather, Rev. Michael A. Remley, came from Virginia early in the nineteenth century and was a Presbyterian minister. He and his wife traveled over the country in a sort of dog cart, finally locating in Jefferson county. Here he engaged in raising silk worms, and the farm where he lived is still known as the "Silk Farm." He also once owned a farm where part of the city of Chicago now stands. Joseph Thomas was a farmer in his early life, but later learned the coopers' trade, at which he worked until his death. He and his wife were the parents of nine children, only three of whom are now living: John W., the subject of this sketch, Joseph and Alice. John W. Thomas received a limited education in the public schools, the years of his youth and early manhood being spent in working on a farm. During the war he was employed on a steamboat, and after the return of peace he went to Arkansas, where he found work as a farm hand. In 1867 he returned to his old home, learned both the carpenters' and coopers' trade, and for several years worked as a journeyman, the last place he was employed being at Frankfort, Ky. Borrowing sixty dollars to start with, he began business for himself in a little shed at Madison, making flour barrels for the mills there. From this modest beginning he has built up his present establishment, manufacturing all kinds of spokes and whisky barrels for a number of the leading distilleries of the country. He ships spokes to several points on the Pacific slope, as well as to a number of European cities. Mr. Thomas is also at the head of the Madison Coal Company, owning the steam towboat *Minnie* and a complement of barges. He is an extensive dealer in real estate, a director of the trust company, vice-president of the People's bank a member of the Commercial club, and owner of five farms in Jefferson county, one of which, consisting of 360 arces, is the largest farm in the county. He also owns a large farm in the State of Arkansas. He served as county commissioner for two terms, and was for eighteen years a member of the city council. Mr. Thomas has always favored every movement for the upbuilding of the city and is regarded as one of Madison's most progressive citizens. No one envies him his success or popularity, for all realize that they have come to him through his energy and perseverance, and are the just reward of untiring industry. He belongs to the Knights of Pythias, the Independent Order of Odd Fellows, the Improved Order of Red Men, and the Firemen, and in all these orders he has a high standing. In December, 1872, Mr. Thomas and Miss Susan C. Smith were united in marriage. Three of the children born to this union are now living, viz.: Gaylord, Raymond and Anna.

CHARLES R. JOHNSON, manufacturer of engines, boilers, steamboat and mill machinery, Madison, Ind., was born in that city, Oct. 8, 1851. His father, William C. Johnson, was a native of Ripley county, Ind., having been born near the town of Versailles. He was a cabinet maker by trade and was for many years one of the leading cabinet makers, furniture dealers and undertakers of Madison. He married Miss Mary Schaffer, a native of Pennsylvania. Charles R. Johnson received his education in the public schools of his native city, afterward learning the trade of a machinist. He worked as a journeyman until 1883, when he embarked in business for himself. At first he conducted his business in a small way but in late years he has had the satisfaction of seeing it grow to generous proportions. There may be larger establishments than his but few are better equipped with modern machinery, and none excel it in the quality of work turned out. He employs a number of skilled workmen and supplies the trade in Southern Indiana and a large portion of Kentucky. Mr. Johnson has always taken a lively interest in promoting the city's interest, realizing that whatever was of benefit to the whole community was also to his private interest. In 1886 he was elected to the city council and has been a member of that body ever since, being the longest continuous service ever accorded to any one man. He has served on all the council committees and during the greater part of his official service has been chief of the fire department. He has also taken an active part toward securing a deep water channel in the Ohio river, being one of the committee to accompany the Cincinnati delegation to Washington to present the matter to the national authorities, and has attended conventions at Cincinnati, Paducah, Evansville, and other points to aid the undertaking. He was largely instrumental in securing the establishment of the Madison electric street railway, of which his son, Charles R., Jr., was treasurer and general manager for six years. He formerly owned the steam towboat *Minnie,* plying on the Ohio and Kentucky rivers. This vessel he sold in 1903. He and his son lease the Beech Grove driving park and conduct the annual county fairs. Mr. Johnson is a member of Madison Lodge, No. 72. Independent Order of Odd Fellows; Juniata Tribe, No. 24, Improved

Order of Red Men; Syracuse Lodge, No. 104, Knights of Pythias; Indianapolis Lodge, No. 13, Benevolent and Protective Order of Elks, and of the Royal Arcanum. In 1874 Mr. Johnson and Miss Virginia Gaumer, a native of Madison, were united in marriage. They have three children: Charles R., Margaret, and Rosetta. The son is associated with his father in business. Margaret has achieved a wide reputation as a vocalist, having studied under Professor Ernestinoff, of Indianapolis, and is now the leading singer in the choir of the Second Presbyterian church. Rosetta was for three years the secretary of the Madison Light and Railway Company.

·ELMER E. SCOTT, wholesale grocer, Madison, Ind., is a native of that city. He is a son of John W. and Sarah A. (Protsman) Scott, and was born Sept. 28, 1863. His father was born in Jefferson county, Ind., though his ancestry came from Scotland, and his mother, who was of German parentage, was a native of Switzerland county. John W. Scott followed blacksmithing during his early life but in later years engaged in farming and conducting a retail grocery in Madison. During the Civil war he was a member of the Indiana Home Guards. In 1876 he was elected treasurer of Jefferson county, the first Democrat to hold that office in twenty years. He devoted his attention to the payment of the county debt, amounting to $178,000, and in two years succeeded in almost wiping it out. He was re-elected in 1878 but was counted out. His death occurred in 1902. He was a prominent Knight Templar Mason and a member of the Methodist Episcopal church. His wife also died in 1902. They were the parents of nine children, seven of whom are living. Elias J. is the bookkeeper for the Indiana Fuel & Supply Company, of Indianapolis; William A. is state agent for the Great Western Seeding Company, with offices in Indianapolis. The others are Elmer E., Ida M., now Mrs. Patton; Anna, Nora, now Mrs. Gordon, and Bertha E. Elmer E. Scott was educated in the Madison schools, and at the Ryker's academy. Upon leaving school he was associated with his father in the grocery for several years. In 1888 he embarked in the brokerage business, having at that time a working capital of $78.00. He prospered, however, and in 1894 began the wholesale business in a limited way, covering a small territory and buying just what his trade demanded. His patronage has grown until it is one of the largest in Southern Indiana. Although a busy man Mr. Scott finds time to devote to the public welfare. Politically he is a Democrat and although his county is Republican by about 900 he was elected a member of the county council and is now president of that body. He is also a member of the city council, having been elected from the Fifth ward, which, although a Republican ward by 125, elected him by a majority of 18 out of a full vote. In the city council he occupies the important positions of vice-president and chairman of the finance committee. Under his supervision a thorough investigation of the city's finances was made, resulting in the finding of a shortage of $18,651.58 in the accounts of the treasurer, all of which was collected and returned to the treasury where it belonged. Out of several shortages that have occurred in this city and county this is the first time the community has enjoyed the full settlement of a like deficit in the public funds. This result is due in a great measure to the persistent and intelligent work of Mr. Scott, who stands for the same honest administration of public affairs that he applies in his private business. Mr. Scott is a member of the Masonic fraternity and the Methodist Episcopal church, in which he is president of the board of stewards and superintendent of the Sunday school. He was married on Aug. 9, 1888, to Miss Emma M. Davis, of Madison. She was born in Cincinnati, but came with her parents to Madison when she was but three years of age. They have two children, Margaret Marie and John Elmer.

HARRY SUTPHIN HATCH, M.D., a well known and popular physician, of Madison, Ind., was born in Butler county, Ohio, Jan. 21, 1867. He is a son of Metcalf B. and Martha A. (Sutphin) Hatch, the former a native of Leroy, N. Y., and the latter of Butler county. Dr. Hatch's maternal grandmother, whose maiden name was Jane Patten, was the first white child born in Butler county. Daniel Buell, a great-uncle on the paternal side, was a captain of infantry in the war of 1812 and was killed at the battle of Chippewa. His body was never found. Metcalf B. Hatch served three years as county commissioner of Butler county, and his brother, Hobart H. Hatch, served with distinction in the Seventy-seventh Illinois infantry as captain of a company. General Hatch, who is still in the service, is a cousin to the doctor, and Rufus Hatch, of Wall street fame, is a relative of the family. Doctor Hatch received his primary education in the public schools of Middletown, Ohio, afterward taking the degree of Ph.B. at Worcester university. In 1889 he entered the Pulte Medical college of Cincinnati, graduating with the degree of M.D. in 1892. The same year he located at Madison, where he has built up a large practice, being regarded as one of the most progressive physicians in the city. He is a member of both the Ohio and Indiana State Medical societies, and has served as secretary of the Jefferson county board of health. He keeps in close touch with the progress of his profession, is conscientious in his methods of treatment, which inspires the confidence and esteem of his patients. Doctor Hatch is a member of all the Masonic bodies of Madison, a Knight of Pythias, a Redman, and a Modern Woodman. In all these orders he enjoys a high standing and is a welcome visitor to the lodge meetings when his practice will admit of his attendance. He is also a member of the board of stewards of the Methodist Episcopal church. On Jan. 23, 1896, he was married to Miss Helen N., daughter of the late Capt. William H. and Elizabeth (Cooper) Daniel. Mrs. Hatch's father was a native of Louisville. He was a large stockholder in the People's steamboat line and was one of the best known men on the river. He became a resident of Madison about forty years ago. Her mother was born in Lexington, Ky. Mrs. Hatch is one of twins, the youngest children of her family. Doctor and Mrs. Hatch have one daughter, Helen Martha. The mother is a member of the Methodist Episcopal church.

LAWRENCE W. NIKLAUS, wholesale grocer, of Madison, Ind., is probably the youngest wholesale merchant in the country. For three generations his family have been engaged in the business on the same site where his store now stands. His paternal grandparents were natives of Canton Berne, Switzerland. They came to Madison, some time in the forties, where his grandfather, John Niklaus, put up a blacksmith shop on the present site of the store. A few years later he engaged in the wholesale grocery business, adding rectifying to it in 1870, and in 1884 turned the whole business over to his son, Edward G., who was born soon after the family came to Madison. The son conducted the business until his death, which occurred Feb. 22, 1904, when it fell to the subject of this sketch. During his life Edward G. Niklaus was one of Indiana's prominent Democrats. He was a delegate to several national conventions of his party and was postmaster under Cleveland's second administration. He was also prominent in secret and benevolent orders, being a member of the Cincinnati Lodge of Elks, a Redman, and major of the First battalion, Fourth regiment, Uniform Rank Knights of Pythias. In 1879 he was married to Miss Mary Wharton, daughter of William G. and Ann R. Wharton, one of the old and honored families of Madison. Lawrence W. Niklaus is the only child born to this marriage. He was born July 8, 1882, and received his education in the Madison public schools, a preparatory course at Hanover college, and the mechanical course at Purdue university. Two years before the death of his father he entered the store, and since his father's death has had charge of the business, though his mother still holds an interest in it. Thus at the age of twenty-two years he has succeeded to an undertaking, the responsibilities of which might cause many an older or more experienced man to hesitate. But so far he has been equal to every emergency, and being a young man of exemplary habits and great energy it is safe to predict his future success. Mr. Niklaus is a member of the Benevolent and Protective Order of Elks, and of the Phi Delta Theta college fraternity.

CHARLES B. MELISH, founder and proprietor of the Charles B. Melish Pearl Button Company, of Madison, Ind., was born in the city of Cincinnati, Ohio, Jan. 16, 1856. He was educated in the public schools of his native city and at Denison university, Granville, Ohio. For sixteen years he was connected with the Cleveland Rolling Mill Company, now a part of the American Steel and Wire Company, as superintendent of the Southwestern agency, with offices in Cincinnati. After the absorption of his company by the American Steel and Wire Company he determined to embark in business for himself. He began the manufacture of pearl buttons on a small scale in Cincinnati and finding the industry one of great promise he removed to Madison in 1901 and founded the company of which he is still the head. Buildings were erected and equipped with new and modern machinery, skilled workmen were employed and the products of the factory soon found favor with the trade all over the country. The factory employs about one hundred operatives when running to the full capacity. Mr. Melish has by his sagacity and enterprising spirit thus turned the hitherto worthless musselshells of the Ohio river into an important article of commerce and spread the name of his adopted city abroad. In Masonic circles Mr. Melish is well known, being a Knight Templar and a Thirty-second degree member of the Scottish Rite.

GEORGE E. DENNY, M.D., a leading physician and surgeon of Madison, Ind., was born at Bryantsburg, Jefferson county, Ind., March 23, 1870, and is a son of John W. and Victoria (King) Denny, both natives of Jefferson county. His paternal grandparents came from Kentucky and were among the early settlers of Southern Indiana, while his maternal grandparents came from Belgium in the early part of the nineteenth century. For many years his grandfather, John King, conducted a bakery in Madison. Doctor Denny's father served four years in the Union army during the Civil war. Since that time he has continued in the occupation of farming. He has served as township trustee and is at present one of the county commissioners. Doctor Denny was educated in the common schools and at Hanover and Franklin colleges. After leaving school he taught for three years and then took up the study of medicine. He attended the Ohio Medical college two years and graduated from the University of Louisville in 1893. Locating at Alert, Ind., he practiced there for six years, when he went to Chicago and entered the post-graduate hospital of that city as a resident physician. He remained in this institution for twelve months, being head physician the last half of that period. In 1901 he located at Madison, where he has established a large practice as a specialist in surgery and diseases of women. Soon after coming to Madison he founded Doctor Denny's sanitarium, accommodating ten patients. In this institution he has placed modern scientific apparatus, trained nurses, etc., making it the equal of any in the country. He is a member of the Jefferson County Medical society and of the Indiana Medical association, and is the examiner for the John Hancock Life Insurance Company. Doctor Denny is a member of the Independent Order of Odd Fellows, both the subordinate Lodge and Encampment, the Knights of Pythias, and the Modern Woodmen. When the People's bank was organized he became one of the stockholders and was for a time on the board of directors. On Nov. 30, 1893, he was married to Miss Jennie Childs, of Franklin, Ind., and they have two children, Leota and Neva. The doctor and his wife are members of the Baptist church.

PROF. GARFIELD HOARD, superintendent of the Jefferson county schools, Madison, Ind., was born on a farm in Graham township of that county, Nov. 11, 1878. He is a son of Adam and Electa (Roseberry) Hoard, both natives of the county. His paternal grandfather came from Kentucky at an early date and passed the remainder of his life as a Jefferson county farmer. His maternal grandfather, Samuel Roseberry, also a farmer, was one of the first settlers of the county, taking land from the government. During his life he was a prominent citizen, holding several local offices. Professor Hoard's father still resides on his farm in Graham township. Like most farmer boys, Professor Hoard received his primary education in the district schools. After graduating from the Central Normal college, at Danville, Ind., he took a course in the medical department of the Kentucky university. Giving up the notion of becoming a physician he returned home and for several years was engaged in teaching in the common and high schools of his native county. In June, 1903, he was elected to his present position, being the youngest man to ever hold the office. His youth seems to be in his favor, however, as he brings to the office vigor and ambition, as well as a practical experience of the needs of the public schools. Professor Hoard is a member of the Masonic fraternity, and of the Improved Order of Red Men. Politically he is a Republican and takes an active interest in his party's success. He has frequently been called upon to serve as a delegate to conventions and stands high in the councils of his party. On June 15, 1903, about two weeks after assuming the duties of his office, he was united in marriage to Miss Emma C. Lamb, a native of Spencer county, Ind., and a highly esteemed young lady.

JAMES WHITE, contractor and builder, Madison, Ind., is a native of Scotland, having been born at Blackwood, Closeburn parish, Dumfrieshire, April 17, 1842. When he was about nine years of age his parents, James and Elizabeth (Gibson) White, came to America. On New Year's day, 1851, they embarked on a sailing vessel at Liverpool and after a very tempestuous voyage, during which they had to put into port at the Island of St. Thomas, Danish West Indies, for water, they landed at New Orleans. From there the family proceeded up the Mississippi and Ohio rivers to Madison, where they arrived on March 22d. The father found ready employment in a sash and door factory and later as a carpenter at the shipyards, where he assisted to construct the marine ways. In the old country he was what is known as a wood forester on a large estate, where his father before him had served in a similar capacity. His duty was to look after the cutting and replanting of trees, the repairing of all buildings on the estate, and protection of the fishing, etc., the estate being on the river Nith only a short distance from the sea. For ten generations the eldest son of the eldest son in this family has borne the name of James. The subject of this sketch received his first schooling in the primary schools of Scotland, and finished his education in the public schools of Madison. He then served an apprenticeship at carpentering with his uncle, Alexander White, who was at one time mayor of the city. On July 22, 1862, he enlisted in Company E, Seventieth Indiana infantry, commanded by the late President Benjamin Harrison, and served until June 25, 1865, when he was mustered out at Washington, D. C. During his military service he was an orderly sergeant, in the department of the West, and marched with Sherman to the sea, taking part in all the engagements of that memorable campaign. After the war he returned to Madison and resumed work at his trade. In March, 1868, he formed a partnership with a Mr. Cochran, the firm being known as Cochran & White, but after two years he purchased his partner's interest. In 1873 he formed another partnership, this time with Robert H. Rankin, under the firm name of Rankin & White, and this association lasted until the death of Mr. Rankin in August, 1887, since which time Mr. White has conducted the business alone. During the existence of the firm of Rankin & White they built the woolen and cotton mills. Many of the principal buildings of Madison have been erected by Mr. White and his business extends to other towns and cities in Southern Indiana. Mr. White takes a deep interest in all things relating to the municipal welfare and in 1878 was elected to the city council. After a service of twelve years in that body he declined further honors, but in May, 1904, he was again elected to the council on the Republican ticket. He has been an Odd Fellow ever since 1866 and was for over twenty-five years the treasurer of his lodge. He is also a Knight of Pythias, a member of the Grand Army of the Republic and the Benevolent and Protective Order of Elks. On Dec. 4, 1867, Mr. White and Miss Margaret J. Kellaway, a native of Dorsetshire, England, were united in marriage. They have four children living: James K., Jessie M., Margaret E., and Charlotte B. Mr. White and his family belong to the First Presbyterian church and he is well known for his charitable deeds.

JOSEPH H. BARNARD, D.D., pastor of the Second Presbyterian church, Madison, Ind., was born in Juniata county, Pa., Feb. 9, 1838, his parents being Joseph and Elizabeth (Hoke) Barnard, both natives of the Keystone State. His paternal grandfather, also named Joseph, came to this country, early in his married life, his children all being born in this country. He came from the north of Ireland, where a family of English Barnards settled shortly after the time of Cromwell, and who were the ancestors of the family in America. The Hoke family is of German extraction. Joseph Barnard, father of the subject, was a carpenter by trade all his life. He and his wife had five sons and two daughters, only one of whom is deceased. Rev. Joseph H. Barnard received his early education in the old log school house of the country districts. At the age of twelve years he entered the Tuscarora academy, where he studied four years. In 1854 he was admitted to the sophomore class in Lafayette college, graduating from that institution in 1857, standing second in a class of thirty-one and taking one of the honorary degrees. He was also the salutatorian of his class. He then took a three years' course at the theological seminary at Princeton, N. J., graduating in 1860, when he was licensed and ordained by the Presbytery of Huntington, Pa. For a short time he was at Tyrone and Birmingham, Pa., and was then called to the pastorate at Bellefonte in the same state. In 1866 he came West and for about three years was engaged at Waukesha, Wis. He was then called to Kankakee, Ill., where he remained for seven years, at the end of which time he accepted a call to Muscatine, Ia. Here he remained until 1883, when he came to Madison. During the twenty-one years that he has been in charge of his present church he has seen it grow to be one of the most influential congregations in Southern Indiana. In 1888 his alma mater conferred on him the degree of D.D. as a recognition of his distinguished services in the ministry. Dr. Barnard is Dean of the Presbytery of New Albany; one of the trustees of Hanover college; and has been chosen commissioner to the general assembly four times, where he has served on some of the most important committees. He is a member of the Masonic fraternity, and of Juniata Tribe, No. 24, Improved Order of Red Men. On June 6, 1861, Dr. Barnard and Miss Martha Gray Grubbs, of Springfield, Ill., were united in marriage. Four children born to this union are now living. George Grey is one of the most noted of American sculptors, in fact has won the highest honors ever conferred on an American sculptor. He was awarded a gold medal at the Paris exposition of 1900, and received a similar recognition at the Pan-American exhibition at Buffalo in 1901. He is a member of the Societe Nationale des Beaux Arts, Paris; the National Sculpture Society; the National Academy of Design, and the Architectural League of New York. His work may be seen in the art galleries of both this country and Europe. He is now in Paris engaged in making the statuary for the new State capitol at Harrisburg, Pa. Evan, another son, is a prominent ranchman in Oklahoma. May is the wife of James Hargan, a Madison capitalist, and Martha is the wife of William Bancroft, a well known publisher of New York City.

PROF. FREDERICK M. BOOTH, proprietor of the Indiana Business college, Madison, Ind., was born at Moville, Woodbury county, Ia., April 20, 1877. He was educated in Highland Park college of Des Moines, Ia., graduating in 1899, and for the next two years was employed as a commercial teacher in Sioux Falls college. On Sept. 1,

1901, he purchased the Indiana Business college, which was then run on a comparatively small scale, and set about its improvement. Securing new quarters, occupying the entire third floor of the Richert building, 323-325 East Main St., he began to advertise the merits of the institution. Since then the attendance has increased, keeping four teachers employed day and evening. All commercial branches, shorthand and typewriting are the principal studies. Shirley Bondurant, a graduate of this school, is said to be the fastest operator on a typewriter in the world. So far Mr. Booth has been fortunate in placing the graduates of his school in good paying positions. Professor Booth is a young man of more than ordinary ability, and is fired with a determination to rise by his own efforts. As a teacher he is thorough, conscientious and original and the results of his work can be seen in the character of those who graduate from his school. On Aug. 6, 1901, he was married to Miss Rose Cabhal, a native of Des Moines, and they have one little daughter, Edyth Helen. Professor Booth is a Congregationalist and his wife is a member of the Christian church.

CLARENCE J. ROBERTS, a promising young attorney, of Madison, Ind., was born on a farm in Jefferson county, Oct. 21, 1873. He is a son of Daniel A. and Perintha (Robinson) Roberts, the former a native of Ohio and the latter of Indiana. The family came originally from Lancashire, England, some of its members being among the early settlers of Southern Indiana. Daniel A. Roberts has always been a farmer and still resides on his farm a few miles from Madison. He has held the offices of township trustee and county commissioner and was a soldier in the Union army during the Civil war. Clarence acquired his early education in the common schools, after which he attended college at Hope, and at Mitchell, Ind. At the age of sixteen he began teaching in the common schools. Three years later he began the study of law at Madison and in 1894 he was admitted to the bar. In 1896 he was elected prosecuting attorney, holding the office for one term, and is at the present time the county attorney. He has a high standing in the profession for one so young, and he enjoys the respect of both bench and bar in Jefferson and the surrounding counties. Mr. Roberts is a member of the Independent Order of Odd Fellows and the Improved Order of Red Men. He was married May 2, 1897, to Miss Eliza E. Stewart, a native of Jennings county, Ind., and they have two children: Albert S., aged five years, and Bernard S., who is still in his infancy. Mrs. Roberts is a member of the Methodist Episcopal church.

DANIEL W. FISHER was born in Sinking Valley, Blair county, Pa., Jan. 17, 1838. After a common school education he prepared for college partly at Milnwood and partly at Airy View academy in Central Pennsylvania. He entered the sophomore class in Jefferson college, in the autumn of 1854, and graduated in the summer of 1857, receiving one of the honors of his class. He then entered the Western theological seminary of the Presbyterian church at Allegheny, Pa., and completed the course in the spring of 1860. He was licensed to preach by the Presbytery of Huntingdon in the spring of 1859, and spent the summer as a missionary in Jackson county, in what is now West Virginia. In the spring of 1860 he was ordained by the same Presbytery as a missionary to Siam. Providential circumstances hindered his sailing and in the autumn he with his wife whom he had married in the spring, went to New Orleans, where he became the pastor of what is now the Memorial Presbyterian church. The war coming on, about the last of June of 1861 he voluntarily and contrary to the wishes of his people returned to the North. In August he was invited to become the regular supply of the First Presbyterian church of Wheeling, Va., and in January he became the pastor. Here he continued until April, 1876, when he resigned and went abroad for some months. On his return, after some time he temporarily took charge of the Second Presbyterian church of Madison, Ind. In July, 1879, he was elected president of Hanover college, and has ever since continued in that office. Dr. Fisher while a pastor at Wheeling received from Muskingum college the degree of D.D. and he has twice been honored with an LL.D. since he became a college president,—once by the University of Wooster and once by Washington and Jefferson. President Harrison appointed him a member of the commission to examine the United States Mint. He was a member of the committee of the General Assembly of the Presbyterian church which prepared the way for the revision of the Confession of Faith, and also a member of the commission which revised the Confession. He has frequently been a member of the General Assembly of his church, and as such has held important chairmanships.   He was the chairman of the special committee which secured the organization of united Presbyterian bodies on foreign mission fields; has been the moderator of the synods of Wheeling, Pittsburg and Indiana, and was in one Assembly a prominent candidate for the moderatorship.   Dr. Fisher has written and published much, mainly in the line of his church and college work, and for the newspapers and higher periodicals open to such discussions.   He has also published many sermons.   He has three times gone abroad, the last time having with him his wife and daughter and going as far east as Palestine. His wife was Amanda D. Kouns of Ravenswood, W. Va.   They have three children.   The eldest, W. L. Fisher, of Chicago, is well known as the secretary of the Reform League of that city.   The second, Dr. Howard Fisher, is a physician practicing in Washington, D. C.   The third is Edith Fisher, the only daughter.

WALTER HENRY BRIMSON, of Cincinnati, Ohio, general superintendent of the B. & O. Southwestern, was born at Norwalk in that state.   His early education was received in the common schools at Norwalk and later at Norwalk academy, from which he graduated in 1870.   Immediately after graduation he entered the railway service with the Cleveland & Toledo Railway Company as a messenger in the telegraph department.   He served successively as telegraph operator and chief operator on that road; secretary to the superintendent; train despatcher; train master, superintendent of telegraph and superintendent on the Cincinnati, Sandusky & Cleveland; chief despatcher of the Lake Erie & Western; train master and superintendent of telegraph of the Chicago & Indiana Coal Railway; superintendent of the Duluth & Iron Range Railroad; despatcher on the Minnesota division of the Northern Pacific; assistant superintendent of the Pacific division of the same road and from 1892 to Aug. 1, 1895, was superintendent of the Rocky Mountain division of that road at Missoula, Montana.   On Nov. 1, 1895, he was appointed superintendent of the Brainerd & Northern Minnesota railroad, resigning that position in June, 1896.   On May 1, 1897, he went to the Baltimore & Ohio Southwestern at Chillicothe,

O., from which position he was promoted to that of general superintendent at Cincinnati on Feb. 1, 1898. On Oct. 16, 1872, he married
Frances D. Drake of Sandusky, O.

JOHN S. PERNETT, of Jeffersonville,
Ind., sheriff of Clark county, is a son of
Samuel and Naomi (Bowman) Pernett,
both natives of Indiana. The father was
born in Switzerland county, April 5,
1837, and was in later life engaged in
merchandizing at Bethlehem in Clark
county. He died there on Oct. 25, 1873.
The mother was born in Clark county,
Sept. 9, 1840, and is still living. They
had six children, viz.: Edward S., Emanuel, Emma, Charles E., John S. and Eva.
After the death of her first husband the
mother married a Mr. Jackson, and one daughter, Goldie Jackson,
has been born to this second marriage. On the paternal side Mr. Pernett is of Swiss extraction, his grandfather, David Emanuel Pernett,
having been born in that country, March 2, 1797. While still a
young man he came to America and died at Bethlehem, April 26, 1858,
being associated with his son in mercantile pursuits at the time of
his death. The maternal grandfather was John Bowman, a native of
Hamilton county, Ohio, born Oct. 25, 1814, and died Aug. 31, 1889.
The grandmother, Isabella Bowman, was born Jan. 24, 1818, and
died Dec. 10, 1898. John S. Pernett was born at Bethlehem, Sept. 26,
1869. He attended the common schools of his native township, then
in succession the normal school at New Washington; the Borden institute; the Bryant & Stratton business college of Louisville, Ky.;
DePauw university at Greencastle, Ind.; and in 1893-94 was a student
in the law department of the State university at Bloomington. In
1894, soon after leaving college, he was appointed trustee of his township to fill out an unexpired term, and afterward taught for two
seasons in the common schools. Shortly after Herman Rave took
charge of the sheriff's office he appointed Mr. Pernett to the position
of deputy, and in 1902 he was elected on the Democratic ticket to
succeed Mr. Rave, though he did not assume the duties of the office
until January, 1904. He was elected to a second term in 1904. Mr.
Pernett was married on Nov. 12, 1899, to Miss Lotta, daughter of
Charles W. and Mildred Vaughn, of Louisville.

GEORGE W. STONER, recorder of Clark county, Jeffersonville, Ind., is a descendant of one of the oldest families in that section of the state. His great-grandfather, Valentine Stoner, was one of four brothers who came from Germany prior to the Revolutionary war. Upon reaching this country they separated, each settling in a different colony. Valentine served in the Continental army during the Revolution, being at the battle of Lexington, the first outbreak of the war. After the war was over he came West and settled in what is now Clark county. His son, Jacob Stoner, the grandfather of George W., was born after the family came to the county. During his infancy he was hidden in a hollow log to escape the Indians the time of the Pigeon Roost massacre. At the time of his death he owned nine farms of eighty acres each—one for each of his children. Alfred Stoner, the father of the subject of this sketch, was born in Clark county in 1829 and died there in 1900. There are now some of the sixth generation from Valentine Stoner living in the county. George W. Stoner is of the fourth generation and was born on his father's farm, Oct. 9, 1862. He received his education in the public schools and after leaving school engaged in farming and buying timber, continuing in these occupations until elected recorder of the county in 1902. Mr. Stoner has been actively identified with the Democratic party ever since he attained his majority and his election to the office of recorder was but the well merited reward of a faithful supporter of Democratic principles. He took charge of the office in 1903 and is now serving the second year of his four years' term. In 1881 he was married to Miss Maggie B. Dismore, the daughter of one of Scott county's representative citizens. Her father, Richard Dismore, is a son of Nathaniel Dismore, who came over from Ireland in 1798 and settled near Clark's Fort on the Ohio river. There are now some of the fifth generation of his descendants living in the counties of Scott and Clark. To Mr. and Mrs. Stoner there have been born the following children: Elmer, Arthur, Ethel, Bertha, George Dewey, Mattie and Maggie B.

CAPT. EDWARD CLEGG, chief of police, Jeffersonville, Ind., was born on a farm in Clark county, of that state, July 23, 1870. His parents, William Harrison and Mary Clegg, were both natives of Scott county, the father born June 20, 1842, and the mother, April 8, 1845. They had a family of six daughters and three sons. Edward Clegg was educated in the common schools and after leaving school entered the employ of the Ohio Falls Car Works, where he remained for ten years. At the end of that time he was appointed a patrolman on the Jeffersonville police force, and has ever since been connected with the police department of the city. As a patrolman he made a model officer, which led to his promotion in the force. On Jan. 1, 1903, he was appointed chief, a fitting recognition of his fidelity and efficiency in subordinate positions. Politically Captain Clegg is a Republican and in 1902 he received the nomination of his party for the office of sheriff, but was defeated with the rest of the ticket. He is a member of several fraternal organizations, chief among them being the Independent Order of Odd Fellows. Captain Clegg married Maggie Roster, a daughter of John and Ellen Roster. Both her parents, now deceased, were natives of Ireland. To this marriage there have been born four sons: Joseph H., Eugene A., John W., and Franklin E. Captain Clegg has passed his entire life in the county where he was born. He is interested in promoting the general welfare of Jeffersonville and Clark county and realizes that an orderly community is necessary to the industrial and commercial prosperity of the people. Consequently he has introduced various reforms since becoming chief of police that tend to improve the moral conditions of the city and give better protection to person and property.

BERNARD A. COLL, of Jeffersonville, Ind., treasurer of Clark county, was born in the city of Pittsburg, Pa., Oct. 22, 1862. He is a son of Maurice and Maria (Herron) Coll, the former a native of Ireland and the latter of New Orleans, La. Maurice Coll came to America in his early manhood and located at Pittsburg, where he was for many years associated with the foundry and machine works of Maffett, Coll & Nold. In 1869 he came to Indiana as a machinist in the employ of the Pennsylvania railroad company. Bernard at that time was but seven years of age. Soon after coming to Jeffersonville he entered the parochial school of St. Augustine's church and attended that institution until he was about sixteen, receiving a good practical education. He began his business career as a retail grocer in Jeffersonville, and continued in that vocation for twenty years. He then took a position as traveling salesman for the wholesale grocery house of H. C. Armstrong, of Louisville, Ky., but after three years returned to the retail grocery business. Two years later he was elected treasurer of Clark county on the Democratic ticket. At the close of his first term he was honored with a triumphant re-election and is now serving his second term. Mr. Coll is a genial gentleman, who owes his political success largely to his "mixing" qualities. As a public official he has won the reputation of a careful, efficient, and conscientious officer—one who realizes that in his public capacity he is the servant of the people, rather than their master. Consequently his treatment of all who have business with the treasurer's office is uniformly courteous, which has added materially to his popularity. He was married on Feb. 22, 1892, to Miss Carrie A., daughter of Galen and Bridget Meadows, of Clark county. Mrs. Coll died on Aug. 16, 1902, leaving one daughter, Edna K., now twelve years of age.

CAPT. JOHN E. COLE, chief of the fire department of the city of Jeffersonville, Ind., was born in the State of Maryland, Aug. 5, 1857, his parents being Godfrey G. and Mary (Sweeney) Cole. The father was a native of Vermont, a stone cutter by trade, and died in 1857. The mother was born in Ireland, and is still living at the age of seventy-five years, having been born in 1829. Their family consisted of two sons and one daughter. John E. Cole was educated in the Jeffersonville city schools. After leaving school he entered the employ of the Pennsylvania Railroad Company, in March, 1874, and remained with that company until 1883, when he was elected city marshal of Jeffersonville. He served as marshal for eight years, when he returned to railroading as yard master for the Illinois Central until June 23, 1902, at which time he was appointed to a position as pipeman in the Jeffersonville fire department. His promptness, his aptitude and his fidelity won for him the approbation of his superiors, which naturally led to his promotion, and in 1904 he was elected chief of the department. Some years ago Mr. Cole was married to Miss Catherine, daughter of Patrick and Mary Carroll, and to this marriage there have been born the following children: Marie, aged twenty-three years; Amy, aged twenty-one; John, aged nineteen; Edwin, aged seventeen; Harold, aged fifteen, and Clarence, aged thirteen.

HON. HARRY C. MONTGOMERY, judge of the Fourth judicial circuit of Indiana, which is composed of Clark county, was born in Jeffersonville, the county seat of that county, April 9, 1870. His father was Capt. John R. Montgomery, for many years a pilot on the Ohio and Mississippi rivers, a native of Kentucky, who removed with his parents to Clark county in 1840, and served during the Civil war as a captain in the United States navy attached to the Mississippi river gunboat flotilla. After the close of the war he was a pilot in the Cincinnati and New Orleans passenger trade, dying in 1873 of yellow fever, contracted while in that service. Captain Montgomery married Miss Mary L. Mauzy, who was born May 10, 1840, near Salem in Washington county, Ind. Mrs. Montgomery resides with Judge Montgomery in Jeffersonville. He has no brothers; his sisters are Miss Sadie L. Montgomery, principal of the training school for teachers of Springfield, Ill., Mrs. Jessie L. Abbott, and Mrs. May L. Wear of San Angelo, Texas. Judge Montgomery was educated in the public schools of Jeffersonville, at DePauw university, Greencastle, Ind., and at the university of Louisville, Ky., from the legal department of which last named university he graduated in 1895 with the degree of Bachelor of Laws. He was admitted to the bar in Clark county in 1895, since which time he has practiced his profession in Jeffersonville. He was elected prosecuting attorney of the Clark circuit court in 1896 and re-elected in 1898, serving as such until 1900. In 1904 he was elected to the position of circuit judge which he now holds. He has probably a larger acquaintance and more sincere friends than any other man in Clark county. As a man his character is above reproach, as a lawyer he has enjoyed the confidence of all who have had dealings with him, as a judge he has neither friends nor enemies, and cares not whether litigants are weak or powerful, rich or poor, nor what their station in life may be; they have all the same privileges before him, and their causes are decided strictly according to the law. He is a good lawyer, a conscientious judge and an affable gentleman, who has for his friends all law abiding citizens.

VICTOR W. LYON, city engineer of Jeffersonville, Ind., was born in that city, June 26, 1853, his parents being Maj. Sidney S. and Honora (Vincent) Lyon. The father was born at Cincinnati, Ohio, in the year 1807. He was a geologist, paleontologist, civil engineer and artist of some note. In 1848 he located at Jeffersonville, where he passed the remainder of his life. He was prominent in the Masonic fraternity and the Independent Order of Odd Fellows, and was always interested in the promotion of the public welfare. He died June 24, 1872. The mother of Victor W. Lyon was born in Cork, Ireland, in 1818, and died Feb. 22, 1900. Victor was educated in the public schools of his native city, after which he attended the Union College at Ann Arbor, Mich. He began his business career as a clerk in a pork packing establishment at Jeffersonville. In 1880 he was elected surveyor of Clark county and served by re-election for fourteen consecutive years. From 1891 to 1894 he was city engineer of Jeffersonville, and again from 1898 to 1902. He was then appointed railroad surveyor for the Louisville city railroad and served in that capacity until June 3, 1903, when he was again elected city engineer of Jeffersonville, for the term ending in 1905. Mr. Lyon is a member of Myrtle Lodge, Knights of Pythias, to which he has belonged ever since 1880, and he was for some years active in the Uniform Rank of the same order. He is also a member of the First Presbyterian church of Jeffersonville, with which he united in 1892. He was married on Nov. 25, 1886, to Miss Gertrude Pettit, daughter of Thomas and Mary Pettit, of Clark county, and they have two daughters and a son, viz: Mary, aged fifteen years; Mildred, aged thirteen, and Sidney, aged ten.

FRANK M. MAYFIELD, a promising young lawyer of Jefferson-ville, Ind., and prosecuting attorney for the Fourth judicial circuit, composed of Clark county, was born at Little York, Washington county, Ind., July 21, 1870. He is a son of James H. and Mary (Hartley) Mayfield. His father was a native of Tennessee, and was for many years a well known farmer of Washington county, where he died in 1891, his wife having died in 1874. The subject of this sketch was educated in the public schools of Jeffersonville, after which he graduated from the New Albany business college. In 1896 he entered the Indianapolis law school, from which he graduated in 1898. The same year he was admitted to the bar in Clark county, where he practiced his profession until 1900, when he was elected to the office of prosecuting attorney. Being young and ambitious as well as a close student of everything pertaining to his profession, he made an efficient prosecutor during his term of two years. His work received the approval of a re-election in 1902 and he is now serving his second term. Admitted to the bar only six years ago, and having four years of public service to his credit, is a record of which any young lawyer might feel proud. In his practice Mr. Mayfield has won the respect of his brother attorneys by his dignified demeanor and his knowledge of the law, and a successful future is predicted for him by those who know him best. He is a member of the Masonic fraternity, the Knights of Pythias, the Modern Woodmen, and the Benevolent and Protective Order of Elks. On Nov. 16, 1900, he was married to Miss Julia L., daughter of George W. and Lucretia Felker, of Clark county, and to this marriage there has been born one daughter.

THOMAS W. PERRY, city treasurer, Jeffersonville, Ind., was born at Utica, in the same county, Sept. 7, 1860. His parents, William R. and Letitia (Robinson) Perry, were both natives of Clark county, the former having been born at Utica in 1832, and the latter at Bethlehem. The father was for a number of years engaged in the lime business at Utica. He died in 1889, and the mother in 1896. They had nine children, of whom the subject of this sketch and Samuel R. are the only ones now living. Thomas W. Perry received his primary education in the Jeffersonville public schools. In 1887 he entered the Cincinnati school of pharmacy and graduated two years later. In 1891 he embarked in the drug business in Jeffersonville, and continued in that line until 1902, after which he was the local agent of the Standard Oil Company for some time. From 1897 to

1901 he served with distinction in the city council, and in 1902 was elected school trustee. In these official capacities he made friends by his straightforward course in public matters, which led to his election to the office of city treasurer in May, 1904. Mr. Perry is a prominent Knight of Pythias, being a member of both the Lodge and the Uniform Rank. He is also a Knight Templar Mason and a member of the Royal Arcanum. He was married in 1882 to Miss Rosa, daughter of Selby and Anna Bennett, of Prather, Ind. She died in 1890, leaving three children: Ethel, Irvin and Halbert. In 1891 Mr. Perry was married to Cora A. Swartz, of Utica, and to this second marriage there has been born one daughter, Letitia.

HENRY F. DILGER, city attorney of Jeffersonville, Ind., was born in Perry county of that state, Feb. 26, 1865. His parents, Joseph and Rosina Dilger, were both natives of Germany. They moved to Southern Michigan in March, 1865, and remained there until the fall of 1871, when they moved to Spencer county, Ind. The mother died in 1884 and the father in 1891. Henry F. Dilger, the subject of this sketch, attended the country schools of Spencer county until he was fourteen years of age, when he went to work in a sawmill. In 1884, seeing the needs of an education, he started to school again, beginning work where he left off five years before. After two years, during which time he worked as a farm hand in summer, to earn money to carry him through school in winter, he began teaching in the public schools of Crawford county, Ind. After teaching two years in this county he taught one year in Kentucky, and after that two years in Clark county, Ind. In 1892 he began the study of law in the office of H. D. McMullen & Son of Aurora, Ind., and during the school year of 1892-93 was a student in the law school at Danville. He was prevented from completing the course of study on account of friends to whom he had loaned his earnings having become bankrupt. He therefore came to Jeffersonville and entered the law office of George H. Voigt, one of the leading attorneys of the Clark county bar, and in 1894 was admitted to the bar. In 1897 he returned to the school room and taught until 1900. He then resumed the practice of law in Jeffersonville, and May, 1904, was elected to the office of city attorney. Mr. Dilger is a fine example of a self made man. Beginning his career as a helper in a sawmill when only fourteen, he has steadily climbed the ladder to his present position. His success has not made him vain, however, and to his friends he is the same genial gentleman under all circumstances. The only fraternal organization to claim him as a member is the Independent Order of Odd Fellows. In 1899 Mr. Dilger was united in marriage to Miss Annie L., daughter of Christopher and Elizabeth Meyer, of Clark county. To this marriage there has been born one son, Frank H., now four years old. Mr. Dilger owns a beautiful home in Jeffersonville, and is one of the substantial and progressive citizens of the city.

THOMAS J. BROCK, a prominent attorney and representative citizen of Jeffersonville, Ind., was born at Borden, Clark county, Ind., July 9, 1876. His parents, Francis Marion and Abigail (Brown) Brock, are both natives of Indiana, the father having been born at Martinsburg, Washington county, July 22, 1849, and the mother near Borden, Nov. 7, 1854. Francis M. Brock is a minister of the Christian church. Their family consists of two sons, Thomas J., the subject of this sketch, and John B. Thomas J. Brock was educated at the Borden institute, graduating in the normal, scientific and academic courses in 1892. He then studied law in the same institution and in 1898 was admitted to the bar. He established an office in the city of Jeffersonville and began the practice of his profession, soon acquiring a good clientage and winning a high standing at the bar. Upon reaching his majority Mr. Brock cast his political fortunes with the Democratic party, and in every campaign since that time he has been an active factor in shaping the destinies of the Clark county Democracy. In September, 1900, he was elected to the office of city attorney, and held the position until he was succeeded by Henry F. Dilger, who was elected in May, 1904. Mr. Brock is a member of the Free and Accepted Masons and the Knights of Pythias, in both of which societies he is deservedly popular because of his high social attributes and sterling qualities. He was married on Dec. 23, 1894, to Miss Ada Littell, a native of Clark . county, and daughter of Milburn and Rachel (Thomas) Littell. To this marriage there have been born two boys, Howard Curtis, aged eight years, and Byron Jennings, aged six.

CHARLES ZOLLMAN, of Jefferson-ville, Ind., one of the leading lawyers of the Clark county bar, was born at Charlestown, in that county, March 1, 1875. His father, William Zollman, was born in Prussia, Nov. 7, 1842. When he was twelve years of age he came with his parents to America, and after a long and tedious voyage on a sailing vessel landed at New York in 1854. The following year the family came West and settled at Charlestown, where William Zollman grew to manhood and married Elizabeth, daughter of Charles and Elizabeth Bohmer. She was born at Charlestown in December, 1850. To this marriage there were born two sons, Charles and Christopher. The parents still live near Charlestown, where the father is a well known farmer. Charles Zollman received his primary education in the public schools, after which he attended a normal school in Scott county, and in 1898 entered the law department of the University of Louisville. He graduated from this institution in 1900 and the same year was elected on the Democratic ticket to represent Clark county in the state legislature. He began the practice of law in 1901 at Jeffersonville, and in 1903 formed a partnership with Burdette Lutz. In 1902 he was again elected to the legislature. During both terms as representative he served on some of the important house committees and was always alive to the interests of his constituents. When the Clark county Democratic convention met in March, 1904, he received the nomination for prosecuting attorney, and was elected the succeeding November. Mr. Zollman is a member of the Improved Order of Red Men. As an attorney he has a high standing at the bar, as a politician he is recognized as a good organizer and a mixer, and as a man he enjoys the respect and esteem of his acquaintances because of his intellectual and social qualities.

GEORGE W. McKINLEY, of Borden, Ind., county assessor of Clark county, was born in that county, March 3, 1855, his parents being Jeremiah and Elizabeth (Packwood) McKinley. The father was born in Kentucky in 1800, and came with his parents to Clark county when he was but six years of age. There he grew to manhood and was for many years one of the best known farmers in the county. He died March 3, 1883. The mother was born in Virginia on New Year's day, 1807, and died in Clark county on her seventieth birthday. George W. is the youngest of a family of thirteen children. He received a good common school education in the schools of Wood township, and upon reaching his majority adopted the life of a farmer, in which he has been successful. Mr. McKinley has always taken an active interest in public affairs, and in 1895 was elected assessor of his township. In this office he served for five years, or until 1900, when he was elected assessor for the county. His term expires Jan. 1, 1907. He is a member of the Independent Order of Odd Fellows and the Modern Woodmen of the World, and is popular in both of these well known societies because of his genial disposition and his many sterling qualities. He was married in 1877 to Miss Carrie M., daughter of J. B. and Isabel Miller, of Floyd county. Four sons and two daughters have been born to this union, viz.: Evart M., Tollmer, Bertha B., Hattie Z., Jacob and Morris. Their ages are respectively twenty-six, twenty-four, twenty-two, nineteen, seventeen and twelve years.

MICHAEL A. WALL, of Jeffersonville, Ind., deputy sheriff of Clark county, was born in the city where he now resides, April 16, 1870. His parents, John and Elizabeth (Cook) Wall, were both natives of Ireland. They came to America in 1863, and located at Jeffersonville, where the father followed his trade of blacksmithing until his death in 1883. The mother died on the day that Michael was one year old. Michael A. Wall received a good practical education in the Jeffersonville public schools, after which he learned the trade of bolt maker and worked at that occupation until 1895. He was then for about two years in a commission house. In 1897 he was appointed to a place on the police force and served for about six years. When Sheriff Pernett took charge of the office on Jan. 1, 1904, he appointed Mr. Wall to the position of deputy, a position for which his long service with the police department gave him especial qualifications. He was married in 1899 to Miss Lula Gobin, daughter of Adam and Maggie Gobin, of Henderson, Ky. Three children have been born to this marriage: Henry Edward, twelve years of age; Margaret Evelyn, aged seven, and Helen Louise, aged four.

JOSEPH H. WARDER, city clerk of Jeffersonville, Ind., was born in that city, June 17, 1878, and is a son of Luther F. and Elizabeth (Lewis) Warder. The father was born in the State of Kentucky, Dec. 2, 1841, and came to Jeffersonville when he was about twenty years of age. There he was employed in the railroad shops and government work until his death, which occurred June 12, 1902. He took an active interest in public matters, and was for several years mayor of the city. He served one term in that office in the early eighties, and again from 1887 to 1891. His wife was born in Clark county, Ind., Feb. 23, 1842, and is still living. Joseph H. received his education in the public schools, graduating from Jeffersonville high school in 1897. From 1899 to 1901 he was a student in the Louisville, Ky., law school, and in the latter year was admitted to the bar. He began practice at Jeffersonville, and soon won a high standing in his chosen profession. Mr. Warder has always taken an active part in political contests, and is a splendid example of the younger school of Democrats. In 1904 he was chairman of the city central committee, being elected city clerk the same year. Notwithstanding his political activity he has many warm personal friends among the opposition, because of his genial disposition and general good fellowship. He belongs to the Improved Order of Red Men, which is the only fraternal society to claim him as a member.

PORTER C. BUTTORFF, secretary and treasurer of the Indiana Chain Company, and manager of the Indiana Manufacturing Company, Jeffersonville, Ind., was born in Nashville, Tenn., April 12, 1866, and is a son of Henry W. and Mary E. (Nokes) Buttorff. The father was born in Carlisle, Pa., Aug. 18, 1837, and the mother in Virginia in 1845. She died in 1891. Their children were Porter C., Lucy, Ethel, Mary, Lizzie, Hattie, Alice, Henry, Ella and Isabel. Henry W. Buttorff was educated at Carlisle and at the age of twenty, after learning the trade of tinner, went to Nashville. There he worked for a time at his trade, forming a partnership with W. H. Wilson. After a time he bought out Mr. Wilson and formed the firm of Phillips, Buttorff & Co. In 1881 this concern was incorporated under the name of the Phillips & Buttorff Manufacturing Company, with a capital stock of $400,000. Annual dividends of ten per cent were paid up to 1890, when a stock dividend of twenty-five per cent was declared. From that time until Jan. 1, 1904, the annual dividends amounted to eight per cent. At that time a cash dividend of twenty per cent was paid. The stock now amounts to $500,000 and the undivided profits to $850,000 more. Porter C. Buttorff received a high school education in Nashville, and in 1884 graduated from a technical school at Worcester, Mass. For about a year he was engaged with the National Sheet Metal Roofing Company, of New York City, after which he returned to Nashville, where he was associated with his father's company until 1901. About the beginning of the present century he built the works of the Indiana Chain Company, and in 1901 was made secretary and treasurer. Mr. Buttorff's training has been of that character that makes strong and successful business men. Under his direction his company has come rapidly to the front as one of the leading manufacturing industries about the Ohio Falls. He is a prominent member of the Masonic fraternity and the Knights of Pythias. Some years ago he led to the altar Miss Cornelia Johnson, daughter of Stephen Johnson of Nashville. She was born in that city June 20, 1870. To this marriage there have been born two sons: Henry, aged thirteen years, and Gordon, aged six.

BURDETTE C. LUTZ, a popular and successful attorney of Jeffersonville, Ind., was born on a farm near that city, June 28, 1875. His paternal grandfather, Joseph Lutz, was a native of South Carolina, who came to Clark county, Ind., in his early manhood, and there followed the occupation of a farmer for many years. Henry J. Lutz, the father of the subject of this sketch, was born in Clark county in 1845. He married Rhoda B., daughter of William Gibson, one of the old settlers. She was born in 1850. To this marriage there were born seven children, five sons and two daughters. Burdette C. Lutz was educated in the public schools, the Charlestown high school, and in 1900 graduated from the State University of Indiana, at Bloomington, with the degree of LL.B. He first began the practice of law at Sellersburg, in 1901, but in March, 1903, he formed a partnership with Charles Zollman and located in Jeffersonville. Notwithstanding both members of this firm are young men a good clientage has been built up, few firms in the city occupying a higher standing at the bar. On the election of Mr. Zollman as prosecuting attorney of Clark county Mr. Lutz was appointed his deputy on Jan. 1, 1905. Mr. Lutz is a member of the Knights of the Maccabees, which is the only fraternal organization to claim his membership, and he belongs to the Christian church.

GEORGE S. ANDERSON, founder, Jeffersonville, Ind., was born at Port Fulton, in that state, Feb. 1, 1840, his parents being Charles C. and Mary (Lanciscus) Anderson. The father was born in New York in 1811. In early life he came to Cincinnati, where he worked in a foundry until its removal from the city, when he went to Port Fulton. That was in 1832. A few years later he came to Jeffersonville, where he became the head of the firm of Anderson, Robinson & Goss, founders, and continued in that line until his death in 1890. The mother was born in Pennsylvania in 1818, but came to Jeffersonville in her childhood. She died in 1880. George S. Anderson is the second in a family of eight children. After an education in the public schools he began his business career in his father's foundry. In 1884, in company with his brothers, Charles and Robert, he succeeded to the business. Upon the death of Robert in 1903 his interest was taken by W. H. Lang. The foundry is one of the oldest and best established in the city and has an extensive patronage. Mr. Anderson was married in 1862 to Miss Kate S. Watson. Of their family but one son, William, is living. Mr. Anderson is a member of Advent Christian church.

GEORGE H. D. GIBSON, of Charlestown, Ind., is one of the best known lawyers in Southern Indiana. He was born at Charlestown in September, 1851, his parents being Thomas Ware and Mary (Goodwin) Gibson. The father was born in the city of Philadelphia in 1815. When he was six years of age he came with his parents to Indiana, the family locating at Lawrenceburg. He was educated at West Point, studied law and was admitted to the bar in 1837, and from 1851 to 1876 practiced his profession at Louisville, Ky. He was a member of the Indiana constitutional convention of 1851 and was two terms in the state senate. At the beginning of the Mexican war he raised a company in Clark county, and served through the contest, holding a commission as captain. His wife was a daughter of Amos and Amelia Goodwin, of Clark county. She was born May 20, 1820. George H. D. Gibson is one of a family of three children now living, two sons and a daughter. He was educated at the Kentucky Military institute, at Frankfort, and in 1874 was graduated from the law department of the University of Louisville. He practiced at Charlestown from 1874 until 1876, serving as prosecuting attorney of Clark county during the year 1875. From 1877 to 1892 he practiced in Louisville, but resided in Indiana all the time. In 1880 he was elected a member of the Indiana legislature and re-elected in 1882. In 1892 he was elected judge of the Fourth judicial circuit of Indiana, consisting of Clark county, and held the office for a full term of six years. Since his retirement from the bench he has devoted most of his time to agricultural pursuits, especially the raising of Hereford cattle. For many years Judge Gibson took an active interest in political matters. As a Democrat he was called upon to take the stump in every campaign, and few speakers in his section of the state could better hold an audience or make a more instructive speech on public issues. He is a member of the Benevolent and Protective Order of Elks. In 1896 Judge Gibson was married to Miss Virginia C. Van Hook, daughter of William and Martha Van Hook, of Charlestown.

GEORGE W. BADGER, clerk of the Clark circuit court, Jeffersonville, Ind., was born at Charlestown, in that county, Dec. 29, 1860, his parents being Christian G. and Lereen M. (Green) Badger, the former a native of Prussia, and the latter of Clark county. Christian G. Badger was a tool-maker by trade. He came to America when he was eighteen years of age and located in Clark county. There he served as auditor of the county for eight years and as county treasurer for two years. He died in 1887, aged sixty-eight years. His widow is still living with her son, the subject of this sketch, and is eighty-one years of age. George W. Badger was reared in Charlestown and received his education at the Barnett academy and the public schools of that town. At the age of nineteen years he commenced teaching and followed that occupation for about three years, when he began to learn the printers' trade, but later changed to that of wheelwright, learning the latter trade in Indianapolis. After working awhile at his trade in Indianapolis he entered the employ of the Central Ohio Wheel Company, at Galion. After a short period in their shops as a mechanic he entered their office, and from this position became their traveling salesman. In 1886 he left the road and came home, and in the year 1888 was elected trustee of Charlestown township on the Democratic ticket. He served one term of two years and six months. In 1892 he was assistant doorkeeper of the National house of representatives at Washington; from 1895 to 1899 he was superintendent of the Clarksville public schools, near Jeffersonville; was elected county auditor in 1898, taking the office the following year; served one term of four years and two months, and in 1902 was elected clerk, taking office Feb. 27, 1904. Mr. Badger is well calculated by nature for a political leader, and in all the councils of his party he stands high, because of his quick discernment, his sound judgment and his readiness to assist in the execution of any plan proposed for the defeat of the enemy. Few Democrats in Southern Indiana are better known or more generally trusted. The Masonic fraternity is the only secret organization of which he is a member. On Nov. 6, 1887, he was married to Miss Jennie Campbell, of Charlestown, and they have four children living: Amelia, Karl, Maurice and Mildred, aged respectively fifteen, twelve, eight and four years.

GEORGE B. PARKS, auditor of Clark county, Jeffersonville, Ind., was born in that city, Nov. 16, 1876, and is a son of Floyd and Barbara Ella (Lutz) Parks, both natives of Clark county. On the paternal side the ancestry is of English and Scotch origin. William Parks, the great-grandfather of George B., was at one time an extensive land owner on Manhattan Island. His son, Lyman, who was born in New York, married Rachel Lavinia Lewis, a native of Virginia, and this couple came to Indiana, settling in Clark county. They are the grandparents of the subject of this sketch. Floyd Parks is a well known druggist of Jeffersonville. On the maternal side the grandparents, Henry and Mary Lutz, of German descent, were both natives of South Carolina. Floyd and Barbara Parks had seven children: Flora, now deceased, was the wife of F. M. Coots, of Jeffersonville; Lyman, a wholesale coal dealer and alderman of the same city; George B., the subject; Emma, wife of Herbert C. McMillin, a Clark county farmer; Floyd, Jr., a clerk in his father's drug store; Ella, and William, the last named dying in infancy. George B. Parks graduated from the Jeffersonville high school in 1894; spent the years 1894-95 in taking a mechanical course at Purdue university; entered the State university in the fall of 1895; took the four years' course there in three years, graduating with the degree of A.B. in 1898; was elected president of his class in his senior year—a class of 187 members; entered the law department of the University of Louisville in 1898 and graduated in 1900; was immediately afterward admitted to the bar and began practice as the senior member of the firm of Parks & White; took an active part in Democratic politics, and was elected auditor of Clark county in November, 1902, at the age of twenty-six years, receiving a majority of 460 over his opponent. He took charge of the office on Jan. 1, 1904, and enjoys the distinction of being the youngest county auditor in the state. The success of Mr. Parks is due to his intelligence, his thorough training, his indomitable energy and his genial disposition. He is a member of the Improved Order of Red Men and the Benevolent and Protective Order of Elks. In the Red Men he is chairman of the committee on by-laws in the Great Council. On the occasion of the celebration of Jeffersonville's centennial in 1902 he was grand marshal. In politics he has frequently served as delegate to state and congressional conventions, and was a delegate to the national convention at St. Louis in 1904.

HON. GEORGE BENNETT CARD-WILL, ex-judge of the circuit court of Floyd county, Ind., deputy clerk of the United States court for the Southern district of Indiana, and United States commissioner, was born in the city of Cincinnati, O., Sept. 17, 1846, his parents being John H. and Caroline B. (Montgomery) Cardwill, the former born in Rutland county, Vermont, May 18, 1814, and the latter in Sussex county, N. J., born July 14th, of the same year. The father was reared in Central New York, where he learned the trade of tanner and currier, and about 1836 or 1837 he came West. After visiting a number of places, among them Chicago and Indianapolis, then mere villages, he decided to locate at Cincinnati. For some time he pursued his trade there, but later became connected with the firm of A. M. Taylor & Co., wholesale dealers in leather and findings for the shoe and harness trades. In 1850 this firm sent him to Louisville as their representative, and it was in that city that Judge Cardwill received his first schooling. In 1856 the family removed to New Albany, where the husband and father formed a partnership with W. S. Durbin, father of ex-Governor Durbin, of Indiana, for the purpose of conducting a tannery and grist-mill at New Philadelphia, in Washington county, not far from New Albany. This partnership lasted for several years, and the firm carried on a successful business. John H. Cardwill continued to reside in New Albany until his death, Sept. 5, 1899, being at the time one of the oldest and most highly respected citizens of the city. His widow and four children are still living, the eldest being the subject of this sketch; Ann Eliza and Mary E., of New Albany, and John H., of St. Louis, Mo. Mary E. Cardwill is the regent of Piankeshaw Chapter, Daughters of the American Revolution, which chapter she organized. The Cardwill ancestry can be traced back to the middle of the eighteenth century, to William Cardwill, who came from England in 1747, to New London, Conn., where he married Elizabeth Burch, and became the founder of the family in America. His son William married Sybil Griswold, a daughter of Elisha and Susanna (Merrill) Griswold, related to the same family as Governor Griswold of Connecticut. Coming down to the next generation, John Griswold, a son of William and grandfather of the subject, married Rachel Train, the daughter of Isaac Train, an old Revolutionary hero, and a member of the family from which the celebrated George Francis Train descended. William Cardwill, the great-grandfather, was a soldier in the Revolution. On the maternal side the grandparents were William and Ruth (Swezy) Montgomery, both natives of Orange county, N. Y., where the family were among the early settlers. In 1817 William Montgomery left Sussex county, N. J., came West and located on the present site of the Cincinnati zoological gardens, where the girlhood of Judge Cardwill's mother was spent. Judge Cardwill was educated in private schools at Louisville and New Albany and at Wabash college. Owing to his father's financial reverses he was thrown on his own resources in early life. For a time he tried merchandizing, but finding it uncongenial he entered the office of Stotsenburg & Brown at New Albany, read law and was admitted to the bar. His youth kept him from joining the army in the Civil war, but he took part in the famous Morgan raid. Ever since reaching his majority he has been an enthusiastic Republican. He organized and was the first president of the local Lincoln league; was secretary of the Republican county central committee in 1886; represented his district as an alternate to the presidential convention in 1888; nominated for prosecuting attorney the same year, but was defeated owing to the immense majority to overcome; appointed by Governor Chase in 1892 to fill out the unexpired term as judge of the circuit court, the vacancy being caused by the death of Judge George V. Howk; nominated for the legislature as the joint representative of Floyd, Harrison and Crawford counties; elected by a majority of 264 votes, although each of the counties in the district was ordinarily Democratic; appointed deputy clerk of the federal court at New Albany in December, 1897; about the same time appointed United States commissioner; has been active in building up the public library of New Albany; was one of the organizers and third president of the Commercial club; member of the Indiana chapter of the Sons of the American Revolution; also of the Phi Gamma Delta fraternity; one of the promoters of the New Albany Charity organization, and one of the executive committee. A glance at his long and honorable career shows that he is a worthy son of an ancient and honorable ancestry, and a typical American citizen, whose example is worthy of the highest emulation.

FRED D. CONNOR, deputy collector of internal revenue for the Seventh district of Indiana, at New Albany, was born in Perry county, of that state, Feb. 17, 1841, and is the son of Terrence and Nancy (Tate) Connor, both natives of Perry county, born in 1810 and 1820, respectively. His great-grandfather, whose name was originally Terrence O'Connor, was a native of Virginia. He served in the Revolution in Captain Galliher's company of Col. David Morgan's regiment. His name appears on pages 257-264 of Saffell's "Records of the Revolutionary War" as Terrence Connor, the "O" being dropped, and he was an associate of Washington and LaFayette. He was discharged at Bush Creek on North river in 1779. Soon after he married Miss Sarah J. Speaks and came West, settling first in Washington county, Ky., in 1785, and in 1806 he came to Perry county, Ind., where he died Dec. 6, 1841.

The paternal grandfather of F. D. Connor was Samuel Connor, a captain in the war of 1812, under Col. R. W. Evans. He served as a member of the Indiana legislature, was a brigadier-general of the state militia, took part in the battle of Tippecanoe, and died on his farm July 26, 1863. Terrence Connor, the father, was a farmer and river pilot, and ran a line of flatboats on the Ohio and Mississippi rivers for many years. He died on his farm Sept. 10, 1859. His wife died at Leavenworth, Jan. 8, 1879. The subject of this sketch received his education in the common schools of Perry county, and in 1859 received a scholarship in Asbury university at Greencastle. He went to Gibson county and sold books to get the money to carry him through. He was successful and realized about $600, but his father's death, which occurred just at that time, changed the whole course of his life. Fred being the eldest of a family of nine children, it devolved upon him to take care of the family, and the money which he had accumulated was used to pay his father's doctor bills and funeral expenses. The other eight children are John T., now postmaster of Toledo, Ill.; Terrence, a coal dealer at Baxter Springs, Kan.; George H., in the mining business in Idaho; Eliza J., a Mrs. Scribner, of Russellville, Ind.; Catherine C., Mrs. Wilson, of Roachdale, Ind.; Ada, Mrs. Miller, of Hanford, Cal.; Emily A., Mrs. Dodd, of Greencastle, Ind.; Andromedia, Mrs. Hawn, of Leavenworth, Ind. For two years after his father's death, Fred taught school. He enlisted in the Union army in company K, Thirty-fourth regiment, Kentucky volunteers, and served until the close of the war, being discharged June 7, 1865. Although engaged in several battles, he escaped without a scratch, but lost an eye as the result of typhoid fever in 1864. After the war he went to Indianapolis and was engaged as chief clerk in the United States pension office under Col. John W. Ray, pension agent for Indiana. In 1868 he came to New Albany, and later became deputy collector under Col. H. Woodbury. With slight intervals, during the Cleveland administrations, he has held the office ever since, serving under Presidents Grant, Hayes, Garfield, Arthur, Harrison, McKinley and Roosevelt. Mr. Connor's first vote was for Lincoln in 1864, and he has voted the Republican ticket ever since. He is a member of the Grand Army of the Republic, a Knight Templar Mason, and Past Grand Master of the Ancient Order of United Workmen of Indiana. On Oct. 3, 1871, he was married to Miss Harriet Sackett, and they have two daughters, Edna C. and Alma, the latter being the wife of William P. Lewis, a hardware dealer of New Albany.

ROBERT W. MORRIS, postmaster at New Albany, Ind., was born in that city, Nov. 10, 1858, his parents being William D. and Eliza (Cutshaw) Morris, the former a native of Virginia and the latter of Washington county, Ind. The father came to Indiana with his parents while still in his boyhood. His father, George Morris, settled at Greenville, a little village about twelve miles from New Albany, where the father of the subject of this sketch lived until some time in the forties, when he removed to New Albany, and died there on June 5, 1882, in his sixty-third year. His wife died in 1868, at the age of forty-two. Robert W. Morris is one of ten children, the eldest two of whom died in infancy, the others being Frank M., Noble D., James B., Richard A., Rebecca, Maurice, and Nathaniel. James and Rebecca died in later life, leaving six sons living and all are active Republicans. Robert W. was reared in New Albany and received his education in the schools of that city. From the age of nine to sixteen years he clerked in his father's store when not in school, and at the age of sixteen he began the battle of life for himself. His first position was that of driver of a delivery wagon for George W. Grosheider, a grocer, and later was a clerk in the grocery, remaining with Mr. Grosheider for seven years. In 1883 he was elected city clerk and was re-elected in 1885. Before the expiration of his second term as clerk he was elected auditor of the county. That was in 1886 and in 1890 he was re-elected to the auditor's office, holding altogether for eight years. In 1896 he was elected to the legislature from Floyd county, although the county was nominally Democratic, and his various political victories in such a county tell the story of his personal popularity. In 1899 he was appointed postmaster of New Albany by the late President McKinley and took the office March 5, of that year. On Feb. 9, 1903, he was reappointed by President Roosevelt for a second term of four years. As postmaster he has brought a high order of executive ability to the place and has instituted a number of reforms in the office for the betterment of the service. Mr. Morris is a Royal Arch and Scottish Rite Mason, a Knight Templar, an Odd Fellow, a Knight of Pythias, an Elk, and a Red Man. In the Knights of Pythias he belongs to the Uniform Rank, and he is a

Past Exalted Ruler of the Elks' lodge. He is also a member of the New Albany Commercial club. He was married Nov. 30, 1891, to Miss Nellie Emory, an accomplished young lady of New Albany.

FRANK L. SHRADER, ex-mayor of New Albany, Ind., was born in that city, June 23, 1861. His parents, John and Margaret (Smith) Shrader, were both natives of Germany, but came in childhood with their parents to America. The paternal grandfather, Bossler Shrader, settled in New Albany, and there his son, John, the father of Mayor Shrader, was for half a century one of the leading furniture manufacturers and dealers of the city. He founded the well known establishment of the John Shrader, Sr., Company, now incorporated, and of which Frank L. is the president. John Shrader died March 17, 1895, in the seventy-sixth year of his age. His wife died in February, 1901, having passed the age of threescore and ten. They had eleven children, ten of whom are yet living, viz.: George B., John H., Adelia, now Mrs. Webster; William S., Edward N., Magnolia, now Mrs. Joseph Gimnich, of Louisville; Frank L., Susette, Mrs. William Holman, Ella E., the widow of Edward Holman, and Eva, Mrs. Eugene W. Walker. All reside in New Albany except Mrs. Gimnich. Charles died in infancy. Frank L. Shrader attended the public schools until he reached the age of sixteen years, when he entered his father's furniture establishment and has ever since been identified with the furniture business in the city of New Albany. In January, 1885, he severed his connection with his father and embarked in the furniture and carpet business for himself, buying the store formerly operated by his brother, John H. Shrader, the latter retiring from business. For nearly twenty years he has been one of the leading carpet and furniture dealers of the city; was one of the incorporators of the John Shrader, Sr., Company, and for the last three years has been president. Mr. Shrader is a Republican in his political opinions and in 1902 was elected mayor of the city on that ticket. His administration was marked by that high order of executive ability that has characterized his business career, and he was a popular official. He is a member of the Knights of Pythias and the Improved Order of Red Men, in both of which societies he is universally liked because of his genial disposition and sterling qualities. Mr. Shrader was married in October, 1890, to Miss Annella D. Baldwin, a daughter of the late Thomas Baldwin, of New Albany.

HON. THOMAS HANLON, a prominent Democrat of New Albany, and the present auditor of Floyd county, was born in County Clare, Ireland, Dec. 25, 1842, and is the son of John and Helen (Drony) Hanlon, both natives of the Emerald Isle. When Thomas was about ten years of age his mother died and the father married Mary Mahoney. Early in the year 1853 the family embarked on the sailing vessel *Mary Hale,* and after a somewhat tedious voyage landed at Baltimore on March 17th, St. Patrick's day. They settled first at Princeton, N. J., but two years later came West and located at Lafayette, Ind. There the father spent the rest of his life, passing to his rest Sept. 11, 1885, at the age of eighty-four years. His widow still resides in Lafayette. Thomas was but twelve years old when the family located at Lafayette. He did not have the opportunity to attend school, as his father, in addition to being a poor man, was a cripple, and the son had to begin to earn his own living early in life. Not only did he have to support himself but he had to assist in supporting the family. But with true Irish pluck he went to work and few men would have succeeded better than he has done. First he drove a gravel cart on the Wabash railroad, then under construction; then water-boy on the New Albany and Salem railroad, now part of the well known "Monon Route." He remained with this road for twenty years, working his way up from water-boy, through the positions of freight brakeman, passenger brakeman, freight conductor, and in 1861 was placed in charge of a passenger train and continued as a passenger conductor until 1875. In 1874, while running his train he was elected auditor of Floyd county and at the close of his first term was re-elected, holding the office from 1875 to 1883. Since then Mr. Hanlon has been identified with the political affairs of his city, county and state. When his second term as auditor expired he re-entered the employ of the Monon as freight and passenger agent at New Albany. In 1884 he resigned to become a candidate for the legislature. He was elected and made a good clean record as a legislator. In the spring of 1885 President Cleveland appointed him collector of internal revenue for the Seventh Indiana district, with his headquarters in New Albany. A fight occurred in the United States senate over the appointment, the late President Harrison, then a senator from Indiana, opposing his confirmation, because the appointment had been recommended by Senator Voorhees. The fight lasted for over two years but Mr. Hanlon was finally confirmed a short time before the adjournment of Congress in 1887, and he served out the remainder of the term, making his home and office at Terre Haute, Ind. Upon retiring from this position he again entered the railroad service as a passenger conductor on the Louisville Southern railroad. Here he continued until 1899, when he gave up his position to again assume the duties of auditor of Floyd county, to which office he was elected in 1898. In 1902 he was again re-elected and is now serving his fourth term in that office. His present term expires in 1908. If he lives to complete it he will have served seventeen years and two months as auditor. Mr. Hanlon is a Scottish Rite Mason, and is one of the best known and most universally liked Democrats in Southern Indiana, being now chairman of the central committee of the Third congressional district. He has been married three times. His first two wives have been called away by the hand of death and his present wife is a sister of the late Hon. James Rice, formerly auditor of the State of Indiana, and a daughter of Patrick Rice, who in his day was a popular merchant of New Albany. Mr. Hanlon has no living children.

CHARLES B. SCOTT, clerk of the Floyd circuit court, New Albany, Ind., was born at Scottsville, in that county, a village named in honor of his family, Feb. 27, 1866, his parents being Madison M. and Harriet (Goss) Scott. The father was born in Floyd county, Jan. 8, 1842, and died at New Albany, April 20, 1893. The mother was born in Clark county, Nov. 20, 1846, and still lives in New Albany. The Scott family is one of the oldest, the most prominent and the most numerous in the county. The paternal grandfather of Charles B. was Rev. Robert H. Scott, an Adventist minister, and a native of the county. He died in 1904. His father, John Scott, was one of the early settlers and founder of the family. He had a large family of children, all of whom lived to maturity. The descendants of John Scott are more numerous than those of any other of the pioneers of Floyd county. His children were

Emily, Elizabeth, Reasor, Robert H., James V., Harbert, John, David, Wesley and Richard. Six of the sons became local preachers. Robert H. reared a family of nine children, viz.: Madison M., John G., Robert H., Jr., Anna, Jane, Emily, Sallie, Rhoda and Caroline. Harbert Scott had a family of fifteen children, all of whom are yet living, except one who died in December, 1903. On the maternal side the grandparents of Charles B. Scott were Frederick and Cynthia (Campbell) Goss, the grandmother being a cousin of ex-Gov. James E. Campbell, of Ohio. Frederick Goss was a native of North Carolina, where he was born in 1801, and died in Floyd county in 1878. His wife was a native of Ohio, where she was born in 1808, and died in Floyd county at the age of sixty-four. Madison M. Scott, the father of the subject, was for twenty-five years a merchant in New Albany. He and his wife had six children: three died in infancy and those living are Charles B., Arthur E., and Bertha L., all of New Albany. Charles B. Scott was ten years old when his parents removed to the city. He was educated in the New Albany public schools, and after graduating from the high school he took a course in the New Albany Business college. After leaving school he went into the store with his father and remained there until the latter's death in 1893, when he and his brother succeeded to the business. In the year 1891 Charles was a clerk in the Indiana state legislature, and afterward he was appointed assistant postmaster at New Albany, serving until the fall of 1897, when a change in the administration caused his removal. In 1898 he was nominated by the Democracy of Floyd county for the office of clerk, and was elected in November of that year. In 1902 he was re-elected and is now on his second term, which expires Jan. 1, 1907. He served as secretary of the Democratic county central committee for ten years and is always ready to do his part to achieve a Democratic victory. In fraternal circles Mr. Scott is a member of the Uniform Rank, Knights of Pythias, and is a Past Exalted Ruler of his Lodge of Elks. He has been twice married. His first wife was Miss Charlotte Van Dyke, to whom he was united on June 22, 1892. She was the daughter of Rev. David Van Dyke, pastor of the Second Presbyterian church of New Albany. She died Oct. 18, 1894, leaving one son, Van Dyke, now eleven years of age. Mr. Scott was married the second time, on Nov. 29, 1899, to Miss Frances Schindler, of New Albany, a sister of former postmaster and ex-county recorder, Charles W. Schindler. She was born in Floyd county on Jan. 7, 1873; served two terms as deputy recorder, and four years as money order clerk in the postoffice, under her brother. By his second marriage Mr. Scott has two sons, Ivan Lamar, four years old, and Leyden, who was born July 14, 1904. Mr. Scott is a member of the Christian church and ever since his majority has taken an active interest in the welfare of his church. In all of the public positions which he has filled he has made an enviable record and has discharged the duties with credit to himself and to the satisfaction of the patrons. Mr. Scott resides on Silver Hills, west of New Albany, one of the most beautiful suburban sites in the Ohio valley, in an attractive home and surrounded by an interesting and happy family.

LEWIS A. STOY, recorder of Floyd county, New Albany, Ind., was born in Spottsylvania county, Va., July 10, 1869, and is a son of Lewis W. and Mary (Anderson) Stoy, the former a native of Floyd county, Ind., and the latter of Tennessee. The paternal grandfather, Peter Stoy, was a Pennsylvania Dutchman, who settled in Floyd county in 1818. Lewis W. Stoy was born there in March, 1829, and died there, Sept. 10, 1895. During his life he was engaged in business at Galveston, Tex., Spencer, Ind., and in Virginia, where he was engaged as bookkeeper, living on a farm in the meantime. In 1879 the family returned to New Albany, the old home and birthplace of the father and there both parents lived out their days, the mother dying in 1900. They had seven children: Mary A., Henry E., Mattie, Henrietta E., Carrie R., Lewis A. and William V. All are living except Mattie and William. Lewis A. Stoy graduated in the public shools of New Albany at the age of sixteen and commenced the battle of life as a driver of a delivery wagon for the grocery of Charles H. Breetz. After a short time he obtained a position as bookkeeper in one of the departments of the DePauw plate glass works, but three months later returned to the store of Mr. Breetz, where he remained as bookkeeper and clerk until he was twenty years old. He then accepted a place as traveling salesman for the Kentucky Flour Company, of Louisville, and followed that vocation until 1893. For several years, subsequent to this date, he operated a poultry and fruit farm near New Albany. In 1899 he removed to the city and took a position with the Prudential Insurance Company. In the meantime he had been somewhat active in political work as a Democrat, and in 1902 he received the nomination of his party for recorder and was elected. Mr. Stoy is an Odd Fellow and a member of the Improved Order of Red Men, in which he has passed through all the chairs and is a member of the Great Council of Indiana. On March 19, 1890, Mr. Stoy was married to Miss Maggie Hurley, of New Albany, and they have had born to them four children: Carrie Eleanor, Edmund H., Mary A., and Virginia, the last named having departed this life at the age of four years.

RAYMOND J. MORRIS, sheriff of Floyd county, New Albany, Ind., was born at Greenville, in that county, Sept. 16, 1866, and is a son of George W. and Sarah J. (Wood) Morris, both natives of Greenville, and both living, now residing in New Albany. The father is a cooper by trade and is now sixty-four years of age. He is a son of Thomas Morris, an old settler of Greenville, who died when the subject of this sketch was less than three years old. Of the eleven children born to George W. and Sarah Morris, all are living except Arthur, who died at the age of twenty-seven years. Walter M. is the telegraph operator and station agent of the Louisville, Henderson & Texas railway at Hawesville, Ky.; Jesse N. is route agent for the American Express Company at Fort Wayne, Ind.; Raymond is the subject of this sketch; Anna is now Mrs. R. Clark, of Francesville, Ind.; George A. is yard clerk of the Southern railway at New Albany; Olive and Lydia R. are at home; Clarence J. is a brakeman on the Monon railroad; Nancy is a stenographer at New Albany, and Coleman is a student. Raymond J. Morris was reared and educated at Greenville; clerked there in a store for one year; started in business for himself as a dealer in agricultural implements and fertilizers; conducted this business until 1898, when he was appointed deputy sheriff under Louis C. Hipple. Always active in Democratic politics, he made friends by his general good fellowship, and in 1902, after four years in the office as deputy, he was nominated for sheriff and at the election ran 300 votes ahead of his ticket. In 1904 he was again nominated for the office, this time having no opposition. Mr. Morris is a Royal Arch Mason, a Red Man, a Modern Woodman, and a Knight of the Maccabees.

He was married on Oct. 2, 1886, to Miss Henrietta J., a daughter of Stephen P. Main, then of Greenville, but now of New Albany. They have had two children. Virgil R., who died in infancy, and Olive Leona, now twelve years of age.

HON. WILLIAM C. UTZ, of New Albany, Ind., judge of the Floyd county circuit court, of the Fifty-second judicial district of Indiana, was born on a farm in Floyd county, Jan. 30, 1863, and is a son of Kennard and Sarah Elizabeth (Huff) Utz, the former of whom died in 1889 and the latter in 1896. They had a family of six sons, viz.: Monroe, a teacher by profession and died Sept. 16, 1893; Harvey S., a physician, who died Nov. 10, 1888; William C., the subject of this sketch; D. Sherman, a physician, now in Arizona; Henry C., also a physician, died Dec. 6, 1903; and Shelby, who died in infancy. Judge William C. Utz was reared on his father's farm, attending the common schools until he was seventeen years of age. He then entered the Illinois State Normal school, at Normal, where he attended one year, preparing himself for the work of teaching. In the winter of 1881-82 and 1882-83 he taught in the rural districts in Woodford county, Ill., and the succeeding winter was again a student in the normal school, meanwhile reading law. In the spring of 1884 he returned home, remained on the farm for one year, and in the spring of 1885 he went into the law office of Hon. Charles L. Jewett as a student, remaining there until May 12, 1886, when he was admitted to the bar. Soon afterward he went to Wichita, Kan., where for about two years he was associated with the law firm of Dale & Reed. Returning to New Albany in 1888 he opened an office in that city and practiced there until November, 1890, when he was elected prosecuting attorney. He was three times re-elected to this office. Before the close of his last term as prosecutor he was elected to the bench and since then has been judge of the district, taking the office in 1898. In the spring of 1904 he was renominated for the position without opposition. Judge Utz is a diligent student and keeps thoroughly informed on all the decisions of the supreme and superior courts of the country. In addition to this he has the judicial mind and approaches every case absolutely free from bias, rendering his decisions according to the law and the evidence. Politically he is a Democrat, but he never allows his private opinions to influence his official conduct. He is a Knight of Pythias, a Red Man, an Elk, a Modern Woodman, and an Odd Fellow, with a high standing in all the orders. On Nov. 25, 1891, Judge Utz was married to Miss Alice, daughter and only child of Joshua Wiley, a steamboat captain. Mrs. Utz died on April 10, 1903, leaving one son, Wiley, born Aug. 3, 1893.

EUGENE L. BRISBY, city clerk, New Albany, Ind., is a native of that city, having been born there May 7, 1866, and is the second child of James M. and Mary E. (Vanderbilt) Brisby, the former a native of New Albany and the latter of Madison, Ind. James M. Brisby was born Aug. 7, 1838, and died Feb. 18, 1888. His widow, who is still living, was born June 6, 1842. The paternal grandparents were James and Priscilla (Aiken) Brisby and the maternal were Dennis and Mary A. (Gibson) Vanderbilt, all of whom have joined the silent majority. James M. and Mary E. Brisby had six children: Wallace, Eugene L., Mary Estella, Addie Gay, James Archie, and Frank Mayo. Two of these, James Archie and Wallace, are deceased. Eugene L. Brisby has lived in the city of New Albany all his life. He received his education in the public schools, leaving school at the age of fifteen to become a clerk in a drug store. He was with the firm of C. L. Hoover & Sons, as clerk, for eight years, by which time he became a proficient pharmacist. After eight years in the drug trade he took a vacation and then went to work in the De-Pauw Plate Glass Works. Later he went with the New Albany Steam Forge Works, where he remained for two years, followed by a similar length of time with the New Albany Manufacturing Company, in the machine shops. On Feb. 10, 1893, he had the misfortune to be caught in a railroad accident which made necessary the amputation of his left leg above the knee, rendering him a cripple for life. Upon recovery he could no longer follow his old vocations. Having, however, studied music, he worked on the Louisville and New Orleans Packet Line for some time, furnishing music to the passengers. On May 6, 1902, he was elected to the office of city clerk as a Democrat, receiving a majority of 116 votes. In the spring of 1904 he was re-elected, receiving this time a majority of 631, which is evidence of his popularity and efficiency. Mr. Brisby is a member of the Knights of Pythias and the Improved Order of Red Men, in both of which he is a welcome attendant at lodge meetings, and is universally liked by his fraternal associates.

EDMUND B. COOLMAN, city engineer, New Albany, Ind., was born in Portage county, O., Dec. 12, 1845, his parents being William L. and Eliza (Babcock) Coolman, both natives of that county. The paternal great-grandfather, William Coolman, came from Strasburg, Germany, and after several years in Connecticut, settled in Portage county. In Germany the name is spelled Kuhlmann. William Coolman, the grandfather of Edmund, was a prominent man in the affairs of Ohio in his day. He was twice sheriff of Portage county; three times elected to the legislature; one of the proprietors of the Cleveland & Pittsburg stage line; and one of the contractors that built the Cleveland & Pittsburg railroad. The father of Edmund B. was at one time publisher of the *Ohio Star,* at Ravenna, though in later years he gave up the printers' trade and became a carriage painter. He died at Ravenna in 1888, being about seventy years of age. His widow is still living at Ravenna. The Babcocks are descended from the old New England Puritan stock. Edmund B. Coolman was the eldest in a family of four children. Horace C. is a physician at Hudson, O.; Laura A. is a Mrs. Porter, residing in Ravenna, and Eliza died at the age of twelve years. Edmund was educated in the public schools of Portage county and the city of Ravenna. He left school at the age of seventeen and joined an engineering corps then engaged in the construction of the Atlantic & Great Western railway. He remained with this corps for four years, there receiving his first lessons in the work which he has since followed. At the age of twenty-four he taught a term of school; was employed as engineer on various roads in Ohio, until 1871; then came to New Albany as constructing engineer on what is now the Monon railway. Owing to the panic of 1873 work was suspended and he entered the government service as engineer on the White river improvement in Arkansas; returned to Portage county and was engaged in merchandizing for about eighteen months at Atwater; returned to New Albany in 1881, and assisted in completing the road begun several years before—the Louisville, New Albany & Chicago. In 1882 he went to Mississippi and took a contract to build thirteen miles of the New Orleans & Northeastern railway. For three years, from 1884 to 1887, he was a contractor on the Ohio Valley railroad between Henderson and Princeton, Ky., and from 1887 to 1889 he was employed as engineer with the Louisville & Nashville railroad. In 1889 he was elected city engineer of New Albany, holding the office for one term. In 1892 he went to Spokane, Wash., where he had charge of the construction of the water tower and electric transmission plant of the Walla Walla Gas and Electric Company, after which he returned to New Albany. In addition to the numerous services already mentioned he was for twelve years surveyor of Floyd county; in 1902 was again made city engineer, and was re-elected in 1904. Mr. Coolman is prominent in Masonic circles, having taken his first degree in the order while living at Ravenna, joining the lodge of which both his grandfathers were charter members in 1813. In politics he is an unswerving Democrat and is always ready to give his reasons for his political faith. He was married in New Albany, Aug. 16, 1883, to Mrs. Sarah E. McCurdy, widow of Frank McCurdy and daughter of Capt. James C. Bentley. They have one son, William E. Coolman, now nineteen years of age. Mrs. Coolman had one son by her former marriage, now Capt. James F. McCurdy, of New Albany, captain of a company in the Indiana National Guard.

JOHN F. SHUTT, chief of police, New Albany, Ind., was born in Forsyth county, N. C., June 18, 1853, and is the son of Jacob F. and Salina H. (Carmichael) Shutt, the father a native of Pennsylvania and the mother of North Carolina. In 1860, Jacob F. Shutt, being a Union man, and not liking the appearance of the situation in North Carolina, left that state and came North, settling at Hope, Bartholomew county, Ind. When the war broke out he enlisted in Company I, Sixty-seventh Indiana infantry, and served until a sunstroke compelled him to retire from the service. After the war he removed to Indianapolis, where he followed his trade of carpenter for a time; served five years on the police force, after which he engaged in mercantile pursuits, being thus employed at the time of his death, June 5, 1901. The mother of Chief Shutt was born in North Carolina on June 11, 1821, and is still living in Indianapolis, hale and hearty for one of her age. The six children of Jacob and Salina Shutt were Martha J., now the widow of John Hornaday, of Indianapolis; her husband was a veteran of the Civil war; Henry A., deceased; John F., the subject of this sketch; Sarah, now the wife of John A. Kersey, a lawyer at Marion, Ind.; Mary L., now Mrs. John Fleming, of Indianapolis, and James W., who died in childhood. John F. Shutt was seven years of age when his parents came to Indiana. He received the greater part of his education in the schools of Hope; worked with his father and learned the carpenter's trade; was employed for a time in a feed store; became a contractor and builder;

followed this vocation both in Indianapolis and New Albany; removed to New Albany in 1888; was appointed a patrolman in 1893; with the exception of one and a half years has been connected with the force ever since; served as patrolman, sergeant and detective, and in April, 1903, was appointed chief. In all his long career as an officer Mr. Shutt has been a conscientious performer of his duty as he saw it. Courageous, cool-headed in time of danger, and full of resources, he has been an ideal policeman. His promotions tell the story of his faithful service and as the head of the department he has the entire confidence of the people of New Albany. Mr. Shutt is a Knight of Pythias and has a high standing in his lodge. He was married on March 27, 1879, to Miss Georgia Herrell, and they have two children: Lena May and Harry B., aged respectively twenty-four and nineteen years.

THOMAS CANNON, captain of police, New Albany, Ind., and the senior member of the force, was born in Danville, Livingston county, N. Y., April 1, 1851. He is a son of Michael and Bridget (Culkin) Cannon, both natives of County Galway, Ireland, where they were married in 1850 and immediately afterward came to America to seek their fortune. After one year in each of the towns of Danville, N. Y., Mount Morris, Pa., and Chicago, they came to New Albany, where the father died in January, 1897, his wife having departed this life in July, 1895. They had five children, viz.: Thomas, Michael, Charles, Mary, and Cordelia, and all are living except Michael, who was born at Mount Morris and died in New Albany, aged ten years. Charles is a glass blower by trade and lives in New Albany, as do the two sisters, neither of whom ever married. Thomas was less than three years of age when the family came to New Albany. He attended the common schools until he was about sixteen years old, when he went to work to learn the trade of upholsterer, and worked at it for some time, after which he was employed in a glass factory for several years. Then he took service on a steamboat and was for three or four years on the Ohio and Mississippi rivers between Pittsburg and New Orleans. In 1874 he was appointed a supernumerary on the New Albany police force, and with the exception of the years from 1881 to 1886, he has been con-nected with the force ever since. During those five years he filled the office of constable with credit and efficiency. In 1891 he was pro-moted to the chieftainship of the department and held the position for two years. In 1893 he was elected superintendent of the force, holding that position for four years, and since then has been a cap-tain, the change being brought about through the change in politics of the city administration. Captain Cannon is a prominent member of the Improved Order of Red Men and the Benevolent and Protective Order of Elks. He has been twice married. Some time after the death of his first wife he was married to Miss Elizabeth Dingeldine of New Albany, the marriage taking place on Sept. 25, 1883. He has one daughter living, Catherine, now a young lady.

PROF. CHARLES A. PROSSER, su-perintendent of the public schools, New Albany, Ind., was born in that city, Sept. 20, 1871, and is a son of Rees W. and Sarah Emma (Leach) Prosser. The for-mer was born in Wales in November, 1848; came with his parents, Thomas and Margaret (Williams) Prosser, to this country when he was twelve years of age; began learning the trade of iron worker in a rolling mill before leaving his native land; worked at Wheeling, W. Va., New-burg, O., and New Albany, and is now foreman of the American Steel Roofing Company's plant at Middle-town, O. The mother is a daughter of Thomas Leonard Leach, a farmer of Floyd county, Ind. She is still living. Rees W. and Sarah E. Prosser had a family of six children: Enoch, Charles A., Frank, Estella May, Nellie Grace, and Thomas Leonard. Enoch and Frank died in infancy. The others are all living. Professor Prosser gradu-ated from the New Albany high school in 1889 and in the same year from the New Albany business college; was for the two succeeding years superintendent of the New Albany postoffice; from 1891 to 1893, inclusive, was a student at DePauw university; managing editor of the DePauw *Bema* and editor-in-chief of the DePauw *Literary Magazine*; vice-president of the Interstate Oratorical association, composed of ten states; and winner of the first inter-collegiate debate between DePauw and Indiana universities. For want of funds to pursue his college work he left DePauw in his junior year and was for the next two years principal of the West Market street school in New Albany. From 1896 to 1899 he was teacher of physics, chemistry and literature in the high school. During this time he spent four summers doing graduate work in the summer schools at DePauw and Indiana universities; graduated as honor man in the class of 1898 at DePauw, the only time in the history of the institution that this honor was accorded to a non-resident student; elected to the Phi Beta Kappa fraternity on graduation; read law with the Sprague Correspondence school; graduated from the Louisville Law school in 1899, winning the Edgar Thomson prize for the best essay on a legal subject; kept up his duties as science teacher in the New Albany high school while studying law; elected superintendent of the New Albany public schools in 1899; present term expires on June 1, 1905; was president of the Indiana State Teachers' association in 1902, the youngest man ever elected to the position; and is now carrying on post-graduate work at DePauw university. Professor Prosser has been in close touch with high school work ever since he graduated from the university. While doing science work in the New Albany high school he was really the acting principal owing to the advanced age of the nominal principal. Since his election to the office of superintendent he has closely supervised the work entrusted to his care, being filled with a laudable ambition to make the New Albany schools the equal of any in the country. For the past two years he has been at the head of the commission for the revision of the course of study in the graded schools of the state. Professor Prosser is a fine example of the "sound mind in the sound body." He is about five feet seven inches in height; weighs one hundred and fifty-five pounds; excellent health; interested in athletics and while in college played short stop on the base ball team. He was married on Dec. 30, 1896, to Miss Zerelda A. Huckeby, a graduate of the Louisville Kindergarten association and a teacher in the kindergarten of that city. At the time of her marriage she was a kindergarten teacher elect in the Cook County Normal school, of Chicago. She is the daughter of Lawrence B. and Zerelda Ann (Minor) Huckeby, her father being an attorney of New Albany and her mother of the old Minor family of Virginia. Mrs. Prosser is eligible to membership in the Daughters of the American Revolution through her mother's ancestry. Professor and Mrs. Prosser have one son, William Lloyd, born March 15, 1898. Professor Prosser is a Knight Templar Mason and a member of the Phi Delta Theta and the Phi Beta Kappa fraternities.

WILLIAM M. ADAMS, sergeant of the police force, New Albany, Ind., was born near Elizabethtown, Hardin county, Ky., April 25, 1864, his parents being Thomas and Letitia (McMullen) Adams. The father was a wheelwright by trade and died in New Albany at the age of sixty years. The mother died in LaRue county, Ky., in 1873. When William was about twelve years old he came to New Albany, where he made his home with his sister, Mrs. John R. Morris, and started in to learn the trade of shoemaker. After a time at this occupation he decided that he did not like it and went into the blacksmith shop of Samuel Marsh, where he served an apprenticeship of three years. Following this he worked for awhile at his trade in the old New Albany Steam Forge Works. In 1883 he enlisted as a blacksmith in Troop H, Sixth United States cavalry, in the regular army, and served for five years, at the end of which time he re-enlisted in Troop E, of the same regiment, where he served three years and three months, making a total of eight years and three months in the army. Most of this time was spent in Colorado, Nebraska, the two Dakotas, Arizona, and New Mexico. He participated in the White Mountain and Apache campaigns in Arizona, the famous Geronimo campaign in New Mexico, and the Messiah war in South Dakota, being all the time under Gen. Nelson A. Miles, the noted Indian fighter. In June, 1891, he was honorably discharged and returned to New Albany. In 1892 he went to Chicago and joined the World's Fair Columbian Guards, serving as special policeman in Machinery Hall until the following March, when he resigned and came back to New Albany to become a patrolman on the police force of that city, where he has since remained. In 1895 he was made a sergeant; in 1897 he became superintendent and chief, holding the office for six years, when a change in the political complexion of the city administration reduced him to the position of a detective, but after a few months he was again made a sergeant. Sergeant Adams is a member of the Masonic fraternity; the Improved Order of Red Men; the Modern Woodmen; the Benevolent and Protective Order of Elks; and is a stanch Republican in politics. He was married March 17, 1891, to Miss Nancy Elizabeth, a daughter of Capt. John R. Morris, an old steamboat man, now residing in New

Albany.   Mrs. Adams was born in Nashville, Tenn., Dec. 2, 1861, her mother being Margaret E. (Stephenson) Morris, who died Jan. 10, 1901, aged seventy-two years.   Sergeant and Mrs. Adams have had but one child: Cleon, born April 1, 1892, and died March 27, 1895.

W.·G. HARRISON.

NEW PUBLIC LIBRARY.—The New Albany Public Library was organized May 8, 1884, under an act of the legislature approved on March 5, 1883. Until January, 1904, the library occupied rented quarters. In that month it was moved into a magnificent building at the intersection of Bank and Spring streets. This building was the gift of the Hon. Andrew Carnegie, who donated $35,000 for its construction and $5,000 for the proper equipment of the building in book stacks and furniture. The Carnegie Library is especially adapted to all modern improvements in library work. It contains a reading room 31 by 22 feet, in which are kept about fifteen daily papers and thirty magazines, all of which are of free access to the public. The children's department is a room of the same size, in which are kept constantly on file magazines, newspapers and all popular books of a juvenile nature. At the north end of the main floor there is a stack room equipped with metal stacks and having shelving capacity of over 75,000 volumes. The building also has a public hall 50 by 31 feet, with a capacity of two hundred and ten chairs, which is used for educational purposes. The main building is 90 by 75 feet. The officers of the public library are Charles Day, president; William Rady, secretary; George Borgerding, treasurer; Walter G. Harrison, librarian; assistant librarians, supernumeraries from the public schools. The purchasing of books is in the hands of a committee composed of the following members: Dr. J. W. Duncan, chairman; Miss Delia Woodruff, secretary; Mrs. R. L. Stoy, Mrs. James Dunbar, Charles Needham and George A. Briscoe. The library was recently re-catalogued under the Dewey classification, which, with the open shelf system, has proved very satisfactory. The number of card holders now using the library is 3,103. The number of books in the library is 11,525, of which 325 are in the Government room and 1,500 are in the children's department. The library is open from 9 A. M. to 9 P. M. every day, except Sunday. The beginning of the public library work in New Albany was due to the public spirit and generosity of a few of its leading citizens who banded together and raised a subscription of $1,000, which enabled the library to come under the law and be supported by taxation from the city. The librarian, Mr. Walter G. Harrison, whose portrait appears, took charge of the New Albany Public Library in 1896. When it was succeeded by the splendid Carnegie Library Mr. Harrison was retained as librarian and now fills that position with great efficiency, giving it his entire attention. He has a laudable ambition to make the Carnegie Library of New Albany second to none in the country. Mr. Harrison is a Royal Arch Mason and a Knight Templar. He is deservedly popular and is one of the most progressive and highly esteemed young men of his native city.

JOHN S. KRAFT, chief of the fire department, New Albany, Ind., was born at La Grange, Oldham county, Ky., Dec. 23, 1863. His parents, Ferdinand and Sophia (Scharf) Kraft, are both natives of Germany, the former coming to this country at the age of twenty-four, and the latter at the age of two years. They now live in New Albany. They are the parents of eleven children, viz.: Frances, wife of Jacob Kleober, of Louisville, Ky.; Robert, ex-city clerk of New Albany, now deceased; Elizabeth, wife of Captain August Reuter, of New Albany; John S., the subject of this sketch; Louisa, now Mrs. Frank Klumb, of Louisville; Minnie, Mrs. Peter Felter, of New Albany; Ida and Emma, twins, both deceased; Alice Amelia, wife of John Raba, of New Albany; Katherine, died in infancy; and George, now in New Albany. Of the two twins Ida died at the age of eighteen years and Emma became Sister Itta in the Catholic convent at Oldenburg, Ind., where she died at the age of thirty-two. John S. Kraft has lived in New Albany since he was six years old; was educated in the public and parochial schools of that city; learned the shoemakers' trade while still in his boyhood; worked at it until he was twenty-three years of age; was then a short time in the New Albany Plate Glass Works; then for awhile with the N. K. Fairbank & Co. Soap Works, of St. Louis; collector for the firm of Rhodes & Burford, a large furniture installment house of Louisville, for seven years; then in a similar position with John Shrader, Jr., of New Albany; started in the furniture business for himself in 1901 at 1405 East Market street, New Albany, which business he still owns and manages. On May 10, 1904, he was appointed chief of the city fire department. Although he was without practical experience at the time of his appointment he was not altogether a stranger to the duties of the position. On May 31, 1888, he was married to Miss Anna, daughter of William Merker, who was for thirty-two years chief of the fire department, and by association with his father-in-law, Mr. Kraft acquired technical knowledge of the art of fire fighting. Since assuming charge of the department he has won the confidence of the men under him, and by his management and disposition of the force in handling fires he has likewise won the confidence of the public. He is a member of the Improved Order of Red Men, which is the only order to claim his membership. Chief Kraft and his wife have one child, Frances Amelia, born Oct. 6, 1893.

WILLIAM V. GROSE, mayor of the city of New Albany, Ind., a son of Solomon and Naomi (Miller) Grose, was born in Crawford county, Ind., Aug. 8, 1842. His father was a native of Lawrence county, Ind., was a brickmaker and miller by trade, and was killed in 1864, while serving in the Union army during the war. The mother was a daughter of Felty Miller, of Crawford county, and died April 13, 1865, from the effects of a paralytic stroke. William V. Grose has been a resident of New Albany since he was seven years of age. He has had a somewhat checkered career. After learning the trade of brickmaker with his father he enlisted in Company K, Forty-ninth Indiana infantry, as a private; was made lieutenant before the close of 1861; took part in the siege and capture of Vicksburg; the Red River campaign; numerous battles and skirmishes; and was mustered out in 1864. For several years after the war he was manager of the Louisville and New Albany Transfer Company; was for a long time employed in the New Albany Rail Mill, and in 1895 became a solicitor for the Metropolitan Life Insurance Company, which position he held until May 3, 1904, when he was elected mayor of the city for the term beginning in the succeeding September. Mr. Grose's popularity is attested by the fact that he was nominated for mayor by the Democracy, of which party he has for years been an active member, and was elected by a clean majority of 435 votes, although the city is nominally Republican. Mr. Grose is a Mason, a Knight of Pythias, in which order he is a member of the Uniform Rank, and the Rathbone Sisters; and has a popular standing in both societies. He has been twice married; in 1866 to Charlotte Elliott, who died in 1879. Her children living are Carrie, wife of George Hall; John K., Joseph R., and Eddie. Those deceased are William E., Etta and George A. In 1880 Mr. Grose was united in marriage to R. Belle Brown, and to this union have been born two children: Mary E. and Charles Albert. In whatever station of life the lot of William V. Grose has been cast, whether as a brickmaker, a soldier, superintendent of the transfer company, solicitor for a life insurance company, or operative in the rolling mill, he has done his duty faithfully and conscientiously, and as mayor of the city he will not prove a disappointment to those who elected him. Mr. Grose is a member of the Tabernacle Baptist church and invokes the aid of the Master in the performance of his official functions.

GEORGE B. McINTYRE, prosecuting attorney of the Floyd county circuit court, New Albany, Ind., was born in the city of Keokuk, Ia., Jan. 6, 1868, and is a son of Dr. Charles W. and Mary McIntyre, now living in New Albany, where the father is a practicing physician. Besides the subject of this sketch they have two other children: Charles W., Jr., a physician in Louisville, Ky., and Margaret. When George was a small boy his parents removed from Keokuk to Cannelton, Ind., and in 1880 to New Albany. Seven years later he graduated from the New Albany high school; then attended the University of Louisville for two years, after which he entered the law department of the University of Michigan, at Ann Arbor, and graduated from that institution in 1891. Returning home he began the practice of law in New Albany, practicing alone for about one year, when he formed a partnership with John B. James, under the firm name of McIntyre & James, which lasted until 1900, at which time Walter V. Bulliet was admitted to partnership and the firm became McIntyre, Bulliet & James. The firm is one of the strongest in Southern Indiana, having been retained in many important cases and enjoying a large clientage. Mr. McIntyre is also well known in political circles, being one of the active and enthusiastic Democrats of his section of the state. In 1892 he was elected to the legislature, where he made a creditable record although one of the youngest members of the general assembly. In 1896 he was a candidate for presidential elector on the Bryan and Sewall ticket, and in 1898 was elected prosecuting attorney of the Fifty-second judicial district; was re-elected two years later; and again in 1902; and in 1904 was nominated for a fourth term. His record as prosecutor has received the highest endorsement of his constituents, as may be seen by his repeated re-elections. He is able, conscientious and fearless, the three essential qualifications of a good prosecuting attorney. Mr. McIntyre is a member of the Independent Order of Odd Fellows, the Knights of Pythias, the Improved Order of Red Men and the Benevolent and Protective Order of Elks. He was married March 8, 1894, to Miss Nellie Stevens of New Albany, and to this union there have been born two children: Mary, who died in infancy, and Ellen, now seven years of age.

THOMAS E. FOGLE, judge of the police court, New Albany, Ind., is a native of Pittsburg, Pa., where he was born on Jan. 3, 1855, his parents being John K. and Mary Jane (Stewart) Fogle. The father was born in Washington county, Pa., March 26, 1826, and the mother in what is now West Virginia, Nov. 1, 1827. Both are yet living, now being residents of New Albany, where they have lived since August, 1867. For some time before that the father had been associated with the firm of S. W. Dougherty & Co., pension attorneys, now of Columbus, Ind. John K. and Mary Fogle had six children, only two of whom are now living —the subject of this sketch and Daniel S., who holds a responsible position with the great packing house of Armour & Co. of Chicago. At the time the family removed to New Albany, Judge Fogle was twelve years of age. In 1878 he graduated from the New Albany business college and the following year became the bookkeeper in the office of Thomas Baldwin, grand national secretary of the Independent Order of United Workmen of the United States. A little later he was bookkeeper for the firm of Fulton, Smith & Co., hub, spoke and wheel manufacturers of Louisville, remaining with them for two years. From 1882 to 1889 he was employed in the Ohio Falls Iron Works of New Albany. In 1889, through the influence of J. N. Huston, then United States treasurer, he was appointed to a position in the mail service on the Louisville and Evansville Packet Line. This position he held but nine months, however, resigning to return to the iron works.   In 1892 he became manager of the Merchants' Ticket Register Company of New Albany, but six months later the plant was sold.   For several years he was then associated with the building and decorating trades as carpenter and paperhanger.   In November, 1902, he was elected justice of the peace of New Albany township, an office which he still holds, and in addition to those duties he was appointed police judge of the city by Mayor Frank L. Shrader, on Dec. 2, 1902.   Judge Fogle is a Royal Arch Mason and a Knight Templar; a member of the Junior Order of American Mechanics, the Fraternal Order of Eagles and Benevolent and Protective Order of Elks, and in 1877 was the delegate from the State of Indiana to the national convention of the Order of American Mechanics, at Dayton, Ohio, and is also a member of the Tribe of Ben Hur.   In June, 1891, he was a national delegate from New Albany Lodge to the assemblage of Amalgamated Association of Iron and Steel Workers, at Pittsburg, Pa.   He was married on March 4, 1880, to Miss Belle V. Bryant, a native of New Albany, where she was born, of English parentage, April 15, 1856.   To this union there have been born the following children: Carrie C., married, June 2, 1904, to Duke B. Tomlinson; Jennie; David H., married in April, 1904, to Miss Belle Wattam; William A., Diana B., George C. K. and Frank C. B.

FRANK H. WILCOX, M.D., a physician and surgeon of New Albany, Ind., was born in that city, April 21, 1870.   His father, Dr. Seymour C. Wilcox, was born at Franklin, Delaware county, N. Y., in 1818; graduated from the Albany, N. Y., Medical college; practiced for more than sixty years; came to New Albany in 1869, and now lives a retired life in that city, being eighty-seven years of age.   The mother of Dr. F. H. Wilcox was Miss Julia Daniels.   She is still living, aged sixty-four.   Dr. F. H. Wilcox has one brother, George D. Wilcox of Rochester, N. Y.   Doctor Wilcox received his general education in the New Albany public schools; took a course in the New Albany Business college; spent four years in the medical department of the University of Louisville, graduating with the class of 1890.   Locating in his native city he soon built up a lucrative practice, and is today regarded as one of the coming physicians of Southern Indiana.   He is a member and ex-president of the Floyd County Medical society; belongs to the American Medical association; is surgeon of the Louisville & Southern Indiana Traction Company, the Kentucky & Indiana Bridge and Railroad Company, and has a large private practice.   Politically he is a Democrat of the unwavering type, yet he numbers among his personal friends a large number of Republicans. For six years he was a member of the pension examining board and was for a similar length of time the representative of the Seventh ward in the city council. In his political positions, as in his professional career, his labors were marked by a strict adherence to correct business principles, an unswerving fidelity to the cause of those entrusting him with their affairs, and a conscientious and intelligent performance of duty. Doctor Wilcox was married in December, 1892, to Miss Portia May Fullenlove, the daughter of Martin Van Buren Fullenlove of New Albany, and they have two children: Ira F., aged eleven, and Frank Shirley, aged nine.

PROF. IRA G. STRUNK, proprietor of the business college at New Albany, Ind., was born in Center county, Pa., March 22, 1846. His parents, John and Nancy (Henry) Strunk, were both natives of the Keystone state, his father having been born in Berks county, Feb. 17, 1806, and the mother in North county, Oct. 30th of the same year. He died on July 17, 1884, and she on June 17, 1862. They had fifteen children, the dates and births of which follow: George H., Dec. 13, 1828; William, March 27, 1830; Mary Ann, Aug. 14, 1831; John F., Aug. 29, 1832; Margaret Jane, Nov. 27, 1833; James B., Jan. 30, 1835; Susan, April 14, 1836; Robert, Sept. 21, 1837; Thomas, March 16, 1839; Elizabeth Hays, Sept. 6, 1840; Peter W., May 19, 1842; Samuel C., Aug. 29, 1843; an infant daughter, Feb. 19, 1845, and died at the age of two days; Ira G., March 22, 1846, and Nancy C., Oct. 7, 1847. Of these children, nine boys and six girls, seven are still living. Mary Ann Holmes died Jan. 8, 1858, as the wife of John Holmes; James B. died Nov. 27, 1861, a private of the Seventh Pennsylvania cavalry, while in rendezvous at Williamsport, Pa. His was the first death in the regiment; Nancy C. died March 28, 1865; Margaret Jane Seyler, as the wife of John Seyler, died Feb. 22, 1900; Thomas, April 24, 1869; John F., Aug. 6, 1891; William, June 25, 1904. Five brothers of the nine served their country during the Civil war, viz.: James B., Samuel C., Peter W., Thomas and Robert. Samuel C. joined the Seventh Pennsylvania cavalry to take the place of his brother, James B., who had died, and served his country continuously from the day of his enlistment to the close of the war. He was in the thickest of many battles, but always came out unharmed. Ira G. Strunk was reared on the farm near Jacksonville, Center county; attended the village school about five months in the year, after which he went to the Jacksonville seminary, under the principalship of a Miss Brown, a graduate of Oxford college, Ohio. From this school he secured a teacher's license; he taught in the winter and attended normal school in the summer; entered Kentucky university in the fall of 1868, and "bached" the entire year that his scant means might permit him to take advantage of an education. At the close of the first year President Patterson offered him a tutorship in the Agricultural and Mechanical college, which was accepted. At the close of the second year he was forced to leave the university for lack of funds. He was given the school at Leesburg, Ky., and taught it two years, when he was offered six different schools. He declined them all, returned to Lexington, graduated from the Hollingsworth & Co.'s Business college, and was sent to New Albany, Sept. 2, 1872, as principal of one of their branch schools. On November 1st he purchased a half interest, and on the 18th bought the other half. His school continued to grow, and in May, 1876, he admitted Prof. D. M. Hammond as a partner. In May, 1886, he retired from the school on account of ill health, selling his interest to Professor Hammond. In May, 1887, he repurchased a half interest in the college. This partnership lasted until June 18, 1904, when Professor Hammond retired on account of failing health, after a partnership of twenty-eight years. During this time they both labored persistently to keep the New Albany Business college well to the front among schools of its class, and today it enjoys a reputation second to none in the state. Professor Strunk is fitted by nature for the work before him, having had years of experience in the line of accounting, from which he gathered valuable points that were frequently presented in his class work, thereby giving his students the benefit of his experience. He has without doubt taught more students bookkeeping than any other teacher about the Ohio Falls. The longer he is in the work the more enthusiastic he seems to get. He takes an individual interest in all his students, and if he can patronize one of them he will walk out of his way to do it. His students are notably successful and may be found as merchants, bankers, manufacturers, brokers, teachers, etc., filling offices of honor and trust all over the country. He believes that the mission of the business college is not to prepare the students for effective office work alone, but if possible to make them honest, influential, public-spirited men and women.   Professor Strunk is a member of the Second Presbyterian church; belongs to the Independent Order of Odd Fellows and the Benevolent and Protective Order of Elks.   He is a member in good standing of the National Federation of Commercial Teachers' association and has just paid his thirtieth year's membership assessment in the Young Men's Christian association, in which he feels a deep interest.   He is fond of outdoor sports, and especially outdoor work, and is never happier than when planting trees or shrubbery to embellish his home, on Silver Hills, which he has named "Poplar Slope."   Any one who had seen these grounds six years ago, with their luxuriant growth of green briars, blackberry bushes, sassafras and black locust, and see it today, knows that it was the industrious, skillful hand which touched nature that caused the transformation.   Today the carefully trimmed hedge, the well kept lawn, the meandering walks, the shaded nooks, the wide verandas, impress the passer-by on a hot summer day that this air of retirement, restfulness and comfort is nearest to the simple life.   It is here that Professor Strunk hopes to spend his declining years.

CHARLES UMBREIT, beef and pork packer of New Albany, Ind., was born at Darmstadt, Germany, Feb. 1, 1861.   When he was five years of age his parents, John Christ and Mary Umbreit, came to the United States and soon after their arrival in this country they located in New Albany, where both died.   Ever since that time Charles has been a resident of New Albany.   He left school in his teens and learned the butchers' trade, which has been his vocation through life. During the twenty-one years that he has been in the business he has sold many a pound of meat to the people of New Albany, and none of his customers have ever yet made a complaint as to its quality or its short weight.   When Mr. Umbreit commenced business for himself he had but fifty dollars for a working capital.   Unable to hire a carpenter, he tore down the kitchen to his little home and with his own hands converted it into a butcher shop.   From the outset his motto has been the best possible goods for the least margin of profit.   In recent years he has branched out into the packing business, and today he has one of the best equipped plants of its size in the country, and runs two large wagons constantly to supply the local demand.   The kitchen to his house has been replaced by a more modern one, and his packing house at present bears no resemblance to the humble shop in which he began business.   He lives at No. 1513 North State street, where he has a comfortable home, and on the premises adjoining his residence is his packing house, fitted up with all the latest improved appliances for dressing and curing meats. The success of Mr. Umbreit is entirely due to his industrious habits, his thorough knowledge of his business, his courteous treatment of his patrons, and, above all, his sterling honesty. Not a pound of bad meat has ever been sold over his counter or delivered to one of his customers with his knowledge, and few men are better known or have a higher standing with the meat trade of New Albany than Charles Umbreit. Mr. Umbreit is a Democrat in political matters, and is a member of the Lutheran church. He was married, Nov. 8, 1888, to Mary Arnold, a daughter of John and Mary (Weller) Arnold, the former of whom is now deceased. To this marriage there were born two sons: William, Aug. 4, 1889, and Herman, July 16, 1892. His first wife died on Nov. 6, 1899, and on the following New Year's day he was married to Miss Lillian Arnold, a sister of his former wife. By the second marriage he has one son, Otto, born Oct. 25, 1903.

PETER RAYMOND STOY (deceased), son of Peter and Mary Stoy, was born in the city of New Albany, Ind., Feb. 25, 1825, and died there, July 19, 1892. During his long life of more than three-score and seven years he was a useful member of society and was active in promoting all those institutions that contribute to the health, morals and general prosperity of the people. He served fourteen years as a member of the city council, his first election to that body being in 1850; was city commissioner for two years, and county commissioner for three years; as county commissioner he secured the erection of the county asylum, which is a model institution of its kind; was a member of the city school board at the time of his death, and was a potent factor in securing the erection of some of the finest school buildings in the city. Outside of his native city he was known far and wide as a friend to religion and education. Joining the Wesley Methodist Episcopal church at the age of eighteen, he was ever afterward one of its most prominent and active members; for thirty years he was superintendent of the Sunday school; was trustee and treasurer of the church for over forty-five years; served as trustee of the old Asbury university for several years, and after it changed its name to DePauw university he was one of the trustees until his death; frequently served as a lay delegate to the Indiana conference and to the state Sunday school conventions. In business matters he was no less prominent. In 1873 he became one of the directors of the Ohio Falls Iron Works, and it was largely due to his tact, ability and industry that this great concern was kept from disaster during the troublous times that followed the panic of that year. For many years he was a stockholder and director in the First National bank, but in later years transferred his interests to the New Albany National, of which he was a director at the time of his death. But the institution with which he was most inseparably connected is the old established hardware house of P. R. Stoy & Sons, which is still in existence, and is one of the leading hardware houses of Southern Indiana. This concern he founded in 1848, and was associated with it until his death. In all his business transactions he was actuated by a high sense of justice and humanity. While vice-president and manager of the iron works, he often kept the mills running when there was little demand for the product, simply to keep his employes from suffering the stings of idleness and poverty. This was characteristic of his whole life—always a consideration for the comfort and happiness of others. Mr. Stoy was married on May 16, 1850, to Ellen J. Beeler, of New Albany, and to this union there were born ten children. Mary died in infancy; Edward was drowned in 1882; Minnie E. passed to her rest in 1902; Louis R. is now the head of the hardware firm of P. R. Stoy & Sons; William H. died in 1880; Frank M. died in 1897; Walter E. lives at Pittsburg, Pa.; Raymond was killed in a railroad accident in 1898; Julia E. is now Mrs. R. Brude of Elwood, Ind., and Ellen died in 1900.

LOUIS R. STOY was born in New Albany, March 26, 1857; was educated in the public schools, graduating from the high school in 1872; began life as a clerk in his father's hardware store the same fall, and remained there until 1887; was then admitted to partnership, though he had practically managed the business for five years previous, his father being manager of the iron works. Upon the death of his father Louis was retained by the estate to settle up the affairs, and by his superb business business training under his father he built up the business of the old house of P. R. Stoy & Sons, until it occupies a position second to none in New Albany commercial circles. Politically Mr. Stoy is a Republican, though he is by no means what can be called an active politician.   He is a member of the Methodist Episcopal church and is interested in its good works.   On June 6, 1882, he was married to Miss Lillie G., daughter of the late William Jones, who in his day was a well known steamboat builder of New Albany.   Mr. and Mrs. Stoy have no children living.   For almost a century some of the Stoy family have resided in New Albany.   In 1814 Peter and Mary (Wicks) Stoy, the grandparents of Louis R., came from Kensington, Pa., and settled in the city "just below the Falls."   During the three generations the Stoys have been a part of the warp and woof of the business, social, religious and educational life of New Albany, and have always been noted for their public spirit and enterprise.   The mother of Louis R. Stoy is still living, esteemed and respected by a large circle of friends.

ROBERT W. WAITE, vice-president and treasurer of the Louisville & Southern Indiana Traction Company, and also of the United Gas & Electric Company, of New Albany, Ind., was born at Buda, Bureau county, Ill., March 6, 1870, his father being Benjamin F. Waite, a well-known resident of that place.   After attending the public schools of his native town Robert took a full course in stenography in the Eclectic shorthand school of Chicago and began his business life as a stenographer in the Buda Foundry & Machine Works, which soon afterward removed to Harvey, a suburb of Chicago. He remained with this concern for three years, then went to Omaha, Neb., as stenographer for the wholesale brokerage firm of John H. Leslie & Co.; a year later went to the Omaha Coal, Coke and Lime Company as bookkeeper; caught the gold fever and went to Cripple Creek, Col., where he remained for a few weeks, and then returned to Chicago.   Next he took a position with the Edison Electric Company as a substitute stenographer; soon obtained a permanent position with the company; one promotion after another followed, until he was made credit man and head of the mercantile branch of the accounting department; became confidential assistant to the general officers, and one of the most useful men connected with the company.   When the president of the company, Samuel Insull, in company with the Trobridge & Niver Company, also of Chicago, became interested in the gas and electric interests of New Albany and Jeffersonville, in March, 1902, Mr. Waite was made vice-president and treasurer of the company controlling these properties. Since then the company has absorbed the light, heat and power company, and the gas light and coke company of New Albany; the Jeffersonville Light and Water Company and the electric light, gas, heating and coke company of that city. The traction company operates the New Albany street railway under a lease; has built and equipped the Jeffersonville street railway; also the interurban road connecting the two cities; rebuilt a large portion of the tracks in New Albany; opened "Glenwood Park," on the bank of Silver creek, between the two cities, which is fast becoming a popular resort for the people of all three of the cities about the Falls; rebuilt the power plant at a cost of more than $200,000; introduced the most modern cars in the street railway service; has a leased contract over the Big Four bridge connecting Jeffersonville with Louisville; also a franchise for landing its passengers in the latter city, and as soon as the approaches to the bridge are completed will run its cars to the corner of Third and Market streets, in Louisville. Besides all this, the company has under contemplation the building of interurban lines to Corydon, French Lick, Sellersburg, Columbus and Madison, Ind. Large improvements have also been made in the gas plants controlled by the company, and since the advent of Mr. Waite as vice-president the quantity of gas has been doubled and the quality improved. Much of this progress is due to the untiring energy, the sagacity, tact, and superb qualifications of Mr. Waite. The official roster of the company is Samuel Insull, president; R. W. Waite, vice-president and treasurer; J. O. English, secretary. Mr. Waite belongs to the Ancient Free and Accepted Masons, which is the only fraternal organization to claim him as a member.

AUGUST BARTH, deceased, founder of the August Barth Leather Company of New Albany, Ind., was born in Germany in the year 1835. In his native land he learned the tanners' trade, and at the age of nineteen years came to the United States. After a few years in New York and Chicago, he came to Louisville, Ky., and a year or two later he, in company with C. Groscurth, located in New Albany and established the business that still bears his name. The partnership continued until 1885, when Mr. Barth became the sole proprietor. The business prospered from the beginning, owing to the excellent quality of goods turned out by the tannery, the grades of leather being hand-stuffed oak harness, fair saddle seating, whole hide russet collar leather, and the different grades of light bridle leather. Mr. Barth died on Jan. 31, 1902, and on the 11th of February following the business was incorporated by his four surviving sons, with Ernest F. as president, August, Jr., as vice-president, Hugh A. as secretary and treasurer, and Oscar C. as superintendent. Ernest was born Oct. 30, 1872, Oscar in 1873, Hugh A. in 1875 and August in 1879. Thus it will be seen that the plant is now in the hands of young men full of energy and thoroughly acquainted with every branch of the business. The buildings of the company are six in number, two and three stories high, all built of brick and fireproof. A 120 horse power boiler and a ninety horse power and three smaller engines furnish the power to the latest improved machinery for producing leather, while from forty to fifty skilled workmen are employed, the annual capacity of the tannery being 30,000 hides. Ernest F. Barth, the president of the concern, completed the course in the New Albany public schools, took a course in bookkeeping in the business college there, and attended the Kentucky Military institute for two years. He is a gentleman of fine educational attainments and possesses a high order of executive ability. On July 18, 1900, he was united in marriage to Miss Florence Lee of Louisville, and they have three interesting children: Mary Lee, born May 30, 1901; Lucy, born Aug. 20, 1902, and Ernest F., born April 26, 1904.

EDWARD T. SLIDER, one of the largest dealers in coal, lime, sand and cement, etc., about the Falls of the Ohio, was born in the city of New Albany, where he now resides, March 4, 1866, and is a son of John T. Slider, a well-known resident and retail coal dealer. After attending the public schools until he was fourteen years of age he began his business career as the driver of one of his father's teams. The first money he ever earned was as a driver for the Terstegge & Gohmann Stove Foundry. After two years with this concern he bought two teams of his own, hired drivers, unloaded grain in summer and hauled coal in winter, meanwhile attending business college at night until he graduated. Since then his rise in the business world has been almost phenomenal.

In 1888 he bought the teams and business of John Hamilton; the following year he became the owner of a three-team transfer company operated by Everton & Yeaden between Louisville and New Albany; in 1891 he purchased the business of his father, which was his beginning in the coal trade; soon afterward he bought a piece of ground on West Second street, between Main and the Ohio river, for a retail coal yard; in 1895 he purchased the site, docks and elevator of Charles H. Fawcett, on East Fourth street and the river; purchased additional ground in 1896 that gave him railway connection with all the roads centering at New Albany; added lime, cement and sand to his business in 1898, and put on a line of pump boats; also the steam tug *Louise;* put on a steam coal digger the same year, the second machine of the kind below Cincinnati; in 1900 he purchased the property adjoining his yards, and fronting on the river, from the John Plotz estate; put on an additional "digger" to be used for lightening barges, etc.; built the harbor towboat, the *E. T. Slider,* and eight small barges for sand, crossties, etc., and began pumping sand on his own account; has the best equipped pumping outfit about the three falls cities, having a capacity of 800 cubic yards per day; ships both by rail and water to all the surrounding towns; purchased the property of the Republic Iron and Steel Works, better known as the New Albany Forge and Rolling Mills, in March, 1902, and installed a $30,000 unloading plant, with a daily capacity of 25,000 bushels. This property is on East Water street, between Sixth and Eighth streets and adjoined his yards. Its purchase gives him better railway facilities, as it extends from the Pan Handle tracks to the Belt line. He has about 1,300 feet of siding along the former, enough to hold twenty-five cars at one time, and nearly a thousand feet of siding along the Belt line railroad. With his superior unloading facilities the coal can be dumped into these cars after being rescreened, or it can be loaded on wagons for local delivery or dropped in the yard, where he has storage for 1,000,000 bushels of coal and 20,000 tons of sand and gravel. Altogether he has one of the most complete coal, lime, sand and cement outfits on the river, and has the satisfaction of knowing that he has built up this magnificent business by his energy, his strict attention to business, his square dealing and his general superb business qualifications. As he is a young man, with good health, it is more than likely that the future contains for him even greater prosperity than he has enjoyed in the past. Mr. Slider was married in 1888 to Miss Anna Conner and they have six children living.

CHARLES HEGEWALD, president of the Charles Hegewald Company, founders and machinists, of New Albany, Ind., was born in Saxony, Germany, Sept. 18, 1832. He was reared and educated in his native land, there learned the trade of machinist and worked at it as a journeyman long enough to get money to pay his passage to America. About the time he reached his majority he came to this country, and in 1854 he located at New Albany, which city has ever since been his home. His first employment in New Albany was with the Louisville, New Albany & Chicago Railroad Company in the shops. A strike caused him to lose his place there, and he went to work for the Union foundry. In 1856 he went to the American foundry, and was later employed in the works of Lent, South & Shipman, where he remained until the breaking out of the Civil war. He then returned to the American foundry as foreman and stayed with that concern until the year 1873, when he formed a partnership with the late W. C. DePauw, under the firm name of Charles Hegewald & Co. In 1878 N. C. DePauw purchased his father's interest and continued until 1889, when he retired, and the business was incorporated under the name of the Charles Hegewald Company, with the subject of this sketch as president, E. J. Hewitt as secretary, A. F. Hegewald as treasurer, and E. C. Hegewald as assistant secretary. The company does a large business in stationary and steamboat boilers and machinery, glass works machinery, all sorts of brass and iron castings, smokestacks, sheet iron and steel work, and mill supplies. The plant covers half a square of ground at the corner of Lower State and Water streets, and employs from 100 to 150 men, the annual business amounting to over $200,000. The goods turned out by the Charles Hegewald Company have a widespread reputation for being honestly and scientifically constructed, and the name of the company on a piece of machinery is a guarantee of its workmanship. Mr. Hegewald was married in 1855 to Miss Catharine Meyer, and they have four children: Emma is the wife of Edwin Reiley, proprietor of the Boston Shoe Store in New Albany; John F. C. is a graduate of West Point, and now lives in Louisville, Ky., and Arthur F. and Edwin C. are both officers in the Charles Hegewald Company.

I—17

REV. EDWARD M. FALLER, dean of the New Albany district and rector of the Church of the Annunciation of the B. V. M., is one of the oldest and most notable ecclesiastics in the diocese of Indianapolis. He was born at Barr, in the province of Alsace, now a part of the German Empire, Jan. 3, 1824; educated at Strasburg until his sixteenth year; embarked for America, Jan. 19, 1840, and landed at New Orléans on the 11th of April; reached Vincennes on the 1st of May; in the autumn of the same year entered the diocesan seminary there, where he took a course of six years, and was ordained priest by Bishop Hailandiere, July 5, 1846. Since then the life and work of Father Faller have been a part of the warp and woof of the diocese. For nearly threescore years he has followed his holy calling without faltering, though at times the outlook was anything but propitious. His first mission was at Lanesville, Harrison county, Ind., where he began two days after his ordination and continued until October 7th following; then at St. Augustine's, at Fort Wayne, until 1848, when he organized the Mother of God congregation in that city; left this congregation with fairly good buildings and out of debt, in March, 1857; then came to New Albany and took charge of the Annunciation congregation; remained there ten years and one month, during which he paid $2,200 of the debt he found on his arrival, and built the main part of the present church at a cost of $20,000, every dollar of which he paid; next he went to St. Benedict's, Terre Haute, where in four years he improved the grounds, paid a debt of $8,000, half of which was his personal contribution; from St. Benedict's he went to Cannelton, Ind., taking charge there on March 3, 1871, of St. Michael's congregation; here he found a debt of $9,000; paid $4,000 of it in a few months, and with $10,000 of his own money built a new parsonage and improved the church. He remained at Cannelton until November, 1878, also having charge of St. Paul's, at Tell City, during the last twenty-one months of that time. He then removed to Tell City and there remained until Oct. 12, 1882. In that time he finished a church that had been commenced, and paid the debts hanging over his congregation, in all amounting to $21,000. From Tell City he went to St. Michael's, at Madison, Ind. Here Father Faller found a congregation that was under an apathy he was unable to dispel. After nearly three years there he asked for another mission, and in July, 1885, was sent to St. Ann's, in Jennings county. Here he paid a portion of the $1,100 indebtedness, built a new school house, added to the parsonage, and improved the church, all amounting to about $8,000, of which he paid $7,000. On July 14, 1886, he returned to New Albany as rector of the Church of the Annunciation. His predecessor, Father Klein, had commenced the work of enlarging the church, and Father Faller carried out the original designs, later building a new rectory at a cost of $7,500, and spending $5,000 on paintings, statues, organ, etc. At the Fourth Synod of the diocese of Vincennes, November, 1886, he was appointed dean of the New Albany district, composed of the counties of Floyd, Clark, Harrison, Crawford, Washington and Scott. He was not present at the time, and his appointment came unsought and unexpected. Fourscore years have passed since Dean Faller first saw the light of day in the little Alsatian town beyond the sea. Nearly three-fourths of that time has been spent in the business of his Master. As he looks back over the long life he awaits the words of approbation, "Well done, thou good and faithful servant."

THE DAY LEATHER COMPANY of New Albany, Ind., is the oldest concern of its kind in the vicinity of the Ohio Falls, and is generally spoken of as the "Pioneer Tannery." It was founded in 1838 by Theodore Day, who was born in Prussia in 1812 and came to the United States in 1837. It was first located at Lanesville, ten miles from New Albany, but in 1851 was removed to the city. In 1883 the business was incorporated as the Day Leather Company, with Theodore Day as president, and Anthony T. Day, secretary and treasurer. Upon the death of Theodore Day in 1885 the official personnel of the company was changed to Anthony T. Day, president; John I. Day, vice-president, and Charles Day, secretary and treasurer, and has thus remained ever since. The tannery is located at the corner of Fourth and Oak streets, employs about sixty workmen, and has a capacity of 600 heavy hides per week, the product being sold all over the United States. The founder learned the business of leather making in Prussia, Austria and France, and the technical knowledge he acquired has been imparted to his sons, the result being that the leather turned out by this concern has no superior in the markets of the country.

Anthony T. Day, the president of the company, was born near New Albany, May 15, 1844. He was educated in the public and private schools of that city and for two years in his early manhood he conducted a leather store in St. Louis, Mo. In 1871 he sold out this store and returned to New Albany, where he has since been connected with the company of which he is now the official head, most of the time as its active manager. He was married on July 18, 1875, to Miss Elizabeth Poole, a native of Iowa, and they have three children. George H. is a physician of Louisville, Ky.; Clarence C. holds a responsible position with the firm of Hanna & Co., in their extensive saw and planing mills and lumber yards of Cincinnati, and Nellie B. is at home with her parents.

Charles Day, the secretary and treasurer of the company, was born in the city of New Albany, June 13, 1863. After graduating from the New Albany business college he became connected with the business founded by his father, and since 1885 has held his present position. The Day brothers have a high standing in the commercial circles of New Albany, and are regarded as among the representative citizens of the city. Public-spirited, progressive and charitable, they have won a prominent position in the estimation of their fellow-men.

GEORGE M. CLARK, president of the Ohio Falls Iron Company, New Albany, Ind., was born in the city of Cincinnati, March 4, 1855. His father, George W. Clark, was formerly a banker of that city, but at the close of the Civil war moved across the river to Covington, Ky., where the son was reared and educated, graduating from the Hughes high school in Cincinnati at the age of eighteen years. He then went into a brass foundry and supply house, the firm of William Kirkup & Son, Cincinnati, and remained with them until 1881, when he withdrew to become a member of the firm of Clark & Hawley, lead pipe and sheet lead works, and dealers in plumbers' and steamfitters' supplies, in Cincinnati. This business is still carried on under the name of Crane & Hawley. In 1891 Mr. Clark sold out his interest and bought a large share in the well known Mitchell-Tranter Company, manufacturers of iron and steel. Of this concern he was president until 1899, when it was merged into the Republic Iron and Steel Company, Mr. Clark continuing with that corporation as a director and district manager. A little later he severed his connection with the company, however, came to New Albany; bought the idle plant of the Ohio Falls Iron Works; organized the company of which he is now president, and Henry Green vice-president; expended $50,000 in a little over a month in putting the plant in good working condition; and in the latter part of 1899 commenced business. Within less than two years the volume of business had increased to such an extent as to make necessary the erection of a new rolling mill just west of the old one, and since then both mills have been running to their full capacity, the plant employing about 900 men and having an annual capacity of 40,000 tons of bar iron, most of which finds ready sale in the railroad shops and car works of the country, because of its superior quality. Mr. Clark is vice-president of a large mercantile concern in Cincinnati, known as the Cincinnati Iron Store Company, which he was instrumental in organizing in 1901. This company deals in iron and steel and all kinds of structural materials. He is also a director in the First National bank of Covington, Ky. In the business life of Mr. Clark the young man may find an example worthy of the highest emulation. Realizing that we live in a commercial age, he caught in early life the spirit of the time, and has gone steadily forward from one enterprise to another, turning his attention to that which the demands of the day seemed most to justify. By his close observation of the market conditions, he has been able to embark in lines of business that were certain to yield returns; by his industry and well directed efforts he has made those undertakings successful; by his sound judgment and conservative methods he has avoided everything like speculation and confined himself to legitimate schemes; and by his sterling integrity he has made friends in the business world who know that he can always be relied on to carry out his contracts to the very letter. Mr. Clark is a prominent member of the Masonic fraternity, being a thirty-second degree member of the Scottish Rite and a Noble of the Mystic Shrine. He was married Dec. 20, 1876, to Miss Ada Tranter of Covington, Ky., and they have three children: Lucy is now the wife of William F. Streich of New York, and the two sons, Clifford E. and James T., are associated with their father in business.

WILLIAM A. M'LEAN, vice-president and general manager of the Wood-Mosaic Flooring Company of New Albany, Ind., and Rochester, N. Y., and also vice-president of the Hugh McLean Lumber Company of Buffalo, N. Y., was born near Montreal, Canada, May 31, 1868. He was reared and educated in Canada, and at the age of sixteen years began his business career. At the age of twenty-one he went to Buffalo, N. Y., and secured a position in a hardwood lumber concern, remaining there for three years, in which time he learned the details of the business. In 1892 he formed a partnership with his three brothers, Hugh, Angus and Robert D., under the firm name of the Hugh McLean Lumber Company, with headquarters in Buffalo. It carries on an extensive lumber business all over the country, with branch offices at Louisville, Ky.; New Albany, Ind.; Chattanooga, Tenn.; Bedford, Ind., and Rochester, N. Y. Angus McLean is president and general manager of the Hugh McLean Lumber Company, Hugh is treasurer, William A. is the vice-president, and Robert D. is the secretary. At the New Albany branch of the company they are operating a large plant known as the Wood-Mosaic Flooring Company, of which C. E. Rider of Rochester is president, William A. McLean vice-president and general manager, Angus McLean secretary and treasurer. Besides the plant at New Albany, the company has factories at Buffalo and Louisville. Mr. McLean came to New Albany in 1900. He is fond of sports, particularly hunting, and every autumn he joins a party of friends for a deer hunt in Canada, where the four brothers have a game reserve of 121 square miles. He is a Knight Templar.

HENRY GREEN, vice-president of the Ohio Falls Iron Company, was born Dec. 16, 1846, in Shropshire, England, on a farm which had been in the possession and the residence of some of his family name for two hundred and forty-five years. Upon the death of his father Henry decided to learn the business of iron making, and at the age of sixteen years he entered a rolling mill, where he served as an apprentice until he was twenty-three. He then left his mother country and drifted into foreign lands. First he went to St. Petersburg, Russia, but not understanding the language he made but a short stay and came to America, landing in New York in June, 1869. Mr. Green went direct to Pittsburg, where he took charge of the roll turning department of the Phillips & Jordan mills; then to the Fulton rail mill of Cincinnati; next the Swift Iron and Steel Works of Newport, Ky., and in 1873 he assumed the charge of the Mitchell & Tranter rolling mills, in Covington, Ky. For some time he continued in charge of all four of these plants, and in 1876 became one of the organizers of the Anchor Iron and Steel Works of Newport, remaining a stockholder in the concern during the period of its existence. About the same time he became interested in some coal mines near Terre Haute, Ind., but as they were eighteen miles from a railroad the project was abandoned. In 1890 Mr. Green severed his connection with all the mills except the Mitchell-Tranter Company, in which he then became a stockholder, and remained with the company until it was merged into the Republic Iron and Steel Company in 1899, and he still retains his stock in the latter corporation. While with the Mitchell-Tranter Company, Mr. Green formed the acquaintance of George M. Clark, president and general manager of the company, and has ever since been closely associated with him in business. (See sketch of Mr. Clark.) In 1899, in connection with Mr. Clark, he assisted in organizing the Ohio Falls Company and has been vice-president from the incorporation of the company. His company makes a specialty of bar iron, used by railroad shops and car works, and of special iron and steel machinery used in such works. For some time they have run night and day to keep up with their orders, and finally built a second rolling mill to supply the demand. In 1870 Mr. Green took the degrees of Masonry in Colonel Clay Lodge, No. 159, of Covington; was made a Royal Arch Mason in Covington Chapter, No. 35, the same year; received the degree of Knight Templar in Covington Commandery, No. 7, in 1876, and in 1893 became a member of Syrian Temple, Nobles of the Mystic Shrine, in Cincinnati. He still holds his membership in these different Masonic bodies, and is a Knight of Pythias, being one of the charter members of Myrtle Lodge, organized at Covington in 1874. The following year he became an Odd Fellow in Kenton Lodge, No. 24, of Covington, and in 1901 he joined New Albany Lodge, No. 270, Benevolent and Protective Order of Elks. Mr. Green has never married. He is a bachelor from choice, though he enjoys the society of refined ladies and has the highest respect for womanhood. Although a resident of New Albany but for a short time, he is frequently spoken of as one who has done more to put new life into the city than any one else. He is a stockholder in a number of business enterprises and is a thorough-going business man—one of the twentieth century kind. Genial and generous, he is popular with his acquaintance and associates, and his well established reputation for honesty and integrity only adds to this popularity.

FRANK MANUS, head of the firm of Frank Manus & Son, beef and pork packers, New Albany, Ind., was born in that city, Feb. 25, 1856. His father, whose name was also Frank, was a native of Germany, a butcher by trade, and followed that occupation for several years in New Albany. The son received his education in the New Albany public schools and the business college there, and then learned the butcher business before he was twenty-one years of age. In the fall of 1876 he started in the business for himself. Being young, ambitious and desirous to please, he soon came to be one of the most popular butchers in the city, many a woman advising her neighbors to try "the Dutch boy" if she wanted to get good meat. As the years went by his popularity did not wane, as he had learned that it paid to give the best meats to his customers for a reasonable price. In more recent years he has turned his attention more to the wholesale meat trade. He has a well equipped slaughter house on State street, where he slaughters about one hundred hogs a week, besides a number of cattle. Not far from his packing house he has a comfortable residence, one which he has paid for out of the proceeds of his own labor and which is one of the modern homes of the city. Mr. Manus was married on April 29, 1879, to Miss Eva C. Endres of Lanesville, Harrison county, Ind., and they have three children living and three deceased: Frank, Jr., is the junior member of the firm, and the other two living are John L. and Lulu May. Those deceased were Rudolph, Andrew and Lorena. Mr. Manus is a member of the Improved Order of Red Men and the Benevolent and Protective Order of Elks. In his lodges, as well as in the community, he has a high standing, and is regarded as one of the reliable and substantial citizens of New Albany.

GEORGE MOSER, senior member of the firm of George Moser & Co., tanners and leather manufacturers, New Albany, Ind., was born in Germany in the year 1850. In 1867, at the age of seventeen years, he came to the United States and shortly after his arrival in this country he located at New Albany, which city has ever since been his home. For over ten years he was employed in the tannery of August Barth, but in 1878 he decided to embark in the business for himself.

He accordingly purchased the tannery of Lockwood Brothers, on East Eighth street. This tannery was established in 1848 and has therefore been in existence and active operation for over half a century. Upon taking hold of the concern Mr. Moser set about enlarging and improving it, and during the time that he has been in possession he has added greatly to the efficiency of the plant by the introduction of improved machinery, new buildings, etc., and it is now an up-to-date tannery in every respect. The business was carried on under the name of George Moser until 1891, when his nephew, John M. Moser, was admitted to partnership and the firm of George Moser & Co. came into existence. In 1900 John M. Moser withdrew from the firm, his interest being taken by his brother, Charles E. Moser. George Moser is a tanner of the best kind. What he does not know about making leather, according to present established processes, is hardly worth learning. His firm makes a specialty of high grade collar leather, and while there may be larger tanneries, there are none whose products command a better place in the market. Mr. Moser is married and has a family of four children, three sons and a daughter. Charles E. Moser, the junior partner, was born in New Albany, March 31, 1874; was educated in the public schools and the New Albany business college. He is a fine representative of the younger school of business men and has a high standing in commercial circles. He is married and has two children.

FRANK ENSLINGER, of the firm of Schueler & Enslinger, butchers and dealers in meats, New Albany, Ind., was born on a farm near that city, June 24, 1863. He is a son of Frank Enslinger, a farmer, born in Germany in 1813, who came to America and settled in Floyd county about 1840. He died there in 1876, his wife, the mother of the subject of this sketch, having died in 1869. Frank is the youngest of their ten children, the others being Pauline, now the widow of Philip Scharf; Joseph; Adam; Mary, now Mrs. John Lich; Fannie and Frank, living, and Helena, Catharine, August and Eva, deceased. The last named died as the wife of Joseph Fein. At the age of seventeen years Frank left the farm; came to New Albany and clerked in a grocery to the age of twenty-four; then learned the butchers' trade with the late John Shueler, the father of his present partner, and upon the death of Mr. Shueler in 1893 formed the partnership with his son Joseph, which arrangement still exists. The firm of Shueler & Enslinger commands a good portion of the retail meat trade of New Albany and vicinity, and they have one of the best appointed meat markets to be found anywhere. Mr. Enslinger was married on Jan. 24, 1888, to Miss Anna Barbara Shueler, the sister of his partner, and to this union there have been born three children: John Frank, Herman Joseph and Karl Edward. Mr. Enslinger is a member of St. Joseph's Society of the St. Mary's Catholic church and of the Improved Order of Red Men. His partner, Joseph Shueler, was born in New Albany, March 16, 1869, his father, John Shueler, having been born in Germany in the earlier part of the nineteenth century, and locating in New Albany about the close of the Civil war. Joseph learned the butchers' trade with his father; at the tender age of sixteen he embarked in the business for himself, and since 1893 he has continued in it, as the partner of Mr. Enslinger. He is one of the best known butchers in the city, and one of the most proficient in his line of work.

JOSEPH T. KREMENTZ, grocer and butcher, of New Albany, Ind., was born in that city, Aug. 3, 1862. His father, Joseph Krementz, was a native of Germany and a butcher by trade. He died when Joseph was about two years old. The subject of this sketch has lived in New Albany all his life; attended the public schools there; learned the butchers' trade while still in his boyhood; and about fifteen years ago embarked in the business for himself. Since then he has made it a point to carry nothing but the best goods to be found, either in meats or groceries, and his large and constantly growing patronage demonstrates the wisdom of his course. In 1900 he bought a fine piece of business property, with residence attached, at No. 615 Vincennes street, where he has one of the best appointed grocery stores and meat markets in the city. Mr. Krementz takes great pride in his business, prompt attention to his customers, quick delivery of goods ordered, and a nice, clean store being some of the points upon which he always excels. He is a Knight Templar

Mason and a member of the Improved Order of Red Men. On Oct. 14, 1884, Mr. Krementz was united in marriage to Miss Louisa Sohn, a daughter of Anton Sohn, a former resident and prominent brewer of New Albany. Mrs. Krementz was born in New Albany, Jan. 26, 1864. During the twenty years of their married life Mr. and Mrs. Krementz have worked together in the upbuilding of the husband's business and the establishment of their home. Two daughters have been born to them, Louise C. and Tillie W. The former died at the age of seven years and the latter is now a young lady of seventeen.

JAMES T. RUBY, bicycle dealer and proprietor of the Crystal Laundry, New Albany, Ind., was born in Wayne county, Ind., June 3, 1851, his parents being William T. and Rose Ann (Fender) Ruby, the former a native of Kentucky and the latter of Wayne county. The mother died in 1887, aged fifty-seven years, and the father on Oct. 20, 1903, aged about seventy-eight. He was the son of John Ruby, who was a son of Joseph Ruby of Pennsylvania, and the father of Joseph came from England. On the maternal side Mr. Ruby's grandfather was Gabriel Fender, a native of North Carolina, and his father was Henry Fender, of German descent. James T. Ruby lived on the farm in Wayne county until he was seventeen years of age, when he went to Richmond and worked at the printers' trade for two years, after which he went into the depot restaurant there as a clerk, and two years later went to Cambridge City, Ind., where he held a similar position for six months, after which he had charge for ten years. In 1882 he went to Dayton, O., and became a collector for the Howe Sewing Machine Company, where he remained one year, was then manager for two years, when he accepted a position as traveling salesman for H. A. Lozier & Co., wholesale agents for the New Home sewing machine, of Cleveland, and for thirteen years covered the territory composed of Ohio, Indiana, West Virginia and Kentucky. He was next two years "on the road" for the Springfield (Ohio) Fertilizer Company, and a similar length of time for the Iver Johnson Arms and Cycle Works, of Fitchburg, Mass., covering the entire Southern states. In 1890 he came to New Albany and opened a bicycle store at No. 139 Market street, and in 1903 he became the proprietor of the Crystal Laundry, at No. 139 Main street. In addition to his business enterprises in New Albany, Mr. Ruby owns a fine farm of 320 acres in Guthrie county, Ia., one of the best agricultural regions of that state. Beginning life without a dollar, he has made his way in the world to his present position by indomitable industry, sheer force of will, and unflinching honesty. Mr.

Ruby is a member of the Masonic fraternity, in which he has a high standing. He has been married three times, his first and second wives having died. He has two sons by his first wife: Edward E., now a professor of Latin and French in Whitman college, Walla Walla, Wash., and Oliver A., who is associated with his father in business. Oliver A. is married and has two daughters, Irma Helen and Lucile Ethel. Mr. Ruby's present wife, to whom he was married on Oct. 16, 1899, was Lunettie Jackson.

EDWARD P. VERNIA, freight agent and general yard master of the Chicago, Indianapolis & Louisville railway, better known as the Monon, at New Albany, Ind., was born in that city, July 23, 1875. His father, the late Lewis Vernia, a wholesale grocer of New Albany, died on Aug. 22, 1902. Edward was reared and educated in the city where he was born, graduating from the Holy Trinity parochial school when he was sixteen years old. About a year after he left school he entered the employment of the Monon Railroad Company as a clerk. In 1899 he was made freight agent at New Albany, and in August, 1903, was made general yard master. Mr. Vernia has been all his active life in the employ of the same company, and when it is remembered that railway corporations are on the lookout for intelligent and trustworthy young men to fill places of responsibility, it speaks well for the character of Mr. Vernia that in the first eleven years of his railway service he worked himself up from a minor clerkship to the position he now occupies. To have done so it was necessary that he should apply himself diligently and willingly to whatever duty might be assigned him, and to always keep his mind upon his business. This he has certainly done, and his promotions have been the just reward of industry and fidelity to his employers' interests. As Mr. Vernia is yet a young man, there is little doubt that still higher positions await him in railroad circles. Mr. Vernia is a member of the Louisville local freight agents' association, the Benevolent and Protective Order of Elks, and the Holy Trinity Catholic church. Politically he is a Democrat, but he is first of all a railroad man, and never neglects his business to participate in politics. He was married on June 15, 1904, to Miss Catharine E. Jackson, an accomplished young lady of Cincinnati.

S. J. GARDNER, a well known foundryman of New Albany, Ind., was born in Paducah, Ky., in the year 1863. He acquired his education in the schools of his native city, and at the age of eighteen started in to learn the trade of machinist. After serving an apprenticeship of four years he worked as a journeyman in railroad shops and manufactories in different parts of the country until 1897, when he came to New Albany and bought the plant of the old Webster & Pitt foundry, on First street, between Main street and the Ohio river. This concern had been standing idle for about three years, and Mr. Gardner spent a considerable sum of money in putting it in good condition, adding new machinery, etc. He has now been operating the plant for seven years, under the name of the S. J. Gardner Foundry and Machine Works, and has built up a good business, particularly on the Lithgow furnace, of which he is the builder, and which has become popular in the Ohio valley, the demand for it rapidly increasing as its introduction is extended into new territory. Mr. Gardner has made his way to the front rank as a manufacturer by his careful and conscientious methods in the construction of his work and his close application to his business. In 1892 he was united in marriage to Miss Maggie Carney of Paducah, and they have two children, Ella Laurence and Edward Merwin.

TOBIAS HOFFER, a prominent wholesale liquor merchant of New Albany, Ind., is a native of that city, having been born there, May 30, 1862. He is a son of the late Frank Hoffer, a native of Germany, who settled in New Albany some time in the fifties, and who was for many years engaged in the wholesale liquor business there. He died on Feb. 24, 1889. Tobias was educated in the public and parochial schools of his native city and the New Albany Business college. In 1882 he went into his father's store as a clerk and was afterward engaged for some time as a traveling salesman for the house. From 1886 to 1890 he was in partnership with his brother in the wholesale liquor trade, under the firm name of Hoffer Bros. Since 1890 he has been in the same line by himself, having been located the whole time at No. 106 East Market street. Mr. Hoffer is a member of St. Mary's Catholic church and is regarded as one of the stanch business men of New Albany. His trade extends over a large section of the surrounding country, and he has one of the leading establishments of the kind about the Falls of the Ohio. He was married on Oct. 12, 1886, to Miss Mary Frances Broecker of New Albany, and they have two daughters, Mary Elizabeth and Estella Johanna.

WILLIAM WIRT ROWLETT (deceased), familiarly known as "Buck" Rowlett, an old time newspaper man of Kentucky, was born in Owen county, of that state, May 24, 1845, and died at La Grange in Oldham county, Feb. 5, 1904. His life was an eventful one. While still in his boyhood his parents removed to Lockport, Ky., where he was educated in the public schools and in 1860 began life for himself as a clerk in a general store. He continued in that capacity until Aug. 7, 1861, when he enlisted in the Union army at Camp Joe Holt and was assigned to duty as corporal of Company C, Second Kentucky Federal cavalry. He was soon promoted to first corporal, and from that position arose to orderly sergeant and later to regimental quartermaster. In 1864, although still in his minority, he was placed in charge of a fund of $30,000 appropriated by the Kentucky legislature to aid the work of the Sanitary Commission. The following year he was recommended by Gen. John Palmer for a captaincy, received a commission from Governor Bramlett, and was given command of Company E, Barracks battalion, at Louisville. In September of that year he became a member of the stock company of the Louisville theater, playing utility parts, subsequently taking the part of a low comedian, and remained with the company until the theater was destroyed by fire. For a time he engaged in school teaching; was then a pilot on the Ohio and Kentucky rivers; in connection with his father, contracted with the state to repair the locks on the Kentucky river, and put in the lock gates; was next in the business of building wooden truss bridges, and in 1871 located in Henry county, where he engaged in the mercantile line. Here he was elected justice of the peace, holding the office for nearly five years. On May 26, 1875, he established the *Henry County Tribune*, at New Castle, which marked his entrance into the field of journalism. The following January he removed to La Grange, and on February 4th the first number of the *Oldham County Era* appeared. From that time until his death he continued to conduct the paper as "The only second class newspaper in the United States," and since his death the publication of it has been continued by his sons, Bushrod and Felix. In 1885 Mr. Rowlett edited and published a book entitled "A Job Lot," being a collection of quaint sayings, witticisms, etc. In the preface he expressed the hope that the book would be read by many who had not purchased it, "for if there is an enemy of mankind it is the book borrower." Mr. Rowlett was a man of brilliant wit and endowed with a generous supply of what is known as common sense. As a conversationalist he was both entertaining and instructive. His original way of expressing ideas frequently aroused the mirthfulness of his listeners and fixed the fact firmly in their memory. During his life he was noted for his public spirit, always being identified with every movement to promote the interests of La Grange and Oldham county. Politically he was a Democrat of the kind that never apologizes for his political views, though he had many warm personal friends in the opposite party. As a Mason and an Odd Fellow he was always a welcome attendant at the lodge meetings because of his genial and sunny disposition, and his sound judgment when business of importance was to be transacted. At the battle of Perryville he sustained two painful wounds, and a short time before his death the government granted him a pension of thirty dollars a month—a somewhat tardy recognition of his valiant services when the nation was in peril. Mr. Rowlett was married in 1870 to Sallie R., daughter of William L. White of Lockport, and to this union there were born the following children: Bushrod; Ella, now Mrs. Clarence Kerr; Alma, Felix, Mamie, Annie, Charles and Robert. The mother of these children died in 1900. The eldest son, Bushrod, was born in Lockport, June 3, 1871; learned the printers' trade with his father; received his education at the Funk seminary at La Grange; from 1893 to 1898 was employed in the government printing office at Washington, and on April 29, 1898, enlisted as a private in Battery A, First District light artillery, for the Spanish-American war. From private he rose to corporal, sergant, sergeant-major, and at the time of his discharge, on Dec. 7, 1898, he was acting commissary. After the war he was at the Garfield Memorial Hospital, in Washington, for three months, ill with typhoid-malaria. On his recovery he returned to his old position in the government printing office, but a few weeks later was discharged to reduce the force. For some time he worked at his trade in different Eastern cities, and in 1900 he returned to La Grange and took charge of the *Oldham County Era*, which he now ably conducts in connection with his brother, as already stated.

JOHN F. GEBHART, general manager of the New Albany Woolen Mill Company, New Albany, Ind., was born at Maytown, Pa., in December, 1831. With a moderate education in the public schools he started early in life to learn the business of making woolen goods with his father, who was the proprietor of a little woolen mill at Maytown. In 1860 Mr. Gebhart came to New Albany, and on the 1st of January, 1861, in company with John T. Creed, started a little woolen mill on State street, in the building afterward used as the Air Line railway station. In 1861 the New Albany Woolen Mill Company was organized, put up a mill on Vincennes street, ran it for about two years at a loss of several thousand dollars, when, to secure the services of Mr. Gebhart, the company bought his concern and consolidated the two mills. Since then the success of the company has been steady and certain. In 1871 the first cotton mill was erected, three others having been built since. By his cool demeanor and sound judgment he kept the mills running through the depression that followed the panic of 1873, although the works had been placed in the hands of an assignee. In 1879 the hosiery department was started, which has since become a separate institution. In order to secure sufficient water supply for the manufacture of fancy plaid flannels, Mr. Gebhart secured the construction of the city waterworks in 1876, although few people believed that the movement was a successful one. Mr. Gebhart has been actively associated with several other enterprises. He was one of the organizers of the New Albany & Eastern railroad, which connects with the Baltimore & Ohio Southwestern at Watson; one of the promoters of the Belt railroad; has served as president of the street railway company; built the Highland railroad to the top of Silver Hills, thus making the hill-top a place of residence and resort; was active in organizing the New Albany Ornamental Brick Company, of which he is now president; and every one of these important industries owes much of its vitality to his sound judgment and superb ability. In church matters Mr. Gebhart has been a prominent figure in the city ever since he came there. For over thirty years he directed the choir of the First Presbyterian church; raised the money and supervised the construction of the pipe organ in the building; served as president of the Y. M. C. A. building committee, which erected the association's handsome building on the corner of Bank and Main streets, and has ever been identified with worthy projects for the improvement of public health and morals. Mr. Gebhart has been married four times. His first wife, to whom he was united on Sept. 4, 1851, was Susan Latchem. She died in 1854, and in 1857 he was married to Rachel Santee, who died in 1861. In 1865 he was married to Amanda Rodgers, and she passed to her rest in 1871. On Nov. 27, 1873, he was united to Miss Rosalinda Ridgway, a native of Delaware, who is his present wife. By his first marriage he has one daughter living, who is the wife of W. A. Hedden of New Albany; by his second wife he has two children living, James, who is superintendent of a woolen mill at Omaha, Neb., and Letitia, now the wife of Edgar S. Crane, a prominent business man of Yazoo City, Miss.; to the third wife was born one son, Frederick, who died in his twenty-third year. By his present wife he has two sons: John Reuben, a traveling salesman for the woolen mill company, and David Ridgway, who is supervisor of music in the New Albany public schools. Both are married and both served in the Spanish-American war as commissioned officers, John R. being in the ordnance department and David adjutant of the One Hundred and Fifty-ninth Indiana infantry. Mr. Gebhart is a prominent member of the Masonic fraternity and is an elder in the Presbyterian church.

J. L. BERRY, proprietor and manager of a large sawmill at Louisville, Ky., was born in Jefferson county of that state, about twenty miles from the city of Louisville, Oct. 23, 1853. He is a son of Leander S. and James Anise (Curry) Berry, the former a native of Virginia and the latter of Jefferson county, Ky. The father was a carpenter and builder who followed that vocation for many years in Louisville and died there about 1890. His wife survived him for about five years and passed her last days in the same city. She was a daughter of Philip S. and Elizabeth (Bean) Curry, both natives of Jefferson county, where the family were among the pioneers. Of their seven children one son, Thornton B. Curry, is now living. In 1861 Leander S. Berry removed with his family to Champaign county, Ill., and there the subject of this sketch grew to manhood, receiving his education in the common schools. In 1879 he went to Indianapolis, Ind., and after a short stay in that city returned to Louisville, where he has been practically all of the time since identified with the lumber and sawmill interests of the cities about the Falls. In 1886 he established his present mill on the block bounded by Third and Fourth avenues and J and K streets. At that time the surrounding lots were nothing but commons. Now the city has extended in that direction until it built up almost solidly all around the mill. Mr. Berry's mill has a capacity of about 20,000 feet of lumber daily, or approximately 4,000,000 feet a year. In the eighteen years that he has been established here it is estimated that he has produced 60,000,000 feet of hardwood lumber alone. Logs are shipped from all parts of Kentucky and neighboring states to supply the demand. Mr. Berry is a member of the Louisville Lumbermen's club, and there are not many points about the lumber trade upon which he is not thoroughly informed. He has been twice married. On Dec. 31, 1879, to Miss Christina Thorn, who died on December 31st, a few years later. A striking coincidence is that she died on the anniversary of her marriage, and almost at the same hour of the day. She left two sons: Morphy Edison, a graduate of the Louisville manual training high school, graduated from the mechanical department of Cornell university in 1904, completing a four years' course in three years and winning a fellowship besides, and in 1905 will enter the department of electrical engineering in Cornell. He was born Nov. 15, 1881, and his brother, George H., was born November 14, 1891, the latter lacking just one day of being ten years younger than his brother. George is now attending the public schools in Louisville.

REUBEN T. DURRETT, lawyer, and author, was born in Henry county, Ky., Jan. 22, 1824. He is the son of William and Elizabeth (Rowlings) Durrett, both of old Virginia families who came to Kentucky about the beginning of the nineteenth century. His early education was acquired in a little country schoolhouse built by his father for the benefit of his own and his neighbors' children. To prepare himself for college he entered Henry academy at New Castle. In 1844 he entered Georgetown college, completing the freshman year. In 1846 he entered the sophomore class at Brown university, Providence, R. I., graduating from the same with the degree of A.B. three years later. Completing the law course of the University of Louisville in one year, he received the degree of LL.B. from that institution. Brown university conferred upon him the regular degree of A.M., and Georgetown college, university of Louisville and Brown university the honorary degree of LL.D. He at once began the practice of law in Louisville and continued it uninterruptedly for thirty years. Retiring on the competency he had by this time acquired, he devoted his time to literary pursuits, for which he had always had a strong desire. Gifted as a writer, orator and poet, he indulged his tastes in each of these lines. He was at one time editor-in-chief of the Louisville *Daily Courier* and wrote much for other newspapers and magazines of his time. His writings were usually distinguished for original research, and his article upon the Kentucky Resolutions of 1798-99, which appeared in the *Southern Bivouac,* may be taken as a specimen. Clearing up the historic errors about these celebrated resolutions, he has placed them where they and their authors should remain in history. Not a few of his court and public addresses were deemed worthy of publication and appeared in newspapers or in pamphlet form. In 1884 he and a few of his associates founded in Louisville the Filson club, a historic and literary association, for the purpose of collecting and preserving the history and biography of Kentucky. For each year of its existence it has published a volume of history and biography, the twentieth volume having now been issued. Of these volumes, Mr. Durrett is the author of the first, fifth, seventh, eighth and twelfth, having written the introduction to all of the others. His literary taste led him to the investigation of various subjects, and, as he bought the books he needed, he soon accumulated one of the largest private libraries in the county, embracing almost every branch of human knowledge. Mr. Durrett has also been active in the establishing of a number of successful business corporations. His benevolence has led him into connection with charitable institutions, causing him to take a prominent part in some of the most worthy institutions of that kind in the state. He has served as a member of the city council and of the board of park commissioners, neither of which were offices of profit, but were deemed by him positions in the interest of the city. When Beriah Magoffin was a candidate for governor of Kentucky, Mr. Durrett took an active part in his behalf and helped to secure his election. After his election the governor sent for Mr. Durrett and asked him what he could do for him. Mr. Durrett replied that he wanted no reward other than the continuance of his good will. Governor Magoffin then said, "Well, I will commission you as a colonel on my staff," and he did so. This title of colonel will, no doubt, stick to Mr. Durrett the remainder of his life. Although advanced in years, the Colonel is still possessed of health and vigor. He stands six feet two inches high, as straight as an Indian chief, and bids fair to outlive many of those around him who are of fewer years. His writings have caused him to be known at home and abroad, entitling him to be made a member of many historic and learned societies.

COL. BENNETT H. YOUNG, lawyer, Louisville, Ky., who has been prominently identified with the development of Southern railway enterprises, and who, in many ways, has contributed vastly to the material prosperity of Kentucky, is of Scotch-Irish descent. He is the son of Robert and Josephine (Henderson) Young and was born in Jessamine county, Ky., May 25, 1843. He was fitted for college at Bethel academy and was preparing to enter Centre college, Danville, when the Civil war began. With other students, Colonel Young enlisted in the Eighth Kentucky cavalry, which became a part of Gen. John H. Morgan's command. He was captured in Morgan's raid across the Ohio, and for a short time confined in the military prison at Camp Douglas. Escaping from prison, he made his way to Canada, and there collected and conducted to the Confederacy, by way of the West Indies, a number of escaped Confederates. Later on he returned to Canada bearing a commission as a Confederate officer, and from that vantage ground organized a series of expeditions into the United States, which at the time attracted much attention and occasioned considerable alarm on the part of the Federal authorities. At the close of the war Colonel Young went to Europe to pursue his studies for three years in the Scotch and Irish universities, supplementing his literary education by a thorough law course. In Queen's college, Belfast, he took the first honors of his class in the law department and the third honors in the literary department. In 1868 he returned to Kentucky, well equipped by education, travel and experience to enter upon his professional career. He located in Louisville, where he soon impressed himself upon the bar and public as an accomplished and resourceful lawyer, and built up a lucrative practice. In 1872 he formed a partnership with St. John Boyle, and with him became interested in railway construction. They operated together in the construction of the Louisville, Evansville & St. Louis railway, now known as the St. Louis Air Line, and now a part of the Southern railroad system. For this important railway connection Louisville is indebted to this firm. Later Colonel Young was called upon to undertake the purchase and reorganization of the Louisville, New Albany & Chicago railway, a project that he conducted to a successful issue. He was general counsel for this railway corporation until 1883, when he became its president, a position he afterwards resigned to give his attention to affairs of great importance to the city of Louisville and the State of Kentucky. Chief of the enterprises that occupied his attention at that time was, perhaps, the building of a second bridge across the Ohio river. This enterprise, which involved an expenditure of $2,500,000, was pushed to completion in 1886 by Colonel Young with characteristic energy. This was the largest cantilever bridge that had up to that time been constructed. To make the Kentucky and Indiana bridge a success, a Southern railway outlet was needed. In company with other Louisville capitalists he inaugurated the Louisville & Southern railway, connecting with the Cincinnati Southern at Burgin, which gave to Louisville another great Southern railway outlet. The completion of this line marked a new era in the development of Louisville and contributed vastly to her commercial importance. Thus without burdening herself with any obligations Louisville secured a trunk line railway connection with the South, similar to that for which Cincinnati a few years before had expended nearly $20,000,000. At a still later date Colonel Young became interested in the organization of the Richmond, Nicholasville, Irvin & Beattyville railway, but left its construction to other parties. To the development of Southern resources and the rehabilitation and rejuvenation of the Southland he has largely devoted his time and energies during the most active period of his life. Still a leading practitioner at the Louisville bar, a large share of his time is devoted to the legal business of corporations. With all movements designed to promote the prosperity of Louisville he has been very actively engaged. In recognition of his services to the city and state he was elected an honorary member of the board of trade, being the youngest man upon whom this honor had ever been conferred. In 1884 he was honored with the presidency of the Southern Exposition. In 1890 he was elected a member of the constitutional convention and was one of its most influential agents in forming the present organic law of the state. Notwithstanding the fact that he was a very busy man in his profession he has found time to devote to literary pursuits. He is the author of a "History of the Three Constitutions of Kentucky," and "A History of the Division of the Presbyterian Church of Kentucky." He has contributed largely to every phase of church work; established and largely endowed the Bellwood seminary and the Kentucky Presbyterian Normal School at Anchorage; was one of the reorganizers of the Louisville public library and has been its president for several years; is president of the Kentucky

Confederate Home; president of the Kentucky institute for the blind; commander of the Kentucky division of the United Confederate Veterans, and has established a reputation as one of the most successful and eloquent lawyers at the Kentucky bar. He enjoys a large and lucrative practice; has declined all political honors; has never held any office, and has persistently declined to seek any political preferment.

EMBRY LEE SWEARINGEN, president of the Kentucky Title Company and the Kentucky Title Savings bank, of Louisville, was born at Millwood, Bullitt county, Ky., Jan. 27, 1863. He is a son of George W. and Mary (Embry) Swearingen, and is of the tenth generation from Gerrit Van Swearingen, the first of the family in America. Gerrit Van Swearingen was one of the younger sons of a Dutch nobleman and a native of Beemsterdam, North Holland. In 1656 he was sent to America in command of a vessel laden with supplies for the Dutch colony at New Amsterdam, now New York. The good ship was lost in a storm off the Atlantic coast, which led Captain Van Swearingen to abandon the sea and the same year he settled in Maryland. His wife was Barbara De Barette, of Valenciennes. Four generations of the family lived in Maryland. Toward the close of the seventeenth century the "Van" was dropped from the name and since that time it has been written "Swearingen." In the year 1804 some of the family came to Kentucky and settled in Bullitt county. At that time William Wallace Swearingen, the grandfather of Embry L., was an infant, having been born in Maryland in 1803. He grew to manhood in Bullitt county and in time became a wealthy farmer and slaveholder. He married Julia F. Crist, daughter of Hon. Henry Crist, a native of Berkeley county, in what is now West Virginia. Henry Crist was one of the distinguished pioneers of Kentucky. He was noted as an Indian fighter and served in the Kentucky legislature continuously from 1795 to 1806. In 1809 he was elected to Congress and served two years. William Wallace Swearingen died in 1869 and his wife in 1838. He was widely known in Bullitt and adjoining counties and was an influential citizen. George W. Swearingen, the father of the subject of this sketch, was born and reared in Bullitt county. He was educated at the Washington academy and Centre college, Danville, Ky., and after leaving school in 1856 taught for a year. In 1860 he purchased the old homestead and conducted it until 1866, when he removed to Louisville and there became actively identified with business enterprises. In 1869 he built the Mellwood distillery, which he successfully operated until 1890, its product being known far and wide as the equal of any in the market. In 1890 he organized the Union National bank and was elected president of the institution, which office he continued to hold by repeated re-elections until the time of his death. He was also one of the organizers of the Kentucky Title Company and was for some time its president. In addition to these two concerns he was connected as a stockholder and in other ways with various undertakings that tended to promote the industrial and commercial prosperity of Louisville. He was recognized as one of the liberal minded, public spirited men of the "Falls City," one who was always willing to contribute from his time and means to the public welfare. He was married in 1858 to Mary Embry, daughter of Samuel Embry, a veteran of the war of 1812, and a granddaughter of Henry Embry, who came from Virginia and settled in Green county, Ky., in 1790. One of her uncles, Ben T. Embry, was a prominent planter in Arkansas, served several terms in the legislature, and was once speaker of the state senate. During the Civil war he commanded a regiment of Confederate cavalry. In this connection it is worthy of mention that some of the Swearingen family have been in every war in which the people of the United States have been concerned since the middle of the seventeenth century. Their names appear on the muster rolls of the early Indian wars, the French and Indian war, the Revolution, the war of 1812, the Mexican war, and the great Civil war, many of them as commissioned officers. Embry Lee Swearingen was prepared for college at the Rugby school in Louisville. In three of the four years' course he carried off the first honors of his class and in the other year stood second. In 1878 he entered the University of Virginia but was soon compelled to leave on account of his health. A year later he returned to the university and after taking the academic course devoted three years to the study of special subjects, graduating from several different departments of the university. He then went to Philadelphia, where he became one of the partners in the establishment of a hosiery and knit goods factory. A year later, after thoroughly familiarizing himself with all the different processes of manufacture, he returned to Louisville and established a factory there for the manufacture of hosiery, knit goods, woolens and jeans, one of the first factories of the kind in the South. He continued to conduct this business for about eight years, during which time he was constantly extending his trade into new territory, until his goods were sold in nearly every state of the Union. Toward the close of that period he employed about two hundred people. Although the concern was a good advertisement for the city the profits were not satisfactory to Mr. Swearingen and he disposed of the plant to become general manager of the Kentucky Title Company. He continued as general manager until 1895, when he was elected to the presidency, and he has been continued in that position ever since. As the chief executive officer of the company he has been brought into contact with the real estate interests and great financial institutions of the city, and has impressed himself upon the managers and directors of these interests and institutions as a man of sound judgment, sagacity, and correct business principles. In 1900 he organized the Kentucky Title Savings bank. Mr. Swearingen is also a director in the Union National bank; was one of the first members of the Commercial club; and an active member of the first City Development committee. In all these capacities his enterprise and public spirit have been made manifest in the promotion of various plans for the advancement of the city's prosperity. He was married in 1887 to Miss Lalla Robinson, daughter of Lawrence and Amelia (Owsley) Robinson, a granddaughter of Rev. Stuart Robinson, and a great-granddaughter of Hon. William Owsley, who was judge of the Kentucky appellate court from 1812 to 1828, and who was elected governor of the Commonwealth of Kentucky in 1844 and served four years. Mrs. Swearingen died in 1897, and in 1901 Mr. Swearingen was married to Miss Ada C. Badger, of Chicago, Ill., daughter of A. C. Badger, who came to Louisville from Portsmouth, N. H., when a boy and soon became identified with the business interests of the city as a partner in the well known banking firm of A. D. Hunt & Co. In 1850 he married Elvira C. Sheridan and in 1861 they moved to Chicago, where he became actively interested in banking and lumber business.

JOHN FREDERICK KELLNER, prominent among the business men of the city of Louisville, and equally prominent in fraternal circles and as a member of the numerous German-American societies of the city, has had a career which illustrates forcibly the strength of the German character and the tenacity of purpose which makes the typical German successful in life. He was born in

Bavaria and is the son of John and Barbara (Boehlein) Kellner. His education was limited to attendance in the schools of his native city until thirteen years of age. In his native land, famous the world over for the excellence of its brews, he learned the art of brewing, or at least laid the foundation of his knowledge of the art. In 1864 he came to the United States, locating at Cannelton, Ind., where he found employment in the Cannelton coal mines. After six months' work in this field he went to Kankakee, Ill., where until 1868 he found fairly remunerative employment in various capacities. In that year he came to Louisville and went to work at his trade in the Zang & Vogt, now the Phoenix Brewing Company's plant. He worked for this firm until 1872, when he obtained a better position in the brewing business just then established by Frank Fehr and Mr. Brohm. He soon became actively identified with the business management of this brewery, and when Mr. Fehr organized and became the head of the corporation known as the Frank Fehr Brewing Company, took full charge of its collections and outside business. During these years of hard, earnest toil he demonstrated that he possessed strong business capacity, and learned how to husband his means, investing his savings in the stock of the corporation with which he was connected. In 1890 he was elected vice-president of this concern. Sharing in its prosperity and in the conduct and management of the business, he has succeeded in building up a fortune which he will know how to enjoy. His thorough knowledge of the business, his high standing in commercial circles and the intimate relationship that he sustained to Mr. Fehr made him the logical successor to the latter as head of the corporation, and on the death of Mr. Fehr in March, 1891, Mr. Kellner succeeded to the emoluments and responsibilities of that office. So successfully has he managed the affairs of the company that he still remains its chief officer. Mr. Kellner has at all times shown a broad liberality and a commendable public spirit. He and his business associates were the most liberal contributors to the entertainment of the thousands of veterans of the Civil war who visited Louisville in 1895, on the occasion of the National encampment of the Grand Army of the Republic. Hundreds of visitors were royally entertained by them, and among the most valuable souvenirs of the occasion was a vest-pocket scroll gotten up by the Frank Fehr Brewing Company, on which were printed the names and dates of all the battles of the great conflict between the states. When in 1901 the Frank Fehr Brewing Company was consolidated with five of the other leading breweries of the city, under the name of the Central Consumers Company, Mr. Kellner's ability as a leader was recognized by his associates, who unanimously elected him to the presidency of the new concern. Mr. Kellner is actively identified with a number of other important interests, one of which is the German Security bank. He is a Knight Templar, a Thirty-second degree Scottish Rite Mason, a Knight of Pythias and holds membership in a number of the leading German societies of Louisville. In politics he is a Democrat. In 1871 he married Charlotte Stigner, who died in 1888, leaving six children. In 1889 he married Anna F. Boschen, daughter of George Boschen, of Louisville. To this union four children have been born.

GEORGE GARVIN BROWN, president of both the Brown-Forman Company, wholesale liquor dealers, and the Brown-Forman Distilling Company, both incorporated, was born in Montfordville, Ky., Sept. 2, 1846. He is the son of John Thompson Street and Mary Jane (Garvin) Brown. His father was born in Hanover county, Va., April 7, 1793, and his mother was a native of Londonderry, Ireland. His paternal grandfather, William Brown, a Virginian by birth, was a son of James Brown, a Scotchman who settled in Virginia about 1740. Wm. Brown with his brother Patrick first came from Hanover county, Va., to Kentucky in 1782. Following "Boone's Trail" or the "Wilderness Road" through Cumberland Gap, they reached Harrodsburg on July 24th, of that year. Here they met their brother James, who had been in Kentucky for several years and who had co-operated with Gen. George Rogers Clark in protecting the settlers and making expeditions against the Indians. James Brown is said to have built the first house in Kentucky in 1774, near the site of Danville. The meeting between him and his brothers proved a reunion and a farewell meeting at the same time. On the following day he left them to go on an expedition against the Indians who had invaded Kentucky under the renegade Simon Girty, and was killed in the battle of "Blue Licks," Aug. 18, 1782. William and Patrick having joined the Logan command, visited the battlefield the following day and buried the victims of the savages. Both William and Patrick were conspicuous in later wars with the Indians, and Col. Patrick Brown was especially famous as an Indian fighter. Major William Brown, the grandfather of George G., was a man of culture and education, as well as an intrepid and enterprising frontiersman. After spending several years in Kentucky he returned to Virginia. In 1790 he made a second trip to Kentucky by way of the Ohio river. Returning to Virginia after an absence of two years, he married Hannah Street, daughter of John and Frances (Park) Street, and granddaughter of John Street, who was born in Bristol, England, and came to Hanover in early manhood. Here he purchased a plantation on which he resided the remainder of his life. After his marriage Major Wm. Brown remained in Virginia until his father's death, after which he returned to Kentucky and settled on a large tract of land near Elizabethtown. Both he and his wife were typical representatives of the fine old Virginia society in which they had been brought up. The maternal grandparents of the subject were High and Mary (Orr) Garvin, Scotch-Irish Presbyterians who emigrated to America in 1828 and settled at Montfordville, Ky., where both of them died. John T. S. Brown, father of our subject, came to Kentucky with his parents in early manhood and settled at Montfordville, where he served as postmaster over fifty years and became the owner of several fine farms. He died in 1875, respected by his fellow townsmen. George G. Brown, the subject of this sketch, was educated in the schools of his native village and the Louisville high school. In 1865 he began his business career as a clerk in the wholesale drug house of Henry Chambers & Co., Louisville, serving as such for nearly five years. He next embarked in the commission and whiskey brokerage business as a member of the firm of J. T. S. Brown & Bro. In 1873 the firm was reorganized as Brown, Chambers & Co., becoming Chambers & Brown a year later. For six years it continued under this name, when George G. succeeded to the business and admitted to partnership some young men who had been in his employ, the firm now becoming Brown, Thompson & Co. In 1889, on the withdrawal of Mr. Thompson, the firm became Brown, Forman & Co. When Mr. Forman died in 1901 the business was incorporated as the Brown-Forman Company, which name it still bears. The high regard and esteem in which Mr. Brown was held by his partners is shown by the fact that as the successor of each firm in the settlement of the affairs of the different firms, when hundreds of thousands of dollars were involved, such confidence was reposed in Mr. Brown that his partners declined to examine the books and accounts, relying solely on his honor for a strict accounting. Mr. Brown has been president of the National Wholesale Liquor Dealers' association and for ten years president of the Louisville Presbyterian orphanage. He is also a member of the Filson, Pendennis and Tavern clubs. On Feb. 1, 1876, he married Mrs. Amelia (Owsley) Robinson, widow of Lawrence A. Robinson, of Louisville, who was the son of Rev. Stuart Robinson, an eminent Presbyterian clergyman of that city. She is the daughter of Erasmus Boyle Owsley and granddaughter of Wm. Owsley, once governor of Kentucky and justice of the supreme court under the old constitution. Mr. and Mrs. Brown have six children living: Mary Garvin, Owsley, Elizabeth Bodley, Robinson Swearingen, Innes Akin and Amelia Bella.

ERNEST CHRISTIAN BOHNE, vice-president of the Southern National bank of Louisville, Ky., was born in Hesse-Cassel, Germany, Feb. 8, 1840. He is the son of Johann J. J. and Helen Maria (Wurtemberger) Bohne. His father was an officer in the army of the great Napoleon, and after the Russian campaign, in which he took an active part, settled in the city of Cassel, capital of Hesse-Cassel. Here he embarked in business as a publisher and bookseller. For twenty years prior to his death he was city treasurer of Cassel. He had served as city counselor for thirty years. Ernest C. Bohne was educated at the gymnasium in Cassel, a famous institution of learning, where the present German emperor and his father were educated. In 1854 he left school and went to Bremen to learn the book trade. This occupation not being congenial, he went to sea as sailor and finally landed at New Orleans in 1856. From New Orleans he came directly to Louisville. Here, until 1861, he served as bookkeeper in a wholesale dry goods house. He next took charge of the office management of the Louisville hotel. During the Civil war he was connected with a company of home guards and saw military service as quartermaster sergeant, which he was enabled to do without relinquishing his position in the hotel. In 1872 he organized the Western German Savings bank, becoming its cashier. Two years later this was reorganized as the Third National bank of Louisville with Mr. Bohne as cashier, a position he held until January, 1905, when he connected himself with the Southern National bank. He has proved himself to be a capable and sagacious banker. A careful study of monetary problems, currency questions and banking methods has caused him to be recognized as an accomplished financier in the broader sense of that term. He has delivered several addresses before the American Bankers' association and, in each instance, has attracted marked attention in banking and financial circles. He has always taken an active part in the work of the Kentucky Bankers' association, frequently reading valuable papers at its stated meetings. In addition to his regular duties he has for several years transacted business for the British consul in Baltimore, the Imperial German consul in Cincinnati and the Imperial and Royal Austro-Hungarian consul in Richmond, Va. Ever since Mr. Bohne became a citizen of Louisville he has taken an active part in promoting the city's welfare. As a banker and business man he has aided in the development of the resources of the city as well as in the expansion of its commerce. As a city official he has aided in the building up and improvement of its civic institutions. He served as school trustee from 1867 to 1870, and as charity commissioner from 1877 to 1880. While on the school board he and Mr. L. L. Warren were instrumental in establishing the Louisville Normal school for teachers. In 1891 he was elected a member of the first board of park commissioners, and it was during his term that the present splendid park system was purchased and sprang into existence. He helped to select the sites of the present Cherokee and Shawnee parks and caused this park system to be placed in the hands of Ohmstead & Co., the most famous landscape gardeners in the United States, for improvement. This same firm laid out and improved the grounds on which the World's Columbian exposition at Chicago was held in 1893. The work done through Mr. Bohne has been highly gratifying to all parties interested in the adornment of the city's parks. As a charity commissioner he was instrumental in bringing about much needed reform at the city hospital and the alms house. He also served for three years on the board of managers of Lakeland Insane asylum, Lakeland, Ky.

SAMUEL GRABFELDER, a prominent merchant of Louisville, Ky., was
born in Rehweiler, Bavaria, Germany,
Sept. 2, 1844. He is the son of Samuel
and Regina Grabfelder. His early education was received in the schools of his
native town. In 1856, when still a boy, he
came to America and the following year
located in Louisville. There he attended
the Louisville high school, where he paid
especial attention to the mastery of the
English language and to those other
branches most essential to his success as a
business man.   Relying entirely on his own resources, and without influential friends to give him a start, he went to work
determined to make a success in life.   How well he succeeded the
sequel will show.   His aptitude in acquiring a correct knowledge
of business methods, his industry and his general intelligence commended him to those with whom he came in contact, hence he had
little difficulty in securing employment.   By the close of the Civil
war he had developed into a capable salesman and business man.
For several years after the war he was employed as traveling salesman for one of the large wholesale liquor houses of Louisville,
his territory being the Southern states.   Wherever he went he
made friends and increased the business of the house he represented.   While employed in this capacity he saved his money, which
fact enabled him to embark in business in 1873 as one of the partners
of the largest wholesale liquor house of Louisville.   After six years'
connection with this firm he withdrew from it to found the house of
S. Grabfelder & Co.   The business of the firm aggregated but fifty
thousand dollars the first year, but gradually increased until now it
does a business of millions annually.   This result has been accomplished through close attention to all of the details of the business,
unremitting efforts and an unswerving determination to be guided
by the strictest principles of integrity and fair dealing.   Traveling
men now represent this house in every state and territory in the
Union, and its famous brands of whiskies are known throughout
the United States.   Among the various houses engaged in the dis-
tribution and sale of Kentucky whiskies, none has a higher standing than that of the firm of S. Grabfelder & Co., and none more
richly deserves abundant prosperity.   Mr. Grabfelder is a member

of the board of trade, of the Commercial club and the Standard club. He is prominent in both business and social circles, and is a worthy Thirty-second degree member of the Masonic Order. In religious affairs he is a Jew, having served for several years as president of the Temple congregation of Louisville, noted among the Jewish churches for the culture, liberalism and intelligence of its members. For some years he served as president of the Old Folks' home of Cleveland, Ohio, a worthy Jewish charitable institution. In politics he is independent, reserving the right at all times to vote as his better judgment dictates. He is the founder and president of the National hospital for consumptives, built in Denver, Col., at a cost of $250,000.

REV. S. S. WALTZ, D.D., pastor of the First English Lutheran church, Louisville, Ky., was born in New Philadelphia, O., Oct. 24, 1847. He is the son of Elias and Mary Waltz, both of whom died after having reached the age of threescore and ten. His father was an honest and industrious farmer, who was always active in church and as a citizen. His mother was a pious and devout woman, whose highest ambition was to train her children to become faithful Christians and good citizens. Doctor Waltz comes of Protestant Swiss stock, his ancestors first settling in Maryland and Pennsylvania and later in Ohio. He received his early education in the public schools of his native town. After teaching school for three years he entered Wittenberg college, graduating in the full classical course in 1872. Having consecrated himself to the ministry, he spent one year at the theological seminary at Gettysburg, Pa., and then completed his theological course at Wittenberg seminary in 1874. During his college course he became one of the founders and first editor of the *"Wittenberger,"* now the college journal of his alma mater. After his ordination to the ministry he became pastor of the Lutheran church at Dixon, Ill., where for five years he conducted the church work in a very successful way. He next succeeded to the pastorate of the First Lutheran church of Kansas City, where he also remained five years. During his pastorate of this church he founded and conducted a mission which has since become a successful and self-sustaining church. He took an active part in all aggressive Christian movements in the city and in the development of the Lutheran church in the West. For three successive years he was elected president of the Synod of Kansas and the adjacent states and was for three years president of the Olive Branch Synod. In the fall of 1883, he resigned his charge in Kansas City to accept a call to the First English Lutheran church of Louisville. This position he still occupies, rejoicing in the abundant evidence of the Divine blessing of his ministry and enjoying the esteem not only of his large congregation but of the general Christian public. During his pastorate of over twenty-one years the English Lutheran churches of the city have increased from two to seven, a considerable part of the nucleus for these several churches coming from the First church. Despite this fact the membership of the mother church has steadily increased. The congregation is now building a new church edifice, which when completed will be one of the finest church buildings in the city. As further recognition of the high standing of Mr. Waltz in the estimation of those who know him best, Wittenberg college in 1892 conferred upon him the honorary degree of doctor of divinity. Several times he has been chosen a delegate to the general Synod. He has been almost continuously a member of the board of college directors. As a minister Doctor Waltz believes that the highest service he can render his city and country is by helping to permeate society with the spirit and principles of the Gospel. Brought up in the Evangelical Lutheran church, he is a firm believer in, and loyal advocate of, the doctrines of the Christian faith as held by that church. Tireless in work for his own church, he always finds time to give a helping hand to all charitable and religious movements of a general character in the city in which he lives. During his residence in Louisville he has done a great amount of missionary work for the Lutheran church in Kentucky, Indiana and Tennessee. In politics he is a Republican. On Sept. 23, 1875, he married Miss Mina L. Hastings, of Springfield, O., the daughter of G. W. Hastings, Esq., for many years proprietor of the *Springfield Daily Republic*. They have two children. Their son, Fred H., is a successful newspaper man in New Orleans. Their daughter, Helen M., is a kindergarten principal in the public schools of Louisville. A happy home, hard work, loyalty to duty and reliance upon God are the elements in Doctor Waltz's life to which his success may be attributed.

COL. BISCOE HINDMAN, of Louisville, is Kentucky manager for the Mutual Life Insurance Company of New York. After graduating from college he taught mathematics and civil engineering at the Kentucky military institute and afterwards became superintendent of public schools in his native town of Helena, Ark., and later professor of mathematics in the male high school of Louisville. He resigned the last position to enter the service of the Mutual Life at Louisville as superintendent of agents in Kentucky. After seven ·months' service in this capacity he became manager for West Virginia, and a year later manager for Tennessee for the same company. Four years later he returned to Louisville as manager for Kentucky and Tennessee, holding this position for nine years, when his brother, Thos. C. Hindman, took charge of Tennessee and he retained Kentucky. Under his management the business of the company has shown a uniformly rapid growth and has been so conducted as to prove satisfactory in every respect to the policy holders and the company. Colonel Hindman has been a lifelong Democrat, believes in strict party allegiance and has always voted a straight ticket. He is a park commissioner for the city of Louisville and is the Democratic executive committeeman for the Fifth congressional district of Kentucky. He is also colonel commanding the First Kentucky infantry, and was instrumental in securing passage of a bill through the Kentucky legislature in 1904 requiring Jefferson county to erect an armory for his regiment, the result being that the fiscal court has contracted for a magnificent armory to be built at once at a cost of about $425,000. Colonel Hindman is a native of Arkansas, but is a Kentuckian in reality, as he has spent nearly all his life in Kentucky, where he has numerous friends in all parts of the state. In 1884 he married Miss Cannie Rodman, a daughter of Gen. John Rodman, of Frankfort. He is of Scotch-Irish descent, the immigrant ancestors settling in Virginia and Maryland in the latter part of the seventeenth century, since which time the Hindmans have been prominent in the history of the country and especially so in its wars. In the Revolutionary war James Hindman was a captain and afterwards lieutenant-colonel of the Fifth Maryland regiment, and Edward

Hindman was a lieutenant in the same regiment. Dr. John Hindman was a surgeon in the Fourth Maryland, while Wm. Hindman was a delegate from Maryland to the Continental Congress and afterwards represented his state for many years in Congress and in the United States senate. Another ancestor was an officer with Commodore Perry on Lake Erie, while his grandfather, Col. Thos. C. Hindman, was colonel of a Mississippi regiment in the Mexican war. The father of Biscoe Hindman was a young lieutenant in the Mexican war, where he was brevetted for gallantry at the age of seventeen, was afterwards in Congress from Arkansas and a major-general in the Confederate army. This officer was a cavalier of distinct personality and a model of courage and military excellence. He won fame on every battlefield where he fought and was severely wounded at Shiloh, Chickamauga and Prairie Grove. He won his commission as major-general at the battle of Shiloh, and it bears the endorsement of Gen. Braxton Bragg: "nobly won upon the field." He was killed at the age of thirty-nine and died a hero's death in the presence of his friends. He was an able lawyer and a brilliant orator, and if he had lived still greater honors would have been added to the laurels that cluster around his name. General Hindman married Mary Watkins Biscoe of Helena, Ark., the beautiful daughter of Col. Henry L. Biscoe, who was a distinguished Mason and a wealthy planter in Arkansas before the war.

WILLIAM W. HITE, a prominent business man of Louisville, Ky., is a descendant of the sixth generation of Hans Jost Heydt (Baron Jost Hite), a native of Alcen, Germany, who came from Strasburg to America in 1710, with two of his own ships. His wife was Anna Maria Dubois, of Huguenot extraction, who died in 1738. Capt. William Chambers Hite, a noted steamboat man, the father of the subject and the son of Lewis and Eliza V. Hite, was born near Brunerstown, Ky., July 23, 1825. In early life he came to Louisville and began his business career as a clerk. With his brother, Lewis Hite, he then embarked in the carpet business. On the death of his brother he became the head of the firm and conducted the business successfully for several years. During this period he became identified with the river interests, his first experience being with Capt. Frank Carter, on the *Alice Gray*. In 1846 he served as master of the steamer *Talma,* having been promoted from a clerkship in that boat. He next served as captain of the, steamer *Peytona*. By this service he became thoroughly familiar with all branches of river traffic. In 1856 he became interested with Capt. Z. M. Sherley in the Louisville and Cincinnati Mail Boat line. The same gentlemen established the line of packet boats between Louisville and Henderson and acquired a large interest in the Louisville & Jeffersonville Ferry Company. Capt. Hite was actively connected with these interests until his death on Dec. 6, 1882. His services as a promoter of steamboat lines made him known to river men from Pittsburg to New Orleans. But his activities were not confined to this field of operations. He was equally energetic in other affairs. From 1861 to 1873 he was connected with the Commercial bank of Kentucky, serving as cashier. His interests continued to broaden until, at the time of his death, he had become a director in thirteen different corporations, chief among them being the Southern Mutual Life Insurance Company, the Kentucky & Louisville Mutual Insurance Company and the Bank of Kentucky, now the National Bank of Kentucky. The captain was a man of positive character, being frank, outspoken and charitable. Owing to his active interest in so many of the most important business concerns of Louisville, his death was a great public loss. In 1850 he married Miss Mary E. Rose and by her had a family of six children, three sons and three daughters. His eldest son, William W. Hite, the subject, was born in Louisville, November 14, 1854, and was educated in the public and private schools of that city. He was, under the guidance of his father, thoroughly trained for a business career. In 1872 he entered the dry goods house of Joseph T. Tompkins & Co., remaining with the firm five years. He next became secretary and treasurer of the Louisville & Evansville Mail Company. In 1878 he became a member of the firm of Gilmore, Hite & Co., which four years later became the firm of W. W. Hite & Co. This firm is widely known as dealers in steamboat, railroad and mill supplies. His connection with the transportation lines during the later years of his father's life brought him into close touch with the river interests, and in 1883, after the death of his father, he succeeded to the presidency of the Louisville & Evansville Mail Company and the Louisville & Jeffersonville Ferry

Company. A year later he became a director in the Mutual Life Insurance Company of Kentucky. He is now a director in the National Bank of Kentucky, president and director of the Northern Lakes Ice Company and vice-president of the Louisville & Cincinnati Packet Company. For twenty-eight years he has been prominently identified with the interests of Louisville, having developed the same business traits that made his distinguished father such a power in the business world. He is a typical representative of the active, progressive and public spirited class of men that are doing so much to promote the growth and prosperity of their native city and to make it one of the leading cities of the South. For seven years he served as director of the Louisville Industrial School of Reform, being vice-president for four years. He is a member and director of the board of trade and of the Pendennis and Filson clubs. On Jan. 4, 1888, he married Miss Carrie Pace, daughter of James B. Pace, Esq., of Richmond, Va. Mr. and Mrs. Hite have one son living, named William W., Jr.

WILLIAM M. SHOEMAKER, head of the firm of W. M. Shoemaker & Co., electricians and electrical contractors, Louisville, Ky., was born in York, Pa., in 1866. He is the son of William H. and Eliza (Boyer) Shoemaker and comes of good old German stock, being of the fifth generation of both the Shoemakers and Boyers who came from Germany and settled in Pennsylvania before the Revolutionary war. Mr. Shoemaker received his education in the public schools of Harrisburg, Pa. After leaving school he learned the art of organ building in his father's factory at Harrisburg. In 1885 he went to Florida, where he was employed for fourteen months as superintendent of his father's planing mill. Coming to Louisville in 1889, he took up the study of electrical engineering. In this capacity he was for the next eleven years employed in some of the largest concerns of that city, among them being the American Tobacco Company and the New Gaynor Electric Company. In April, 1900, Mr. Shoemaker embarked in business for himself. His place of business at 232 Third street has a floor space of more than three thousand feet. It is fully equipped with all the machinery and appliances necessary to run such a plant successfully. The establishment is prepared to do all kinds of repair work and to manufacture all kinds of electric fans, dynamos, motors and electrical supplies. The stock in trade is complete for thoroughly installing electric plants, both light and power. Among the recent contracts secured by this firm are the following: The equipment of the Norton building, the Avery factory and the Hopkins theater. W. M. Shoemaker & Co. do an extensive trade in and about the city of Louisville, requiring the constant service of a dozen or more men. On May 12, 1888, Mr. Shoemaker married Miss Ann Elizabeth Gorgas, of Harrisburg, Pa. In politics he is an Independent. He belongs to Preston Lodge, No. 281, of the Masonic order of Louisville.

JOHN ROHRMAN, Louisville, Ky., popularly known as the "Ice Man," was born in Madison, Ind., May 7, 1862. His paternal grandfather, John Rohrman, born in Alsace-Lorraine, Germany, was one of the pioneer settlers of North Madison, Ind., near which place he cleared and improved a large body of land. When he died in 1889 he was the owner of several of the finest farms in the vicinity of North Madison. The father of the subject of this sketch, also named John, came to this country with his parents when twelve years old. A brewer by trade, he came to Louisville during the Civil war and there worked at his trade. He next entered the employ of the Northern Lakes Ice Company, serving them faithfully for a number of years. In 1889 he erected the Seventh Street brewery in Louisville, which he conducted until his death in 1892. John Rohrman, the subject, was reared in Louisville and educated in its public schools. The first work that he did was for the Northern Lakes Ice Company. In 1894 he embarked in business for himself, which business he has since conducted successfully. Mr. Rohrman is the founder of the National Ice and Cold Storage Company of Louisville, a plant erected at the cost of $150,000. He next founded the Merchants' Refrigerator Company of Louisville, capitalized at $200,000, for the manufacture of ice and for cold storage purposes. These two plants are mammoth affairs and turn out two hundred tons of ice each day. Their terms are so reasonable and their service so thorough that they have a third of the trade of the city. On Nov. 24, 1882, Mr. Rohrman married Sallie, daughter of William and Cynthia (Lancaster) Emerson, of Louisville. He is a Mason, an Odd Fellow, an Elk, an Eagle, a Woodman of the World, and Red Man, having recently passed through all the chairs of the last-mentioned organization. He is also identified with the Mose Green, Delmar and Commercial clubs. In politics he is a Democrat.

JULIUS MUENCH, a prominent and popular restaurateur of Louisville, Ky., is a native of that city, having been born May 10, 1864. He is the son of John Otto and Frederika (Reuff) Muench, both natives of Germany. His father, a baker by trade, settled in Louisville prior to the Civil war, where he founded, built up and conducted successfully for thirty-five years a large baking business. He died in 1894 at the ripe age of seventy-two years. Of his children five are still living: Adolph; Julius; Albert; Emma, wife of K. J. Dietrich, and Ida, widow of Henry Bromfield. The subject after completing his education in the public schools of Louisville, served an apprenticeship at the watchmaker's trade, which vocation he followed for eight years. He then took charge of the business of his father, which for a period of almost half a century has been conducted by the Muench family. The product of this bakery cannot be excelled in Louisville. Among the many excellent restaurants of the city, the one conducted by Mr. Muench takes a high rank. It is the policy of this establishment to cater to the city and traveling public day and night the year round. Mr. Muench was married Feb. 27, 1889, to Elizabeth (Bohardt) Seiffert, of Evansville, Ind. The children living are: Raymond A., Irene, Albert and Julius. In politics Mr. Muench is a Republican. The following are some of the orders to which he belongs: Elks, Mystic Lodge, Knights of Pythias, Fraternal Order of Eagles, and the Knights of Khorassan. He is also quite prominent in the Commercial club.

JOHN H. BREWER, state manager for Kentucky of the Woodmen of the World, was born in Hardin county, Ky., November 11th, forty-two years ago. He is the son of Uriah and Elizabeth (Gohagan) Brewer, both natives of Kentucky, of Dutch and Irish descent. He received his education in the public schools of his home district, learned telegraphy at Cecelian Junction, Ky., studying between school hours and at night, while attending Cecelian college during the day, and followed that calling for three years. Next he served for two years as fireman on the Chesapeake, Ohio & Southwestern railroad, when he was promoted to engineer. After six years' service as engineer he voluntarily resigned and located at Hot Springs, Ark., where he embarked in the hotel business, conducting the National hotel for six years. A part of this time he was engaged in the real estate business and was traveling agent for two of the largest bicycle manufactories in the United States, his territory being the Southwestern states. In 1893 he became interested in the organization of lodges of Woodmen of the World and two years later decided to give all of his time to the advancement of the interests of that order. For a year and a half he was state manager for Arkansas and later for Northeastern Texas. Resigning this position he returned to Hot Springs to look after the improvement of some property there. In 1899 he attended the Sovereign Camp of the Woodmen of the World at Memphis, Tenn., when he decided to move to Louisville, Ky., and take up work for the order as state manager for that state, a work that he has ever since successfully conducted. In 1890 he married Miss Mary Fisher, of Hot Springs, Ark., who died in 1900, leaving two daughters. These children are now being educated at Bethlehem academy, St. Johns, Ky. Mr. Brewer is a thirty-second degree Mason and past chief patriarch of the Independent Order of Odd Fellows. While in Arkansas he was for four years district grand master of the Odd Fellows. He is also a member of the Knights of Pythias, the Woodmen of the World, the Benevolent and Protective Order of Elks, the Louisville Commandery of Knights Templars and the Nobles of the Mystic Shrine. He represented the National Fraternal Congress of America at the World's

Fair, St. Louis, during the week September 26 to October 1, 1904. In politics he is a stanch Jeffersonian Democrat.

THEODORE AHRENS, SR., founder of the Ahrens-Ott Manufacturing Company, Louisville, Ky., was born in Hamburg, Germany, April 28, 1825, and died Jan. 10, 1903. He was the son of Joachim and Dorothy (Greve) Ahrens, the father being for many years in the government service in Hamburg. Theodore was educated in the public schools of his native city. He then served his apprenticeship at the machinist trade, thoroughly mastering the same. Later he broadened his knowledge and increased his skill as a craftsman and by traveling through Germany, Sweden and Norway, working at his trade in the larger cities of those countries. In 1840 he volunteered in the German army, which sought to liberate the provinces of Schleswig and Holstein from the domination of Denmark. This war, which ended the Schleswig-Holstein question, lasted two years, ending in 1850. Mr. Ahrens served throughout this war as a soldier and received a medal for his bravery on the field of battle. In 1850 he first visited the United States, remaining two years. In 1853 he came to America the second time, engaging in the work of machinist and molder; also that of a sailor on an Atlantic coast vessel. On coming to Louisville in 1858 he secured employment as a tool-maker in the iron works of Barbaroux & Snowden. After being connected with the firm for a year he decided to go into business for himself by opening a small brass foundry and finishing shop. Later he made plumbing a feature of his business. This small plant was the foundation upon which the present mammoth Ahrens-Ott manufacturing establishment has since been built. Originally the firm of Ahrens & Ott was a co-partnership between Mr. Ahrens and Henry Ott, but in 1885 it was made a stock company with Mr. Ahrens as president, a position he held until his death. No better illustration of the industrial development of Louisville within the past fifty years can be found among its numerous and varied industries than is afforded by the growth of this enterprise. Starting in business with little capital other than mechanical skill, untiring industry and well balanced judgment,

Mr. Ahrens and those associated with him have built up the largest manufactory of plumbers' brass, iron and enameled goods in the South, if not in the United States. In the little shop, started in 1859, Mr. Ahrens had little assistance and the products of the shop were nearly all the work of his own hands. The successor of this humble institution employs today in its different departments more than one thousand persons and sends its wares to all parts of this country and Canada, thus contributing largely to the material prosperity of Louisville. Mr. Ahrens was born with the love of civic and religious liberty in his heart and, when he began to inform himself regarding the laws, government and customs of the United States, he reached the conclusion that human slavery had no part in the institutions of a free country. As a natural consequence he became a member of the Republican party, assisted in the organization of that party in the city of Baltimore, where he was then living, and in the national election of 1856 was one of the seven men in that city that dared to go to the polls and cast their votes for Gen. John C. Fremont. This was a very unpopular thing for him to do, but it was one of his characteristics through life that he would rather be right than to win favor at the expense of his honest convictions. He was in no sense a politician and never held or sought public office. For many years he was president of the Louisville Turngemeinde and later an honorary member of that organization. He was also an honorary member of the Liederkranz, the most popular and prominent German society of the city. He took an active part in Masonry, being a member of Zion Lodge. In 1853 he married Anna Maria Nebel, of Hamburg, Germany. Her death occurred in 1885. The following year he married Mrs. Amelia Baas, widow of Henry Baas, of Louisville. His eldest son, Theodore Ahrens, Jr., grew up in the business with his father, mastering all of its details, and at the death of the latter succeeded to the presidency of the Ahrens-Ott Company, which position he still holds. Theodore Ahrens is president of the Louisville board of trade and is conspicuous among the leading and progressive business men of the city.

MATHIAS POSCHINGER, proprietor of the Louisville Ice Company and builder of its extensive plant, was born in Rettenbach, Germany, Feb. 7, 1849. He is the son of Mathias and Catherine (Breinbauer) Poschinger. His father was a well-to-do farmer in his native country. Mathias was reared on his father's farm, and received his education in the country schools. At the breaking out of the Franco-Prussian war he joined the Bavarian army and served his country throughout that war. He then went to work in a match factory in Switzerland. Here he afterwards learned the machinist trade, following this vocation for three years. In 1882 he came to America, locating in Frankfort, Ky., where he worked until 1884 as an engineer in a brewery. He then came to Louisville, where he was first employed as an engineer of an ice factory and then as a machinist in a machine shop. In 1894 he erected the extensive ice and refrigerator plant on East Main street, at a cost of $200,000. This plant is one of the most complete establishments of its kind in America. The building is of brick and presents a fine appearance among the other manufacturing plants of the city. Mr. Poschinger was married Nov. 11, 1894, to Elizabeth Schnell, daughter of Nicholas Schnell of the Texas family of Switzerland. Mr. Poschinger is a Democrat and a member of the St. Boniface Catholic church.

JOHN FREDERICK OERTEL, proprietor of the Butchertown brewery, Story avenue, Louisville, Ky., was born in Baden, Germany, Feb. 25, 1855, and is the son of John and Maria (Schmitt) Oertel. He was reared in his native country, where he received a thorough high school education. Here he also served an apprenticeship of about six years at the brewer's trade. In 1880 he came to the United States, located in Louisville, Ky., where for the next seven years he was employed at his trade. In 1887, with Charles Hartmetz as a partner, he established the Butchertown brewery. This partnership lasted three years, and then Mr. Oertel became the sole proprietor by purchasing the interest of Mr. Hartmetz. From that time on he has conducted the business successfully by himself, employing thirty-two men. The brewery has a capacity of three hundred barrels of beer a day. Its product is of the best quality and has a large sale in the principal towns of Kentucky and the Lower Ohio Valley. Mr. Oertel was married in June, 1885, to Sarah, the daughter of Cornell and Francisca Kaisir, of Carrollton, Ill. The names of their four children are as follows: Josephine, Katie, Louise and John F., Jr. Mr. Oertel is one of the most progressive and enterprising citizens of

Louisville. He is a member of St. Joseph's Catholic church, the Young Men's Institute, St. Joseph Orphan society and Catholic Knights of America. He is also an active member of the following organizations: The Benevolent and Protective Order of Elks, the Improved Order of Red Men, the Fraternal Order of Eagles; the Benevolent Society of Gambrinus, the Sons of Herman, the Liederkranz, the Concordia and others. In politics he affiliates with the Democratic party.

SIMPSON SEATON MEDDIS, one of Louisville's most energetic and progressive citizens, was born May 21, 1837, on Frankfort avenue, formerly known as the Louisville and Shelbyville turnpike, and now the Aubindale addition to the city of Louisville. He is the son of Matthew and Apphia (Seaton) Meddis. His father, born in Jefferson county, Ky., first came to Louisville in 1837, where he followed the vocation of contractor for several years. Then for several years he gave his attention to farming in Jefferson county. In 1850 he returned to Louisville and embarked in the livery business at Second and Jefferson streets with Thomas Batman as partner. After conducting this business successfully for seven years, he purchased a farm on the Bardstown road, residing there until his death in 1882. Simpson's paternal grandfather was Godfrey Meddis, who was killed at the battle of New Orleans in the war of 1812. His maternal grandfather was George Seaton, a native of Kentucky and descendant of a prominent English family, whose son, Dr. John S. Seaton, was in his day one of the most eminent physicians of Kentucky. Later in life he was persuaded to visit California and Colorado to look after some mining interest in which he with others had made investments. These mines that he owned at his death were later estimated to be worth $100,000,000. Among them may be mentioned the celebrated Stratton mines at Cripple Creek, since developed. His heirs, however, paid no attention to these properties and permitted them to pass by default into other hands. Simpson S. Meddis was educated in the private schools of Jefferson county, principally under the tutorship of Prof. W. F. Beach, a noted instructor of his day. He began his business career as deputy sheriff under sheriff Charles F. Quirey, of Jefferson county in 1853. Since then he has served under the administrations of S. S. Hamilton, W. S. D. Megowan and J. Wash Davis. After leaving the sheriff's office in 1862, he entered the employ of Hite & Small, Louisville, remaining with the firm about a year. In 1864 he entered the banking house of J. Q. A. Oder, as clerk at a salary of $30.00 per month, which was increased to $175.00 per month after four months' trial. In 1866 this bank was merged with the firm of Burnside, Taylor & Co., Mr. Meddis continuing with them until 1867. At this time he embarked in the real estate business, in which he has since successfully continued. At first he started in on his own account, but afterwards under the following firm names: Meddis & Miller, Meddis, Morris & Southwick, Meddis & Southwick. The firm of Meddis & Southwick did business successfully for seventeen years. The firm then became Meddis, Southwick & Co., Bruce Hoblitzell being the company. Mr. Southwick died in 1891, when the firm became Meddis & Co., Mr. Hoblitzell being the company. In 1892 Mr. Hoblitzell retired, and the business has since been conducted under the name of the S. S. Meddis Company, with S. S. Meddis as president and Geo. H. Fisher as secretary and treasurer. The firm handles every department of real estate transactions in city property of all kinds and in farm lands throughout Kentucky, undertaking for its clients everything that has to do with the purchase, sale or exchange of property. They also possess all organized facilities for the renting and management of all classes of property, the collection of rentals and the care and management of estates of non-residents. Taxes are paid, loan and real estate notes negotiated, making a specialty of selling real estate and live stock at auction. No other firm in the city is better equipped to guard and care for the interests of its customers than the S. S. Meddis Company. Mr. Meddis is considered to be one of the best auctioneers and the best informed men in this line of Louisville. On Nov. 16, 1861, Mr. Meddis married Eliza H., daughter of George W. and Eliza Ann (Hite) Small, of Louisville. They have two sons: Victor M., a prominent physician of Louisville, and George Small Meddis, a lumber merchant, of Mobile, Ala. Mr. Meddis is a member of Calvary Episcopal church. Politically he always has been and still is a true Democrat.

WILLIAM KOPF, furniture manufacturer, and a prominent German-American citizen, of Louisville, Ky., was born at the city of Schramberg, in the province of Wurtemberg, Germany, Nov. 19, 1846, his parents being Joseph and Caroline (Fichter) Kopp,

both natives of Wurtemberg. His father was a prominent manufacturer of furniture at Schramberg for many years and there died.
William received his education in the schools of his native city and
after passing through the high school went into the factory of his
father and learned the trade of cabinet-maker. In 1869 he came to
America and soon after his arrival in this country located at Louisville, where for one year he worked as a journeyman at his trade.
In 1875 he began the manufacture of furniture in a small way on his
own account. At first his business was not large, but by close attention
to it, and by safe and conservative business methods, he has built up
a trade approximating $150,000 a year, and now operates a factory
employing sixty-five skilled men. This growth has been entirely due
to his careful study of the demands of the furniture market and
turning his attention to the production of something that the people
want. Mr. Kopp is popular in German social circles; is a permanent
member of the Liederkranz society, of which he has been president for
eight years, having been elected to his eighth term Dec. 27, 1904.
Politically he is a Republican, and is one of the public spirited and
progressive men of the Falls City. On Aug. 24, 1865, he was united
in marriage to Miss Katie Schmitt, a native of Germany, and they
have three children: Bettie, wife of August Miller; Carrie, wife of
Harry Dunekake, and William Frederick.

FRANK WALTER, of the firm of John
E. and Frank Walter, proprietors of the
Clay street brewery, Louisville, Ky., was
born in Louisville, July 25, 1859. He is a
son of Conrad and Eva (Bessenbacher)
Walter, both natives of Germany. His
father, a distiller by trade, came to America in 1846, locating in Louisville, Ky.,
where for several years he worked at the
carpenters' trade and gardening. In 1858
he established the Clay street brewery,
conducting the same successfully up to
1873, the year of his death. His widow
continued in the business until 1890, when the sons, John E. and
Frank Walter, became proprietors. The same firm has been continued up to the present time, notwithstanding John E. died July 8,
1903. The brewery has a capacity of 112 barrels per day, gives
steady employment to twenty-five men and places on the market

a product of the very best quality. This institution has become one of the leading industries of Louisville and enjoys a large trade in the suburban towns of the city. Mr. Frank Walter, subject of this sketch, is a wide-a-awake, enterprising citizen, and is always ready and willing to contribute toward any movement that will benefit his native city. He is an active member of St. Martin's Catholic church and the Sons of Herman. In politics Mr. Walter is a stanch Democrat.

REMI JEUNESSE, one of the leading contractors and builders of Louisville, Ky., was born at Nancy, in the department of Meurthe-et-Moselle, · Lorraine, France, Oct. 4, 1840. In 1846 his parents, Jean and Annie (Grillott) Jeunesse, came to America and located at Louisville, where the father followed his trade of tailor until he fell a victim to the cholera epidemic of 1847. His mother also died with the cholera at the same time. Of the children Etien died in New Orleans, La., after reaching womanhood; Virginia, Francois, Remi and Felix E. all grew to maturity and one died in early life. Remi Jeunesse was reared in the city of Louisville, attended the public schools, and afterward served an apprenticeship at carpentering with John Story. In April, 1861, he enlisted as a private in Company C, First Kentucky Federal infantry, for the three months' service and at the close of that time re-enlisted for three years in the same company and regiment. He fought with his command at Stone River or Murfreesboro, Shiloh, Chickamauga, Chattanooga, Lookout Mountain, and numerous minor engagements, but came out of the service without a scratch, being honorably discharged in 1864. Upon being mustered out of the army he returned to Louisville and went to work at his trade as a journeyman, in which he continued until 1867, when he embarked in business as a contractor and builder. For nearly forty years he has been connected with the growth and development of the city. In that time he has erected many of the finest residences in Louisville, the St. Boniface Catholic church, the First English Lutheran church, the Doerhoffer block, the Merchants' Refrigerator building, and many others of equal note. His career as a business man has always been marked by a prompt and faithful execution of all contracts, his old customers being his best friends. Mr. Jeunesse is one of the progressive men of the "Falls City," being a member of the Horse Show association, and interested in various movements for the betterment of the moral and commercial conditions. Politically he is a Democrat, but is not especially active in political work. He is a member of George H. Thomas Post, No. 8, Grand Army of the Republic. On May 8, 1866, he married Amelia, daughter of Joseph and Genevieve (Cousins) Roe, of Erie, Mich., and five of the children born to this union grew to maturity: Annie Rosalie, now the wife of Louis Hueper; Francois, who died after reaching manhood; Charles F., Felix A., and Amelia A.

MICHAEL JOSEPH HICKEY, proprietor of "Hickey's Café," Louisville, Ky., was born in that city March 11, 1866, his parents being James and Hannah (Moran) Hickey, both natives of County Cork, Ireland. They came to America in 1860, located at Philadelphia, where the father conducted a dairy for about two years, and in 1863 came to Louisville. There he again engaged in the dairy business and continued in it until his death, which occurred on Jan. 27, 1903. At the time of his death he had one of the largest and best appointed dairies about the "Falls City." The children of James and Hannah Hickey who grew to maturity were Mary, wife of William Wales; Michael J., James J., John T., Hannah, wife of Joseph Faust, and Nellie. Michael J. Hickey received his education in the public schools of his native city and upon leaving school assisted his father in the dairy business until 1892. He then opened his present café and billiard parlors at No. 248 West Main street, and has made it one of the most popular resorts in the city. The management of the place has always been under his personal supervision and his infinite attention to the little details of the business accounts for the popularity of his café. His customers are always greeted with a pleasant smile and a kind word and upon their departure are invited to call again with such evident sincerity that they rarely fail to do so. Mr. Hickey is a Democrat in his political views and takes an interest in furthering the interests of his party. He is a

member of No. 1, Ancient Order Hibernians, the Fraternal Order of
Eagles, of which he is president, and both himself and wife belong
to the Cathedral of the Assumption, of Louisville. On Sept. 27,
1897, he married Miss Mary, daughter of James and Catherine
(Sheridan) Moore, of Louisville. Her parents, like his own, are
natives of Ireland.

WILLIAM AVINGTON SHRADER, carpenter, builder and
millwright, Louisville, Ky., is a descendant of Revolutionary stock,
who were among the early settlers of Kentucky. His great-grandfather, William Von Shrader, was a native of Alsace, a province of
France, and was an ambassador from that country to Philadelphia
at the time of the Revolution. He resigned his commission, took
the oath of allegiance to the United States and entered the Continental army. His son, the grandfather of the subject of this sketch,
also entered the army, rose to the rank of colonel, and was in some
of the principal engagements of that historic struggle. After the
war he received from the United States government a tract of land
for his services. This land was located in what is now called Pewee
Valley, where he settled in the latter part of the eighteenth century,
and where both he and his father died. After coming to Kentucky
he married Martha Hardin, sister of Ben. Hardin, the celebrated
criminal lawyer of his day. Colby Shrader, the father of William A.,
was born in Pewee Valley, and upon reaching manhood learned the
carpenters' trade, but spent most of his life in mercantile pursuits.
He started the first wholesale liquor and grocery house in Louisville
and later followed the river for some time, making fifty-two trips to
New Orleans. Toward the close of his life he retired to a farm in
Jefferson county, where he died and is buried at Goshen, in Oldham
county. He married Martha Priest, whose father, Fielding L. Priest,
was one of the pioneers of Louisville. He was a native of Culpeper
county, Va., a carpenter by trade, and erected the first store house
that was ever built in the city of Louisville. Colby and Martha
Shrader were the parents of eight children, viz.: Fielding M., William A., Josephine, Benjamin, Charles M., John O., Richard A., and
Cornelius C. Of these Fielding, Josephine and Benjamin are deceased. William A. Shrader was born and reared in Kentucky, educated in the common schools and at Goshen college, after which he
served an apprenticeship at the carpenter trade. He has followed this
vocation all his active business life, making a specialty of millwright
work, in which he has won a reputation for being a skillful and

ingenious workman. Mr. Shrader is a member of the Masonic fraternity. While he takes a commendable interest in all questions touching the public welfare, he does not belong to any political party to the extent that he always "votes his ticket straight." On the contrary, he believes in doing his own thinking, and votes according to his judgment.

JOHN M. ADAMS, for eight years magistrate for the Eleventh and Twelfth wards of the city of Louisville, Ky., was born in that city Dec. 8, 1852. He is a son of Wesley and Mary Jane (Dowdell) Adams, both natives of Louisville, where for many years the father was engaged in mercantile pursuits as the proprietor of a store on Main street. During the last sixteen years of his life he was gauger and inspector for the city, being repeatedly appointed by the city council. He died in 1875, leaving five children: Charles K., John M., Robert N., Frank G., and Lizzie. John M. Adams was educated in the public schools of his native city, and upon the death of his father he was appointed by the city council to fill out the unexpired term. After that he served twenty-two full terms, being elected by the city council for that number of times. In 1897 he was elected magistrate for the Eleventh and Twelfth wards, and was re-elected in 1901. During all these years he has been active in promoting the cause of Democracy and stands high in the councils of his party. Early in 1905 his name was prominently mentioned as a candidate for county assessor for Jefferson county. Mr. Adams is prominent in fraternal circles, being a member of the Heptasophs, the Improved Order of Red Men, the Royal Arcanum, the Knights and Ladies of Honor, the Woodmen of the World, the Fraternal Order of Eagles, the D. O. O. K., the Pathfinders and the Mose Green club. For two years he acted as county judge in the purging of registration and for seven years he was a member of the fiscal court. His long connection with official life and his membership in social and fraternal organizations have given him a wide acquaintance, so that he is one of the best known and also one of the most popular men in the city. On May 9, 1876, he married Miss Katherine, daughter of Henry and Magdalena Eberhardt, of Louisville.

I—20

Her father was born in Germany. During the war he was a soldier in the Federal army and died of disease contracted while in the service. He rests in Cave Hill cemetery. Mr. and Mrs. Adams have the following children: Clara B., wife of Harlan Turpen, Wesley F., Andrew, Katie May, Mary Elizabeth, Edward Goddard and John Carson.

JOHN P. DANT, distiller, wholesale dealer and jobber of Kentucky whiskies, Louisville, was born in Marion county, Ky., Dec. 4, 1855. In this county his grandfather, John B. Dant, for many years farmed on an extensive scale and afterward removed to Davies county, where he died at the mature age of ninety-six years. He is the son of Joseph W. and Catherine (Ballard) Dant, both natives of Marion county. In 1836 Joseph W. Dant and Raymond Hayden embarked in the distilling business in Nelson county, Ky., operating that plant until 1850. For the next ten years Mr. Dant operated a distillery at the headwaters of Pottinger's creek in Marion county. Then he removed to Dant, Ky., a village named after him, where in 1860 he erected the well known Dant distillery, which he operated until his death in 1890. Since that time this great plant has been operated by his sons under the name of the Dant Distilling Company. The output of this establishment amounts to 1,500 barrels of sour mash whisky of the finest quality, so fine that it has a national reputation for excellence and purity. John P. Dant was reared in Marion county and educated in its public schools. His first work in the distilling line was done as an employe of the establishment located at Dant. After serving in this capacity for fourteen years he removed to Lebanon, Ky., where he conducted a retail liquor business for seven years. From 1891 to 1905 he was engaged in the retail liquor business in Louisville, but in the latter year he embarked in the wholesale and jobbers' trade, making a specialty of the celebrated Dant whisky, the product of the distillery established by his father. It can be truthfully said that Louisville has no more popular, progressive and enterprising citizen than John P. Dant. After having thoroughly mastered the distilling business, he made it a rule early in life to manufacture only the purest goods, knowing full well that he must build up a strong reputation if he would succeed, and the result is that his whiskies enjoy a reputation second to none throughout this country. He deserves success because he has given his undivided attention to his business and has always striven to please his numerous customers. It is his full determination to improve his whiskies from year to year until they are pronounced the best manufactured in the country. In politics he is actively identified with the Democratic party, supporting it liberally in the way of donations, but never seeking an office. He is an ardent, earnest, consistent Catholic, taking a deep interest in every branch of the work of that great church. On Nov. 28, 1883, he married Miss Janie Smith, the daughter of William H. and Rosella (Lancaster) Smith, of Chicago, Ky. They have four children living, named Katie R., Louise, John P., Jr., and Marie.

CHARLES JACOB FEGENBUSH, magistrate for the Third magisterial district of Jefferson county, Ky., with offices in the city of Louisville, was born in that county Dec. 2, 1861. He is of German ancestry, his grandfather, Tobias Fegenbush, coming from the Fatherland in 1814, and locating in Jefferson county, where he followed farming all his life. His wife's maiden name was Maria Mann. They reared a family of seven children, who grew to maturity, viz.: Tobias, Theodore, Daniel, John, Philip J., Joseph, and Elizabeth, who married Joseph Schmeltz. Philip J. Fegenbush, the father of Charles J., was born in Jefferson county, Sept. 13, 1825, and followed farming all his life. His death occurred Jan. 20, 1904. He married M. Frederika Zucker, whose parents were natives of Germany, and they had the following children: John, Charles J., Caroline, deceased, Mary M., George P., deceased, William F., Edward J., Emma, and Margaret, the last named being the wife of S. Edward Vogt. Charles J. Fegenbush was educated in the public schools, and began life as a farmer. In 1890 he left the farm and embarked in the life insurance business with the Ætna Life of Hartford, Conn. He remained in this vocation for ten years. In 1890 he was first elected to the office of magistrate for the Third district and has been three times re-elected. About the beginning of 1905 his name was prominently mentioned in connection with the office of county assessor as a candidate on the Democratic ticket, to which party he belongs. Mr. Fegenbush is a member of the Highland Baptist church, Preston Lodge, No. 281, Free and Accepted Masons, and Pawnee Tribe, No. 42, Improved Order of Red Men. He has been twice married.

His first wife was Miss Mary F. Hite, a member of the well known Louisville family of that name. His second wife, to whom he was married on Aug. 10, 1898, was Miss Minnie M., daughter of Joab and Elizabeth Rehm, of Louisville, and to this union there has been born one daughter, Dorothy E.

THE VERY REVEREND LAURENCE BAX, pastor of St. John's Catholic church of Louisville, Ky., was born at Leende in the Netherlands on April 15, 1828. He was educated at the seminary of St. Michael's and Haren, North Brabant. As soon as he had graduated he came with Archbishop Spaulding as a missionary to Kentucky in May, 1853, and for three years taught in St. Thomas' seminary. He was then appointed pastor of St. John's congregation of Louisville, in which capacity he is still serving. In 1858, by his indefatigable industry and untiring energy, he built the present church edifice, a magnificent structure, the priest's residence, the school house and all the other buildings that go to make up a complete establishment. All this has been accomplished without incurring a single dollar of indebtedness. The church property is estimated to be worth fully $100,000, the interior of the church edifice being pure Gothic and the furnishings of the most precious character, corresponding in every respect to the building itself. The school is, without a single exception, one of the most thorough in the city, and has an average attendance of 300 pupils. This great church has at present a membership of 300 families. In the years 1873-74 Father Bax occupied the chair of moral theology in Preston Park seminary. At the golden jubilee celebration of his priesthood in 1903, the most reverend archbishop of Cincinnati presiding, there were present fully 100 priests, representing as many different churches. Father Bax has visited his native country and Rome three times, in the years 1867, 1883 and 1900, and it is his intention to go there again in 1905. Although he is about seventy-seven years old he is considered a marvel of health and strength and still gives his personal attention to most of the work connected with the parish. When he took charge of the work in Louisville there was but one other English speaking Catholic church, whereas there are now twenty-five. The work accomplished by this divine has been simply wonderful. He has never tired of pushing the good work, and to-day he can look back over his past life and truthfully say that he has done his whole duty. No other priest in Louisville stands higher in the estimation of the higher church dignitaries and of the people of Louisville than Father Bax. He has done so much for the city and his parish that he is esteemed and reverenced by all. It is to be hoped that his life may be spared for years to come and that the work of the parish under his direction may continue to grow.

HENRY A. J. PULS, the leading dyer and cleaner of wearing apparel for both men and women, Louisville, Ky., was born in Holstein, Germany, Feb. 17, 1855. In 1872 his parents, August and Mary (Sattel) Puls, came to America and located in Chicago, where the father opened a dyeing establishment and conducted it until 1879, when he removed to Alabama. There he engaged in farming until his death, which occurred in 1897. Henry A. J. Puls was educated in the schools of his native land before coming to this country. He learned trade of dyer with his father and for several years worked at it as a journeyman in Chicago. In 1886 he went to Evansville, where he managed a dyeing establishment for five years. At the end of that time he came to Louisville and opened a dye-house of his own. It was soon discovered by the people of the city that his work was of a high order and the natural result was to bring him a large volume of business. His trade extends not only to the city of Louisville, but to a large number of the surrounding towns in Kentucky and the adjoining states, his plant being thoroughly "up-to-date" and probably the best of its kind in the entire Lower Ohio Valley. Politically Mr. Puls is a Democrat, but can hardly be called an active party worker. He is a thirty-second degree Mason, a Knight of Pythias, and a member of the Improved Order of Red Men. On June 21, 1887, he was married to Miss Anna, daughter of Frank Sattel, of Bavaria, Germany, and has two children: Luella and Walter.

JACOB A. TOGGWEILER, shingler, with the Ewald Iron Company, Louisville, Ky., and colonel of the Twelfth regiment of the Kentucky Uniform Rank, Woodmen of the World, was born at Zurich, Switzerland, Oct. 23, 1869, his parents being Albert and Mary A. (Kung) Toggweiler. Until he was seventeen years of age he continued to live in his native city, receiving his education by attending school two days in the week, the remainder of his time being devoted to learning the tinners' trade. For this privilege he paid the sum of $200. In 1886 he came to America and soon after his arrival in this country made his way to Louisville, where for the next six years he worked at his trade. He then entered the employ of the Ewald Iron Company, with which concern he has been connected, with the exception of short intervals now and then, ever since. At the present time he holds the position of head shingler with the company, having charge of that division of the work. Prior to the Spanish-American war he was a member of the Kentucky State Guards and on June 5, 1898, was mustered into the Federal service as a member of Company A, First Kentucky volunteers, to serve in the war, the regiment being mustered in at Lexington. The regiment was ordered to Chickamauga Park, where it remained from June 11th to July 25th, when it was ordered to Porto Rico, arriving on that island August 17th. When peace was declared, on Dec. 5, 1898, it returned to the United States and was discharged from the service in February, 1899. Colonel Toggweiler is prominent in fraternal circles, being a member of Modoc Lodge, No. 102, Improved Order of Red Men; Live Oak Camp, No. 6, Woodmen of the World, which enjoys the distinction of being the largest camp in the State of Kentucky and to the Amalgamated Association of Iron, Steel and Tin Workers. On Dec. 2, 1903, he was elected major of the Twelfth regiment, Uniform Rank, Woodmen of the World, and served in that capacity until in June 8, 1904, when he was promoted to the colonelcy to succeed S. J. Hall, who was promoted to the rank of brigadier-general, commanding the First brigade. In October, 1891, Colonel Toggweiler was married to Miss Lizzie, daughter of Henry and Anna (Hudson) Gottschalk, of Louisville, her father being a native of Germany and her mother of Kentucky. To this marriage has been born one son, Arthur M. Both

Colonel Toggweiler and his wife belong to the Church of Christ and are consistent practitioners of the precepts of their religious faith. In politics Colonel Toggweiler is a Republican; is recognized as one of the progressive men of the city, and is universally popular because of his many sterling qualities.

AMOS LEMMON, assistant clerk of the circuit court of Harrison county, Ind., was born in that county, Aug. 3, 1850, and is a son of John and Elizabeth (Johnson) Lemmon, both natives of Shelby county, Ky. Both of his grandfathers, James Lemmon and Henson Johnson, were soldiers in the Revolutionary war. His ancestors on his father's side emigrated from Europe in 1763, being two brothers. They settled at Baltimore, remaining there a number of years agitating the question in favor of American liberty, and when the war came on they were at the front and in the heat of battle and were present at Braddock's defeat and the surrender of Lord Cornwallis. James, being a youth of twelve years, officiated as a message-bearer between his father and General Washington during the struggle of the Revolution. After peace had been established the family remained in Pennsylvania until 1786, when they removed to Kentucky, where John Lemmon, the father of the subject of this sketch, was born in 1804. When John was twelve years of age his parents came to Indiana, settling in Harrison county. He was a life long Democrat and a recognized leader of his party. He served as county commissioner for a number of years, was elected to the legislature in 1852, re-elected two years later and again in 1862 as the representative from Harrison county, and elected in 1864 as the joint representative from Washington and Harrison counties. John Lemmon was an ordained minister of the regular Baptist church, preaching in Indiana and Illinois for twenty years previous to his death. John and Elizabeth Lemmon were the parents of ten children, four sons and six daughters. James W. was a merchant at Rockport, Ind., until his death in 1886. He was also active in politics and in 1862 was elected a member of the legislature from Spencer county, serving in the same session with his father. Henson Lemmon died in 1892, being for many years a prominent liveryman of Corydon, Ind. Daniel F. is a prominent attorney at law, was superintendent of the public schools of Harrison county for twelve years, and was also clerk of the Harrison circuit court for four years. Four daughters, Mary E. Pfrimmer, Ellen Pfrimmer, Sarah J. Zenor and Martha E. Hess are living and two, Annie Benson and Eliza C. Zollman are dead. Amos, the subject of this sketch was educated in the common schools, afterward attending the Hartsville university at Hartsville, Ind., and for about one year taught in the public schools of Harrison county. In 1871 he went to Rockport, where he entered the employ of his brother James and was in the store with him until 1883. He then returned to Corydon in his native county and a year later was appointed deputy clerk of the Harrison circuit court. Since that time he has been continuously in the public service either as assistant to the clerk or the auditor. In 1892 he was elected clerk of the circuit court of his county and served one term of four years. His long service stands as a testimony, not only as to his expertness and efficiency as an accountant, but to his popularity as a Democrat and citizen. Mr. Lemmon has not forgotten his early training, however, and still retains his farm near Corydon and there makes his residence. On June 2, 1877, he was married to Miss Caddie, the daughter of Morris Sharp, a merchant of Rockport. She died without children in 1882 and on June 15, 1884, Mr. Lemmon led to the altar Dora, daughter of John P. and Sarah (Faith) Sonner, of Harrison county. To this marriage there have been born three children: Walter Wesseler, born March 9, 1886, and died at the age of one and one-half years; Georgia Hess, born February 18, 1888, and Hardin John, born October 24, 1890. Mr. Lemmon and his family are attendants at the Presbyterian church; he is a member of Gregg Lodge, No. 235, Independent Order of Odd Fellows located at Corydon; and is popular in the community at large, because of his genial disposition and general good-fellowship.

PLEASANT JENKINS, of Corydon, Ind., one of the best known educators in that section of the state, and now superintendent of the Harrison county schools, was born in that county, June 2, 1869. His parents, Leroy and Charlotte (Baylor) Jenkins, were both natives of Indiana, the former of Clark and the latter of Harrison county. But little is known of the Jenkins family, further than it originated in Virginia, as all reliable records of the ancestry have been lost. Leroy Jenkins was a soldier in the Mexican war, serving under Gen. Zachary Taylor, and while in the military service he received an injury that gave him trouble all his subsequent life. Pleasant Jenkins received his primary education in the public schools of his native county, afterward attending the Central Normal college at Danville, Ind. Upon leaving school he adopted the profession of teaching and taught for fifteen years in the Harrison county schools. In June, 1903, he was elected superintendent of the county schools, a position for which his long experience as a teacher, and his intimate knowledge of the needs and character of the schools, gave him a peculiar fitness. The field of his labors is a large one, there being thirteen townships in the county, but his duties are performed with an efficiency and conscientiousness that fully demonstrates the wisdom of his selection. Mr. Jenkins is not a pretentious individual. He believes in doing rather than talking. In his visits to the schools his mission is improvement. The teachers know that his criticisms of their methods are made with a view to that end and not simply for the purpose of showing off his superior position. Consequently there is always perfect harmony between him and those under his supervision. In addition to his school duties he owns and manages the old homestead formerly owned by his father. As a farmer he is as thorough as he is in teaching, giving that attention to details that brings success. He is a member of Georgetown Lodge, No. 641, Independent Order of Odd Fellows, in which he has a high standing and a due measure of popularity. On April 12, 1896, Mr. Jenkins was married to Miss Lizzie K., daughter of Harvey and Nancy (Bryerly) Johnson, natives of Harrison and Floyd county, respectively, Mr. Johnson being now a prominent farmer of the former county. Mrs. Jenkins is a member of the Christian church.

JOHN F. HABERMEL, Corydon, Ind., assessor of Harrison county, was born on a farm in that county, Oct. 24, 1856. His parents, Joseph and Catherine (Gettlefinger) Habermel, were natives of Germany, but came to America in 1856, settling upon a farm in Harrison county, where the father died some years later. They had three children: Frederick, now living upon the old home farm, which he manages; Josephine, also living upon the homestead; and John F., the subject of this sketch. In 1865 Mrs. Habermel, the mother of these children, married John Geppner, of Dubois county, Ind., and by this marriage has the following children: John, who lives on the home place, Maggie, wife of Richard B. Dewess, of Jeffersonville; and Theresa, wife of Joseph Granger, a grocer at Howard Park, in Clark county. John F. Habermel attended the public schools of Harrison county until he was fourteen years of age, when he went to Mobile, Ala., where he was for some time employed in a store conducted by his uncles, the firm being J. J. Diemer & Co. While in Mobile he attended school and completed his education. After five years in Mobile he returned to Harrison county and in 1875 the family removed to Indianapolis, where he found employment in a wholesale grocery house, remaining there two years, when the family returned to the farm. In 1881 Mr. Habermel took up his residence in Bradford, a village of Harrison county, where he opened a general store. His experience in Mobile and Indianapolis gave him excellent qualifications for a mercantile life, and the result is he has been prosperous in the undertaking. Shortly after locating at Bradford he began to take an active part in the politics of his county. In 1886 he was elected township assessor for Morgan township, and continued to hold the office until 1895. In 1893 he was appointed postmaster at the capitol, during the session of the legislature, and while in this position he made many new friends by his genial disposition and his uniform courtesy and kindness. In 1900 he was elected to the office of county assessor, which position he holds at the present time and in which he has fully demonstrated that he is the right man for the place. In order to give more attention to his official duties he sold his store in 1902 and removed to Corydon. In politics Mr. Habermel is a Democrat of the rock-ribbed type, and is always ready to defend his political views. He was married, June 14, 1881, to Miss Clara, the daughter of William Brockman, of Louisville, Ky., and to this union there have been born seven children, viz: William, born Oct. 29, 1882, a teacher in the Harrison county schools; Katie, born in April, 1884; Zetta, July 1, 1885; Susie, in November, 1887; America, in 1889; Clara, in December, 1897, and John, in March, 1900. William, the eldest son, was married in November, 1903, to Miss Katie Baker of Bradford. Mrs. Clara Habermel studied medicine before her marriage and began practice in 1879. As a homeopathic physician she has few equals and since her marriage she has continued to practice her profession. In addition to a technical knowledge of the science of medicine she has all the gentle nature of the wife and mother, which plays an important part in winning the confidence of the patient and in this way contributes to her success and popularity. Mr. and Mrs. Habermel are both members of St. Joseph's Roman Catholic church at Corydon.

Hiram Akers

HIRAM AKERS, whose portrait appears on the opposite page, was a member of one of the oldest and most prominent families of Clark county, Ind., and a man who, in his day, wielded a great influence in the development of the material resources of the country in the vicinity of the Falls of the Ohio. About the beginning of the nineteenth century his father and grandfather left their homes in Virginia to seek their fortunes in the Ohio Valley, which was then almost unknown to civilized men. After living for several years in Shelby county, Ky., they crossed the river and located permanently near Muddy Fork Blockhouse, in what is now Wood township, Clark county. That was in 1809, and from that time to the present some representatives of the family have been identified with the growth and development of that region. Hiram Akers was born near the blockhouse on Feb. 26, 1812. He grew to manhood without those conveniences in the way of schools that boys of the present generation enjoy, but the education of the frontier made him a strong, self-reliant man. What he lacked in book learning he more than made up in force of character. He was an upright Christian man, was one of the founders of the old State Run church, where his remains now rest in peace near his old home. In his later life he became the owner of a considerable tract of land in Jeffersonville township, near the Floyd county line, where he also held important milling interests. The old brick house, which he erected in 1848, and which was built of brick manufactured on the place, is still standing. It is one of the landmarks of the neighborhood, a silent but at the same time eloquent witness to the industry and frugality of one of the early settlers. Mr. Akers was married on Oct. 10, 1833, to a Miss Amelia Garrittson, of Floyd county. A son, Reason L. Akers, was born to this marriage on Jan. 9, 1837. He grew to maturity in Clark county and, like his father, was a potent factor in shaping the affairs of the community. When the dread news spread in the spring of 1861, that the Confederates had fired upon Fort Sumter, he was one of the first to offer his services to his country for the suppression of the rebellion. He was connected with various volunteer organizations raised in Floyd county and made an honorable record as a soldier. After the war he engaged in the cement business in Clark county, which he continued to follow until his death, Nov. 23, 1878. His father, Hiram Akers, died May 22, 1856. Reason L. Akers married Miss Louisa Miller, of Clark county, on Sept. 28, 1865, and to this union were born a son and daughter: Matthew L., now living in Louisville, Ky., where he holds a responsible position in the service of the Big Four railway, and Miss Minnie Akers, residing in New Albany, Ind. Thus for four generations the family have been a part of the warp and woof of Clark county and the immediate vicinity. In all that time the representatives of the family have occupied a high place in the general esteem. Hiram Akers is still spoken of by old settlers as a man of the highest ideals and the most spotless integrity. These qualities he has transmitted to his descendants, and the name of Akers is one that is honored and respected in the three cities around the Falls of the Ohio.

JAMES HARGAN (deceased), who was for many years one of the leading business men of Madison, Ind., was a native of Ireland, having been born near Londonderry, in 1828. In his early youth he came to America with his parents, who settled in Cincinnati, where James received his education and learned the trade of locksmith. Later he came to Madison, and engaged in the retail grocery business, where he continued to live until his death, May 8, 1898. While living in Cincinnati he was married to a Miss Symms, and by this marriage he had one son, George Symms Hargan, now one of the leading wholesale grocers of Madison, and also a dealer in liquors at wholesale, as a member of the firm of Hargan & Johnson, the business having been established by his father. James Hargan's first wife died in Cincinnati, and after coming to Madison he married Mary Louise Luck, a daughter of Jacob and Louise (Cudlipp) Luck, both natives of England. Jacob Luck came to Baltimore in his youth, there learned the hatters' trade, and was for many years a member of the firm of Bartlett & Luck, dealers in hats and caps at Madison. He and his wife both died soon after the Civil war, in which he served for about six months. By his second wife Mr. Hargan had three children, viz.: Louise, now the wife of Greenville Johnson, of the firm of Hargan & Johnson, and the mother of two children, Corinne and Helen; Harvey W., engaged in the hardware business at Madison; his wife was Miss Caroline Howe, a daughter of S. Q. Howe, of Patriot, Ind., and a descendant of Lord Howe of Revolutionary fame; they had three children, Mary F., Caroline V., and James; James, now engaged in the drug trade, married May Barnard of Madison and they have three children, also: Gladys B., Joseph, and Martha L. James Hargan, during his life was a representative business man and a model citizen. He was a prominent member of the Independent Order of Odd Fellows, and nearly all the family are members of the Episcopal church.

WILLIAM S. NYE, manufacturer of and dealer in monuments, marble and granite work, etc., Corydon, Ind., is a native of the Keystone State, having been born near Brady's Lake, Pa., Oct. 9, 1862. He is a son of Seth S. Nye, a prominent minister of the Christian church, who came to Harrison county, Ind., in 1868, and though now in his eightieth year he is still hale and hearty, taking an active interest in his church work. William S. is the fourth child in a family of five. Herman M. is now in the milling business at Elmwood, Neb.; Wilbur C. is in the hotel and livery business at Bickelton, Wash.; Alva Austin is a contractor of stone work at Georgetown, Ind.; and Stella is the wife of Leonard C. Keller, a member of the mercantile house of the W. H. Keller Company, of Corydon. William S. Nye attended the public schools of Harrison county until he was about sixteen years of age, when he began life on his own account as a farm hand. After a short season at this occupation he went into the marble cutting establishment of H. Byrn & Son, of Corydon, and there learned the trade of marble cutter. Forming a partnership with J. M. Shaw the firm embarked in the monument business at Corydon. At the close of the first year Mr. Nye purchased his partner's interest and since then has been the sole proprietor of the business. In every cemetery around Corydon may be seen the handiwork of Mr. Nye in the monuments of chaste and tasteful design that mark the last resting place of those who have joined the silent majority. Mr. Nye takes a commendable interest in political affairs and in 1900 was elected coroner of the county, which office he held for one term. He is a member and one of the principal officers of Gresham Camp, No. 3270, Modern Woodmen of America, of Corydon. In 1893 he married Miss Lena, daughter of Levi W. Mauck, a prominent farmer of Harrison county and a member of the family from whom Mauckport received its name. Mr. and Mrs. Nye have had born to them five children: Nellie G., William J., deceased, George M., Daisy C. and Russell.

WILLIAM DANIEL, M.D., of Corydon, Ind., one of the leading physicians of Harrison and adjoining counties, was born at Milltown, Crawford county, Ind., Oct. 7, 1852, his parents being William S. and Sarah C. (Russell) Daniel, the former a native of New Albany, Ind., and the latter of Shenandoah county, Va. In 1851 Doctor Daniel's father located at Milltown, where he engaged in the harnesss and saddlery business until 1890, when he retired and now lives on a fine farm near that place. He has been three times married. His first wife, who was the mother of Doctor Daniel, bore him four children, viz.: William, the subject of this sketch; Oliver, deceased; John, a physician of Georgetown, Ind., and a second son named Oliver, who lived in Floyd county. The mother of these children died in 1871 and in 1875 Mr. Daniel married Julia Westfall, of Harrison county, who died within a year after the marriage. In 1880 the father married Julia Cole, of Crawford county, and they have one child, Olive, now the wife of Doctor Rhodes of Milltown. William S. Daniel served a term in the regular army in his youth and was one of the first men to volunteer in the Civil war, enlisting on April 19, 1861, in Company G, Twenty-third Indiana infantry, as an orderly sergeant. At the battle of Holly Springs, Miss., he was promoted for gallant conduct on the field, and at the close of the war was mustered out as a sergeant-major. Doctor Daniel received his primary education in the public schools and attended the Marengo academy, giving music lessons and teaching in the public schools to earn sufficient funds to pay his way through medical college. In September, 1873, he entered the Louisville Medical college and graduated in February, 1875, with the degree of M.D. During the last year he was in college he served on the staff of the public dispensary and after his graduation, by competitive examination, was awarded a place as resident physician of the Louisville city hospital. He resigned the position, however, in July of the same year, and came to Corydon, where he became associated with Dr. Harvey Wolfe in the general practice of medicine. After a year with Doctor Wolfe he went to Marengo and practiced there until 1886, when he returned to Corydon and bought the good-will and practice of his old partner, Doctor Wolfe, remaining there ever since. In 1886 Doctor Daniel took post-graduate work in the hospital college of medicine of the Central university at Louisville, receiving the Ad Eundem degree. As a physician he has built up a lucrative business and ranks as one of the successful practitioners of Southern Indiana. He is a member of the Indiana Medical association; the Mississippi Valley Medical association; the Medical Society of the Mitchell district of Indiana; and the Medical Societies of Floyd and Crawford counties. In 1899 he was appointed secretary of the Harrison county board of health, and still holds that position. He is a member of Pisgah Lodge, Free and Accepted Masons; Gregg Lodge, Independent Order of Odd Fellows; and the Tribe of Ben Hur, at Corydon. He is also a member and one of the trustees of the Methodist Episcopal church, and has been for several years superintendent of the Sunday school. On March 16, 1875, Doctor Daniel was united in marriage to Miss Frederica Martin, a daughter of Frederick and Barbara (Keller) Martin, of Milltown, and to his marriage there have been born five children: Frederick Martin, a dentist at Elwood, Ind., and who married Caroline Clark of Indianapolis; Grace, wife of George W. Applegate, Jr., of Corydon; Catherine, now Mrs. Charles Buchanan, of Corydon; William Victor, deceased; and John Carleton, a student in school.

WALTER MUNDT, president of the Mundt & Hidden Candy Company, of Madison, Ind., was born in Germany in 1862. When he was about four years of age he came to America with his parents, Charles and Bertha (Krahn) Mundt. The family located at Cincinnati, O., where the father followed his trade as millwright until his death, which occurred at Lockland, O., in 1881, in the forty-fifth year of his age. The mother returned to Germany after his death with her two sons, Walter and Edward. After a short visit Walter came back to this country, leaving his mother and brother in Germany. Walter started to learn the confectioners' trade at Covington, Ky., in 1873. After working in that city for nine years he went to Cincinnati as foreman for the firm of A. & J. Doescher, manufacturers of confectionery. While in this position he superintended the making of all the ice cream and confections used at the centennial exposition at Cincinnati. He then came to Madison and opened a retail store at 321 West Main street, which he conducted for ten years. After selling the business he organized the Mundt-Hidden candy company with a capital stock of $20,000. The officers of the company are: Walter Mundt, president; R. H. Hidden, vice-president; C. H. Robinson, secretary and treasurer, and Edward Mundt, director. The trade of the company is steadily growing owing to the high quality of their goods, and the disposition to treat their customers fairly. Mr. Mundt is a popular member of several secret and fraternal organizations, viz: the Independent Order of Odd Fellows; Knights of Pythias; the Improved Order of Red Men; the Modern Woodmen and the Good Samaritans. Politically he is a Republican, but never neglects his business to become a participant in political work. He was married in Newport, Ky., to Annie Hidden, and to this union there have been born four children: Lena, Bertha, Walter, Jr., and Richard.

JOHN ORRILL.

ANDREW RIEDEL, a farmer on Ryker's Ridge, near Madison, Ind., was born in Germany in the year 1838. When he was about three years of age his parents, Martin and Barbara (Arnold) Riedel, came to the United States and located at Cincinnati, where the father was employed as a stonemason's helper in the construction of the city water works. In 1848 the family came to Ryker's Ridge, where Martin Riedel bought thirty-three acres of land and followed truck farming until his death, at the age of eighty years, his wife having died some years before. Andrew received the greater part of his education in the common schools of Madison township. In 1861 he enlisted as a private in Company E, Sixth Indiana infantry, which was the first company to be organized in Jefferson county, Ind. He served with this regiment through the three months service, taking part in the battle of Philippi, W. Va., on June 7, 1861. At the end of three months he returned home but shortly afterward enlisted in the Thirteenth United States regular infantry for three years. His company was honored by being chosen to act as body guard to Gereral Sherman, and was in the battles of Chickasaw Bayou, Arkansas Post, Champion Hills, Black River, Jackson, Tenn., Colliersville, Tenn., and Mission Ridge, and several of lesser note. He was discharged in 1864. Mr. Riedel is a member of Bachman Post, No. 26, Grand Army of the Republic, and of the Methodist Episcopal church. In political matters he is one of the unswerving Republicans of his township and county and always takes an interest in political campaigns. In 1869 Mr. Riedel was married to Kate Lott, a daughter of Abner and Mary Frances (Orrill) Lott. Abner Lott was a descendant of an old Virginia family living in King and Queen county. His parents were John and Phoebe (Lott) Lott, his maternal grandfather having been a veteran of the Revolutionary war. Mary Frances Orrill was a daughter of John Orrill, whose portrait appears at the head of this sketch. He was a veteran of the war of 1812. Some of the Orrill family or their immediate relations have been in every war that ever occurred in the United States, or in which this nation was engaged. Mrs. Katharine (Bird) Orrill, the wife of John Orrill was the daughter of Philip Bird, who lost his life in the war of the Revolution. Her husband was in the war of 1812. She had one son in the Mexican war, three sons and four grandsons in the Civil war and a great-grandson in the Spanish-American war. She and her husband were from Virginia. Mr. and Mrs. Riedel have the following children: Annie Frances, Grace, Charles B., who served in the Seventh Ohio infantry in the Spanish-American war, and Clara Pearl, who married Edward Phillips, an Indianapolis machinist. They have one boy named Raymond Edward. The Lott family are noted for their longevity, Abner Lott dying in his seventy-ninth year and his grandfather living to be one hundred and three years old.

ERNEST J. SHERLOCK, a farmer located near Madison, Ind., was born in that city, Feb. 14, 1855. His parents, Henry E. and Eugenia (Barchall) Sherlock, were both natives of Hanover, Germany. His maternal grandfather died in Germany, at the age of one hundred and three years, and his grandmother came to America, bringing her family. His mother also came to America with her father and his parents were married at Cincinnati. Eugenia Sherlock died at the age of seventy-two years, and her husband is still living in Indianapolis at the age of eighty-one. The paternal grandmother of Ernest lived to the age of ninety-one years. Ernest J. Sherlock was educated in the public schools and has been a farmer the greater part of his life. He is now engaged as a truck farmer and has a highly cultivated farm of a little over twenty-eight acres, on the Ryker's Ridge road, two and a half miles from Madison. Mr. Sherlock is a member of the Methodist Episcopal church and is a Republican in his political affiliations. He is also a member of the Modern Woodmen. In the fall of 1876 Mr. Sherlock was united in marriage to Miss Annie Fewell, daughter of William Fewell, who was a native of Madison. To Mr. and Mrs. Sherlock there have been born two children: George, aged twenty-six, and John Hodges, aged twenty-four. George is a member of the Modern Woodmen and the Independent Order of Odd Fellows. John Hodges married Sallie Cochran, a daughter of Edward Cochran, a resident of Jefferson county, Ind. Mr. Sherlock has all the industrious habits and thrift that distinguish the German people, and is one of the prosperous farmers and worthy citizens of his locality.

ORRIN MARSHALL (deceased), for many years a well-known citizen of Madison, Ind., was born in the city of Cincinnati, O., in the year 1827, and died on his farm near Madison, of pneumonia, in January, 1904, aged seventy-seven years. He was a son of Addison and Margaret (Patten) Marshall, the father being a native of Virginia, who came to Cincinnati in early manhood and was for a long time a steamboat engineer on the Ohio river. When the subject of this sketch was about three years of age the family settled in Madison, where he received his education, after which he adopted his father's calling and became an engineer on the river. He was the first engineer on the ill-fated *United States*, at the time that vessel collided with the *America*, which resulted in the loss of several lives. Later he was first engineer on the *General Lytle*, one of the largest and finest boats on the river. In 1882 he gave up the business of engineer and established a laundry at Madison, which he conducted for sixteen years. At the end of that time he removed to his farm, a short distance from the city, and lived there until his death. On both sides his parents lived to a good old age. His father died at the age of seventy-seven, and his mother died in 1890 at the age ci eighty-four. In 1857 Mr. Marshall was married to Julia, daughter of C. A. and Huldah (Hall) Wise. Her father was a native of Jefferson county, Ind., and was for a number of years in the livery business in Madison. After disposing of this business he went to Louisville, where he was for a long time manager of the St. Cloud and Alexandria hotels. At the time of his death he was seventy-six years old, his wife having died some time before at the age of fifty-nine. Mrs. Marshall was the eldest of nine children, all of whom survived their parents. Mr. and Mrs. Marshall had the following children: Carrie; Frank B., a boiler inspector at Cincinnati; George B., who died at the age of twenty-five years; Charles E.; Virginia, who married B. T. Millican and has three children; Nadine, aged fifteen; Jean, aged twelve; and Mary, aged nine. Orrin Marshall, the youngest of the family, and who bears his father's name, is now the proprietor of the laundry his father established years ago. During his life Mr. Marshall was a stanch Democrat, an honored member of the Independent Order of Odd Fellows, and enjoyed the confidence and esteem of a large number of friends. His widow still lives and is loved by many for her amiable and womanly qualities.

GEORGE D. SCHWAB, one of the best known and most popular young business men of Madison, Ind., was born in that city, Nov. 21, 1874, his parents being William A. and Margaret (Thorne) Schwab. William Schwab was born in Würtemberg, Germany, in 1838. When he was but six years of age he came with his parents to America, stopping for a few years in New York, but coming to Madison in 1850, where he was reared and educated. In 1861 he enlisted in the Fourth Indiana cavalry and after a month's service received a wound which necessitated his discharge. He died in 1875 at the age of thirty-seven years. His widow and all of their six children are still living, the children being Margaret, Lenora, Emma, William, Stella and George D. Emma is the wife of G. L. Spaulding, a photographer of Madison; William lives at Seattle, and the others are at home. George D., the youngest of the family and the subject of this sketch, received his education in the schools of his native city and at the age of twenty-one embarked in the dry goods business for himself. In 1896 he formed a partnership with George M. Daily, under the firm name of Daily & Schwab. Later he disposed of this business, went to Marietta, Ohio, where he was employed in a dry goods house until 1900; returned to Madison and for two years was deputy sheriff of Jefferson county; then engaged in the laundry business for about two years, and is now in charge of a corps of men engaged in placing on the market the products of the Sulzer Medical company of Madison. Mr. Schwab is also the owner of the formula for a preparation known as Dr. Langee's nerve tonic, which he is making arrangements to place on the market, having purchased the rights and good will of the former proprietor. In his political views Mr. Schwab is a firm Republican and in fraternal circles he is a member of the Knights of Pythias, the Improved Order of Red Men, and the Benevolent and Protective Order of Elks. In all these societies he is a popular fellow, because of his genial disposition and generous nature. He is brim full of energy, has rare tact and ability in what he undertakes, is not easily discouraged, and it is safe to say that he will make his mark alongside the progressive men of his day.

CHARLES AUGUST JAHRRIES, a popular merchant tailor of Madison, Ind., was born in that city, Feb. 7, 1874. His grandfather, Frederick Jahrries, was born in Saxony, Germany, in 1812; came in his early manhood to the United States; located at Madison, where he worked at the trade of stonemason until his death, which occurred in 1883 in the seventy-second year of his age. He was married at Madison in 1846 to Dorothy Geyer, a native of Baden-Baden, who died in 1903, aged seventy-seven, leaving four children: Frederick, the father of the subject; Louise, now Mrs. Charles Hahn, of Louisville; Henrietta and William, both now living at Denver, Col. Frederic Jahrries, the father, was born in the city of Madison, May 23, 1847; there grew to manhood and received his education; learned the trade of harness maker, which is still his occupation, and lives in one of the handsomest residences in Madison. He married Ann M. Klein, who was born in Madison on May 9, 1853. She is a daughter of the late Ferdinand Klein, a native of Germany and a merchant tailor, who spent the greater part of his life in Madison, where he was well known, being a Mason, an Odd Fellow, a Knight of Pythias, and an active Democrat. He died in 1896, aged sixty-two. Frederick and Ann Jahrries have reared a family of six children, viz.: Charles, Frederick, Albert, Howard, Franklin and Mary. Frederick, the second son, was a soldier in the Spanish-American war and spent a year in the Philippines. Charles A. Jahrries received his education in the Madison public schools and at the age of seventeen years started in to learn the tailors' trade. He soon mastered the intricacies of the business and since going into business for himself has built up a good patronage. He displays good taste in the selection of goods, takes pride in giving his customers a good fit in every instance, and has acquired a reputation for honest work. Politically he is a Republican though he can hardly be called an active worker in political contests. In religious matters he is a member of the Lutheran church.

JOHN C. ELLSPERMANN, a florist, located at No. 2005 East Virginia street, Evansville, Ind., was born in that city in 1857, his parents being Martin and Catherine (Magin) Ellspermann. His father was a native of Germany, married in the Fatherland, and came to the United States about 1850 with his wife and three children —George, Catherine and Adam. The last named now lives in Evansville and the other two are deceased. After settling near Evansville, where the father followed the occupation of market gardener, four more children were born to them, viz.: Daniel, Joseph, John C., and Mary, all of whom are yet living, John C. being the subject of this sketch, and Mary the wife of Philip Seitz. The father of these children died in 1892 at the age of seventy-one years and the mother on Aug. 10, 1900, in her seventy-eighth year. John C. Ellspermann was educated at St. Mary's school at Evansville and upon leaving school started in to learn the trade of florist with J. D. Carmody. After thirteen years with Mr. Carmody he went into business for himself, not far from his present location. He has been successful and his success is due to his thorough knowledge of his business, his fair dealing and his untiring industry. Mr. Ellspermann was married to Miss Katie, daughter of Rupert Buchenberger, who was for many years connected with the brewing interests of Evansville. He was a native of Germany, came with his parents to America in his boyhood, married Mary Eva Wintz in Evansville, who came from Germany three years after he did. He died in 1875, aged forty-five years, and his wife died in 1900 in her seventy-first year. They had four children, Mrs. Ellspermann being the youngest of the family. Mr. and Mrs. Ellspermann have the following children: Joseph, born June 20, 1883; Mary, born March 27, 1885; Carl, born Jan. 25, 1889; and Theobald, born Sept. 3, 1891. Mr. Ellspermann is a Republican in his political affiliations, a member of the Catholic church, St. Boniface and St. Michael's societies, and the Sunrise Benevolent Society.

THEODORE KEVEKORDES, of Evansville, Ind., recorder of Vanderburg county, was born in that city in the year 1875 and is the son of Leo Kevekordes, one of Evansville's substantial business men. Theodore was educated in the public schools of his native city

and after graduating from the high school there attended DePauw
university during the years 1893-4, and later attended Butler college
at Indianapolis, now the classical department of the University of
Indianapolis. Upon leaving school he established himself in the
music business in Evansville, in which he continued for about four
years, after which he became associated with his father in the furniture business. Upon retiring from the furniture store he was employed in the office of the city water-works for eighteen months and
during this time became somewhat active in political work with the
result that in 1902 he was elected recorder of the county for a term
of four years, taking the office on the first of January, 1903. Mr.
Kevekordes is a member of the Benevolent and Protective Order of
Elks and is one of the official board of St. John's Evangelical church,
in which he is one of the active members. He is a fine example of the
German-American citizen. Educated to love the traditions of the
Fatherland, he is at the same time a loyal American citizen, fully imbued with the spirit of this country's free institutions and always
ready to do his part to insure their perpetuation. He is what is generally called a "good mixer" and owes his political preferment to
his genial disposition, his persevering spirit and the high order of his
executive ability.

MARK GRANT, a prominent contractor
and builder of Evansville, Ind., and one of
the commissioners of Vanderburg county,
was born in London, England, July 24,
1827. When he was five years of age he
came with his parents to this country.
After six months in New York the family
removed to Cleveland, where they lived for
three and a half years and then came to
Evansville. Here Mark was educated in the
common schools, learned the trade of carpenter and has assisted in the erection of
some of the largest buildings in the county.
For over thirty years he has been in the business of contracting and
building for himself. He framed the structure at the salt-wells, near
the Maryland street bridge, and has built many of the finest residences in Evansville. When the One Hundred and Forty-sixth Indiana infantry was organized during the Civil war he enlisted as a
private in Company C and served until the close of the war, being

most of the time with Hancock in the Shenandoah Valley. Mr. Grant has always taken a commendable interest in public affairs, served two years as a member of the Evansville city council, was elected county commiss:oner in 1898, and is now serving his second term in that position. He is a member of Farragut Post, Grand Army of the Republic, and of the Old Soldiers' Republican club. In 1855 he was united in marriage to Miss Elizabeth Pritchett, of Evansville, who died about two years after their union. In 1858 he was married to Miss Nancy A. Bell, of Evansville, and they have four children living. Jeannette is the wife of William A. Gillett, a carpenter of Evansville; Samuel N. is in the plumbing business in that city; U. S. is assistant chief of the Evansville fire department, and Dora is the wife of Frank Britton, the custodian of the Vanderburg county court house.

HARRY W. STAHLHEFER, city clerk of Evansville, Ind., is a native of that city and is a son of the late Joseph Stahlhefer, who was born in Germany, but came to America in early manhood and who was one of the builders of Evansville. Harry has lived all his life in Evansville, was there educated in the public schools, after which he entered his father's store. Ever since reaching his majority he has been interested in political work. In 1896 he was appointed deputy sheriff and continued in this position for about five years. In the city election in the spring of 1901 he was chosen vice chairman of the Republican city central committee and had charge of some important work during the campaign. After having helped conduct a successful campaign he was elected by the city council to the office he now holds. Mr. Stahlhefer is also, by virtue of his office, the clerk of the police court and of the board of public safety. In the several official positions that he has occupied his work has been distinguished by promptness, correctness and simplic:ty. His records are always kept up to date and in such a way that any one who can read can understand them. Personally Mr. Stahlhefer is a gentleman of pleasant demeanor, one of the sort that people like to meet a second time, and the longer one knows him the better he is liked. He is a member of the Benevolent and Protective Order of Elks, is always a welcome figure at the club house of that society because of his genial disposition, and is a ready and cheerful participant in the order's numerous and worthy charities.

EBEN C. POOLE, justice of the peace, Evansville, Ind., is a native of Bangor, Me., and comes of that old New England stock that played so important a part in the early history of this country. When sixteen years of age his parents removed to Boston, Mass. When he was about twenty-five years of age he went to Jersey City, N. J., and engaged in business with his brother. He left this position to become a Pullman conductor, and for the next twelve years he traveled in that capacity nearly all over the United States. His first visit to Evansville was on the occasion of a reunion of the Blue and the Gray. Liking the city and its people, he made up his mind to become a resident of the place, and a few months later found him installed there as the local agent of the Monarch Palace Car company. Since that time he has continued to live in Evansville, where he has made friends by his genial ways, his correct habits, and his many sterling qualities of both head and heart. Some time after taking up his residence in that city he began to take an interest in political affairs, and the result has been his election for three successive terms of four years each to the office of justice of the peace. He conducts the affairs of his court with a dignity and decorum that would reflect credit on some of the higher judicial officers. His decisions have been distinguished for their simple justice and close adherence to well established precedents. Mr. Poole is a Knight of Pythias, a Buffalo, and a charter member of Pioneer Court of Honor, and charter member of No. 122, Tribe of Ben Hur, as well as several other social organizations.

WILLIAM J. HARRIS, senior member of the firm of Harris & Shopbell, architects, Evansville, Ind., was born in the city of Louisville, Ky. His father, Edwin Harris, a retired business man of Louisville, was born in California. William J. received his education in the Louisville public schools, graduating from the high school in 1887. Upon completing his education he entered the office of one of the leading architects, where he was employed for six years. During that period he had ample opportunity to become thoroughly acquainted with all lines of architectural work. He improved his chances, and at the end of his apprenticeship, if such it might be called, he possessed a technical knowledge of architecture that few men excel. For several years he traveled over the country, working in the offices of prominent architects in different cities, going across the continent in his travels, and in 1895 located in Evansville, where he opened an office of his own. Two years later he formed the partnership with Clifford Shopbell, which is still in existence. (See sketch of Mr. Shopbell.) Many of the finest churches in the state have been built according to designs furnished by this firm. Nine Carnegie library buildings have been erected under their supervision, that at Shelbyville, Ind., being regarded by many as being the finest in the state, if not in the United States. Both members of this firm are practical men, both are thoroughly in love with their profession, and consequently keep themselves fully informed as to new methods of construction, etc., which marks them as being progressive and competent architects. Mr. Harris is a member of the Masonic fraternity, the Knights of Pythias, and the Benevolent and Protective Order of Elks. He was married in 1894 to Miss Bell Hawley, of Louisville.

CLIFFORD SHOPBELL, junior member of the firm of Harris & Shopbell, architects, Evansville, Ind., was born at Princeton, in that state, Dec. 8, 1871. His father, George W. Shopbell, was born in the city of Fort Wayne, and followed the business of contractor and builder, so that the son from his childhood has been surrounded by an atmosphere of architecture. After graduating from the Princeton high school, in the class of 1889, Clifford went to Indianapolis, where he was for five years in the office of W. Scott Moore, one of the leading architects of that city, and one year with the Big Four railroad company. In 1894 he returned to Evansville and became associated with C. A. Brehmer in architectural work. This association continued until 1897, when the firm of Harris & Shopbell was formed. From the start they have given their attention to the designing and erection of public buildings, and numerous churches, school and court houses have been built according to their plans and under their supervision. Their business extends over a large scope of territory, and, considering the length of time that the partnership has been in existence, few firms in the Middle West are better or more favorably known. In recent years Harris & Shopbell have made a specialty of the Carnegie library buildings, nine of which have been designed by them, viz.: Shelbyville, Greensburg, Franklin, Seymour, Salem, Princeton, Mt. Vernon and Poseyville, Ind., and Henderson, Ky. Mr. Shopbell is a thirty-second degree Mason and a Noble of the Mystic Shrine, and is a prominent member of the Knights of Pythias. He belongs to the Crescent and Country clubs, and to the Evansville Business Men's association. He was married in 1897 to Miss Winifred Dunlap, of Indianapolis.

BYRON PARSONS, the subject of this sketch, was born in Rodman, Jefferson county, N. Y., Dec. 15, 1835, and is of Scotch-English descent. Just when the traditional three Parsons brothers came to New England is not known, but a deed now in his possession, bearing date of Oct. 30, 1718, clearly proves that his ancestors were early settlers there. This deed is signed by Samuel Parsons, and conveys land located upon the east bank of the Connecticut river, in Hampshire county, to his son Samuel Parsons, Jr. This ancient document had been handed down to him through the oldest sons of succeeding generations. His father Elam Parsons, was born in Connecticut in 1809, and moved with his father, Samuel Parsons, to Jefferson county, N. Y., about the end of the first quarter of the nineteenth century. His mother was the daughter of Capt. Samuel McNitt, who served this country in the war of 1812, and distinguished himself in the battle of Sackett's Harbor in May, 1813. Byron Parsons was the only son born to Elam Parsons by the first wife. Soon after his birth his father moved to Ellisburg, Jefferson county, N. Y., where he grew to manhood. His early life was spent on a farm, and his education was obtained in the country schools and Belleville Union academy. In the spring of 1856, and prior to his twenty-first birthday, he caught the Kansas fever, and left the paternal roof to seek his fortune in the Far West. At this time the Kansas-Nebraska act, which had become a law in 1854, began to bear fruit, and Kansas became the battle ground for the settlement of the great slave question. Settlers in great numbers were pouring into the territory from both north and south; those from the north for the purpose of organizing a free state, and those from the south for the purpose of organizing a slave state. About this time Rev. Henry Ward Beecher, from his pulpit in Brooklyn, N. Y., declared that settlers to Kansas should go armed with a Bible and a Colt's revolver. Mr. Parsons took his advice. He journeyed by rail to St. Louis, and from thence to Wyandotte by river, on a steamboat loaded to the guards with emigrants and supplies destined for the "New Eldorado." The staterooms did not hold half of the passengers, and Mr. Parsons was obliged to sleep on a cot in the cabin with many others, who were no more fortunate than himself. On landing at Wyandotte he put up at the Free State hotel. He soon learned that the feeling between the pro-slavery and anti-slavery factions was already at fever heat. Late in the day he was advised that he had better seek lodgings elsewhere, as the pro-slavery mob from the other side of the river, that two days before had gone to Lawrence to pillage and burn that town, were expected back that night, and the hotel would probably be destroyed, as it was owned by a free state man. The mob returned as expected, armed with all sorts of firearms and bearing banners with various pro-slavery mottoes, but they did not molest anything. They went on board a ferry-boat, and with three cheers for Lawrence, pulled out into the stream and left for their homes in Missouri, on the other side of the river. On the following day, he joined a party of ten in the purchase of two ox teams and a "prairie schooner" with which to transport baggage and supplies. With these they set out for the uninhabited prairies of Southeast Kansas, which were fast being settled. At Ossawatomie a halt was made and a quarter section of land pre-empted. He at once went to work, cutting down trees with which to build a house, in order to hold his claim, but had scarcely more than got the logs up, before rumors were current that a Missouri mob might be expected at any time. A vigilance committee was organized and Mr. Parsons was called upon to do his first duty in defense of right and free institutions, under the direction of Capt. John Brown, later of Harper's Ferry notoriety. The mob came as expected, and Capt. Brown, with his unorganized force, did what he could in defense of the town and postoffice, just established, but was overwhelmed by superior numbers, the town taken and pillaged and the postoffice robbed. Captain Brown lost one son, killed in the fight, and several others of his unorganized force were wounded. From that time on he was known as Ossawatomie Brown. At this time Mr. Parsons was sick at the home of a Quaker, two miles away but distinctly remembers hearing the fusilade, which lasted for about half an hour. Letters for him were found opened in the streets of the town after the mob had finished their pillage and left. Owing to continued illness he returned to his father's home in Jefferson county, N. Y., in the winter of 1856-57. In the spring of 1857 he accepted a position as clerk in a general merchandise store in Ellisburg, at a salary of $75.00 per year, and was so employed until the early fall of 1859, when he accepted a position as traveling salesman for a wholesale boot and shoe house in New York City. The firm failed in the early part of 1860, and he accepted a similar position with Lewis Brothers of Utica, where he remained until October, 1861, when he returned to his native town, in Jefferson county, to assist in raising a company of volunteers for the 94th regiment, then being organized at Sackett's Harbor, N. Y. He enlisted as a private October 16th, and on the organization of Company C, was elected second lieutenant and mustered into the United States service Feb. 14, 1862. On March 15, the regiment was ordered to Washington, and was immediately assigned to duty as provost guard at Alexandria, Va. It did duty there during the embarkation of McClellan's army for Fortress Monroe but soon after joined McDowell's army on the Rappahannock, opposite Fredericksburg. It was with McDowell's corps in its fruitless march to the Shenandoah Valley, after Stonewall Jackson, from May 25th, to June 18th. The regiment was first under fire at Cedar Mountain, August 9th, and almost daily thereafter until the great battle of Bull Run, in which it participated August 30th. First Lieutenant B. D. Searles, then commanding the company, was wounded in that engagement and the command devolved upon Lieutenant Parsons. He remained in command until Lieutenant Searles' return about October 1st. He participated with his command in the battles of Chantilly on September 1st; South Mountain September 14th, and Antietam September 17th, where he was promoted to first lieutenant and was with his command during the march of the army down through northern Virginia, taking part in the battle of Fredericksburg, December 13th. He was promoted to captain Jan. 6, 1863; participated in Burnside's "mud march" January 20th, to 24th; in Hooker's Chancellorsville campaign April 27th, to May 6th; also in the Pennsylvania campaign, and was wounded in the first day's battle of Gettysburg. He was granted leave of absence for thirty days and at its expiration was detailed on special duty at Elmira, N. Y., and subsequently at Riker's Island, New York harbor, until November 25th, when he was detailed on general court-martial which convened at Fort Hamilton and adjourned to New York City. He served on that court until Jan. 16, 1864. On January 22d, he was detailed as second in command of a cargo of conscripts to Fortress Monroe and Alexandria, Va., and subsequently went with another cargo in the same capacity. He rejoined his command then doing duty at Camp Parole near Annapolis, Md., February 12th and on the 19th of May left with it to join the army of the Potomac, then fighting the battles of the Wilderness under Grant. His command reached the front on the line of the Tolopotomy May 30th, and was assigned to the first brigade, second division fifth army corps. Thus organized, his command participated in the general movement towards Petersburg, and was hotly engaged in the swamps of Chickahominy on the 13th, holding the enemy in check while the main army was crossing to the James river. He reached the front before Petersburg on the 17th, and participated in the advance and final unsuccessful assault upon the enemy's works on the 18th. He was continually with his command during the investment of that city; participated in the movement for the possession of the Petersburg and Weldon railroad that began August 18th, and was taken prisoner in the battle that gave the Federals permanent possession on the afternoon of the 19th. He was a prisoner of war at Belle Isle, Libby, Salisbury, N. C., and Danville, Va.; was paroled from Libby prison Feb. 22, 1865, and was discharged on application by reason of expiration of term of service, March 10th. He was then appointed major, rejoined his command April 13th, and served in the field until mustered out with his regiment July 18th. While in Libby prison he formed the acquaintance of Capt. Jesse Armstrong of Evansville, Ind., who became one of his messmates in that noted hostelry. Captain Armstrong was enthusiastic in his praise of Evansville, and the acquaintance thus begun resulted at the close of the war in a correspondence with Coolidge Bros., who were formerly of Watertown, Jefferson county, N. Y., but at this time the leading dry goods men of Evansville. Thus it was that Major Parsons together with Capt. C. E. Scoville and Col. S. A. Moffett were persuaded to come to Evansville. These three young men had been comrades in arms and officers in the same regiment for nearly four years. This close relationship resulted in a mutual understanding that when the war was over they would enter into business together. So after being mustered out of service, they came to Evansville, arriving here in the latter part of August, 1865. October 12th, they bought out William Riley, then doing a retail grocery and feed business at 124 Main street and commenced business under the firm name of Parsons, Scoville & Moffett. Since then Major Parsons' life has been an open book to the people of Evansville, except for the most part of the time from the summer of 1885 to the spring of 1893, while engaged in developing a salt industry in Texas. Major Parsons was the pioneer in the salt business in that state and in company with Mr. Frederick R. Blount succeeded in building up a large and lucrative salt industry, which was incorporated, in 1889, under the name of the Lone Star Salt Company, and Major Parsons was made its president. This corporation is now one of the large industrial enterprises of that great state. The firm of Parsons Scoville & Moffett took front rank in the retail grocery business of that city from the beginning. In the spring of 1871, Parsons & Scoville bought Colonel Moffett's interest in the business and he moved to Chicago. The new firm of Parsons & Scoville gradually merged the wholesale business into their extensive retail trade until their warehouse, No. 127 Main street, was inadequate to their growing business. They, therefore, July 17, 1881, sold a one-half interest in their retail business to Mr. Ezra Lyon and established the wholesale grocery house, corner of Second and Sycamore streets. July 1, 1882, they sold their other one-half interest in the Main street business to David Bros., and since then have conducted an exclusive wholesale grocery business. In July, 1894, they incorporated under the name of Parsons & Scoville Company. Captain Scoville died in January, 1902, thus terminating a most harmonious business association of more than thirty-six years. At the time of his death it was believed that he and Major Parsons were the oldest associated business co-partners in the city of Evansville. Major Parsons has been the president of the Parsons & Scoville Company since Captain Scoville's death. The concern ranks today among the foremost jobbing grocery houses of the Ohio Valley. In politics he has always been a stanch Republican. He has been frequently asked to accept office at the hands of his party, but has steadfastly declined all political honors. Major Parsons is a man of progressive ideas, a clear thinker, a thorough business man, well read, active in all worthy enterprises for the good of the city and the well being of his fellow citizens. He is a man of high moral principles and for many years has been a member of Walnut street Presbyterian church. He is a comrade of Farragut Post No. 27, Grand Army of the Republic; also a companion of the Indiana commandery of the Military Order of the Loyal Legion of the United States. His wife, Oella Howard, was born in Ellisburg, N. Y., Jan. 13, 1841. Her father, Daniel Howard, was born in Connecticut June 16, 1796. He removed to Ellisburg, N. Y., when a small boy and at the early age of sixteen was a minute man under the command of Capt. Gad. Ackley, in the war of 1812. Her mother was Phebe Winters, who comes of Revolutionary stock, thus making her eligible to membership in the Daughters of the American Revolution. But one child was born to Major and Mrs. Parsons, and it died in infancy.

JAMES D. SAUNDERS, a well-known civil engineer and surveyor of Evansville, Ind., is a native of that state, having been born at Bloomington, Dec. 4, 1853. His immediate ancestors on both sides were civil engineers. His father, whose name was also James D., was born at Manchester, England, in 1829, and was the son of a civil engineer. He learned the business with his father and in 1850 married Mary Sweeney, a native of County Donegal, Ireland, and emigrated to America. Her father was a civil engineer and was employed on the ordinance survey of Ireland. When James D. Saunders, the father, and his young wife came to this country they located at Bloomington, Ind., where he was employed as one of the engineers in the construction of what was then known as the New Albany & Salem railroad (now the Monon). In 1854 he came to Evansville as the engineer of the Evansville, Indianapolis & Cleveland railroad, generally referred to as the "Straight line." The next year he was elected surveyor of Vanderburg county, and in 1857 was made city engineer and surveyor. From that time until 1861 he held both positions, but resigned at that time to become a member of Company D, Forty-second Indiana infantry. He was afterward promoted to captain and served with that rank until 1862, when he resigned and returned to Evansville. Soon after his return he was again elected city engineer, and held either that position or county surveyor until his death, which occurred on June 6, 1880. His three sons, Miles S., George W. and James D., all became civil engineers. James D., the subject of this sketch, received a common school education, after which he studied his profession under his father's instruction, and became a skillful and proficient surveyor and engineer. In 1872 and again in 1876 he was elected county surveyor, but resigned in 1880 to accept the place of city engineer, which had been made vacant by his father's death. He was re-elected to the place at each succeeding annual election until 1887, when he was defeated by a majority of 200, though the rest of his ticket was defeated by about 1,400. For many years Mr. Saunders has been actively identified with the Democratic party in political contests. His ability as an organizer has been frequently called into play in such cases, and in 1904 he was the choice of the party for the position of chairman of the county central committee. Mr. Saunders is a member of several fraternal organizations. He was married in 1886 to Miss Lizzie McQuigg, of Ironton, O.

MAJ. HAMILTON ALLEN MATTISON, a prominent attorney of Evansville, Ind., and ex-judge of the circuit court of Vanderburg county, was born at South Berlin, Rensselaer county, N. Y., Sept. 23, 1832, his parents being Allen J. and Lucy (Thomas) Mattison. Major Mattison's grandfather, Allen Mattison, was a Rhode Island Quaker. In 1775 he joined the American army under Gen. Nathaniel Greene, fought at the battle of Bunker Hill, and at various other places during the war for Independence. After the Revolution he removed his family to South Berlin and lived there until his death in 1854. Major Mattison was reared on his father's farm, receiving his early education in the district schools. At the age of nineteen years he entered the New York conference seminary at Charlottesville. While completing his education in this institution he earned enough as assistant teacher to pay for his tuition and living expenses. After a thorough preparation in the seminary he entered Union college, while Dr. Eliphalet Nott was president, and graduated from that institution in 1860. For the next two years he was the principal of the Bacon seminary at Woodtown, N. J. In July, 1862, he gave up the school room for the tented field by enlisting in the Union army. In this action he was only true to his inheritance, nobly defending the institutions his grandfather had fought to establish. He was empowered to raise a company, which was afterward mustered in as part of the Twelfth New Jersey infantry, with him as second lieutenant. His natural talent for military affairs, and his strict adherence to duty, led to his rapid promotion through the rank of first lieutenant and captain to that of major. He served on the staff of Generals Alexander Hayes and Nelson A. Miles and was in twenty-five of the greatest battles of the war. At Chancellorsville he was wounded three times; in the battle of the Wilderness he had his horse shot from under him, was twice wounded and captured. Soon after his capture he was introduced to Gen. Robert E. Lee on the field, and has a distinct recollection of his conversation with the famous Confederate commander. He was taken first to Lynchburg, then to Macon, Ga., where he was confined until the following July "on short rations." He was then taken to Savannah, and was one of the fifty officers sent from that city to Charleston and placed under the fire of the Federal guns that were shelling the city from Folly Island. Some weeks later he was confined, with other prisoners, in an open pen at Columbia, S. C., where, with scant food, no shelter, and ragged clothing, he was kept until November 28th, when he and another prisoner, Rev. John Scamahorn, managed to make their escape. Notwithstanding they were half starved and half naked they took to the woods, determined to intercept Sherman's army, then on its way to the sea. Traveling by night and concealing themselves by day, they succeeded in crossing the State of South Carolina and reached the Savannah river. There they procured a small boat, succeeded in eluding the Confederate guards and gunboats, and finally reached Savannah, which had in the meantime surrendered to Sherman. Thus, after tramping nearly fifteen hundred miles through the enemy's country, they found themselves once more under the protection of the old flag. Major Mattison was sent home to recuperate, and ordered to report to the army of the Potomac as soon as he was able for duty. Accordingly he joined that army about March 1, 1865, and was engaged in all the military operations about Richmond until the final surrender. Shortly after he was mustered out he entered the Albany law school and graduated in 1866 with the degree of Bachelor of Laws. He began practice in partnership with Hon. Marinus Fairchild at Salem, N. Y., but in February, 1868, came to Evansville, where he has ever since made his home. In the campaign of that year he took an active part, advocating the election of General Grant. In 1870 he was appointed county attorney. The following year a vacancy occurred in the office of prosecuting attorney in the Vanderburg county criminal court and he was appointed by Governor Baker to fill out the unexpired term. At the election in the fall of 1872 he was elected by the people to the same office for a full term of two years. Not long after the expiration of this term he was appointed register in bankruptcy by Chief Justice Waite of the United States supreme court, and held this position until the office was abolished by an act of Congress. In 1887 he was appointed city attorney of Evansville, and reappointed the following year. He retired from the office, however, before the expiration of his term, to become a member of the law firm of Mattison, Posey & Clark, later Mattison, Posey & Chappell. In 1896 he was elected judge of the Vanderburg circuit court for a term of six years, being the first Republican ever elected to that office. Upon retiring from the bench he again resumed the practice of his profession, and since February, 1903, has been the senior member of the firm of Mattison & Curry, with offices at 125 Upper Fourth street. Judge Mattison joined the Masonic fraternity at Troy, N. Y., in 1862. After coming to Evansville he transferred his membership to Reed Lodge, No. 316, and also acquired membership in the higher Masonic bodies of the city. He is a Past Master of Reed Lodge; Past High Priest of Evansville Chapter, No. 12, Royal Arch Masons; Past Illustrious Master of Simpson Council; and Past Eminent Commander of La Valette Commandery, No. 15, Knights Templars. Not long after coming to Evansville he became a member of Trinity Methodist Episcopal church, and has taken an active interest in church and Sunday school work. In 1866 he was married to the daughter of Hon. Marinus Fairchild, his first law partner, and one daughter was born to the union. The wife died in 1873, and the daughter in 1892, aged twenty years. On Feb. 7, 1878, Judge Mattison was married to Miss Henrietta M. Bennett, of Evansville, formerly of Brooklyn, N. Y. Although past the age of threescore and ten years, he is still one of the active attorneys at the Evansville bar, with an honorable record both as a private counselor and a public official.

ALBERT J. OTT, president of the Crescent Handle Works, of Evansville, Ind., was born at Tell City, Perry county, in that state, in the year 1870. His father, Conrad Ott, was for many years engaged in the planing mill business in Tell City, and died there in 1875. The son was reared in his native town and there received his primary education. At the age of seventeen years he entered the business department of the Central Normal college, Danville, Ind., and graduated the following year. He then went to Indianapolis, where for the next thirteen years he was in the employ of the Vonnegut Hardware Company, one of the largest concerns of the kind in the state, in various responsible positions. While with the hardware company he learned the possibilities of the handle trade, and in 1901 established a factory at Washington, Ind. The business was soon removed to Evansville, where it has become one of the substantial manufacturing concerns of the city. The product embraces all sorts of handles for farming tools, shovels, etc., and elm hub blocks for wheels, the principal purchasers being the jobbing trade, tool and wheel manufacturers. The establishment has been "running on orders" almost ever since its organization four years ago. Since coming to Evansville he has identified himself with the progressive element of the city, and is a member of both the Manufacturers' and Business Men's associations. He is also a member of the Walnut Street Presbyterian church, and vice-president of the Men's club of the church. In 1891 Mr. Ott was united in marriage to Miss Anna L. Marsh, of Danville. She died in June, 1896, and subsequently he was married to her sister, Miss Victoria Marsh.

GEORGE W. VARNER, M.D., one of the most popular and successful physicians and surgeons of Evansville, Ind., was born on a farm in Spencer county of that state, in the year 1862. After the acquisition of such an education as the common schools afforded he graduated from the National Normal university at Lebanon, O., and took up the profession of teacher. While engaged in teaching he devoted his leisure hours to the study of medicine, and in 1886 graduated from the Kentucky School of Medicine at Louisville with the highest honors of his class for general proficiency in his work. He also received the highest honors for the best work in anatomy, and was awarded two gold medals in token of these honors. He was also the recipient of the appointment as interne or house physician at the Louisville city hospital for one year, an honor much desired by the students because of the experience to be obtained. At the close of his year in this position he was appointed interne in the New York

Hospital for the Relief of Ruptured and Crippled Children, where he served for one year, gathering a fund of useful knowledge from his experience there. In 1888 he took a post-graduate course in the New York Polyclinic school. Again in 1895 he took post-graduate courses in New York and Vienna and in the latter place took special courses in surgery and gynecology. This course has marked him as one of the most progressive physicians of the day, and has been an important factor in building up his magnificent practice. Doctor Varner located at Evansville in 1888, where he began the practice of his profession, establishing his office on the West Side, in which locality he has ever since remained, though his patients are to be found in all parts of the city. In the fifteen years that have elapsed since that time he has steadily grown in his profession until he is regarded as one of the most eminent physicians of Evansville, if not of Southern Indiana. Certain it is he is one of the busiest, his professional skill and services being called into demand almost night and day. In addition to his private practice he is surgeon to St. Mary's hospital; visiting physician and surgeon to the Vanderburg county orphan home; medical examiner for the Royal Arcanum, the Ancient Order of United Workmen, Knights of Honor, Woodmen of the World, Degree of Honor, and several of the old line life insurance companies. Doctor Varner is a member of the American and Indiana State Medical associations, the medical society of Vanderburg county, and has one of the most extensive libraries both literary and medical in Evansville. Outside of his profession, Doctor Varner is one of the progressive men of Evansville. He has taken an active part in municipal and county affairs and is one of the most influential citizens of the West Side. When the West Side bank was organized he was one of its most enthusiastic advocates, and has been vice president of the institution ever since it opened its doors for the transaction of business. As he is just in the prime of life, with studious habits and a laudable desire to excel in his profession, it is almost certain that his professional reputation will be greater in the years to come. The winning of honors, however, has never turned his head nor made him vain of his powers. His genial disposition and his natural sympathetic nature have been potent elements in building up his present lucrative business, and to his friends and patients he is always the same. Consequently his patrons have learned to love and trust him, and his brother practitioners have the highest regard, both for his personality and professional standing.

CHARLES J. THUMAN, superintendent of the city water works, Evansville, Ind., was born in that city in 1861. He received his education in the public schools, and has passed his whole life in his native city. When he was sixteen years of age he went into the Mechanics' foundry, in which his father was one of the partners, and there learned the art of fashioning iron. From the foundry he went into the machine shop and learned the trade of machinist, becoming a skillful mechanic. He next went into the Bernardin bottle cap works and took charge of the mechanical department, remaining with the concern for eleven years. When Mayor Covert came into office he appointed Mr. Thuman to the position of water works superintendent, which he has filled with signal ability ever since. The water works plant in Evansville is the property of the city. At the time Mr. Thuman took charge of it the equipment was new, and under his control nothing about the place has been allowed to go to decay for want of proper care. The polished portions of the machinery are always kept bright, the floors are always clean, driveways bordered with flowers encircle the building, an artificial lake, stocked with goldfish, all contribute to the comfort of the employes and add to the attractiveness of the place. Speaking of this recently Mr. Thuman said: "I enjoy these pretty things. They do not cost much, entail very little labor to maintain; an order tomorrow to do away with them would meet with a protest, loud and strong, from the men who work with me. These clean rooms, pretty driveways, flowers, fish and the like have a most refining influence on the men. They like to work among them, and the people like to come out here to be with us and enjoy our surroundings." The works stand upon an elevation, from which a fine view of the beautiful Ohio river and the surrounding country can be obtained, and many people visit the place for that purpose. The water works plant of Evansville is one of the model institutions of its kind in the country. The men who operate it are paid good wages and take a pride in their work. Under the efficient superintendence of Mr. Thuman it has been brought as near to a state of perfection as possible, and the revenue derived by the city from it annually amounts to about forty thousand dollars. Mr. Thuman has recently built a new home on the site of the old John H. Roelker homestead on Mary street. Into this home he has carried his artistic inclinations, and few homes in the city are more cozy or attractive. In politics Mr. Thuman is a Republican but in his official capacity he realizes that he is a servant of the whole population of the city. He is a member of the Knights of Honor, the Benevolent and Protective Order of Elks, and the Buffaloes, in all of which he enjoys a well deserved popularity, because of his genial disposition.

SAMUEL W. LITTLE, treasurer and general manager of the Little Coal & Coke Company, Evansville, Ind., was born in the State of South Carolina, May 17, 1832. When he was about three years of age his parents removed to Indiana and settled on a farm in Monroe county. There the subject of this sketch grew to manhood and engaged in farming until 1853, when he went to Iowa. After three years in that state he returned to Indiana and located at Evansville, where he was employed in the old Canal Flour Mills until the commencement of the war. He enlisted in the Union army as a sailor in the Mississippi flotilla, but after his return to Evansville began the manufacture of staves and shingles and in operating a cooper shop. He succeeded well in this line of business and in 1871 engaged in the lumber business, with which he was actively identified for a number of years. He was the first to introduce the band-saw for manufacturing lumber, and continued in the lumber business until August 1888, when his mill was destroyed by fire. In the fall of that same year he opened a coal mine on a piece of land in Pike county, Ind., which he had bought for the timber. After running the coal business alone for several years, the S. W. Little Coal Company was organized, of which Mr. Little is principal owner and general manager. This company has a large acreage of coal lands, a large stock farm and is also engaged in mercantile business. For several years Mr. Little has been in his present position, the company with which he is connected being one of the largest dealers in coal and coke in the city of Evansville. He is one of the most public-spirited men in the city and is always ready to join in any movement for promoting the industrial and commercial interests of Evansville, or for improving the social and moral conditions of the people. He was married in 1870 to Miss Mary E. Macer, daughter of Thomas Macer, of Evansville, and they have two sons, Charles S. and Harry W., both of whom are graduates of Wabash college of Crawfordsville, and Johns Hopkins Medical school at Baltimore. The elder is practicing his profession in Indianapolis and the younger is at present in business with his father. Mr. Little and his family are members of the Presbyterian church.

EDWIN C. HENNING, a brilliant and successful lawyer of Evansville, Ind., is a native Indianian, having been born at Cannelton, Perry county, Jan. 20, 1873. He is a son of Judge William Henning, who in his day was one of the best attorneys in Southern Indiana. Edwin C. Henning received his early education in the public schools of his native city, reading law in the office of his father as oppor tunity offered. After graduating from the high school he entered the University of Michigan, and was graduated from that institution in both law and literature in June, 1894. He immediately began the practice of his profession in Cannelton, and was soon honored by an election to the office of prosecuting attorney of the second judicial circuit, embracing the counties of Perry, Spencer and Warrick. While serving in this office he made a splendid reputation as a capable and painstaking official, and won marked distinction by his successful prosecutions of offenders against the law. On March 1, 1900, he opened an office at 321 Upper Third street, Evansville, where he is still engaged in practice. Mr. Henning makes a specialty of insur ance and corporation practice, though he attends to all lines of legal business and has a large and constantly growing clientage. As a criminal lawyer he won a wide reputation by his defense of Wilbur Sherwell , charged with the murder of three women, and by his asso ciation with the defense in the trial of Caleb Powers, charged with complicity in the killing of Gov. William Goebel, of Kentucky. As a counselor Mr. Henning is considered one of the safest in the city, for the reason that he never hazards an opinion offhand, unless he is absolutely certain he is right. As an advocate few men of his age and experience can claim to be his equals. He is a polished and eloquent speaker, but at the same time his oratory is forceful and earnest, and rarely fails to impress a jury. Industrious, studious, and filled with a laudable ambition to excel in his profession, the future doubt less holds greater honors in store for him.

CAPT. CHARLES H. MYERHOFF, secretary and treasurer of the Evansville Stove Works, Evansville, Ind., was born in the city of Cincinnati, O., March 10, 1842. When he was about six years old his mother died and from that time until he was fourteen he lived with an uncle and a lawyer named Cummings in Jackson county, Ind. In 1856 he went to live with his father, who had married again in the meantime , but two years later the father also died and young Myerhoff found em ployment with a gardener near Newport, Ky. He worked there but a short time, however, when he went to live with a sister at Grand View, Ind., where he worked on a farm until 1859. In that year he made a trip to Vicksburg, Miss., and being fond of adventure soon afterward started out with three com panions in a sailboat to see the world and to find employment at such occupations as presented themselves . This experiment soon taught him the truth of the old saying, " A rolling stone gathers no moss, " for after several hardships he returned to Evansville with all his worldly possessions tied up in a bandanna. At that time his brother, John H., was foreman for the Armstrong Furniture Company, and here he found employment until the commencement of the great Civil war. Not long after the commencement of hostilities he attended a meeting in the old Crescent City hall , when the first two companies of home guards were organized. He enrolled his name as a member of General Blythe's company, but when the announcement was made that Dr. Noah S. Thompson had been commiss oned to organize a company of volunteers to go to Washington, D.C., in defense of the national capital he arose, withdrew his name from the muster roll of the home guards, and a few minutes later presented himself to Dr. Thompson and requested that his name be enrolled as one of the volunteers. At first his request was denied, because of his youth and delicate physique, but he persisted and upon examination was found so familiar with military tactics that the objections were withdrawn and he was the first man accepted in the first company that left Evansville for the war. While the company was being drilled in Klausman's hall he was detailed to guard the front entrance, and there his general bearing and strict adherence to orders made a deep impres sion, both on the boys of the city, who were thus denied the privilege of seeing the soldiers drill, and his superior officers. The company was mustered into the service as Company E, Fourteenth Indiana infantry, and Captain Myerhoff has the distinction of being the first man to enlist in the first company that left the city. He participated in all the battles in which his regiment was engaged, except what time he was in prison or on duty as a recruiting officer; was appointed corporal; promoted to sergeant at Cheat Mountain; to orderly sergeant, on Oct. 1, 1862; and to first lieutenant on May 7, 1863. About this time he was sent back to Evansville on recruiting service, but was in command of the company in the famous charge of Carroll's brigade, on East Cemetery hill at Gettysburg. Subsequently he was in command of Company H at the battles of the Wilderness, Spottsylvania, North Anna River and Cold Harbor, where he was severely wounded in a lunette, between the lines. Some idea of the fighting in which his command took part may be obtained when it is known that of the twenty-three men of his company with whom he started on May 4, only two were left on duty when the regiment's term of service expired on June 7, 1864. Captain Myerhoff was at that time in the hospital on account of the wounds received at Cold Harbor. While in the hospital he brought about some much needed reforms and won the thanks of the patients. When he was discharged he came to Evansville and was for a short time interested in a sawmill in Spencer county, but not yet having fully recovered from the effects of his wounds he gave it up and re-entered the service in the employ of Philip Decker, the sutler of the Tenth Tennessee infantry, at Nashville. On his way to Nashville to accept this position he was arrested three times, but was soon released each time. Soon after joining the regiment it moved to Knoxville and then to Greenville, where Captain Myerhoff slept for several months upon the tailor's table formerly used by Andrew Johnson. When the war closed he again returned to Evansville, took a course in bookkeeping in Behm's Commercial college, and entered the employ of Keller & White as bookkeeper. About a year later he went to the well known hardware firm of Boetticher, Kellogg & Co., in the same capacity, and remained with this house for nearly twenty-one years. While with them he was secretary of the Evansville Union Stock Yards. In 1888 he became interested in the Evansville Stove Works as secretary and treasurer, and has been treasurer of the associated charities of the city since organization. As a drill master Captain Myerhoff has few equals, and it was in this connection that his name became widely known. For three successive terms he was captain of the Evansville Light Guards.

During the same period he was also Sir Knight commander of the Orion drill corps, Knights of Pythias, and so thorough was his work with this organization that it won three prizes in competitive drill, and he was awarded a gold medal as the best commander at St. Louis in August, 1880. In political campaigns his companies, such as the "Red Shirts" and "Zouaves," always attracted favorable notice. He has frequently been called upon to act as grand marshal in political and Memorial Day processions, also on Dewey Day and the return of the volunteers from the Spanish-American war. He was on the staff of National Commanders Kountz, Fairchild, Walker and Blackmar, of the Grand Army of the Republic; and also on the staff of several of the commanders of the department of Indiana. Besides being a staff officer he was also a member of the national council of administration, and has frequently been district delegate to national encampments. He was the second commander of Farragut Post, in which he holds his Grand Army membership. Captain Myerhoff was married in 1867 to Miss Jennie, daughter of Alexander Sharra, of Evansville.

CHARLES H. DAVIES, senior member of the firm of Davies & Scarborough, contractors and builders, Evansville, Ind., was born in the city of Chester, England, in 1861. He is a son of Thomas and Sarah (Fellows) Davies, both natives of England, where the Davies family has been for generations one of the highly respected families of Great Britain. Charles H. Davies was reared and educated in his native land. In 1883 he came to the United States, and two years later located in Evansville, where he found ready employment at his trade of bricklayer. After two or three years he formed a partnership with James Scarborough, a fellow-countryman, for the purpose of carrying on a general contracting business. The firm of Davies & Scarborough soon began to make itself felt in the building trades of Evansville, and today no concern of its kind has a higher standing in the city. This is due to the square dealing that has always characterized the individual members of it, and to the prompt manner and skillful workmanship displayed in executing their contracts. Some of the most pretentious buildings in the city have been erected by them and each time a contract is finished the owner of the building becomes an advertisement for the firm. On Dec. 21, 1887, Mr. Davies was united in marriage to Miss Ada, daughter of George Wolf, a native of Germany, but for a number of years a resident of Evansville.

JAMES SCARBOROUGH, of the firm of Davies & Scarborough, contractors and builders, Evansville, Ind., is a native of Huntingdonshire, England. When he was about eleven years of age he came with his parents to America, and after two months in the city of Cleveland, O., the family located in Evansville, where Mr. Scarborough has ever since continued to reside. He received his education in the public schools and for several years after leaving school followed the business of teaming. In 1875 he went into the Evansville fire department as driver of the No. 6 hose wagon, and was afterward captain of the company. In the meantime he learned the trade of bricklayer, and upon leaving the fire department went to work at this occupation. He was elected president of the bricklayers' union, and represented the Evansville union in the national conventions of Washington and Boston. About 1889 he formed a partnership with C. H. Davies and J. Oakley for the purpose of carrying on a general contracting business, and during the last fifteen years a number of the substantial edifices of Evansville have been erected by this firm, which has won a well deserved reputation for honest work and promptness in executing contracts. Mr. Scarborough has been honored with the presidency of the Evansville Builders' and Traders' Exchange, and was for six years a member of the board of public works of the city of Evansville. He is a member of the Independent Order of Odd Fellows and the Benevolent and Protective Order of Elks, and is a deacon in the Calvary Baptist church. He was married in 1877 to Miss Anna R., daughter of Alexander Tiepman, a veteran of the Civil war and an old resident of Evansville. Mrs. Scarborough died in March, 1904, leaving four children: Ella, wife of J. T. Cadick, of Evansville; Charles Silas, associated with his father in business, and a member of the bricklayers' union; May Viola, and Artie James.

WILLIAM G. RALSTON, M.D., of Evansville, Ind., is one of the oldest physicians in that section of the state. His grandfather, William Ralston, was a soldier under Washington in the Revolution, and was present at the surrender of Lord Cornwallis at Yorktown. He afterward served with distinction in the war of 1812. His son, Andrew R., father of Dr. Ralston, also served in the American army during that war, enlisting when he was but eighteen years of age. In 1818 Andrew R. Ralston was married to Miss Patsy, daughter of Maj. Joseph Neely, of Kentucky. Her father was a major in one of the Continental regiments during the Revolutionary war, and was also present at the siege and surrender of Yorktown. Soon after their marriage Andrew and Patsy Ralston settled at Princeton, Gibson county, Ind., and there Dr. Ralston was born in February, 1819. His early life was spent upon his father's farm, assisting in the farm work in the summer time and attending the imperfect district schools in the old log school house during the winter months. In this way he received his elementary education, and in 1840 taught school for one term. In 1841 he went to Posey county and took up the study of medicine under the instruction of Dr. Joseph Neely, one of the popular physicians of that period. Here he studied for four years, at the end of which time he located at Boonville, Warrick county, and there practiced his profession until 1863. He then attended a course of lectures in the Ohio Medical college at Cincinnati, and subsequently graduated from the medical college of Evansville. At the beginning of the Civil war Dr. Ralston was appointed surgeon of the Eighty-first Indiana infantry by Governor Morton, and served about a year with his regiment in the army of the Cumberland. He was then appointed by the secretary of war to the position of surgeon to the board of enrollment of the First congressional district of Indiana, and in that capacity examined something like ten thousand volunteers, conscripts and substitutes. He remained in this position until April 14, 1865, when he located at Evansville and resumed private practice. For four years he was surgeon of the United States Marine hospital at Evansville, and he has been for a number of years one of the board of pension examiners. Dr. Ralston, although more than fourscore years of age, is a man of remarkable energy. While engaged in the active practice of medicine he has found time to devote to scientific research, and is the inventor of the Ralston bed-warmer, a device for producing the comforts of a warm bed at nominal cost. As a sick room appliance and sanitary help it is one of the most important of the simple inventions of recent years. For more than sixty years Dr. Ralston has been an active and helpful member of the Cumberland Presbyterian church, and he is one of the veteran members of Crescent Lodge, No. 22, Independent Order of Odd Fellows. In 1850 he was united in marriage to Miss Isabelle, daughter of R. C. Matthewson, and after thirty-two years of happy wedded life she joined the silent majority in 1882.

SAMUEL G. RICKWOOD, of the firm of Lannert & Rickwood, general contractors in stone work, Evansville, Ind., also president of the Evansville Builders' Exchange and secretary of the Manufacturers' Association, is a native of England. When he was about nine months old his parents came to America and settled in Evansville, where both died when he was about two years old. Samuel grew to manhood and received his education in the public schools. Upon leaving school in the fifteenth year of his age he went into the monumental works of Stahlhefer & Nightingale, and there served an apprenticeship, continuing with this firm five years. He was then for three years with H. H. Uhlhorn in the same line of work. In 1882 he formed a partnership with Adam Lannert for the manufacture of all kinds of building stone work, plain and ornamental. That partnership has continued ever since, and the firm is one of the best known in the entire Lower Ohio Valley, as their business extends into several states. Their success is due to their fair dealing and skilful workmanship, and their best advertisement is the recommendation of those for whom they have done work. Mr. Rickwood is a member of the Court of Honor, and the Tribe of Ben Hur, also a member of the Park Memorial Presbyterian church, of which he is treasurer and one of the board of elders. He is also superintendent of the Sunday school; is a director in the Young Men's Christian Association, and one of the trustees of the Deaconess' hospital. Mr. Rickwood was married in 1880 to Miss Louise Alt, daughter of John

Alt, an old resident of Evansville, and they have four children living, as follows: Mabel, wife of W. E. Miller, of Pike county; Ruth, wife of C. H. Hitch, secretary of the Builders' Exchange; Roland, and Lela. Four children died in early childhood.

ANDREW KOCH, a retired citizen of Evansville, Ind., was born in Albig, Germany, in 1841. Two years later his parents, Philip and Margaret Koch, came to America, locating first in Evansville, but removing to Posey county in a short time, where the father followed farming for about four years, returning to Evansville in 1847. There he opened a cooper shop and did a good business for about three years, when his buildings were destroyed by fire. He then turned his attention to the brewing business, established the old Eagle brewery and conducted it until 1858, when he sold out and started a brewery on the West Side, which he ran for several years. Philip Koch died in 1889, leaving five sons: Philip is the trustee of Perry township, Vanderburg county, Ind.; Henry is a successful tinner in Evansville; Andrew is the subject of this sketch; George and William have both died; one daughter, Elizabeth, is now the wife of John Ingle, manager of Rosenberger Park. Andrew Koch acquired a meager education in the common schools, but the greater part of his information has been obtained by self-study, so that it may be said he is a self-educated man. As a boy he worked in the cooper shops and brewery of his father until 1862, when he enlisted in Company D, Ninety-first Indiana infantry, and served until June, 1865, when he was discharged a short time before the expiration of his term of enlistment, because of a wound received in the leg in front of Atlanta. During his term of service he was in the battles of the Atlanta campaign, marching from Chattanooga to Atlanta; was at Franklin, Nashville and Murfreesboro; and in numerous skirmishes in which his regiment took part. He was wounded on June 6. 1865; was mustered out on the 26th of the same month; and received his discharge on July 6. After the war he engaged in the grocery and saloon business at what became known as "Koch's Stand," West Heights, and continued in that occupation until 1881. He then became interested in the sand business and followed that until 1899, since which time he has been on the retired list. Mr. Koch has always taken a deep interest in public affairs, and has been active in political campaigns. From 1868 to 1872 he held the office of justice of the peace. In 1892 he was a candidate on the Republican ticket for the office of county commissioner, but was defeated. At the Republican convention held on April 7, 1904, he was nominated for commissioner for the Third district of Vanderburg county, receiving his nomination on the second ballot. He is one of the charter mem· bers of Farragut Post, No. 27, Grand Army of the Republic, is a member of the Old Soldiers' Republican club, and belongs to St. John's church, with the other members of his family. Mr. Koch was married in September, 1867, to Miss Katharine Klein, and they have the following children: John A., a bricklayer and contractor; Philip, also a bricklayer; Jacob, a bookkeeper; Garfield, a plumber; Elizabeth, wife of John Kronshagen, a bricklayer; Emma, wife of Charles Waterman, a farmer of Vanderburg county; and Helen, a trained nurse in Louisville, Ky.

BEN S. ROSE, M.D., a well known and successful physician, of Evansville, Ind., was born near that city, in Vanderburg county, in the year 1869. He is a grandson of Rev. Benoni Stinson, whose power as a minister and orator will be remembered by all of the older citizens, far and near, and a son of Conrad and Octavia (Stinson) Rose, the father being of the successful agriculturists of Vanderburg county. Dr. Rose obtained his elementary education in the public schools. When he was twenty-two years of age he entered the Ohio Medical college, at Cincinnati, and for two years was a student in that institution, afterward graduating with high honors from the Louisville Medical college in 1894. For eleven years he has practiced his profession with unvarying success in Evansville. That success is due to the fact that he is fully abreast of his profession, keeping well informed as to new methods of treatment, etc., to his untiring industry, and to his sympathetic nature and the ease with which he makes friends and wins the confidence of his patients. He is one of those physicians who understand the true character of the Hippocratic oath, and never turns a deaf ear to the appeals of the afflicted. As a member of the Indiana State

Medical association and the local medical society he enjoys the full confidence and respect of his brother physicians, and occupies an honorable place among them. He is a member of the staff of the Deaconess' hospital, lecturer to the training school for nurses and surgeon for the various liability insurance companies doing business in the city. Dr. Rose is one of the progressive men of the city outside of his profession. He is a member of the Evansville Business Men's association, where he is always to be found advocating those measures that will redound to the material interests of the city. In fraternal circles he belongs to the Benevolent and Protective Order of Elks, and few members of that society enjoy a greater degree of popularity at the lodge and social meetings. Politically he is an unswerving Republican, but seldom takes an active interest in political contests. He was married in 1898 to Miss Helen M. Hewson, and their home is the social center of a large circle of friends.

W. FRANK LITTLE, president of the United Typewriter Company, of Evansville, Ind., is a native of White county, Ill., where his father, G. R. Little, has for many years been one of the well-known and influential citizens. The subject of this sketch was educated in the public schools, graduating from the Carmi, Ill., high school in 1894. Before he had attained his majority he took a position as traveling salesman for the United Typewriter and Supply Company, of New York, working for two years out of the St. Louis office and then one year out of Chicago. He was then for about two years with the Smith Premier Typewriter Company, in charge of their office at Peoria, Ill., after which he came to Evansville, where he was associated for a year with the Remington Typewriter Company. In October, 1901, the present company was incorporated, with a capital stock of $10,000, for the purpose of handling all kinds of typewriters and supplies, and dealing in a general line of office furniture. The officers of the company at the present time are W. Frank Little, president; J. J. Little, secretary and treasurer. The company employs a number of traveling salesmen, who cover a large territory in the states of Indiana, Illinois and Kentucky. Although only a little over three years old, it is one of the substantial business concerns of the city. In addition to his interests in this company Mr. Little is an extensive operator in Evansville real estate. He has the additions of Jackson Park and Maple Grove, besides other desirable city property. He was married in January, 1901, to Miss Edna Damron, of Evansville. In fraternal circles he is well known and popular, being a Knight of Pythias, an Elk and a member of the Royal Arcanum.

LAURENCE B. BITZ, M.D., of Evansville, Ind., is a native of Germany, having been born Dec. 6, 1839, in the village of Weisenheim, a berg in the county of Durkheim, Rhein Province of Bavaria. When he was about seven years of age his father, Simon Bitz, came to America, located in Warrick county, Ind., and there followed farming and shoemaking until his death, which occurred on April 23, 1857. Dr. Bitz grew to manhood in Warrick county, received his education in the public schools there, and followed farming until 1864, when he enlisted in Company G, Forty-fourth Indiana infantry, and served with the regiment in Tennessee and Georgia until mustered out in 1865. During his military service his health was impaired by the hardships of a soldier's life, so that he soon gave up farming after the war and took up the study of medicine. In 1867 he entered the Miami Medical college of Cincinnati, and received the degree of M.D. from that institution in 1869. He first located at Blairsville, in Posey county, and there practiced for twenty-one years, building up a lucrative business. In 1890 he removed to Evansville and located at No. 816 Franklin street, where he has ever since practiced his profession. Dr. Bitz is a member of the State Medical association, the Vanderburg County Medical society, and has belonged to the American Medical association ever since 1878. He belongs to that nationality which has produced so many eminent physicians, and with the true German love for investigation he has never ceased to be a student of those things pertaining to his chosen calling. This has marked him as one of the progressive physicians of his time, and has been instrumental in bringing to him a large degree of success. On July 6, 1871, Dr. Bitz was united in marriage to Miss Mary Marvick, who was born Nov. 15, 1851, in the village of Wertel, Westphalia, Prussia, of Saxon parentage, but was reared in Paducah,

Ky. Of the children born to this union six are living: Frederick C. is in business in Evansville; Laurence B., Jr., is attending school in St. Louis; Minnie R., Julia F., Mary K., and Cornelius Anton are at home.

ELI D. MILLER, president of the Eli D. Miller & Co. furniture factory, of Evansville, Ind., was born in that city, in the year 1866, and is a son of Edward Miller, a native of Illinois. Eli received his education in the schools at Mt. Carmel, Ill., and there commenced at the age of nine years to learn the trade of cabinet maker. From that time until he was twenty-one he worked at this occupation, except what little time he was in school, receiving only his board and clothes for his labor. He profited in another way, however, for he acquired a knowledge of the manufacture of furniture which few men excel. In 1890 he came to Evansville, where he continued to work at his trade until August, 1894, when he opened a retail furniture store at 1500 Main street. He commenced this business without a dollar, but by strict attention to business and square dealing he has built up a fine trade. In April, 1901, upon the incorporation of the United States Furniture Company, Mr. Miller was elected secretary and manager. Some eighteen months later he sold out his interest in the concern and in March, 1903, began the manufacture of furniture in a modest way at 1705 Main street. In May following the business was incorporated with the following officers: Eli D. Miller, president; John Schwan, vice-president; George L. Miller, secretary; S. W. Powell, treasurer. These officers, with the addition of Louis A. Wallenberger, constitute the board of directors. The capital stock was at first fixed at $15,000, but in February, 1904, this was increased to $35,000. Soon after the incorporation the factory at 1705 Main street was erected, as well as the one on Morgan avenue. The latter is a fine modern brick structure, with about 36,000 square feet of floor space. It was built and equipped with all its machinery in ten weeks, establishing a new record for such work. The company makes a specialty of folding beds, and already has a large and constantly growing trade. Mr. Miller still retains his retail business. He is an active Republican, a Knight

Templar Mason, a Knight of Pythias, a Buffalo, a member of the Improved Order of Red Men, the Travelers' Protective association, the Royal Arcanum, the Tribe of Ben Hur, and the Trinity Methodist Episcopal church. In all these societies he is popular because of his many sterling qualities. He was married in 1899 to Miss Kate E., daughter of Frank Weil, a merchant tailor of Evansville.

JOHN A. KOCH, senior member of the firm of Koch & Griesbacher, contractors of all kinds of brickwork, Evansville, Ind., was born in that city in 1868, his parents being Andrew and Katharine (Klein) Koch. (See sketch of Andrew Koch elsewhere in this work.) He was educated in the common schools, and after leaving school served a five years' apprenticeship at the bricklayers' trade with Wilhelm Meier. In 1891 he commenced contracting for himself, the first building he erected being the three-story brick building at the corner of Third avenue and Penn street, now occupied by H. C. Koch & Sons, all the brickwork being done in five weeks. In 1893 he formed his present partnership with George Griesbacher, and since then they have erected many of the largest and most pretentious buildings about the city. Among them may be mentioned the large addition to the Evansville cotton mills; the new wing of the State insane asylum; the Palm Garden building, the second story of which was put up in eighteen hours; the Sunnyside flour mills; the George Misker building; the Vulcan plow works; the Hercules buggy company; the Lincoln cotton mills; the brickwork on the Louisville & Nashville railroad station; the mason work, sewers, etc., of the F. W. Cook brewing company; and a large number of fine residences. In addition to their work in the city several large contracts have been executed elsewhere, notably among them the large school building at Owensville, Gibson county. On the West Side they put up the Jacob Folz business block and Curry's drug store, and they erected nearly all the brick buildings in the suburban town of Howell. Mr. Koch has taken an active part in politics ever since he became a voter, giving freely of his time and money to further the interests of the Republican party. In 1891 he was married to Miss Barbara Dauble, a daughter of Christ Dauble, a well known carpenter of

Evansville. To this marriage there have been born two children, Johnnie and Elfrida. Mr. Koch is a member of the Builders' Exchange and of the German Lutheran church.

CHRIST KANSLER, president of the Mechanics' Planing Mill Company, and one of the leading contractors and builders of Evansville, Ind., was born in Germany in 1850. He received his education in the schools of his native land, and there learned the trade of carpenter. In 1870, when he was but twenty years of age, he came to this country, and soon after his arrival in the United States came to Evansville. There he found ready employment at his trade and worked at it as a journeyman until 1879, when he began contracting for himself on a small scale. The following year he formed a partnership with Jacob Bippus, which association lasted for eleven years. During that time they erected a large number of fine buildings in Evansville and vicinity, acquiring a reputation for honest workmanship of which any builder might be proud. It has been said that when Christ Kansler is the contractor the owner of the building does not need a supervising architect to see that the contract is carried out. No better recommendation of his integrity is needed than this simple statement. Mr. Kansler was married in 1873 to Miss Margaret Sniger, and his eldest son, Gus Kansler, is now associated with him in business, being the secretary and treasurer of the planing mill company, and a young man of fine business qualifications. Mr. Kansler is a splendid example of the thrift and industry of the German people. Coming to this country a little more than thirty years ago, with no capital but his trade and a willingness to work, he has by his energy and square dealing built up a magnificent business, and enjoys the full confidence and respect of the good people of Evansville.

ANTON KESSLER, the leading contractor and builder of Evansville, Ind., was born in Bavaria, Germany, in 1864. Having completed a thorough course both theoretically and practically in his adopted trade, stonemasonry, in the Fatherland, he came to America when about twenty years of age. This was in the year of 1888, and soon thereafter he came to Evansville. For the first year, he did not follow his trade, but worked at various occupations, at the end of which year he formed a co-partnership with his brother, Philip, carrying on a general contracting and masonry business under the firm name of Kessler Bros., and until the death of Mr. Philip Kessler in 1897 this partnership continued as originated. Since then Mr. Kessler has conducted the business alone, increasing his business and territory year by year. His connection with the erection of some of the largest and finest buildings in this city indicate the character of work done by him. Among them are the two fine churches, St. Anthony's and St. Boniface, the high school building, the manual training school and a number of other school buildings. The furniture factories of the various Karges company's plants, and also the factories of the Crescent and Evansville Furniture Companies, the children's public home, the Rathbone home, the St. Mary's hospital and a number of the largest and finest residences. Mr. Kessler is recognized as one of the most up-to-date builders, and by his carefulness in executing his work and his faithful adherence to contracts, he has acquired his well deserved reputation of fairness, honesty and punctuality. He was married in 1893 to Miss Carrie Fischer, of Evansville, and they have four children: Emma, Anton, Helena and Franz. He is a member of St. Anthony's church, and takes an interest in its charitable work.

WILLIAM T. VARNER, M.D., a promising physician of Evansville, Ind., was born in Spencer county of that state in 1866. After the usual preliminary education of the American boy in the common schools he entered the Indiana State university, at Bloomington, and graduated with the degree of A.B. with the class of 1891. For the next two years he was county superintendent of schools in his native county, having previously taught in the public schools. Upon the expiration of his term as superintendent he entered Barnes' Medical college of St. Louis, Mo., and graduated from that institution with the degree of M.D. in 1896. In April of that year he located in Evansville, where he has been in constant practice ever since. By his close attention to his business, his high order of professional skill, and his genial personality he has established a lucrative practice and has won for himself a name among the leading physicians of the city. He is a member of the American, the Indiana State, and the Ohio Valley Medical associations, and of the Vanderburg County Medical society, and for the past four years has been one of the city physicians. Doctor Varner takes an active interest in public affairs, his voice and vote always being on the side of municipal progress and the general improvement of the public health and morals. He is a prominent member of the Masonic fraternity. In 1890 he was married to Miss Frances Salm, daughter of Solomon Salm, of Troy, Ind., and occupies one of the coziest homes in the city of Evansville, where Mrs. Varner is popular in social circles.

THEO. E. RECHTIN, dealer in lumber and building materials, Evansville, Ind., was born and reared in that city, and received his education there. His father, John T. Rechtin, was a native of Germany, who came to Evansville in 1848, where he was identified with the sawmill and lumber interests until 1894, when he retired, living a quiet life until his death in 1902. Theo. E. Rechtin became associated with his father soon after leaving school, and has been intimately connected with the Evansville building trades ever since. In 1897 he bought out all the interests in the plant formerly conducted by his father, and now has the largest and best equipped building supply concern in the city, as well as one of the largest in the Lower Ohio Valley. His establishment is located on Lower Seventh street and occupies one-half of an entire square. Everything that goes into the construction of a building can be found there. Mr. Rechtin's trade extends to many of the surrounding towns and cities, and is constantly on the increase. Aside from his private business interests he is considered as one of the most progressive and public spirited men in Evansville, always ready to lend his aid to any enterprise for promoting the city's welfare. He was married in 1887 to Miss Catherine M. Tisserand, of Evansville, and they have one daughter, Lucy Adaline.

ADAM H. SCHROEDER.

ADAM H. SCHROEDER, president of the Schroeder Headlight Company, Evansville, Ind., was born in Germany in the year 1836. When he was about seventeen years of age he came to America, and for twelve years was engaged in iron work in Cincinnati. In 1866 he located in Evansville, where he became a maker of house fronts, his reputation as a skilled mechanic in this line soon bringing him all the business he could attend to. In 1884 he took up the business of electro-plating on a modest scale and continued in that line with success until 1893, when he organized the Schroeder Headlight Company for the manufacture of locomotive headlights, switch and signal lamps. The company was incorporated in 1899 with a capital stock of $10,000, with Mr. Schroeder as president and his son, Charles F., as secretary and treasurer. The goods turned out by this company have found favor with railroad men and the demand for the Schroeder lights is constantly increasing. In whatever department of industry Mr. Schroeder has engaged he has been successful because of his native ability, his indomitable energy and his inherent honesty. He was married in 1858 to Miss Mary Wolke, also a native of Germany, and they have three children living: Charles F., Anna, and Lizzie, now Mrs. Rieger.

CHARLES F. SCHROEDER.

CHARLES F. SCHROEDER, the secretary and treasurer of the company, was born and reared in the city of Evansville. At the age of twelve years he became associated with his father in the plating business, and when the headlight company was incorporated was made secretary and treasurer, which position he has held ever since. He is a fine representative of the younger school of business men, with progressive ideas and believes in modern methods. In 1901 he was married to Miss Louise, daughter of Henry Doench, of Evansville.

MAJ. JOSEPH B. COX, a prominent citizen of Howell, Ind., is a native of Vanderburg county, having been born in Perry township in 1830, and has been a resident of the county all his life. His parents, Col. James and Frances M. (Miller) Cox, were among the pioneer settlers of Southwestern Indiana. The father came to Vanderburg county in 1818, where he followed farming and operated a wood yard, selling wood to the steamboats on the Ohio river near the Ingle coal mines. For some time he held the rank of colonel in the state militia. The maternal grandfather, George Miller, came from Kentucky in 1809 and settled where the city of Evansville now stands. As far as known he was the first white man to settle there, and it is very likely that his solitary log cabin was the first house in the city. Col. James Cox died in 1834 and his wife in 1886. She had been a resident of Perry Township for seventy-six years. They had a family of five children, of which Maj. Joseph B. Cox is the only survivor. He was educated in the common schools of his native county; attended the Cincinnati high school; passed one term in St. Xavier's college of Cincinnati, and graduated from Bacon's Business college in 1849. Upon leaving school he engaged as second clerk on a steamboat running between Cincinnati and New Orleans. He was soon promoted to the position of head clerk and for the next eight years followed the river. He was then elected township trustee of Perry Township, and served one year as a member of the board when there were three trustees, and was the first trustee of the township under the law changing from three trustees to one. After serving one year as trustee he went into the sheriff's office as deputy and served there for two years, or until the breaking out of the war. In 1861 he raised a company which was afterward mustered into the service as Company F, Sixtieth Indiana infantry. He was elected captain of the company at the time the regiment was organized and a few months later was made major. For a time his regiment was stationed at Indianapolis, guarding Confederate prisoners, and was then sent to Kentucky, where it participated in the campaign. After thirteen months of service Major Cox resigned on account of his health and returned to Evansville, where for the next two and a half years he was chief deputy in the county treasurer's office. He was then deputy sheriff for six years, and during President Cleveland's first administration he held the position of surveyor of customs for the port of Evansville, serving in that capacity for four years and one month. Since that time he has been engaged in looking after his large farming interests and in real estate operations. As president of the Howell Land Company he superintended the laying out of the town of Howell, and has been identified with its growth ever since it started. Major Cox is also a director in the Evansville, Suburban & Newburg railroad, and a stockholder in the City National and West Side banks of Evansville and the Fair Ground association. His connection with these institutions marks him as a man of enterprise and public spirit. Major Cox has been twice married. In 1863 he was married to Miss Amanda W. Sirkle, who died in 1868, leaving one son, Dr. D. A. Cox, one of the leading physicians of Howell. In 1871 Major Cox was married to Miss Martha J. Angel, and to this union there have been born two sons: Robert M., a farmer of Union township, Vanderburg county, and Joseph B., a practicing physician of Posey county, Ind. Major Cox is a member of the General Baptist church of Howell and takes an interest in promoting its good works.

THOMAS RUSTON, a well known citizen of Evansville, Ind., was born in Cambridgeshire, England, in 1853. When he was seventeen years of age he came to America, and for a year worked on a farm in Warrick county, Ind. He then came to Evansville, where he was associated with W. J. Newitt in the floral business until 1873, when he went to St. Louis. There he followed the same line of work for two years, at the end of which time he went to Chicago, where he was for a year with a floral company, and then took charge of John Hanson's place at Rose Hill cemetery. He remained with Mr. Hanson about a year and then returned to Evansville, which city has, with the exception of a short time, ever since been his home. In May, 1878, he was united in marriage to Miss Elizabeth Graves, of Evansville, and for the next seven years was in charge of Dr. Walker's greenhouses. In 1884 he went to Chicago again, where he was for a short time with the floral establishment of

Charles Reisig, the finest in the city. After leaving Mr. Reisig he was with A. P. Jackson at Bowmanville for a little while, and then came back to Evansville. For the last nine years he has been engaged in the work of contracting for the building of roads, and the greater part of that time has held the position of road supervisor. Mr. Ruston is a Republican in politics, and at the Vanderburg county convention of his party in April, 1904, he was nominated over four popular candidates for the office of county commissioner from the First district. He is a member of the Ancient Order of United Workmen, has gone through the chairs and served as delegate to the Grand Lodge twice. Mr. and Mrs. Ruston have three children: Annie May, wife of Will Carleton of the Associated Press; Florence Maud, wife of John Granelswith, and Inez May.

GEORGE GRIESBACHER, of the firm of Koch & Griesbacher, contractors of brickwork, Evansville, Ind., was born in that city in 1858. His father, Charles Griesbacher, was a native of Alsace-Lorraine, Germany, but came to America in his early manhood. At one time he owned a lot in New York City where Madison Square garden is now located. About 1855 he came to Evansville, where he became one of the leading brick contractors, and followed that vocation until his death in 1884. George Griesbacher received his education in the parochial schools of Evansville, and at the age of thirteen years started in to learn the trade of bricklayer with his father. He cont'nued to work with his father until the latter's death, and for the next ten years worked as a journeyman bricklayer for different employers. In 1894 he formed a partnership with John Koch which still exists. As both members of the firm are practical mechanics and take pride in the punctual execution of their contracts the new firm soon came to be one of the most prominent in its line in the city of Evansville. In recent years they have been entrusted with the erection of some of the largest public and private buildings in the city, and in every instance their work has been well done and done on time. (See sketch of John Koch for some of the most important structures.) Mr. Griesbacher is a member of the Builders' Exchange, the Business Men's association, and the Citizens' Alliance, and belongs to the Trinity German Lutheran church. He was married in 1884 to Miss Henrietta Weber, a daughter of John Weber, one of the old residents of Evansville. He was born in Germany and settled in Evansville about the same time as the father of Mr. Griesbacher.

JOHN H. OSBORN, an old and well known resident of Evansville, Ind., has been for several years prominently identified with the manufacturing interests of the Lower Ohio Valley. He was born in Boone county, Ill., but when three years of age came with his parents, William and Ann (Burrell) Osborn, to Cannelton, Ind., where he grew to manhood and obtained his education. He learned the trade of machinist, worked in different shops in Louisville and Owensboro, Ky., and for nearly fifteen years was connected with the cotton mills at Cannelton. In 1875 he came to Evansville as master mechanic of the Evansville Cotton Mills. Nine years later he was promoted to the responsible position of superintendent of the mills, which he has ever since held, his previous practical training giving him especially high qualifications for the place. Mr. Osborn was one of the organizers of the White Oak Handle Company, which was incorporated in 1902 with a capital stock of $35,000, and has been president of the company since the formation, W. H. Patrick being the secretary and treasurer. The company manufactures plow handles exclusively and the demand for its products is constantly increasing. Aside from his private business interests Mr. Osborn finds time to assist in the promotion of any enterprise tending to advance the commercial prosperity of Evansville, and to devote to public affairs. Although he is an ardent Republican, and has frequently been urged to accept a nomination for public office, the only political position he ever held was that of trustee of the Evansville waterworks, being a member of the board at the present time. In 1875 he declined to accept the nomination for Congress, though in 1904 he was a delegate to the national Republican convention which nominated Roosevelt and Fairbanks. It is therefore from no lack of loyalty to his political convictions that he declines political honors, but simply from his devotion to his business undertakings. Mr. Osborn has served with marked ability as a director of the Central Trust and Savings Company, the Union Savings Company, and the Evansville Business Men's association. In fraternal circles he is a well known figure, being a member of the Knights of Pythias, the Ancient Order of United Workmen, and the Benevolent and Protective Order of Elks. He is also a member of St. Paul's Episcopal church and is a liberal contributor to the charitable work of his church. In June, 1878, Mr. Osborn was united in marriage to Miss Mary A. White, of Evansville.

JOSEPH SCHAEFER, an undertaker and embalmer of Evansville, Ind., is of German lineage, his parents, Benedict and Katharine (Miller) Schaefer, both having been natives of the Fatherland. The father came to America in 1834, locating first at Pittsburg, Pa., where he remained for about three years, and where he was married. In 1837 he came down the Ohio river to Vanderburg county, Ind., where he obtained a farm in German township and followed farming until 1854, when he removed to Evansville and died there in 1860. The mother died in 1886. They had a family of four children, viz.: Martin, now a retired contractor living on Ingle street in Evansville; Katharine, who married Chris. Schulte, of Evansville, and died in 1898; Elizabeth, now the wife of Peter Leonard, of Evansville, and Joseph, the subject of this sketch. Joseph Schaefer was born on the farm in German township in 1841. He continued to live on the farm until he was almost nineteen years of age, securing such an education as the common schools of that day afforded. When he was nineteen years old he commenced serving an apprenticeship at cabinet making, and subesquently learned the carpenters' trade, at which he worked until 1872. He then embarked in business for himself as a contractor and builder, later adding that of undertaking, and since 1883 has devoted all his time and attention to the latter branch of the business. In 1882 he took a course in the art of embalming under Professor Clark, of Cincinnati, and in 1897 took a course in the embalming school of that city, receiving his diploma on the second day of May. On July 12, 1901, he received an embalmer's license, which gives him the authority to prepare bodies for shipment as well as burial. He has the oldest undertaking establishment in the city and does an extensive business. On Oct. 5, 1863, Mr. Schaefer was married to Miss Elizabeth Bitz, a native of Germany, but who came to Warrick county, Ind., when she was but four years of age. To this marriage there have been born the following children: Mary, wife of Edward Mathews, a marble cutter, of Evansville; Anna T.; John A., a plumber of Evansville; Benjamin T., in St. Louis; Edward M., in partnership with his father in the undertaking establishment; Aurelia, wife of Olaf Olsen, who is employed in the Chicago offices of the Illinois Central railroad. Mr. Schaefer is a member of the Holy Trinity Roman Catholic church.

J. RICHARD ANDERSON, general contractor and builder, of Evansville, Ind., was born at Springfield, Tenn., in 1863. His father, W. T. Anderson, was a farmer of Cedar Hill, in the same county as Springfield. The subject of this sketch obtained his education in the public schools and worked on a farm until he attained his majority. He then entered the employ of John S. McCorkle, with whom he served an apprenticeship at carpentering, after which he came to Evansville, where he was for four years in the coach building department of the Evansville & Terre Haute railroad shops. He left this position to take charge of the wood working department of George T. Mesker's architectural iron works. Here he remained until about 1898, when he commenced contracting for himself. While Mr. Anderson can erect any kind of building he makes a specialty of fine residences, and some of the most pretentious homes of Evansville owe their existence to his architectural taste and skill. Among them may be mentioned the residences of the late Jabez Wooley, at Fulton avenue and Maryland street; O. C. Hauserman, on Campbell street; Henry Folz; Charles W. Wittenbraker, and Dr. Kelsay, as well as a number of others. Mr. Anderson does the greater part of his own designing and his large patronage is due to his exquisite taste in the arrangement and decoration of the home. He is a member of the Evansville Business Men's association, is a stockholder in the Princeton oil field, belongs to the First Baptist church in which he was an official for several years, and is one of the all round progressive men of Evansville. He was married on June 6, 1891, to Miss Annie Taylor, a native of Kentucky, but who was reared in Evansville. She died on Jan. 14, 1901, leaving one son, Roy Taylor.

RANE CLAY WILKINSON, a well known and popular member of the bar of Evansville, Ind., was born in Gibson county of that state, his parents being Aaron B. and Lucinda Wilkinson. He was reared on a farm and received his elementary education in the common schools of his native county. In 1862 he enlisted as a private in the Eighteenth Indiana infantry for "three years or during the war." His regiment was attached to General Schofield's division and during its three years of active service was in some of the hardest fought battles of the war. Mr. Wilkinson made an honorable record as a soldier, receiving four wounds while in the army. At Perryville, Ky., Oct. 8, 1862, he was slightly wounded, but was soon again on duty. In the charge on the Confederate fortifications at Resaca, Ga., in May, 1864, he was shot three times within a few minutes and was left on the field for dead. His splendid constitution pulled him through, however, though he still carries a bullet in his right shoulder as a memento of that terrific charge. After the war he returned to Indiana, and for the next two years was a student in a select school, where he finished his education. He then took service with the Evansville Journal Company and remained in their employ for five years. At the end of that time he entered the law office of Mattison and Gilchrist as a student, and in due time was admitted to the bar. Shortly after his admission he formed a partnership with Maj. H. A. Mattison, and this association lasted until 1883, since which time Mr. Wilkinson has practiced alone. Mr. Wilkinson takes an interest in public questions, though he is not an active politician. During the administration of Gov. Alvin P. Hovey he was commissioned colonel and chief of staff, and accompanied the governor on his trip through Mexico. As an attorney Mr. Wilkinson stands well among the attorneys of Southern Indiana, and as a citizen he is regarded as one of the representative men of Evansville.

C. E. LAUGHLIN, M.D., superintendent of the Southern Indiana hospital for the insane, at Evansville, was born in Lawrence county, Ind., in 1855. His father, Dr. E. D. Laughlin, was a practicing physician, and was for many years located at Orleans, in Orange county, where the subject of this sketch received his general education in the public schools. After a preliminary study with his father he entered the Miami Medical college, at Cincinnati, O., from which he graduated with the degree of M.D. in 1878. He began the practice of medicine at Orleans, where he was associated with his father, and soon won popularity by his close attention to business and his professional skill. Doctor Laughlin has been actively identified with the Republican party ever since attaining his majority, and on June 1, 1903, he was appointed superintendent of the insane hospital, succeeding Doctor Stoner, who had held the position for two and one-half years. He is a firm believer in the efficacy of association as a means of promoting good feeling among physicians, and for the purpose of elevating the standard of professional ability. He is therefore a member of the American, the Indiana State, the Mississippi Valley, and the Ohio Valley Medical associations, and the medical society of Vanderburg county. While practicing at Orleans he was honored with the presidency of the Orange County Medical society, and he has frequently served on committees in other medical societies. Doctor Laughlin was married in 1878 to Miss Emma Brown, of Mitchell, Ind., and they have three children living: Ruth, Edward and Genevieve. Ruth is now Mrs. M. Mayer, of Covington; Edward is in the railroad service, and Genevieve is at home.

EDWARD W. HOLTZ, vice-president of the Riechman Furniture Company, of Evansville, Ind., was born in that city in December, 1872, and has there spent his entire life. He is a son of the late Henry Holtz, a native of Germany, who was for a number of years one of the prominent figures in Evansville circles. The subject of this sketch attended the Evansville schools until he was about fourteen years of age, when he went to work for the Indiana Furniture Company and remained in their employ for about two years. He then went to the Karges Furniture Company, with which he was associated in various capacities for thirteen years. During that time he learned the furniture manufacturing business, and when the Riechman Company was organized he was made vice-president. The company makes a specialty of wardrobes and kitchen cabinets and enjoys a large and constantly expanding trade. Evansville is noted far and wide for its furniture factories. Almost everything in the way of office and residence furnishings is manufactured in the city. Of the men who are active in turning out this immense product few are better qualified or more practical than Mr. Holtz. Ever since the company was organized he has discharged the duties of general superintendent, and the success of the company is due in a great measure to his able assistance, and to his motto: "Honesty is the best policy." Mr. Holtz takes a commendable interest in public affairs. Although he is a firm believer in Democratic principles he is not particularly active in politics, but he keeps in touch with public events and fearlessly discharges his duty as a citizen.

THEODORE E. RAUSCHENBACH, president of the Anchor Roofing and Paving Company, of Evansville, Ind., was born in the city of St. Louis, Mo., in 1868. His father, August Rauschenbach, was a native of Germany. He came to St. Louis in 1854, and there followed his profession of civil engineer. For forty-five years he was city engineer of St. Louis, and at the time of his death, in May, 1900, was actively connected with municipal affairs. Theodore received his education in the schools of his native city. After completing the course in the grammar schools he attended Toensfeld's Military academy for young men, and then took a course in telegraphy, shorthand and typewriting. For two years he was in the main office of the Western Union Telegraph Company as money order clerk, and following that was for two years in the commission department of a wholesale grocery house. In 1887 he went into the cement business in St. Louis and continued in that line until 1896, when he came to Evansville, where he was associated with the Anchor Supply Company until 1902. In that year he and H. D. Baldwin bought out the paving business and on Jan. 1, 1904, in company with Arthur Funkhouser and R. Baumgartner, organized the Anchor Roofing and Paving Company, with a capital stock of $10,000. Mr. Rauschenbach was made president and Mr. Baldwin secretary. The company does a large business in cement work, many of the sidewalks in Evansville being of their construction. Mr. Rauschenbach is a member of the National Union and the Benevolent and Protective Order of Elks. He was married in 1895 to Miss Nettie Parmley, of Mount Vernon. Ill.

EDWARD R. SMITH, vice-president, secretary and manager of the E. Q. Smith Chair Company, of Evansville, Ind., was born and reared in that city, the only son of Edward Q. and Marian W. (Ray) Smith. His father was born at Hunter, Green county, N. Y., Feb. 7, 1828. Beginning at the age of fourteen years he learned the trade of millwright with his father, Jeremiah Smith, who was a skilled mechanic, and in 1848 started west to seek his fortunes. Some time was spent in Milwaukee and the pineries of Wiscon-

EDWARD Q. SMITH.

sin, after which he wended his way south-ward, working in both Memphis and St. Louis. From the latter city he went to Cincinnati to assist in building the machinery for the first machine chair factory in the west. He next went to Detroit, where he remained for about two years. On March 29, 1852, he was married to Marian W., daughter of Elijah Ray, of Vermont, and for the next six years lived in Cincinnati, where he had charge of the largest chair factory in the city. In that time he enlarged the plant

EDWARD R. SMITH.

so that the capacity was doubled, and invented three machines that have since been generally adopted by chair manufacturers. In 1857 he came to Evansville, and there established the first steam chair factory west of Cincinnati. From that time until his death, March 10, 1903, his business career was a part of the warp and woof of the industrial and commercial life of the city. His first factory was located on the canal, at the corner of Ohio and Indiana streets, where he remained until 1866, when he built a new one at the corner of Third and Division streets. In 1880 he acquired the property at the corner of Oak and Waters streets and there erected a sawmill for the purpose of supplying the materials for chair manufacture. Ten years later he built the factory adjoining the sawmill, where the business is still conducted. In 1888 the E. Q. Smith Chair Company was incorporated with himself as president and his son, Edward R., as vice-president and manager. Since the death of the founder of

I—24

this business his widow has succeeded to the presidency. Edward R. Smith was educated in the Evansville schools, and from the time he left school, with the exception of one year, he has been identified with the chair factory. He began at the bottom of the industry and has worked his way up, step by step, through every process of chair manufacture. There is not a piece of machinery in the establishment with which he is not perfectly familiar, and he can take the timber "from the stump" and convert it into a chair of any style or quality as well and as quickly as any skilled artisan in the country. His company makes all grades of chairs, from the cheapest wood seats to the finest polished and upholstered rockers. Mr. Smith is a member of the Trinity Methodist Episcopal church, and like his father before him is prominent in Masonic circles, both attaining the degree of Knight Templar. He was married in 1889 to Miss Amelia Neekamp, and to this union there have been born two children: Edward and Floyd.

GEORGE LAUT, for more than half a century a resident of Evansville, Ind., was born in Huntingdonshire, England, in March, 1828. He is one of five children born to William and Jemima Laut. The three daughters died in England and the two sons, William and George, came to America while they were still young men. In January, 1851, George Laut came to Evansville, and ever since that time he has been a resident of the city and an active member of its business population. Before coming to this country he had been a sub-contractor under the British government, and after coming to Evansville he took up the work of bricklaying, soon becoming a contractor of all kinds of brickwork. He built the first brick school house in Evansville, as well as the first brick structure to be used for mercantile purposes and the first brick sewer. During his long and active career he has probably participated in the erection of more buildings in Evansville than any other man now living in the city. In 1885 he established the brick manufacturing plant now known as the Evansville Pressed Brick Company, which he conducted until his retirement from active business affairs in 1901. Mr. Laut is a member of the Trinity Methodist Episcopal church and has for years been a contributor to its charitable works. He has been twice married. In 1853 he was united in marriage to Mary Ann Stratton, who died in 1864. Three of the children born to that marriage are yet living: Elizabeth, now the wife of Elisha Stevens; Emma, wife of William Vickery, a grocer of Evansville, and Alice. In the fall of 1865 Mr. Laut was married to Elizabeth Storton and they have three children living: Charles S., Herbert S., and Fannie. Charles S. is at home; Herbert S. is president of the brick company, and Fannie is the wife of George Daum, bookkeeper in the Old National bank.

Herbert S. Laut was born in the city of Evansville in the year 1871. After obtaining his education in the public schools he learned the brick manufacturing business with his father, and when the company of which he is now president was incorporated in 1901 he was elected president and W. S. Gilbert was elected secretary. The company makes a specialty of bricks for street paving and for foundations in heavy buildings. Their trade extends over Southern Indiana and Illinois, but their principal market is St. Louis. Mr. Laut is thoroughly familiar with every detail of brick making and he does not permit any inferior goods to leave the factory, a fact to which the popularity of the Evansville pressed brick is largely due. His thoroughness and energy have placed him among the foremost and most progressive business men of Evansville. He is a member of the Trinity Methodist Episcopal church and the Knights of Pythias. In 1893 he was united in marriage to Miss Delia Smith, daughter of the late Edward Q. Smith, whose sketch appears elsewhere in this work. To this marriage there has been born one daughter, named Winifred.

JOHN A. SCHWAN, vice-president of the Eli D. Miller Furniture Company of Evansville, Ind., is a native of Fayette county, Ill. His father, Charles Schwan, was a farmer, a native of Germany, but came to America in his early life, settled first at Mayville, Wis., then in Fayette county, Ill., and there lived until his death, which occurred in 1878. John A. Schwan grew to manhood in Fayette county, receiving his education in the public and parochial schools. In 1892 he came to Evansville, where he learned the trade of cabinet maker with the Karges Furniture Company. He remained with this company for eleven years, or until 1903, when he formed a partnership with Eli D. Miller for the manufacture of folding beds. Later the business was incorporated and

Mr. Schwan was made treasurer of the concern, a position he held until the beginning of the year 1904, when he was elected vice-president. The first factory of the company was located at 1307-1309 Main street. The new factory is located at the corner of Elsas avenue and Morgan street, and is a two-story brick, 128 by 150 feet, where seventy-five skilled workmen are employed. The offices are at the corner of Main and Franklin streets. As both Mr. Schwan and Mr. Miller are practical furniture men, with an ambition to build up a successful business, it is safe to say that no imperfect or inferior goods are sent out from their works. Mr. Schwan is a member of the German Lutheran Trinity church, of Evansville.

LOUIS KRAMER, president and manager of the New York Dimension Supply Company, of Evansville, Ind., was born in the city of New York in 1852. His father, Frank Kramer, was a native of Germany, who came in his early manhood to America. During the Civil war he served in a New Jersey regiment and died soon after being discharged from the service, his death being precipitated by the hardships encountered and wounds received while in the army. Louis Kramer was educated in the public schools of New York and in 1872 came to Evansville, where he has ever since been engaged in the lumber business in some form. For two years immediately after coming to Indiana he was interested in a sawmill on Green river, Ky. In 1896 the Dimension Supply Company was organized and incorporated under the laws of New York, for the purpose of manufacturing all grades of wood mantels, the woodwork for all kinds of plumbers' fixtures, and extension tables. all of which is finished in the white and the greater part of which is shipped to eastern markets. The capital stock was fixed at $5,000 and Mr. Kramer was elected president. The mills and lumber yards of the company are located at Evansville. Mr. Kramer takes a keen interest in every movement for the advancement of Evansville's commercial and material prosperity. He is a member and was for some time a director in the Evansville Business Men's association; a director in the traffic bureau; and a member of the Tri-State Fair association. In 1879 he was united in marriage to Miss Helen, daughter of Philip Auler, who was for many years identified with the Springfield Fire Insurance Company, and one of Evansville's representative citizens. Mr. and Mrs. Kramer have three sons. Frank lives at East Orange, N. J., and is the champion bicyclist of America; Edward is in charge of the company's yards at New Harmony; and Louis, Jr., is connected with his father in business.

JOHN R. BRILL, junior member of the law firm of Spencer & Brill, Evansville, Ind., was born near Center Valley, Hendricks county, of the same state, Dec. 26, 1863, his parents being William and Jeannette (Matthews) Brill. His father was a native of Frederick county, Va., and in his earlier years was a millwright. After coming to Indiana he followed farming until his death, which occurred when the subject of this sketch was about ten years old. The mother was born in Scotland, but when she was about twenty years of age she came with a sister to this country, two brothers having previously come over the water. She died at the home of her son, in Evansville, April 10, 1904. John R. Brill is the third child in a family of six, four sons and two daughters, five of whom are yet living. George W. Brill is a prominent lawyer at Danville, Ind.; William T. is an undertaker in the same city; Rachel Jeannette is the wife of Frank Sparks, of Hendricks county; and Betsey Virginia lives in the same county. After the death of his father John R. assisted his brother in conducting the farm until he attained his majority. During that time he attended the district school until he was proficient in the common branches, and then went to the Central Normal college, at Danville, two winter sessions. In 1884 he entered the Indiana State university, at Bloomington, and graduated in 1889 with the degree of A.B. He then went to Arkansas and was principal of the public schools at Eldorado in that state for one year, when he returned to Indiana, and in the fall of 1890 entered the law department of the State university, graduating with the degree of LL.B. in June, 1891, as the orator of his class. On July 12, of the same year, he located in Evansville and the following fall formed a partnership with John W. Spencer, under the firm name of

Spencer and Brill, which still exists, being one of the leading law firms of Southwestern Indiana. In politics Mr. Brill is a Democrat and has taken an active part in political matters ever since coming to Evansville. He served four years as deputy prosecuting attorney and was chairman of the city central committee two terms. In 1894 he was the nominee of his party for the office of prosecuting attorney for the First judicial district, composed of the counties of Vanderburg and Posey, but was defeated by 251 votes, although he led the ticket. The Republican state ticket that year carried Vanderburg county by about 1,100 votes, yet Mr. Brill's opponent carried the county by only 351, thus demonstrating his popularity with the masses, as well as his reputation as a lawyer. Mr. Brill is a prominent Knight of Pythias and a member of the Benevolent and Protective Order of Elks. He was married on June 29, 1899, to Miss Mary Baird, of Evansville, and they have three little daughters: Mary Jeannette, aged five years; Martha Virginia, aged three, and Katherine Elizabeth, aged one year.

HON. FRANK B. POSEY, surveyor of customs, lawyer and ex-Congressman, of Evansville, Ind., is a native of the Hoosier state, having been born at Petersburg, the county seat of Pike county, April 28, 1848, and is a son of Dr. John W. and Sarah (Blackburn) Posey. For more than a century the name of Posey has been closely interwoven with the growth and development of Indiana and the nation. The grandparents of Frank B., Richard and Frances (Allen) Posey, came from Abbeville district, S. C., in the year 1804 and settled at Bruceville, in Knox county. The grandfather was a cousin of Gen. Thomas Posey, a brigadier-general on the staff of George Washington during the Revolutionary war, and from whom Posey county, Ind., took its name. Richard Posey was the son of John Posey, a native of North Carolina, and his father was a native of Sussex county, Va. At the time Richard and Frances Posey came to Indiana Dr. John W. Posey, Frank's father, was an infant. He received such an education as the schools of that day afforded, took up the study of medicine and after his graduation located at Petersburg, where for more than fifty years he was one of the leading physicians. As a skilled surgeon he was known all over Southern Indiana. He died at Petersburg in 1884. On the maternal side the mother of Mr. Posey was a member of the same branch of the Blackburn family as United States Senator J. C. S. Blackburn of Kentucky. She died on Aug. 12, 1851, when the subject of this sketch was but a few months over three years old. Frank B. Posey is the youngest of six sons and is the only surviving member of his family. He received his primary education in the common schools of his native town and at the age of fifteen entered Asbury—now DePauw—university, attending that institution from 1864 to 1867. For the next two years he was deputy auditor at Petersburg, studying law during his leisure time, and in 1868 he entered the law department of the Indiana State university at Bloomington, graduating therefrom in 1869. Being admitted to the bar immediately afterward he established himself in practice and soon became well known over all the southwestern portion of the state. At the age of twenty-five years he had a clientage that extended to five county courts. Before he reached his majority he was appointed district attorney for Knox, Daviess, Martin and Pike counties, by Governor Baker, to serve out an unexpired term. In early manhood Mr. Posey cast in his lot with the Republican party. In 1872 he was nominated by acclamation for representative to the state legislature; was defeated by two votes in a county where the Democratic majority generally ran into the hundreds; was again nominated for the same office in 1878, without opposition, but was defeated with the rest of his ticket. In 1880 he was one of the presidential electors for Indiana and cast his vote for Garfield and Arthur. He was nominated for this position by a convention at which he was not present. Two years later he was chosen as his party candidate for state senator for the district composed of Pike and Warrick counties—a district in which the Democratic majority was about 1,000, yet Mr. Posey was defeated by only 150 votes. In 1888 he was the Republican nominee for Congress, against Judge W. F. Parrott, of Evansville, and was defeated by only twenty votes in a district where the normal Democratic majority was at least 1,000. In January, 1889, a special election for a congressman to fill out the unexpired term of General Hovey, who had been elected governor, was ordered, and Mr. Posey and Judge Parrott were again made the opposing candidates. This time the Republicans were successful and Mr. Posey was returned by a majority of 1,300. In 1892 Mr. Posey located in Evansville, where he soon became one of the most prominent attorneys at the local bar and a leading citizen in other ways. He was a candidate for the congressional nomination in 1892, but was defeated on the eighty-seventh ballot by Hon. James A. Hemenway. In 1899 Mr. Posey's name was presented to the general assembly as a candidate for United States senator, the other candidates being J. Frank Hanley, now governor of Indiana; Maj. George W. Steele, for many years congressman from the Eleventh district; and Albert J. Beveridge, of Indianapolis, who was finally elected, although Mr. Posey received a flattering vote. In 1902 President Roosevelt appointed Mr. Posey surveyor of customs, which position he still holds, and in which he has instituted a number of important reforms. In addition to his legal and political career Mr. Posey is popular as a lecturer on literary and classical subjects; is a director in the Lincoln Mining Company, one of the largest coal mining concerns of Southern Indiana, and the Indiana vice-president of the Ohio River Improvement Association, which is composed of the progressive men of the large cities of the Ohio, from Pittsburg to Cairo, the object being to secure a nine foot stage of water between those two cities. As a campaigner Mr. Posey is recognized as one of the most forcible and convincing speakers in his party and has a reputation-that extends far beyond the state lines. He is a Knight of Pythias, an Odd Fellow and a member of the Benevolent and Protective Order of Elks. On Jan. 21, 1878, Mr. Posey led to the altar Miss Harriet E. Brown of Petersburg, and they have four children: Helen, Francesca, Myrtle and John A.

CAPT. JAMES W. WARTMAN, deputy clerk of the United States courts for the district of Indiana, and United States commissioner at Evansville, was born at Lewisburg, Greenbrier county, W. Va., Feb. 7, 1832, the county being at that time in Virginia. His grandfather, Lawrence Wartman, was a native of Switzerland, a fine scholar, spoke seven languages and was a journalist by profession. In 1821 he established the *Rockingham Register* at Harrisonburg, Va., which was owned and published by two of his sons for more than fifty years. Frederick Wartman, the father of the subject, was a painter by trade, and while the Captain was still in his boyhood removed to Cincinnati, where the son graduated from the Woodward college in 1847. For some years after that he was engaged in business in Cincinnati, after which he removed to Spencer county, Ind., and took up the study of law under L. Q. DeBruler. Upon being admitted to the bar he began practice at Rockport; was provost marshal of the First district of Indiana in 1864, with headquarters at

Evansville; became commissioner for the board of enrollment for the district and during the drafts of 1864-65 he performed his delicate and important duties to the satisfaction of the national authorities and without friction. After the war he returned to Rockport, where he formed a partnership with T. F. DeBruler and practiced law until 1871, when he was appointed deputy clerk of the Federal district court at Evansville. In September of the same year he was appointed United States commissioner, and for almost a quarter of a century he has efficiently discharged his duties in both positions. Captain Wartman is a Republican and never shirks his duty as a citizen. He has a pleasing personality, is a good judge of human nature, a quick grasp of business and public problems and is a man of unquestionable integrity in all his transactions. In fraternal circles he is well known, being a member of the Independent Order of Odd Fellows and for many years has been a member of the finance committee of Eagle Lodge, Knights and Ladies of Honor. He belongs to the Methodist Episcopal church and takes an active interest in its good works. In January, 1857, he was married to Miss Mary Graham, of Rockport, and of the five children born to this marriage three are living. John G. is a wholesale grocer in Los Angeles, Cal.; Harry W. is president of the Ryan-Hampton Tobacco Company of Newburg, Ind., but resides in Evansville, and Sarah D. is at home with her father, Mrs. Wartman having died on March 31, 1897.

JOHN W. SPENCER was born on the bank of the Ohio River, at Mt. Vernon, Ind., on March 7, 1864, on the border line, during the terrible struggle between the states; his primary education was limited to such schools as his home town afforded; his collegiate course consisted of a short term at the Central Normal college of Danville, Ind.; he acquired some commercial knowledge by two years of service as assistant bookkeeper for the Mt. Vernon Banking Company, after which he began the study of law in the office of his father, Elijah M. Spencer, who was one of the pioneer lawyers of Southern Indiana. By close application to his studies, he was far enough advanced in the law to be admitted to practice when he was twenty-one years old; at the age of twenty-six he was elected prosecuting attorney of the First judicial circuit of Indiana, composed of the counties of Vanderburg and Posey, which position he held for two terms. He moved to Evansville in September, 1891, and there has since resided and practiced his profession, with marked success, as a member of the law firm of Spencer & Brill. For four years he was a member of the Democratic state central committee of Indiana, and in 1902 he was the unanimous nominee of his party for Congress. On Dec. 12, 1882, he married Miss Lillie Lichtenberger, of Mt. Vernon, Ind., and they have two children, Alethea Lowry and John W., Jr.

CAPT. ISIDOR ESSLINGER, deputy collector of internal revenue for the Seventh district of Indiana, located at Evansville, is a native of Germany, having been born at Stuttgart, in the province of Würtemberg, Jan. 11, 1833. After a primary education in the regular schools he prepared for college in the Stuttgart gymnasium. He then attended the Heidelberg university for one year and after a three years' course in the university of Tuebingen graduated from the latter institution at the age of twenty-two. He studied law at both Heidelberg and Tuebingen and came to the United States in 1857, when only twenty-four years of age. After a year in Cincinnati he came to Evansville, where he has ever since made his home. His first employment in Evansville was as a dry goods clerk. In 1861 he left the counter to take up arms in defence of his adopted country and enlisted as a private in Company K, Thirty-second Indiana infantry. Shortly afterward he was made sergeant, then first lieutenant of Company K, and in 1862 was promoted to captain and given command of Company E, of the same regiment. He served the full term of his enlistment for three years, participating in all the battles and skirmishes in which his regiment was engaged. For twenty-one years succeeding the war he was the editor and proprietor of a German daily paper called the *Union,* which he ably conducted and made a power among his German fellow-citizens. Early in the administration of President Harrison he was appointed deputy collector of internal revenue and served until the inauguration of President Cleveland in 1893, when he was removed. In 1901 he was again appointed to the position which he now holds. The interim between his removal and re-appointment was occupied by the management and proprietorship of a job printing office. Captain Esslinger is an unwavering Republican in his political affiliations and is a charter member of Admiral Farragut Post, No. 71, Grand Army of the Republic. Soon after leaving the army in 1864 he visited his mother, then a widow, in the Fatherland, and while in Europe formed the acquaintance of Miss Jeannette Guth, of Switzerland, to whom he was married on June 24, 1864, bringing her to Evansville on his return. Captain and Mrs. Esslinger have four children living—three sons and a daughter, Julius A., Frederick, Oscar N. and Nora—all grown and living at home with their parents. Julius A. is deputy county clerk of Vanderburg county. Captain Esslinger's career has been marked by a strong personality and an unimpeachable reputation for honesty. Though positive in his likes and dislikes he has a host of friends who know him for an honorable and worthy man.

CAPT. THOMAS BOLUSS, wharf master at Evansville, Ind., was born in the city of New York in the year 1832, of English parentage. His father, whose name was also Thomas, came to America in 1831, and the mother came the following year. Thomas Boluss, Sr., was a builder of rolling mills in this country for English capitalists and his occupation took him from one place to another, so that the early life of the subject of this sketch was spent in various cities of the Eastern states. At the age of fifteen he started to learn the trade of steamboat engineer on one of the Ohio river boats and worked at this until 1851. In that year the father came to Evansville to construct the city's first gas plant, the son coming with him to assist in the work. Here he worked with his father until 1853, when he returned to the river as an engineer, continuing in that occupation until 1857. He then started a brass foundry in Evansville, which he conducted for about two years, when he sold out and again returned to the river, this time as a steamboat captain. For the next forty years he was a captain and pilot on the Ohio and Mississippi rivers, few men being better known in river navigation. In the spring of 1901 Captain Boluss became wharf master of the port of Evansville, a position he still holds and one for which his long experience in river matters has eminently fitted him. At every landing between Pittsburg and Cairo, and at many points on the Mississippi he has acquaintances that he formed while a master or pilot, and to be acquainted with Captain Boluss is to be his friend. He was married in 1852 to Anna Gilman, who died in 1882. Captain Boluss has two children, Sophia, wife of a Mr. Skinner, and Thomas, both living in Evansville.

THE CITY NATIONAL BANK of Evansville dates its existence back to Jan. 21, 1850, when the Evansville Insurance Company was granted a perpetual charter with banking privileges, and commenced business under that charter as the "Canal Bank." The entire capital of the insurance company and the bank at the beginning was $250,-000. John M. Stockwell was elected president and James G. Jones secretary. Mr. Jones was soon thereafter succeeded by W. T. Page. The bank operated under the banking law of Indiana for several years but in 1863, on the enactment of the national banking law, the officers of the Canal bank made application for a charter and the institution was incorporated as the First National Bank of Evansville. It was the first bank in Evansville and in fact the sixth in the United States to make application for a charter under the national law. It started with a capital of $250,000, which was subsequently increased to $500,000. H. Q. Wheeler was the first president of the national bank with W. T. Page as cashier. The first board of directors was composed of Gillison Maghee, Robert Barnes, Charles Viele, John S. Hopkins, John Ingle, M. J. Bray, S. M. Archer, H. Q. Wheeler and William Brown. All were men of great prominence in Evansville financial circles. In 1865 Mr. Page was succeeded as cashier by James H. Cutler and in 1867 Mr. Wheeler was succeeded in the presidency by John S. Hopkins. Mr. Hopkins was succeeded as president in 1880 by Charles Viele. In 1882 the original charter expired and a new one was secured. The bank was then reorganized with Charles Viele, president; James H. Cutler, cashier; Will Warren, assistant cashier; Thomas E. Garvin, John Ingle, Chas. Viele, M. J. Bray, Isaac Keen, F. J. Reitz, Cyprian Preston and James H. Cutler, directors. In 1893 Mr. Viele was succeeded as president by Francis J. Reitz. On April 21, 1902, the City National bank of Evansville was organized and succeeded to the business of the First National, whose charter expired by limitation, with the same officers and directors. The present officers of the City National are: Francis J. Reitz, president; James H. Cutler, vice-president; F. A. Foster, cashier; John H. Dippel, assistant cashier; the directors being Francis J. Reitz, Thomas E. Garvin, James H. Cutler, M. J. Bray, George L. Mesker, O. F. Jacobi, D. Kronenberger, Geo. A. Cunningham, A. F. Karges, and F. A. Foster. At the present time the capital stock paid in is $350,000, the total assets amount to over $3,500,000, the surplus fund is $65,000, and the deposits $2,900,000. From the very commencement of business, this bank has enjoyed a successful career and large dividends have regularly been paid on its stock, which has always been considered most valuable property.

M. CARNEY, an old resident and prominent business man of Shawneetown, Ill., was born June 24, 1856, not far from Athens, O., and is of Irish extraction. His grandparents both lived and died in Ireland, and his father, whose name was John Carney, was born in the County of Tipperary in, 1830. In 1852 he came to the United States and located at Circleville, O., where he worked as a stone mason on railroad construction for some time, after which he located at Big Run, in Athens county. There he lived until 1869, when he came to Shawneetown, where he continued to follow railroad building until his death at the age of fifty-seven years. With the exception of a short residence in Cairo he lived at Shawneetown from the time he first came there until his death. Soon after coming to America he was married to Margaret Euright, who was born in County Limerick, Ireland, and came to this country in 1851 with a brother. Of the children born to this marriage Mary and Ellen are deceased; William lives in Cincinnati; the subject of this sketch; and Josephine is a Mrs. Ward, of Danville, Ill. The mother of these children died in 1875. Mr. Carney was denied the privilege of attending school, for at the age of nine years he began life as a driver of a cart in railroad building. However, he has by self-study kept up with the world's progress, and today has a more practical education than many whose opportunities far excelled his own. He continued to drive carts on the railroad for three years, and when he came to Shawneetown in February, 1869, he was employed as a teamster on the Springfield & Illinois Southeastern, now part of the Baltimore & Ohio Southwestern railroad, which was then under construction.   From that time until now he has been connected with the road in various capacities, though he is also interested in other enterprises.   On Jan. 1, 1901, he was made general superintendent of the Bruns-Bowersox Lumber Company at Shawneetown, which position he still holds.   He has also been engaged in the grocery business, and dealer in coal and ice.   For several years he was superintendent of the Bowlesville Coal Company, and owns and oversees several farms.   Although Mr. Carney had the misfortune to lose his left leg by an accident, he is one of the most active men in Shawneetown, and successfully conducts his various interests.   In political matters he is a Republican, and has held the following offices: Tax collector, 1892; alderman, 1893-97; mayor, 1897 to 1901.   His administration as mayor was marked by the big flood of April, 1898, which did great damage to Shawneetown and vicinity, a number of lives being lost.   In this emergency Mayor Carney was prompt to devise measures for the relief of the sufferers, and the progress of the city since that unhappy event is due in a great degree to his wise course at the time.   He is a member of Lodge No. 838, Independent Order of Odd Fellows, in which he is popular for his genial disposition and many good qualities.   On April 15, 1879, Mr. Carney and Miss Belle Ward, a native of Ohio, were united in marriage.   They have three children, Charles H., William F. and John M., all at home with their parents.

CHRISTIAN KRATZ, prominently identified with the lumber and sawmill interests of Shawneetown, Ill., was born Aug. 6, 1864, in the city of Evansville, Ind.   His parents, Christian and Philipine (Krug) Kratz, were both born in Germany.   The father learned the trade of machinist in his native land, and in 1858, when about sixteen years of age, came to America.   Soon after reaching this country he located at Evansville, where he followed his trade until he retired from the active pursuits of life.   He was married at Evansville, his wife having come over in 1853.   They had eight children, all living.   All except the subject of this sketch live at Evansville.   Mary is a Mrs. Hartman; Tillie a Mrs. Wade; Philip; Edward; Elizabeth is a Mrs. Smith, and Emma is at home with her father. The mother died in 1896. The family belong to the German Lutheran church. Christian Kratz was educated in the public schools and in 1881 graduated from the Evansville Commercial college. He then served an apprenticeship as a machinist and followed that trade several years, after which he engaged in the planing mill and hardwood lumber business at Evansville. In 1898 he came to Shawneetown and commenced operating a sawmill on the Wabash river, later dealing in lumber in the town. Since then he has built several mills in the county, and has recently erected a new one at Shawneetown. He is also connected with the dressed lumber and commission business as a member of the firm of Kratz & McMurchy. Mr. Kratz is a member of the Masonic fraternity and the Knights of Pythias, and belongs to the Presbyterian church. Politically he is a Republican, and while living in Evansville served two terms as councilman at large. In 1886 he was married to Miss Ella Casper, and they have three children, Christian, Walter and Elenora, all at home with their parents.

J. W. WILKINS, who conducts a blacksmith and general repair shop at Shawneetown, Ill., was born in Muhlenberg county, Ky., Feb. 19, 1859. His father was born in Muhlenberg county, though the ancestors came originally from England, and were among the early settlers of Kentucky. James W. Wilkins, the father of the subject of this sketch, married Margaret J. Latham in Muhlenberg county and lived there until 1860, when they went to Union county of the same state and lived there until 1871, when they came to Gallatin county, Ill., bought a farm near Kedron and lived there until the death of the father at the age of sixty-three years. The mother died in Shawneetown at the age of forty-eight. Of their ten children only three are living: Jefferson D., who lives near Kedron; Nathaniel, who is in Columbus, O., and the subject of this sketch. J. W. Wilkins received a very limited education in his youth, but he has managed to gather a valuable fund of information by self-study and by associating with well-informed men. In 1875 he left home and went to White county, where he found employment in a sawmill. Some time later he went to Hamilton county and took charge of a sawmill there until 1884, when he returned to Gallatin county and followed farming until 1897. He then removed to Shawneetown and engaged in his present line of business, in which he had just got a good start when the great flood came and swept away every thing he had accumulated. With commendable enterprise he started over again, and by industry, honest dealing and a close attention to business has built up a good trade, requiring the assistance of two workmen all the time to keep up with the demand. Much of his success is due to his personal popularity, as few men in Gallatin county are more universally liked. In 1879 he was married to Mrs. Margaret Sullivan Hoskins, a native of Hamilton county and a widow with one child, Sarah Elizabeth. Mr. and Mrs. Wilkins have five children living, viz.: William, Oma, Virginia, Paul and Wilmer. Mr. Wilkins takes considerable interest in political affairs as a Democrat, but is not a seeker for office. His wife belongs to the Methodist Episcopal church.

WILLIAM CAMPBELL, M.D., who has practiced medicine at Equality, Ill., for almost forty years, was born two and a half miles west of that town Nov. 12, 1842. His father, William C. Campbell, was born in Virginia about 1789 and came in early childhood to Kentucky with his parents, who settled near Lexington. There he grew to manhood, married Mary Guard, and soon afterward came to Gallatin county, Ill. His wife died shortly afterward and he subsequently married Mrs. Sallie Gillette Hewitt, the widow of William Hewitt, and a native of Vermont. They continued to live on the farm until 1858, when they removed to Equality and there spent their declining years. He died at the age of eighty years and she at eighty-two. Of their two children Doctor Campbell is the only one living. Dr. William Campbell received his elementary education in the public schools of Equality, and began his business career as a clerk in a store. While thus employed he commenced the study of medicine, and after 1864 devoted his entire time to the acquirement of a professional education. In 1867 he was graduated from the Cincinnati College of Medicine, and soon afterward opened an office in Equality, where he has ever since practiced his profession. Doctor Campbell is one of the oldest practicing physicians in his section of the state, has a lucrative business, is recognized as one of the successful men in the treatment of diseases, and stands high with both the public and his brother physicians. He was one of the organizers of the Gallatin County Medical society, to which he has belonged ever since its formation. As a member of Lodge No. 19, Independent Order of Odd Fellows, he has filled all the chairs, and has taken considerable interest in promoting the good works of the Methodist Episcopal church, of which he is a member. In 1867 he was married to Miss Rose Norcross, a native of Evansville, Ind., and they have three daughters and a son living. The three daughters live at Equality, where Nellic is a Mrs. Purcell; Mary a Mrs. Dempsey, and Nora a Mrs. Wathen. The son, William A., is an engineer on the railroad and lives at Danville, Ill. Doctor Campbell is one of the public spirited men of the town, and as a Democrat takes a keen interest in political questions, though he is not what could be called a practical politician.

WILLIAM McINTIRE, senior member of the firm of McIntire & Son, brick and tile manufacturers, Equality, Ill., was born near Laconia, Washington county, Ind., June 4, 1844. When he was about seven years of age his father died and the following year the mother removed with her family to Equality. Here he grew to manhood and obtained a good practical education in the common schools. While still a boy he commenced working on a farm at $6 a month during the summer seasons, and when only ten years old began to learn the coopers' trade. He worked at this until 1862, when he enlisted as a private in Company G, One Hundred and Thirty-first Illinois infantry, and was mustered in at Metropolis City. The regiment took part in the siege of Vicksburg and was at Arkansas Post, after which it was consolidated with the Twenty-ninth Illinois infantry, and fought at Natchez, New Orleans, Mobile, at various points in Texas, and was mustered out in November, 1865. Mr. McIntire held the rank of corporal at the time he was discharged. After the war he worked at his trade in Paducah, Ky., for some time, then came back to Equality and in 1869 started a cooper shop of his own, which he conducted until 1880, when he established a brick yard in connection with Mr. Proctor. Two years later he bought out his partner and in 1885 located where he now is. In 1903 he took his son Thaddeus into partnership and added lumber to his business. The yards have a capacity of twenty-five thousand brick and a car load of tile every day, and the trade in lumber is constantly increasing. Mr. McIntire is a director in the First National bank, is a Republican in his political affiliations, and was for several years president of the town board. In 1868 he was united in marriage to Miss Sarah A. Seeley and they have two children: Lizzie is the wife of R. E. Reed, of Equality, and Thaddeus is in partnership with his father as the junior member of the firm.

CAPT. A. A. VINYARD, a well known farmer, living three and a half miles north of Karber's Ridge, Hardin County, Ill., was born in that county, not far from the Old Illinois Furnace, June 17, 1828. His grandparents were natives of Virginia, of German descent. They left Virginia and lived for a while in Kentucky, but in 1811 came to Hardin county. One of their eight children was Eli Vinyard, who was born in Hardin county, Ky., Nov. 5, 1806. After he grew to manhood in Illinois he was married to Miss Sarah Hill, a native of Georgia, and began farming about three miles north of the Old Illinois Furnace. In 1829 they removed to another place, not far from Karber's Ridge, and there they passed the remainder of their lives, he dying at the age of eighty-two years and she at the age of sixty-seven. Of their nine children five are living. Capt. A. A. Vinyard is the subject of this sketch; Elizabeth is a Mrs. Moore, living in Hardin county; Daniel lives in Saline county; Rufina married a man named Tyer and lives in Hardin county, and John lives in the neighborhood of Karber's Ridge. Captain Vinyard received his education in the old subscription schools and upon arriving at manhood became a farmer. In 1861 he enlisted in Company C, Forty-eighth Illinois volunteer infantry, was mustered in at Camp Butler, and for a time was stationed at Cairo. In 1862 he was promoted to first lieutenant, and in 1864 became captain of his company. He was with his regiment in the engagements at Fort Donelson, Shiloh, the siege of Vicksburg, Jackson, Miss., Missionary Ridge, and marched with Sherman to the sea, taking part in the engagement before Atlanta on the occasion of Hood's first sortie, July 22, 1864. He also participated in numerous minor engagements and skirmishes. The regiment was mustered out at Little Rock, Ark., Aug. 16, 1865, and Captain Vinyard returned home, where he again took up the life of a farmer. He married Emeline M. Patton, a native of Gallatin county, Ill., and they began their married life on a farm of 80 acres, all in the woods, where he now lives. At the present time he owns 320 acres, part bottom land, and all under cultivation. Besides this he has given over 400 acres to his children, viz.: Katherine, Jane, Harriet, John C., Andrew, Ira and Manning. Katherine is a Mrs. Brinkley; Jane a Mrs. Williams; Harriet is at home with her parents, and the others all live in the vicinity. They are members of the Social Brethren church. Captain Vinyard has always taken an active interest in public matters and has held some office in local affairs since the war. For twenty-six years he has been township treasurer, and has frequently been a delegate to Republican conventions. His home is noted for its hospitality.

CAPT. PHILIP J. HOWARD, operator of a large stone quarry at Rosiclare, Ill., is a descendant of one of the oldest families in that section of the state. His grandfather, John Howard, came from Virginia while he was still quite a young man, and settled in what was then Pope county. He married a Miss Robinett and they lived their whole lives in the vicinity of the Old Illinois Furnace, in what is now Hardin county. They had four sons and one daughter, all now deceased. One son, Joshua, was at one time sheriff of Pope county, before Hardin county was organized. John Howard lived to be seventy years of age and his wife reached the age of seventy-five. Their son, Philip J. Howard, father of the subject of this sketch, was born six miles north of Elizabethtown, grew to manhood on his father's farm, married Miss Minerva McFarland, and lived his whole life on a farm near that town. Minerva McFarland was a daughter of James and Elizabeth McFarland, who built the first rude log house where the town of Elizabethtown now stands. As the settlement grew and the town began to take form, it was named after Mrs. McFarland. The old log house gave way in time to a commodious brick dwelling, which is still standing and is now used as a hotel. James McFarland was a farmer and flatboatman, making several trips to New Orleans by that means before the advent of railroads. Philip J. and Minerva Howard had three children, Elizabeth, Philip J., and one deceased. Elizabeth is now a Mrs. Dunn, living in Kansas. The father died at the age of thirty-five and the mother lived to the age of seventy-nine years. After the death of her husband she married a second time, her second husband being James Kirkham, and they had five children, two of whom, James H. and Pinckney, now live at Smithland, Ky., and the others are deceased. Captain Howard was born near Elizabethtown, March 11, 1840, received his education in the common schools, and on July 29, 1861, enlisted in Company A, Twenty-ninth Illinois volunteer infantry, under Capt. Charles M. Ferrill. The regiment was mustered in at Camp Butler, and after a short stay at Cairo joined the forces in West Tennessee. It was at Fort Henry, Fort Donelson, Belmont, Mo., Pittsburg Landing, Corinth, and Holly Springs. At Holly Springs a portion of the regiment, among them Captain Howard, was captured and held prisoners at the parole camp at St. Louis for about five months. In June, 1863, they were exchanged and rejoined the command in front of Vicksburg. After that the regiment was at Fort Blakely, Mobile, and numerous minor engagements, not being mustered out until December, 1865, when it was discharged at Hempstead, Tex. For gallant conduct at Fort Donelson and Pittsburg Landing Private Howard was promoted from the ranks to the office of captain, and commanded his company the rest of the time he was in the service. In November, 1865, he was married to Miss Jennie Howe, a native of Harrison county, Ind., and for two years they lived on a farm in Saline county, Ill. They then removed to Rosiclare, where they have lived ever since, now being the oldest residents of the place. For some time he was in the hotel business; was then manager of the Pell Mining Company's interests for fourteen years, and since then has been engaged in the stone business. Captain Howard has taken an active part in politics ever since the war, and is one of the leading Republicans of the county. In 1886 he was elected sheriff of the county against large odds and held the office for four years. He was for sixteen years the postmaster at Rosiclare, and has held some of the minor offices of a local character. He is a member of the Masonic Lodge, No. 276, at Elizabethtown; Empire Lodge, Independent Order of Odd Fellows, also at Elizabethtown, and with his family belongs to the Christian church. He is also a member of the Grand Army of the Republic. Captain Howard and his wife have five sons: Charles L., Philip J., John R., William H. and Walter P., all living at Rosiclare.

HENRY M. WINDERS, attorney at law and postmaster, Elizabethtown, Ill., is a native of the county where he now lives, having been born near Cave in Rock, April 14, 1848. His grandfather, George W. Winders, was born in Logan county, Ky., about 1787, and there grew to manhood. He married Mary Hughes, whose parents came from Ireland, and settled in Crittenden county, on what is now known as the "Wilson Farm," almost opposite Cave in Rock. They had nine children, viz.: William, Washington, Richard, Timothy, Charlotte, Francis M., Melvina, Mary, and Henry. George W. Winders was a farmer by occupation, and was a zealous worker for the advancement of the Methodist church. After the death of his wife he made his home among his children, and died in 1857, while staying with his son, Francis Marion. This son was born in Crittenden county, Ky., May 30, 1822. While still a young man he crossed the river into Illinois, where he was employed in various occupations until his marriage in 1845 to Miss Elizabeth J. Scarborough, who was born Nov. 29, 1829, in Morgan county, Tenn. Her father was John Scarborough, and her mother's maiden name was Clay. They came to Illinois soon after her birth and settled in Hardin county. Francis M. and Elizabeth Winders located on a farm near Cave in Rock, and lived there all their lives. In his day he was one of the active Democrats of that section of the county. They had two children, Silvester, now deceased, and Henry M. Francis M. Winders died on April 26, 1876, and his widow made her home with the subject of this sketch until she, too, passed away in 1889. Henry M. Winders obtained such an education as most farmers' sons do in the public schools, but to this he added by self-study at home. On July 27, 1863, he enlisted in Company D, Forty-eighth Kentucky mounted infantry, went into camp on August 29th, and was mustered into service on October 26th. From that time until Dec. 16, 1864, the regiment was on guard duty at various points in the State of Kentucky, among them Russellville, Bowling Green, on Elkhorn Creek, Bacon Creek, Munfordville, Cave City and Fredonia. Young Winders remained with his command all the time, with the exception of eight days spent in the hospital at Munfordville with the mumps, although at the time of his enlistment he was but fifteen years of age. After his discharge from the army he returned home, continued his studies, and in 1867 commenced teaching, which occupation he followed in connection with farming until 1880. On Dec. 28, 1868, he married Mrs. Mary J. Caltrin, *née* Dunn, and located on a farm five miles north of Cave in Rock, where they lived for six years, when they separated. Subsequently he married Mrs. Mary F. Irrion, *née* Lamb, and in 1886 removed to Elizabethtown, where he began the study of law. In 1889 he was admitted to the bar and practiced his profession until Aug. 1, 1902, when he was appointed postmaster, which position he still holds. Mr. Winders has been active in the political affairs of Hardin county ever since he became a voter, and is one of the Republicans who always has a voice in shaping the destinies of his party. He has served as county surveyor four years; was township treasurer for three years; township trustee for two years; was four terms justice of the peace; has been his party nominee for state's attorney and county judge, but was defeated with the rest of the ticket. He belongs to the Grand Army of the Republic and has served as commander of his Post; is a Past Master in the Masonic Fraternity, and for five years was treasurer of his lodge. His wife is a member of the Methodist Episcopal church. They have no children.

TONY R. KERR, of Golconda, Ill., clerk and recorder of Pope county, was born December 24, 1861, in Hardin county, Tenn. When he was about four years old his parents came to Massac county, but three years later returned to their old home in Tennessee. There Tony received a common school education up to the age of sixteen, when his mother died and he returned to Pope county, taking up his residence at Rosebud. From that time until the spring of 1886 he was employed as a farm hand. He then married Miss Melissa Hornberg, a daughter of John F. and Sarah J. Hornberg, old residents of the county. On June 14, of that year, he was appointed township treasurer, and later was elected road clerk of District No. 6. He continued to hold both these positions until 1896, when he was elected on the Republican ticket to the office of clerk and recorder. Mr. Kerr has been twice re-elected, in 1900 and 1904, each time running ahead of his ticket. As a public official he has made a record for being trustworthy and efficient, while his uniform courtesy to all with whom he comes in contact has added to his personal popularity and contributed to his triumphant victories in being re-elected. In addition to his official position Mr. Kerr is interested in mining operations and was one of the leading spirits in securing the right of way for the Illinois Central railroad through the county. He is a member of the Independent Order of Odd Fellows, the Modern Woodmen of America, and the First Baptist church. He and his wife have four children: Clarence C., Jennie R., Penn H. and Henry G., all living at home.

GEORGE F. DIMICK, dealer in general merchandise, Rosiclare, Ill., was born one and a half miles north of that place Sept. 22, 1846. He is a son of Franklin and Amanda J. (Chancy) Dimick, the former a native of New Hampshire and the latter of Illinois. Franklin Dimick was born in 1820, and came with his parents in his childhood to Illinois, settling in that part of Pope county now included in Hardin county. His father, Jeduthun Dimick, was a surveyor and civil engineer, as well as a farmer, and many of the early surveys in that part of the state were made by him. Franklin and Amanda Dimick commenced their married life on the old home place, and lived in that immediate vicinity all their lives. In addition to farming he also worked at carpenter work, and was one of the first Christian, or Campbellite, preachers in that section. It was principally through his efforts that the first stone church was erected in Hardin county. For many years he held the office of justice of the peace, served one term as county judge, and was one of the very few men in Southern Illinois to vote for Abraham Lincoln in 1860. From that time until his death he was a steadfast Republican. He died at the age of sixty-five years and his wife at the age of sixty. Their children were: Mary L., George F., Jeduthun C., Sarah E., John F., Maria J., Charles C., and Alice. Mary, Sarah, Maria, and Alice are deceased; Jeduthun lives in Texas; John F. is on the old home place; Charles lives in Rosiclare. George F. Dimick was educated in the public schools, and at the age of twenty-one years began his business career as a clerk for J. B. Pell at Rosiclare. In 1871 he was married to Miss Alice Madden, left the store, and for several years lived on a farm near his father. His wife died in 1878, the mother of two children, Carrie B. and Daisy E., both now deceased. After the death of his wife he lived with his parents for three or four years, when he again married, his second wife being Miss Sarah Rose, and returned to his farm. Subsequently he came to Rosiclare, where he formed a partnership with his brother in the merchandizing business, under the name of C. Dimick & Bros. This partnership lasted until 1902, and since then he has been in business for himself. The firm is now G. F. Dimick & Son, his son Walter having been admitted as a partner. In addition to his mercantile interests Mr. Dimick still owns and manages his farm. He is a Republican in his political belief and has held some of the local offices. Since he was twenty-three years old he has been a member of the Christian church. He and his second wife have had three children. Etta and Raymond are deceased and Walter is in business with his father.

CHARLES C. DIMICK, proprietor of one of the oldest mercantile establishments in the town of Rosiclare, Ill., was born a mile and a half north of that town, Sept. 1, 1862, his parents being Franklin and Amanda J. (Chancy) Dimick. (See sketch of George F. Dimick for family genealogy.) Charles C. Dimick was educated in the common schools and lived with his parents until Nov. 10, 1880, when he married Kittie Wood, daughter of Alfred and Sarah (Madden) Wood, old residents of Hardin county. After his marriage he lived a year on a farm near his father, then a year on Dr. White's farm, near Elizabethtown, when he settled on a farm given him by his father near the old home place, and lived there for seven or eight years. He then came to Rosiclare, where he was connected with the mines for about two years, at the end of which time he engaged in mercantile pursuits in connection with his brother, George F., under the firm name of C. Dimick & Bro. In 1902 the partnership was dissolved and he succeeded to the business, which he still conducts. By his conservative and safe business methods he has acquired considerable wealth and owns some of the best property in the town where he lives. Mr. Dimick is a Republican and takes some interest in political affairs. He was appointed postmaster under President McKinley's first administration, having been assistant for two years, and still holds that position. He is also freight agent for the Evansville & Paducah Packet company, and has held some of the minor offices of the town. In church matters he has accepted the faith of his father and is a deacon in the Christian church. He belongs to Lodge No. 54, Independent Order of Odd Fellows, and is always a willing helper in the benevolent work of the order. Mr. and Mrs. Dimick have two daughters, Ethel V. and H. Audrey. Ethel V. was born Dec. 5, 1883, and H. Audrey Feb. 25, 1894. On Dec. 11, 1904, Ethel was married to Austin D. Knight.

JOHN G. MOBLEY, a farmer living two and a half miles south of New Haven, Gallatin county, Ill., was born in that neighborhood, Nov. 11, 1855. He is a son of William Mobley, who was born in White county in 1818, his father being one of the pioneers of that part of Southern Illinois. William Mobley married Cynthia Hughes, a native of Hamilton county, and lived in the Wabash bottoms for several years, after which he went to Iowa for two years, but at the end of that time returned to Gallatin county and settled on what is known as "The Knoll," where he died in 1866. Of the children born to William and Cynthia Mobley, Francis, James E., Sarah J., and two who died unnamed are deceased. Those living are Alexander, who resides in Jefferson county, Ill.; Mary, married and living near New Haven; Martha, wife of William A. Smith, of New Haven; John G., the subject of this sketch; and Rebecca, wife of James D. Radsner, living in Missouri. John G. Mobley attended the common schools in his boyhood and while still in his 'teens commenced working out by the month, which he continued for three years. He then went back home and took charge of the farm for his mother, and has lived on the old home place ever since. His mother died in 1892, at the age of seventy years and he has bought the interests of the other heirs, now being the sole owner of the old homestead of 300 acres, 100 of which are in the Wabash bottoms, and 250 under cultivation. Mr. Mobley has a fine residence, good barns and out-buildings, and is one of the live farmers of his part of the county. Politically he is a Republican, has served one term as township commissioner and three years as director. In 1882 he was married to Miss Eliza Moye, and to this union have been born the following children: Essie, Raymond, Mattie, Willie. Horace, Lemuel, and two who died in infancy unnamed. Lemuel is also deceased, Essie is the wife of Lawrence Givens, and the others are at home.

ALLEN T. SPIVEY, editor and proprietor of the Shawneetown, Ill., *News-Gleaner,* was born six miles west of that town April 5, 1875. He is a son of Thomas J. and Sallie (Smyth) Spivey, and a grandson of Thomas S. Spivey, who was born in North Carolina, of English ancestry, and who was one of the pioneers of Southern Illinois, settling in Gallatin county in 1832. There he took up a tract of government land and followed farming all his life. He was an influential man in his day and one of the leading Democrats of the county, serving as justice of the peace and in other minor offices until 1850, when he was elected county judge for one term. He was also active in building up the Presbyterian church. At the time of his death he was sixty-two years of age, but his wife lived to the advanced age of eighty-four. They reared a family of three sons and seven daughters, only two of whom now survive, viz.: Carrie Spivey, of Shawneetown, and Louise, who is a Mrs. Kanady, of New Albany, Ind. Thomas J. Spivey was born in North Carolina in 1830. He came to Gallatin county with his family when two years of age. When about nineteen years of age he crossed the plains to California, where he followed mining for about two years, when he returned home via the isthmus, and for the rest of his life followed farming with the exception of the last four years. His wife died in 1879, aged forty-five years. In 1893 he removed to Junction City. He died in Shawneetown in 1897. Like his father before him, he was an unswerving Democrat and a member of the Presbyterian church. Of the children born to him and his wife Quinton is in Alaska; Minnie is a Mrs. Smyth of Gallatin county; Margaret is Mrs. Loomis, of Evansville, Ind.; Addie married a Mr. Willis and lives at Mt. Vernon, Ill.; Anna married a Mr. Kanady and is now deceased; Walter W. lives at Shawneetown; Samuel S. is at Paducah, Ky.; Gertrude is a Mrs. Kanady and lives in Gallatin county; Allen T. is the subject of this sketch; and Marshall lives at McLeansboro, Ill. Allen T. Spivey received his education in the public schools, graduating from the Shawneetown high school in 1893. He then went to Evansville, Ind., and took a complete course in the commercial college of that city, graduating in 1895. For about a year he was employed as a bookkeeper, but in 1896 started in to learn the printers' trade in the office of the *Gallatin Democrat*. After three years in that office he went to Henderson, Ky., where he became the city editor of the *Daily Gleaner*. In 1900 he went to St. Louis for a short time, but returned to Shawneetown, where for a few months he was employed as a reporter on the *Democrat*. Next he served as a bookkeeper in a hardware store for a short time, but the journalistic instinct had been developed in his make-up, and in November, 1901, he started the *Shawneetown Gleaner*. The following March he bought out the *News* and consolidated the two papers under the present name. Mr. Spivey is one of the youngest and most aggressive journalists in Southern Illinois. His paper is fearlessly Republican in its politics, and it is the official organ of the party in Gallatin county. Personally he has been somewhat active in political affairs, and held the office of city treasurer for one term. He is a member of the Modern Woodmen of America and the Presbyterian church. On Christmas day in 1901 he was married to Miss Mollie Wright, a native of McLeansboro, and they have one child, Mittase Wright, born Sept. 10, 1902.

JOSEPH FOSTER, a prominent farmer, living near Ridgway, Ill., is a native of the Buckeye State, having been born near Monterey, Clermont county, O., Oct. 17, 1844. He is one of a family of nine children, five sons and four daughters, born to Dennis and Abigail (Whitaker) Foster, natives of Ohio. Joseph Foster received a common school education and grew to manhood on his father's farm. When the One Hundred and Fifty-third regiment Ohio volunteer infantry was being organized he enlisted as a private in Company I, for the one hundred days' service, and was stationed with his regiment on the Potomac river guarding the line of the Baltimore & Ohio railroad. Prior to his enlistment in this regiment he had been a member of the Ohio State Guards. His brother Frank was also in the service. In 1865 Dennis Foster removed with his family to Gallatin county, Ill., his son Joseph accompanying them. The father settled upon the farm adjoining the one where Joseph now lives, and there passed the remainder of his life, dying at the age of sixty-five years. In 1867 or '68 Joseph Foster bought a tract of forty acres where his residence now stands, though at that time the land was covered with timber. He built a hewed log house sixteen by eighteen feet, with one room and only one window, and in 1867 married Julia A. Moye. They began their married life in this humble home, but by a life of industry and frugality they have prospered, so that now in their declining years they can enjoy the fruits of their labors. Mr. Foster now owns 400 acres where he lives, about 300 acres of which is in a high state of cultivation, and at other points in the county he owns 205 acres more. All this has been accumulated by his industry and foresight, and he is one of the finest examples of self-made men. He takes a laudable interest in public questions, and in political matters in identified with the Republican party. He and his wife are the parents of the following children: Alverson, living near Ridgway; Ida J., wife of Frank Miner, of Gallatin county; Abbie, wife of George Bell, residing near Ridgway; Charles, a farmer near his father; Lola, wife of Richard Alwalt, near Asbury; Lulu, wife of John Hardy, also near Asbury; Russell, Lane and George, the last named born March 23, 1892, and died September 22d, of the same year.

GEORGE T. EDWARDS, a farmer and stock raiser of Ridgway township, Gallatin county, Ill., was born on Aug. 16, 1865, near Blairsville, Posey county, Ind. His great-grandfather is said to have been the first settler in that part of the Hoosier State, and his grandfather, Richard Edwards, was born there about 1809, some seven years before the state was admitted into the Union. Both Richard Edwards and his father became large land owners, the latter buying government land in that early day as low as twenty-five cents an acre. Richard Edwards lived to be seventy-five years of age, and in his day was an influential citizen of Posey county, where he passed his whole life. George T. Edwards now owns 166 acres of land that formerly belonged to his grandfather, who bought it years ago for $15 an acre. Isom Edwards, the father of the subject of this sketch, was born on the same farm as his father, and there grew to manhood. On Feb. 2, 1854, he married Miss Esther, daughter of George T. and Lucetta (Culley) Downen, old residents of that section. Her grandfather, Timothy Downen, was one of the first settlers there. Isom Edwards and his family lived in Posey county until his death, when his widow removed to Gallatin county, Ill., and located on the farm where her son George now lives. On Aug. 11, 1891, she was married to Abner Crunk, who is now eighty-two years of age. The children born to Isom and Esther Edwards were George, Jane, wife of William Roark, living near Ridgway; and John, also a resident of Gallatin county. George T. Edwards obtained his education in the common schools and lived with his mother until 1884. He was then united in marriage to Miss Ollie E. Downen, and soon afterward located on the farm where he now lives, a tract of 166 acres all under cultivation with the exception of about eleven acres. At the time he settled on the place there were only about thirty acres cleared. He has made all the improvements on the farm, devotes a great deal of his time to the raising of registered Hereford cattle, and is regarded as one of the progressive farmers of the county. Politically he is a Democrat and he and his wife are members of the regular Baptist church. They have had three children: Clara, Edith and one other who died in infancy and Cora, now living.

J. LOUIS DEVOUS, a well-to-do farmer, living one mile east of the town of Ridgway, Ill., was born in Brown county, O., Sept. 5, 1852. His parents, Isadore and Catherine (Bartell) Devous, were both natives of France. (For an account of ancestry see the sketch of Joseph Devous elsewhere in this work.) When he was about six years of age his parents removed to Gallatin county, where he grew to manhood. He acquired his education in what is known as the Lane school house, in Equality township, and remained at home with his parents until 1880. On April 30, of that year, he married Miss Susanna Wargel and located on part of the farm that he now occupies, just across the road from his present residence. The house in which he went to housekeeping was an old school house, one of the first frame school houses in that part of the country. It is still standing. In 1885 he bought a tract of sixty acres where he now lives, and two years later built his present dwelling, which is one of the best in that part of the county. Altogether he owns 124 acres, well improved and nearly all under cultivation. Mr. Devous is a Democrat in his political affiliations, though the only office he has ever held was that of school director, which he held for several years. The children born to him and his wife are Thomas, Julia, Leonard, Stella, Rosella, Isadore, Harry and Louis. Of these Thomas, Julia, Leonard and Stella are now living, the others being deceased. Mr. Devous and his family belong to the Catholic church and take a deep interest in its many worthy charities.

JAMES J. LOGSDON, one of the largest farmers and land owners of Gallatin county, Ill., living on the New Haven road, five miles from Shawneetown, was born on May 14, 1838, near Napoleon, Ripley county, Ind. His father, Thomas B. Logsdon, was born on what is known as "Sandy Ridge," near Shawneetown. When he was about nineteen years of age he went to Ripley county, where he married Miss Mary Muir, and was for some time engaged in conducting a general store at a place called Tall Bridge, not far from Napoleon. He died there in October, 1846. James J. is the eldest of five children. Joseph M. was killed in 1872, by the recoil of a gun; Thomas B. is a retired farmer of Shawneetown; Prudence is the wife of J. W. Gregor, of Indianapolis, Ind.; and Mary lives with her brother James. When about eight years of age James J. Logsdon had the misfortune to lose his father by death, and about three years later his mother remarried, her second husband being William Love. In the spring of 1861 James went to Indianapolis, and in the fall of that year came to Gallatin county. On March 21, 1861, he was married to Nancy A., daughter of Joseph Logsdon, and a native of Gallatin county. (For a more extended account of the family genealogy see the sketch of Joseph Logsdon.) To this marriage there were born two children, both of whom died in infancy. His wife died early in 1863, and about a year afterward he went back to Indiana. There he was married in the spring of 1865 to Miss Prudence Elizabeth Muir, and soon after his marriage returned to Shawneetown. They remained there but a few weeks, however, going to Raleigh, Ky., where he conducted a general store for about two years. At the end of that time he again returned to Shawneetown, rented a farm from his brother for one year, and in October, 1869, settled on the farm where he now lives. To his second marriage there have been born the following children: Margaret, Robert L., James J., Jr., William, Joseph, Rosa, Thomas B., Fannie M., and Annie. Margaret is the wife of James Gray, living near her father; Robert also lives in the vicinity; James J. is at home, and the others are deceased. Annie was the wife of Douglas Case. Mr. Logsdon owns 800 acres in his home farm, 500 of which is under cultivation; 60 acres near Round Pond; 96 acres in another tract; a half interest in another farm of 160 acres; and is one of the heirs to 1,400 acres in the river bottoms, 600 of which is under cultivation. One of the farms he owns is that where his father was born. Until quite recently he was active in buying and selling live stock, but in more recent years has devoted most of his time and attention to looking after his farming interests. In politics he is a Democrat, and was for ten years the supervisor of the poor. He is a member of the Shawneetown Lodge, No. 838, Independent Order of Odd Fellows, and is always a welcome attendant at the lodge meetings.

EDGAR RIDER, a farmer living near Shawneetown, Ill., was born on June 3, 1839, in what is now Harrison county of West Virginia. At the age of twenty-one years he left his father's farm and went to Cincinnati, where he worked with an uncle in a blacksmith shop one winter, and in March, 1861, came to Gallatin county. During the spring and summer of that year and also a part of the following year he worked on a farm. In the fall of 1862 he helped to organize the First Illinois heavy artillery, but as one hundred and fifty men were required and that number could not be easily obtained the organization was merged into the Fifty-sixth infantry. The officers who could not get positions in the infantry were released, Mr. Rider being one of the number. He then enlisted as a private in Company K, One Hundred and Thirty-first Illinois volunteer infantry. He was soon afterward made corporal and went through the entire war with that rank. His first engagement was at Chickasaw

Bayou, after which he was at Arkansas Post, the first battle of Vicksburg, the siege of that place that followed, Spanish Fort, Fort Blakely, and was then in Texas until September, 1865, when he was discharged. After the siege of Vicksburg, where his regiment and the Twenty-ninth both suffered severe losses, the two were consolidated, afterward being known as the Twenty-ninth. After the war he returned to Shawneetown and opened a retail meat market, which he conducted successfully for seventeen years. He was then engaged in buying and shipping stock for a while, after which he turned his attention to farming. In this line he has been successful, being the owner of 170 acres of good land which he cultivates according to the most approved methods. Mr. Rider is a Republican and while living in Shawneetown was a member of the board of aldermen for eight years. He also served nine years as road commissioner. He is a member of the Independent Order of Odd Fellows and the Grand Army of the Republic. On May 10, 1867, he was married to Miss Isabelle O. Seeley, and their children are: Emma, wife of William Rosolott; Oliver, John, Bertha, wife of Edward Slaton; Med; Jessie, wife of James Logsdon; Edith, who married Charles Martin and afterward died; June, the youngest, who died in early childhood, and one who died in infancy.

JOHN R. LOGAN, a farmer near Junction City, Ill., was born near Moundsville, Marshall county, W. Va., though at the time of his birth the county was in the Old Dominion. He is a son of James and Belle (St. Clair) Logan, and is one of a family of seven children, five sons and two daughters. In 1855, he came with his parents and brothers and sisters to Gallatin county, Ill., being at the time about fifteen years of age. They settled in Gold Hill township, where the father died in the year 1876. On Aug. 15, 1862, John R. Logan enlisted as a private in Company D, One Hundred and Twentieth regiment Illinois volunteer infantry, and was mustered in at Camp Butler "for three years or during the war." For some time the regiment was assigned to the unromantic duty of guarding railroads, its first real service being at the siege of Vicksburg during the latter part. After the fall of Vicksburg it was sent back to Memphis and there did provost duty until the men were discharged in 1865. After the war he returned to Gallatin county, where he has ever since lived. In 1872 he was married to Miss Mary Munch, and commenced farming for himself. He and his uncle bought 80 acres, all in timber, for $5 an acre, and built a hewed log house. Mr. Logan now owns a well improved farm of 100 acres, and although other men may own more land few have their farms in a higher state of cultivation than he. He is a member of the Grand Army of the Republic, belonging to the post at Shawneetown. Mr. and Mrs. Logan have had the following children: James, Charles, Annie, Edward, John A., David, Minnie, Fred and Bertha. James is in Minnesota; Annie is the wife of Edgar Kanady; John is a school teacher; Edward and Bertha are deceased, and the others live at home.

ROBERT B. CASH, a native and old resident of Gallatin county, Ill., was born at Shawneetown, the county seat of that county, Dec. 9, 1843. His father, William T. Cash, was one of the early settlers in that section of the state. In August, 1861, Robert B. Cash enlisted as a private in Company C, Twenty-ninth regiment Illinois volunteer infantry, and was mustered in at Springfield. He received his baptism of fire at Fort Donelson, and at Shiloh was severely wounded by a gun shot in the left thigh. He was placed on board a transport and sent to St. Louis, where he soon afterward received a furlough for fifty days to come home and recover. As soon as his furlough expired he rejoined his command. His next engagement of any consequence was at Holly Springs, Miss., where he was captured, but was paroled, sent to St. Louis, and was soon afterward exchanged. Again he joined his regiment, fought at Spanish Fort and Fort Blakely, then at Mobile, after which the regiment was sent to Texas and kept on duty there until the close of the war, not being mustered out until November, 1865. He was at Mobile when a large quantity of captured ammunition exploded and assisted in taking the dead and wounded from the ruins, and in moving the debris. Upon receiving his discharge he returned home, and in 1867 bought the farm where he now lives. He was married in that year to Miss Serena Hall, of Tennessee, and to this marriage there have been born nine children.

Mr. Cash is a member of the Ridgway Post, Grand Army of the Republic, and of Junction Lodge, No. 434, Independent Order of Odd Fellows. In his political views he is a Republican and takes an active interest in winning victories for his party.

JOHN W. ROGERS, farmer and stock raiser near Junction City, Ill., was born near Harrisburg, Saline county, of that state, Jan. 31, 1851. His father was born at Chattanooga, Tenn., in 1807. In 1845 he removed to Saline county and bought a farm not far from the present Eagle post office and lived there until the fall of 1851, when he came to Gallatin county and bought 160 acres adjoining the farm on which John W. now lives. Only a few acres were cleared at that time, but he improved the farm and brought most of it under cultivation before his death, which occurred on Jan. 18, 1889. He was twice married. Before leaving Tennessee he was married to Elizabeth Booten, and two daughters, Catherine and Polly, both now deceased, were born to that union. His wife died after coming to Illinois and he was married to Mrs. Eliza A. Colbert, widow of Allen Colbert and a daughter of Joseph Logsdon, whose sketch appears elsewhere. His second wife survived him, dying Feb. 19, 1903, at the age of eighty years. She had two children by her first husband: Margaret, now the wife of Thornton Bennett, of Denver, Col., and Allen, who died in infancy. John W. Rogers is the eldest of a family of four children: William T. died June 28, 1897; Matilda is the widow of George Borroughs of Shawneetown; and Marinda is the wife of James White of Gallatin county. The parents of these children were both members of the Presbyterian church. John W. Rogers received his education in the district schools near his father's home, and spent one year in the schools of Ewing, Franklin county. At the age of twenty he commenced teaching and followed that occupation for nine years, also assuming the management of his father's farm after he had reached the age of twenty-two years. On Jan. 25, 1880, he was united in marriage to Miss Lucy, daughter of Bluford and Amanda J. (Rose) Robinett, and since then has devoted the greater part of his time to farming. He owns in all 600 acres, 550 of which are under cultivation. One of his farms is that formerly belonging to his father, and which adjoins the one on which he lives. All the improvements have been made since the land came into his possession. In recent years he has given considerable attention to the breeding of fine horses, Polled Angus and Hereford cattle, and he is generally regarded as one of the most intelligent and progressive farmers in his neighborhood. Mr. Rogers is a Democrat and for eight years held the office of justice of the peace. He and his wife are both members of the Presbyterian church, in which he holds the position of deacon. The church to which they belong stands on his farm. Mr. and Mrs. Rogers have had ten children. Bluford was drowned when he was four years of age; three died in infancy; Daisy is the wife of Casper Fink, of Equality; Joseph, John, Virgil, James and Tessie are at home with their parents.

ISAAC N. BOURLAND, M.D., a physician and druggist of Equality, Ill., was born at Cottage Grove, Saline county of that state, Jan. 5, 1858. The founder of the family in America came from Ireland during the Colonial period. William Bourland, the grandfather of Dr. Bourland, was a native of South Carolina. He served in the war of 1812, after which he lived for a short time in Kentucky, and then located in Saline county. He had learned the trade of bricklayer before leaving South Carolina. In 1829 he entered a tract of government land in Saline county and followed farming, in connection with his trade, the rest of his life. He was also interested in the manufacture of charcoal. The first brick building in Equality was erected by him. It is still standing and in a good state of preservation. He married Rachel Slaten, a native of Kentucky, and died at the age of seventy-three years. She lived to be ninety-four, and died at the home of her daughter, Mrs. Susan Moore. Of their children, Ebenezer, John and Francis are deceased; Susan is a Mrs. Moore, living in Gallatin county, Ill., and the others live in Saline county. William Bourland and his wife were members of the Old School Baptist church. James A. Bourland, a son of William and Rachel Bourland, was born on the old homestead in Saline county, Nov. 30, 1830. He received a limited education in the schools of that day, married Nancy Strong, a native of Kentucky, and commenced farming on the place adjoining his father's. There he lived until the death of his father, when he removed to the old home farm where he was born, and where he is now living. Of the children born to James A. and Nancy Bourland, Gabriel A. lives in Equality; Emma is a Mrs. Proctor, of

Mount Vernon, Ill.; Isaac N. is the subject of this sketch; Timothy D. lives on the old home place; Elizabeth is a Mrs. Guard, of Equality, and Gertrude a Mrs. Pierce, living in Saline county. The mother of these children died in 1869. She was a member of the Methodist Episcopal church. The father is hale and hearty for one of his age and still takes considerable interest in politics as a Democrat. Dr. I. N. Bourland attended the common schools of his neighborhood in his youth, and afterward attended the Harrisburg high school and Ewing college in Franklin county. He then taught one term, after which he remained at home on the farm until 1880, when he commenced the study of medicine. In 1884 he was graduated from the Miami Medical college of Cincinnati and commenced practice in the vicinity of his father's home. Six months later he went to Eldorado, where he practiced for about fourteen months, at the end of which time he came to Equality. While at Eldorado he became interested in the drug business, and upon removing to Equality he brought his stock of drugs to that place, where he still continues to conduct a drug store in connection with his practice. Dr. Bourland is a member of the American and the Illinois State Medical associations, and of the Gallatin County Medical society, of which he now holds the office of president. He is medical examiner for several of the leading life insurance companies, and is one of the most popular physicians in the town. Politically he is a Democrat, and in fraternal matters is a member of the Free and Accepted Masons, now holding the office of treasurer in Lodge No. 2. In 1875 he was married to Miss Ella A. Greer, who was born in Equality, and to this union there have been born the following children: Allie, Frank, John A., Anita G. and Herbert C., twins, and Bernardine. The last named is deceased and the others live at home with their parents.

W. SMITH McGEHEE, a farmer, living four and a half miles west of Shawneetown, Ill., was born April 16, 1850, on the farm adjoining the one where he now lives. His grandfather, William McGehee, was born in Scotland, but came to America in his early manhood, locating in Maryland. There he married Catherine Little and in 1806 settled in Gallatin county, Ill. He entered a tract of land 320 acres in extent, paying twelve and a half cents an acre for it. Game was plentiful in Southern Illinois at that time and he made quite a reputation as a hunter and marksman. He died when about fifty years of age, but his wife lived to the age of eighty-four. They had eleven children, all of whom grew to maturity. One of these children was Charles W., the father of the subject of this sketch. He was born on Gold Hill, Gallatin county, Sept. 10, 1820, not far from where his son, W. Smith, now lives, and there grew to manhood. He married Mahala Moreland, who was born in the same neighborhood in 1823, and followed farming all his life. His wife died in March, 1865, and he passed away in 1887. She was a member of the Baptist church and he was a Presbyterian. They always lived in Gold Hill township, where he was a successful farmer and stock raiser, owning at one time 900 acres of land. They had the following children: Angeline, Samuel, George, Catherine and Nora, all deceased; Emily, wife of William Miller, living in the vicinity; Francis M., living at Cisne, Ill.; Lizzie, wife of Benjamin Smith; W. Smith; Charles, a farmer of Gold Hill township; and John, also a farmer in that township. W. Smith McGehee was educated in the common schools and has followed agricultural pursuits all his life. On Sept. 23, 1873, he was married to Miss Jennie Pellum, of Ridgway, and about a year later settled on the farm where he now lives. He owns 400 acres, more than three-fourths of which lies in the valley, and devotes considerable attention to raising stock. He is a member of the Knights of Honor and is a Republican politically. His wife and children belong to the Presbyterian church. Their children are: Hettie, Mrs. Edward Dale; Nora, who died in infancy; Edward S. of Junction City; Ethel and Gilbert, at home.

THOMAS J. FROHOCK, a farmer living near Junction City, Ill., is a native of Tennessee, having been born in Smith county of that state, Feb. 28, 1841. He is one of a family of fourteen children, seven sons and seven daughters. All the sons and five of the daughters grew to maturity, but only three are now living. Those are Mrs. A. G. King, Thomas J., and David Franklin, a farmer not far from Junction City. When the subject of this sketch was about fifteen years of age his parents removed to Kentucky, and there he grew to manhod. In 1866 he came to Gallatin county, Ill., where for about fifteen years he worked by the month for the farmers of Eagle Creek township. He then bought the farm where he now lives, consisting of 160 acres, though at the time there was but very little cleared land on the place. By his industry and good management he has now one of the best improved farms in the neighborhood, and in addition to his home farm owns 200 acres elsewhere, which he has accumulated by his thrift. Young men can learn from his career the lessons of economy and self-denial. Beginning life a poor boy, he had only his will and determination to succeed for a start in life. But by the proper exercise of these qualities, and by denying himself many of the so-called pleasures of youth, he is to-day one of the substantial citizens of the community in which he lives. Mr. Frohock is a Democrat in his political opinions and takes a laudable interest in public questions. In 1869 he was married to Miss Mary S. Strickland, a native of Saline county, and to this union there were born the following children: John H., Thomas G., Dallas, Lee, Franklin, George, David, Charlie and Mary A., all living in the immediate vicinity, and all useful members of society.

DAVID A. LOGAN, a farmer near Junction City, Ill., and trustee of the township in which he resides, was born, March 11, 1843, in what is now West Virginia. When he was about twelve years of age he came with his parents to Gallatin county, Ill., and lived there with them until Aug. 15, 1862, when he enlisted as a private in Company D, One Hundred and Twentieth Illinois volunteer infantry. The regiment was mustered in at Springfield for "three years or during the war," and soon afterward sent to Memphis on guard and patrol duty. There Mr. Logan contracted smallpox and before he fully recovered he was taken ill with typhoid fever. The two maladies kept him in the hospital for nearly five months. A few days after the fall of Vicksburg he reported there for duty and rejoined his regiment at Lake Providence, La., where it was stationed on guard duty. In September, 1863, it was ordered back to Memphis, after which it was at Corinth, Miss., Lagrange, Tenn., again at Memphis, then on the Guntown raid through Mississippi, and up the Tennessee river. It was mustered out at Memphis, Sept. 10, 1865, and the men returned to their homes. Since the war he has devoted his attention and energies to farming, and although he has but 100 acres he has one of the best improved farms in the neighborhood. In his political convictions Mr. Logan is a stalwart Republican, and for the last twenty years has held the office of township trustee. No better recommendation of his honor, popularity, and trustworthiness is needed than this long record as a public official, during which he has ever maintained the confidence and respect of the citizens who have entrusted him with the administration of township affairs. He is a charter member of M. K. Lawler Post, Grand Army of the Republic, at Junction. Shortly after the war he was married to Miss Elizabeth Munch, and to this union there have been born the following children: Alfred, Moses, Arthur, Chester, Harrison, Walter, Clarence, and twins who died in infancy. Alfred and Arthur are in the State of Washington, Chester is at home, and the others live in the vicinity. Mr. Logan has lived on the farm he now occupies ever since his marriage.

W. J. WILKS, a farmer near Shawneetown, Ill., was born on March 10, 1860, not far from Madisonville, Hopkins county, Ky. He is the youngest of twelve children, six sons and six daughters, born to H. J. and Pauline Wilks. Only two of the family are now living. When he was about two years of age his mother died and in 1866 his father came with the family to Gallatin county, Ill., where he bought 120 acres of land in the river bottoms and died there the following year. After the death of his father the subject of this sketch lived with a family named Duvall, working for his board and clothes, with the privilege of attending school a few months each year, until he was seventeen years old. He then commenced life on his own responsibilities as a farm hand, which occupation he followed for several years, saving his money with a view to some day becoming a farmer on his own land. On Aug. 12, 1888, he was united in marriage to Mrs. Laura Meek, a daughter of Thomas Logsdon, and for the next four years was the manager of Charles Carroll's farm. At the end of that time he bought the farm where he now lives, five miles from Shawneetown, and began farming on his own account. Since then he has bought and paid for 80 acres in New Haven township. On the two farms he has 150 acres under cultivation. Mr. Wilks is a Democrat in politics, though the only office he has ever held was that of school director, which he occupied to the entire satisfaction of his neighbors for three years. He is a modest, unassuming gentleman, whose chief aim in life seems to be to mind his own business, and it is to this trait of character that much of his success in life is due. Naturally such a man possesses the confidence and respect of the people around him, and few men in the community stand higher in a general way than Mr. Wilks.

MARTIN DOHERTY, a farmer and stock raiser, six miles east of Ridgway, Ill., was born on a farm in County Kilkenny, Ireland, not far from the city of Waterford, Dec. 19, 1838. He is the second of six children born to James and Nellie (Merry) Doherty. Mary the eldest, lives in Ireland; Ellen and Stephen came to America in 1863 and both died in this country; Richard died at the age of eighteen months, and one other died in Ireland. When he was sixteen years of age Martin Doherty commenced learning the trade of ship carpenter. For the first year and a half he received no wages. Then he received a dollar a week, with an increase of twelve and a half cents a week each year during the rest of his four and a half years' apprenticeship. On June 29, 1860, he set sail for America, on one of the old sailing vessels of that day, and after a voyage of six weeks and four days he landed in Quebec. From there he came to the United States, working in the city of Cincinnati at anything he could find to do, then in the boat yards at Evansville, Ind., and in the spring of 1865 came to Shawneetown, Ill., where he helped to build a wharf-boat. He then went to Golconda, where he aided in the building of another wharf-boat, and in April, 1867, located on the farm where he now lives. However, he continued to work at his trade that year, not taking up farming for a livelihood until the following spring. Mr. Doherty now owns 408 acres of land in Ridgway township; 240 in New Haven township, and 40 in Gold Hill township. For the last twelve years he has been raising registered Hereford cattle, in which he has been quite successful. In politics he is a Democrat and for thirteen years held the office of justice of the peace. In 1904 he visited his native land, and by a coincidence sailed on June 29, the same day that he first left Ireland for America. Instead of a voyage of six weeks and four days he made the trip in six and one half days. After his return from Ireland he visited the great World's Fair at St. Louis. Mr. Doherty has been twice married. His first wife, to whom he was united on Sept. 6, 1866, was Miss Mary McGuire. To this marriage there were born the following children: John, who attended Notre Dame university and now lives near Ridgway; Eliza, wife of Arthur Maloney, also in the vicinity; Hannah, educated at the St. Vincent convent, in Union county, Ky., now the wife of John Duffy; Stephen, a midshipman in the United States navy at Annapolis; James, who died at the age of nineteen years; Ella, who married William Maloney and died in September, 1896; May, who died at the age of fifteen months; Maggie, who died at the age of nine months, and Mary, who died at the age of six months. Stephen is a noted athlete. He is one of the foot ball team of the naval academy and has won numerous medals for running, broad jumping, hurdle races, etc. The mother of these children died in July, 1883, and in June, 1885, Mr. Doherty was united in marriage to Margaret, daughter of Thomas R. Lawler, and a niece of Gen. M. K. Lawler, whose sketch appears in this work.

JOHN DAILY, a farmer, living in what is known as the "Pond Settlement," near Ridgway, Ill., is of Irish descent. His father, William Daily, was a native of Queen's county, Ireland, a cousin of Gen. M. K. Lawler, and came to Amer.ca about the same time. The voyage was made on a sailing vessel and he was nine weeks on the water. He reached Gallatin county, Ill., with something like $10 in his pocket, and commenced working by the month for the farmers living in the vicinity of Shawneetown. After several years in this way he purchased a tract of 120 acres, about a mile from where the subject of this sketch now lives, and began farming for himself. At the time of his death in 1858 he was the owner of about 1,000 acres of good land and was one of the leading stock raisers of the county. He was married three times. His first wife was Sylvelia Cusick, and to this union there were born the following children.: Thomas, died young; John and Mary, twins, the latter of whom died at the age of twelve months; Sarah and Margaret, also twins, both deceased; William and Joseph. The subject of this sketch is the only one now living. William Daily's second wife was Martha Huston, by whom he had four children, Hannah, James. Samuel, and one who died in infancy. The mother of these children died .from the effects of a mad dog's bite, and although John and his father were both bitten by the same dog, neither became affected with rabies. The third wife was a Mrs. Mary Luttrell, who is still living in White county, Ill., at the age of eighty years. She had one child, now deceased. John Daily was born on the first farm his father ever owned, June 9, 1839. His first school was in a log house that stood on his father's farm. It had no floor and the seats were made of sassafras saplings split in halves with pins driven in the half-round sides for legs. The next school was a mile and a half away, but the house had a puncheon floor, which was at that time regarded as a luxury in a school house. The teacher of this school was a man named Watkins. When only nineteen years of age Mr. Daily commenced farming for himself, on-the place where he now lives. The following year he was married to Miss Eleanora Stout, who was born near Mansfield, O., her parents being William and Mary (Van Horn) Stout. Mr. and Mrs. Daily began keeping house in a box frame dwelling with but one room and a kitchen, and only fifteen acres of cleared land upon which to raise a crop. But by the exercise of industrious habits and good judgment they have prospered until, in addition to his home place, Mr. Daily owns another farm of 80 acres. Politically he is a Democrat who always stands up for his principles, and with his family belongs to the Catholic church, of which his father before him was an honored member. Mr. and Mrs. Daily have had the following children.: William, who now has charge of the **farm**; Henry, who died in 1898; Aaron, who died at the age of twenty-three years; twins, who died in infancy; Mary A., wife of John Frey; John, Jr., who married Eunice Harrelson, and lives on a farm near his father; Sarah, wife of Leonard Frey; Thomas, an attorney at Shawneetown; Carrie, wife of Peter Zirkelbach, of Evansville, Ind.; Charles, at home with his parents; and one who died in infancy. Mary A. and Sarah Frey are both living in the same neighborhood as their parents.

ALOIS WINTERBERGER, a farmer and grain dealer, living near Junction City, Ill., is a native of the historic province of Alsace-Lorraine, where he was born April 4, 1845, of French parentage. In 1854, in company with his parents, two brothers and two sisters, he came to the United States. For about a year after arriving in this country his father followed his trade of gunsmith in Cincinnati, at the end of which time they came on to Shawneetown, Ill. There the father worked at his trade until about 1856, when he bought a farm of fifty acres near Junction, and died there Sept. 21, 1899, aged seventy-nine years. The mother died on April 4, 1902, in the eighty-fourth year of her age. Alois was eleven years of age when the family settled at Shawneetown. He attended the common schools and on Aug. 15, 1862, enlisted in Company D, One Hundred and Twentieth Illinois volunteer infantry, as a private. In May, 1863, he was made a corporal, and on April 6, 1864, was promoted to orderly sergeant, which rank he held for the remainder of his service. The regiment was mustered in at Springfield, sent to Memphis, Tenn., on patrol and provost duty, then to Vicksburg, where it participated in the siege. After the fall of Vicksburg it was on guard duty at Lake Providence, La., Memphis and Lagrange, Tenn., Corinth, Miss., and in June, 1864, took part in the famous Guntown raid. He was once severely wounded by a ball which struck him in the back of the head, passed under the scalp, and killed the next man in the line. On Sept. 10, 1865, he was mustered out with the regiment at Memphis and returned to Gallatin county. He soon returned to Memphis, however, where for three years he worked at the trade of carpenter. From that time until 1880 he was engaged in contracting and building in Gallatin county. During the next five years he worked as a millwright in different parts of the country. In 1885 he built what is known as the "Little Gem" Flour mill at New Haven and conducted it in connection with a grain buying business until 1892. He then removed to the farm where he now lives, though he still does considerable business as a grain buyer at Junction City. Mr. Winterberger owns 165 acres in the home farm, and fifty acres in another tract. He has made all the improvements on his farms, among which may be especially mentioned several thousand rods of tile drain, his farm in this respect being one of the best supplied in the county. Politically he is a Republican and from 1898 to 1902 held the office of township supervisor. At the present time he is one of the three drainage commissioners for the Cyprus special drainage district. He is a Royal Arch Mason and Knight Templar; served as Worshipful Master of Warren Lodge, No. 14, Free and Accepted Masons, of Shawneetown in 1876; and is a Past Commander of Rhodes Post, No. 586, Grand Army of the Republic, of New Haven. In 1877 Mr. Winterberger and Miss Kate Wallace were united in marriage and they had two sons: Louis, deceased, and Ralph, now in the United States navy on board the steamship *Tacoma.* He attended the State university for two years before entering the navy. The mother of these two boys died in 1881 and in 1883 Mr. Winterberger was married to Miss Mary Krauser, a native of Portsmouth, O.

INDEX, VOLUME I

www.ingramcontent.com/pod-product-compliance
Lightning Source LLC
Chambersburg PA
CBHW030234030426
42336CB00009B/92